PARNASSUS
REVISITED

PARNASSUS REVISITED

MODERN CRITICAL ESSAYS
ON THE EPIC TRADITION

Edited and with an Introduction by

ANTHONY C. YU

The University of Chicago

AMERICAN LIBRARY ASSOCIATION / Chicago
1973

Library of Congress Cataloging in Publication Data

Yu, Anthony C   1938–   comp.
  Parnassus revisited: modern critical essays on the
epic tradition.

  Bibliography: p.
  1. Epic poetry—Addresses, essays, lectures.
I. Title.
PN1305.Y8   809.1'3   73-11013
ISBN 0-8389-0132-8

Printed in the United States of America

CONTENTS

PREFACE

PARNASSUS REVISITED is an anthology of essays written by modern scholars on the major epic poems and the epic tradition of the West. The scope of the selections is determined by such important critical issues common to both "primary" and "secondary" epics as the narrative technique, the epic hero, language, and the problem of generic definition. I have sought to present in the Introduction a compendious review of one aspect of recent Homeric scholarship—the discussions of oral tradition, "oral poetics," and their wider implications for literary criticism. A selected bibliography of books and articles devoted to the study of the epic is included at the end.

Even in so modest an undertaking, I have experienced the wisdom of an ancient observation that whenever one walks along with three persons, it is likely that one's teacher is to be found therein.* I would be grossly ungrateful were I to remain silent on how much I have learned from my colleagues at the University. Special thanks are due to Professors Nathan A. Scott, Jr., David Grene, Elder Olson, Charles Long, and Giles B. Gunn for their discerning criticism and enthusiastic support. I am grateful also to my secretary, Mrs. Donna Guido, for invaluable assistance in the typing of the manuscript. Finally, I wish to express my deepest gratitude to my wife, Priscilla, who is as always "the best judge, the best critic, the best observer, the best believer."

ANTHONY C. YU

The University of Chicago

* *Analects of Confucius,* VII, 21.

·I·

INTRODUCTION

Anthony C. Yu

HOMER
AND THE SCHOLARS
ONCE MORE

I

Of all the great forms of imaginative literature, the epic is perhaps the most expansive, the most exalted, and the most enduring. Writing in *Feeling and Form*, Susanne Langer has remarked that the epic

> is the great matrix of all poetic genres. All devices of the art occur in it sooner or later—but never all of them at once. There are lyric verses, romantic quests, descriptions of ordinary life, self-contained incidents that read like a ballad. In the Greek epic one finds political conflicts, personal histories, characters growing with their actions; in the Edda there are riddles and proverbs, in the Kalevala cosmological fantasies; and in all epics, invocations and praises of the gods. The epic is a hodge-podge of literary creations, vaguely yet grandly spanned by a story—the all-inclusive story of the world.[1]

What is even more amazing about this form of literature, however, is that the epic, despite its long and august tradition, has been considered by many to be moribund for centuries. Homer himself, frequently and incontestably acknowledged as one in whom Greek epic poetry had reached its zenith, is recognized more readily as the preserver of a bygone heroic culture than its creator. The poets of subsequent generations, lacking steadily the access to his Weltanschauung, could neither recapture his unified mythic sensibility nor repeat his poetic accomplishment. Similarly, Vergil is said to have celebrated the virtus of Rome only in the aftermath of Augustan grandeur, when it was dimmed by popular unrests and the weariness of war. The literary and historical impulses, which shaped and perfected the Vergilian enterprise of presenting simultaneously a critique and an affirmation of Augustan values, were denied the poets coming after him. Similarly, too, the achievement of Milton appears all the more impressive if it is seen in that moment of history when the writing of epic was fast becoming impossible.[2] Forces at work in the seventeenth century led to the epic's attenuation, giving some justification to Dr. Johnson's later attempt to interpret Milton's cryptic "age too late" in Book IX of *Paradise Lost* as the expression of "some fear that his book is to be written in an age too late for heroic poesy." And since the time of Poe, who regards epic as "the art of being dull in verse," more than one critic in the modern world has sung the requiem for the long poem.

Yet, for all the gloomy forecasts and conclusions made by historians of literature, the epic's capacity for survival is a constant cause of wonder. Phoenix-like, the form that seems doomed to oblivion in one era will emerge anew with more luminous splendor in another. From such ancient poems as the *Mahābhārata* and the *Epic of the Gilgamesh* to modern ones like Spitteler's *Olympische Frühling,* Pound's *Cantos,* and *The Odyssey* of Kazantzakis, the history of the genre spans more than three millennia, embraces a multiplicity of civilizations and languages, and sustains numerous formal modifications and transformations. Though it is undeniable that countless specimens of that history are hardly read today, and were not read even at the time when they were written, it is equally undeniable that the monuments continue to inspire and instruct. "The classical books," wrote Gilbert Murray,

> are in general the books which have possessed for mankind such vitality of interest that they are still read and enjoyed at a time when all the other books written within ten centuries of them have long since been dead. There must be something peculiar about a book of which the world feels after two thousand years that it has not yet had enough.[3]

Murray's statement was, of course, directed primarily to the Homeric poems, but this capacity to engender a permanent quality of interest surely may be felt in such works of lesser antiquity as the *Divina Commedia,* the *Faerie Queene, Paradise Lost,* and *The Prelude* as well.

These remarks about the age and abiding appeal of certain epics also point up, however, the immense difficulty which their study presents to the modern student. The sheer length of the works themselves, the tremendous diversity of the languages in which they were originally composed or written, the vastness of the historical and cultural materials that have gone into their making, and in many instances, the strangeness of the poetic medium all tend to prohibit facile reading and, frequently, intimate knowledge. This is not to say, of course, that the formidable subject has been in want of scholarly devotion and scrutiny. On the contrary, the past few decades have witnessed a steady harvest of important studies on a single author or work, or on comparative topics, themes, and texts. But apart from one anthology in print, *Perspectives on Epic,* edited by Candelaria and Strange,[4] there has been little attempt, similar to that exercised on behalf of such other literary genres as prose fiction, tragic drama, or lyric poetry, to make more readily accessible to students some of the results of this research on the epic. Moreover, the selection by chronology and the brevity of the selections themselves in the aforementioned anthology have prompted a different approach in this volume.

The present undertaking emphasizes the writings of modern or contemporary scholars on certain critical issues and problems which cut across the temporal and literary boundaries of "primary" and "secondary" epics. And, though the contents of any anthology are of necessity truncated to some extent, every effort has been made to provide sufficient space for the essays of each section to treat their subjects in detail and depth. It should be self-evident also that a book of this nature cannot possibly aspire to be comprehensive in its coverage of so vast a topic. The selected essays are deliberately limited to studies on Western imaginative texts belonging in the main to that tradition which Mark Van Doren has aptly designated as that of "The Noble Voice."[5] These are the records of great story and great poetry, and they form part of our permanent curriculum of litterae humaniores. The relative familiarity of most of the primary texts is expected to facilitate the reader's journey through various segments of critical discussion, while the present introduction and terminal bibliography hope to alert him to other texts and criticism not included in the essays.

Though the contents of this volume are devoted to modern criticism of the epic, there is no intention to slight the wisdom of the past. Indeed, anyone familiar with the history of criticism in the West knows with what intensity and relentlessness this form of literature has been scrutinized.[6] The writings of Aristotle, the Italian and French theorists of the Renaissance, and the German authors of the last century (e.g., Goethe, Schiller, Richter, Schlegel, Schelling, and Hegel) continue to possess relevance for any study of the subject. However, if the distinguished classical scholar Wilamowitz-Moellendorff is not overly exaggerating in his oft-quoted assertion that "die Geschichte des Epos, das is die homerische Frage," then twentieth-century investigations of that question are of peculiar importance. In certain respects, the scholarly labor of the last four or five decades has not only proved to be revolutionary for Homeric criticism; it has also stimulated new ways of studying the literature of other epochs and cultures as well.

II

One of the brightest luminaries on the horizon of modern Homeric scholarship is undoubtedly Milman Parry, who, at the time of his lamented death at the age of thirty-three, had already altered radically the course of Homeric research. So momentous and influential have been the results of Parry's findings that he has been called "the Darwin of Homeric Studies."[7] His elaborate and meticulous examination of Homeric style by establishing the formation and function of the noun-epithet formulas has presented overwhelming, if not completely irrefutable, evidence for considering the two Greek epic poems as oral compositions.[8] The method developed in these studies and subsequently in the research on contemporary oral poetry in Yugoslavia has been extended and applied by scholars to the study of late classical and modern Greek poetry, biblical literature, Anglo-Saxon and old French epics, non-Western literary materials, and even the technique of contemporary American folk preaching.[9]

It is not the purpose of this introduction to review the history of Homeric criticism since 1928, when Parry first published his two French doctoral dissertations in Paris (*L'Épithète traditionnelle dans Homère; Essai sur un problème de style homérique* and *Les Formules et la métrique d'Homère*). That history has already been rehearsed repeatedly by more competent specialists,[10] and many of the technical complexities necessarily associated with all phases of that history are beyond the interests of the general student. What

I would like to highlight here, rather, are the crucial implications for criticism occasioned by the work of Parry and followers. For, although Parry's writings have largely rendered obsolete the older dispute of whether the Homeric poems were of single or multiple authorship,[11] they have in fact raised with far greater urgency the hermeneutical question of understanding. Beyond the tabulation and analysis of formulas and formulaic expressions, there is the literary-aesthetic consideration of the poems qua poems. What is the significance of the statement that the *Iliad* and the *Odyssey* "are in essence oral poetry, the end product of a long tradition of songs improvised by illiterate but highly skilled singers"?[12] And what are the distinct possibilities and limitations inherent in criticism of this kind of literature? The problem of an "oral poetics" has become increasingly more controversial among classical scholars, and the student of literature can hardly afford to ignore a debate which, in terms of some of our most cherished literary inheritance, poses once more the fundamental issues concerning verbal art itself.

Milman Parry began his career in the heyday of the Unitarian-vs.-Analyst controversy in Homeric scholarship. At bottom the argument is not simply over the poems' authorial origins on the basis of textual analysis. What is at issue ultimately is the greatness of the poet. In antiquity and in the Renaissance, Homer had enjoyed unrivalled esteem, though for reasons not always poetic. Nonetheless, critics from Plato to Dryden, with a few notable exceptions, voiced unfeigned praise for this, "the best of poets."[13] With the rise of historical criticism, however, Homeric writings, along with many other ancient documents, were subject to critical and, frequently, skeptical scrutiny. The beliefs in a historical Homer and in the poems' unity and single authorship were challenged on historical and textual grounds. The strictures of Abbé d'Aubignac (1604–76)[14] on poor plot construction, banal characterization, and repugnant theology in Homer might indicate not so much astute criticism as a manifestation of Zeitgeist typical of the seventeenth century's quarrel of the ancients and the moderns. But Richard Bentley's remark that Homer had written "a sequel of Songs and Rhapsodies, to be sung by himself for small earnings and good cheer, at Festivals and other days of Merriment," and that "these loose songs were not connected together in the form of an epic poem till Pisistratus's time about 500 years later"[15] already anticipated somewhat Robert Wood's speculations a few decades later. Wood's *An Essay on the Original Genius and Writings of Homer* of 1767[16] continues to attract modern critical attention because he was the first in the modern era to enunciate the possibility of Homer's being an illiterate poet, working in an "unlettered state of society" with only the help of a vital memory. Wood's essay, translated in 1773, directly influenced F. A. Wolf, the first in a succession of great German scholars of Homer. For the next century and a half, German higher criticism of the Homeric poems, paralleling in many ways the practice of Biblical criticism, sought from the study of textual problems to recover the Sitz im Leben of the poems themselves.[17] To be sure, such an effort did not result in any clear consensus on the original form of the Homeric compositions or on the kind of literary tradition within which the poet lived and worked. Nevertheless, the sustained examination of internal difficulties and discrepancies in the poetic details no less than the copious analyses of different cultural and linguistic stratifications within the poems all convinced most critics that neither the *Iliad* nor the *Odyssey* could possibly have come from a single hand.[18]

The success in eliminating the figure of the single poetic author in this instance unfortunately presents only dubious gains for literary criticism. None can deny, of course, that historical scholarship has advanced immensely our knowledge of Homeric life, language, and culture, and this knowledge in turn may enrich our understanding of the poems themselves and many of their particular episodes. But the archeological discoveries, the analysis of dialects, or the study of weaponry can point to irreconcilable differences in the texts, thus necessitating explanations by means of the hypothesis of interpolations and gradual accretion of disparate materials. This view of a poem's syncretic growth understandably appears troublesome to a critical tradition which since Aristotle's *Poetics* has given weighty emphasis to the organic form of a literary text. That form is significant because it reflects, in the last analysis, the shape and creative intelligence of a peculiar authorial will.[19] The Unitarians' objection to the work of the Analysts and their own appeal to the elements of design, structure, and symmetry in the Homeric poems are thus representative of the persistent attempt to account for why and how the poems have affected the readers across the centuries in such a powerful manner. Basic to this consideration is the question of whether a poem of the *Iliad*'s magnitude can conceivably come into its final form without some control from a single artistic mind, be it that of Homer or that of a nameless final redactor. Does the discussion of the poet's genius possess any genuine significance when the poems are regarded as nothing more than a fortuitous collection of folk songs? Is it at all meaningful to attribute the greatness of the *Iliad* to an "intensity of imagination," as Gilbert Murray does, when this imagination is then seen as the attainment by "many writers at their most exalted moments," the common possession of "generation after generation of poets, trained in the same schools and a more or less continuous and similar life"?[20]

That Milman Parry was highly conscious of such vexing problems from the early days of his graduate study was evident from the very opening paragraph of his Master of Arts thesis of 1923. Setting out to examine diction as an element of Homeric style, Parry was concerned already to relate the poetic medium to personal talent, and to delimit as precisely as possible that verbal tradition wherein Homer's superiority as an artist may be given its fullest appreciation.[21] Even in the most exacting inspection of formulas later in his Paris dissertation, Parry was aware of the need to move from statistical analysis to the creation of "an aesthetics of traditional style."[22] Whether he succeeded at all in even taking a first step toward that direction is open to debate. But Parry's intention is unambiguous throughout his writings, though it has not perhaps received its due recognition in the subsequent heated discussions among his followers and critics.

Parry began his study of Homeric style with one of its most obvious characteristics: the large quantity of repeated expressions found in the poems. Anyone reading Homer must be struck by how often Odysseus is called "resourceful" and how frequently "young Dawn appeared with her rosy fingers ($\mathring{\eta}\mu o\varsigma$

δ' ἠριγένεια φάνη ῥοδοδάκτυλος Ἠώς)." It has been estimated, in fact, that "about one-fifth of the Homeric poems is composed of lines wholly repeated from one place to another, and that in some 28,000 lines there are some 25,000 repeated phrases."[23] The immediate scholarly predecessors of Parry had already used the term "formula" to describe such Homeric repetitions.[24] But it remained for Parry to give the term a more precise definition by decisively linking the formation of certain types of these repetitions to the inherent demands of Homeric verse, the dactylic hexameter.

In the dissertation, Parry's detailed catalogs of several of the epithets for heroes and gods are employed to demonstrate how their particular constructions are adapted to the exigencies of versification. For example, the metrical requirements between the bucolic diaeresis (word break after the fourth metron) and the end of the line, and between the hephthemimeral caesura (pause within foot 4) and the end of the line, are —xx— — and xx—xx— — respectively. In the poems we find the noun-epithet combination of "divine Odysseus" in the nominative case (δῖος Ὀδυσσεύς) filling the first position sixty times and "Pallas Athene (Παλλὰς Ἀθήνη)" thirty-nine times. In like manner, the second position is filled eighty-one times by "resourceful Odysseus (πολύμητις Ὀδυσσεύς)," twenty-six times by "gleaming-eyed Athene (γλαυκῶπις Ἀθήνη)," and thirty times by "cloud-gathering Zeus (νεφεληγερέτα Ζεύς)." Such noun-epithet units, moreover, may be joined conveniently with another stock phrase of fixed metrical character. A simple expression such as "thereupon so and so replied to him (τὸν δ' ἠμείβετ' ἔπειτα)" may be combined with an expanded formula like "the gleaming-eyed goddess Athene (θεὰ γλαυκῶπις Ἀθήνη)"—seven times, or "the god-like old man Priam (γέρων Πρίαμος θεοειδής)"—five times, to form a complete line. Again, the phrase "long-suffering divine Odysseus (πολύτλας δῖος Ὀδυσσεύς)" can be linked with twenty-four different hemistichs of exactly alike metrical quality—for example, "thus spoke so and so shuddering (ὣς φάτο, ῥίγησεν δὲ)" and "thereupon he rejoiced (γήθησέν τ' ἄρ' ἔπειτα)" —to create a formulaic system.[25]

On the basis of this form of vigorous investigation, Parry defines "formula" as *a group of words which is regularly employed under the same metrical condition to express a given essential idea.*"[26] Thus, what the poet meant to convey in a clause like "the young Dawn reappeared with her rosy fingers" is not any particularized description of morning but simply "when day broke."[27] Similarly, a formulaic system is "a group of phrases which have the same metrical value and which are enough alike in thought and words to leave no doubt that the poet who used them knew them not only as a single formula but also as a formula of a certain type."[28] Further analysis reveals that while there are a vast number of formula types in Homer (e.g., a noun-epithet combination in the nominative case, beginning with a single consonant, which occupies the position between the trochaic caesura of the third foot and the end of the verse), there is relatively little duplication of interchangeable phrases with identical metrical value and meaning.[29] These two features of the verse, called by Parry "length" and "thrift" of the Homeric system of formulas, led him to conclude that Homeric diction had to be traditional diction, a product of many generations of poets. The twofold operative principle of Homeric poetry is thus deduced: only the severity of metrical pressure can adequately account for the frequencies and locations of the formulas, and only the work of many minds over a long period of time can build up such a vast and intricate schematization of formulaic systems.[30]

If the question is raised as to why, even after making due allowance for the complexity of the Homeric hexameter, metrical considerations should be so determinative in the operation of formulas, the answer is that their function points to a peculiar process of composition which imposes special demands on versification. It is at this point that Parry moves from a study of Homeric style to inferences about its origin. For his examination of what he calls the "ornamental" epithets of Homeric heroes, gods, and even of things leads him to maintain that such epithets have no independent existence of their own.[31] They combine with the nouns or proper names to form a unit whose function is to convey an "essential idea," not particularized meaning.

Ships in Homer are often "swift," regardless of whether they are actually beached, sailing, or burning in front of Troy. Similarly, a reader may be startled at first encounter by this description of battle—"still speaking, his head fell to the dust (φθεγγομένου δ' ἄρα τοῦ γε κάρη κονίησιν ἐμίχθη)." (Iliad. X. 457). But when he learns that another warrior in the Odyssey (XXII. 329) perished in exactly the same manner, the awful realism of the sentence is quickly eroded by the realization that it is perhaps no more than a typical representation of someone killed in action. However, the expression "long-suffering divine Odysseus" is not merely indicative of stock phraseology, for its very syntactical predictability implies that its meaning is strictly subordinated to metrics. The poet's (or poets') choice in utilizing these vast and varied formulas is governed more by metrical convenience than by apposite significance. Now, asks Parry,

> What was this constraint that thus set Homer apart from the poets of a later time, and of our own time, whom we see in every phrase choosing those words which alone will match the color of their very thought? The answer is not only the desire for an easy way of making verses, but the complete need of it. Whatever manner of composition we could suppose for Homer, it could be only one which barred him in every verse and in every phrase from the search for words that would be of his own finding. Whatever reason we may find for his following the scheme of the diction, it can be only one which quits the poet at no instant. There is only one need of this sort which can be suggested—the necessity of making verses by the spoken word. This is a need which can be lifted from the poet only by writing, which alone allows the poet to leave his unfinished idea in the safe keeping of the paper which lies before him, while with whole un-hurried mind he seeks along the ranges of his thought for the new group of words which his idea calls for. Without writing, the poet can make his verses only if he has a formulaic diction which gives him his phrases all made, and made in such a way that, at the slightest bidding of the poet, they will link themselves in an unbroken pattern that will fill his verses and make his sentences.[32]

It should be noted that this forceful claim that the traditional Homeric style must be also an oral style was deduced solely from internal statistical investigations. In the same essay, however, Parry was well aware that to achieve greater understanding of this style, wider comparative study was imperative. The early history of the epic must supply us with a better knowledge of "the relation between the formulas, the dialectic forms, and the hexameter," while the stylistic likenesses between the Greek epic and the oral epics of other nations "must form the basis of any attempt to judge Homer by what we know about these other poems."[33]

His return to Europe in 1933 resulted in the extension of Parry's research to a published comparison of formulaic verses in Greek and South Slavic epics. What is important in this essay is that Parry feels compelled by his analysis to draw firmly the categorical distinction between two kinds of poetic form: *"the one part of literature is oral, the other written."*[34] If the essential quality of oral poetry is a traditional formulaic diction, then the Homeric poems possess demonstrable linguistic affinities in far greater abundance with oral poems of other cultures than with epics known to have been written. To further understand that affinity, Parry's two trips to Yugoslavia before his death were occupied by intensive field work consisting of interviews and recordings. The collections resulting therefrom provide the foundation for comparative study by placing at its disposal the record of a living tradition of heroic singers—their compositions, their techniques, and the actual condition in which they practiced their art.

Parry's explicit purpose in making such a collection of South Slavic poetry was to discover how that poetic tradition might assist him to define more precisely the whole genre of oral poetry. However concise his work on Homer might have been, Parry rightly saw that the statistical and stylistic analysis of the ancient documents could yield no more than the probability of their having been composed orally. Since it was impossible to recover the historical setting in which the Homeric poems came into existence, Parry turned to materials which not only could provide a compelling analogy to clinch his argument about Homer, but also permitted better empirical control in his investigation.

The body of South Slavic poetry was to furnish him "with an exact knowledge of the characteristics of oral style, in the hope that when such characteristics were known exactly, their presence or absence could definitely be ascertained in other poetries, and those many large and small ways in which the one oral poetry differed from written poetry for its understanding could be carried over to the Homeric poems."[35] This projected endeavor was cut short by his untimely death in 1935, but over 3,000 twelve-inch aluminum phonograph discs had been made from the performances by and conversations with the Yugoslavian singers, forming now the Milman Parry Collection at the Harvard University Library. The transcription, translation, and publication of this collection have been under the supervision of Parry's former student, A. B. Lord, whose book of 1960, *The Singer of Tales,* constitutes a major effort in continuing and advancing the work of his distinguished teacher. Lord's chapters on the Homeric poems, a portion of which is included in this volume, are directly based on the knowledge gained from his study of modern oral poets.

The significant element in the first part of Lord's book consists in his helping us to understand more clearly the characteristics of oral composition by clarifying the difficult process of the singer's training and the conditions of his performance. The singer's journey from youthful apprentice to mature entertainer has to be lengthy and arduous precisely because the very nature of his profession, at least within the South Slavic cultural milieu, denies him the resources available and crucial to the writing artist: time and verbal permanence in the form of a text. The oral poet, who in this case is also an illiterate performer, has neither the leisure to compose at whatever pace he chooses nor the mnemonic support of a model document. His total resource resides in a linguistic tradition wherein the architectonic profiles of certain stories and tales are enshrined in various systems of thematic, syntactic, and metrical patterns. To become proficient in his profession, the oral poet must learn to compose with a set of given linguistic materials; for, every occasion he sings means at once a rehearsal of known materials and a creative adaptation of the tradition to the exigencies of that particular performance. Though he must of necessity develop a prodigious memory, the singer's chief concern is not memorization by rote.[36] Rather, his is an "improvisatory" recital of a story governed by the restrictions of a particular style. The temporal pressure of rapid composition thus demands the use of "traditional," and therefore, preexistent linguistic formulations, but the need to fully engage a live audience, characterized unavoidably by its variety and instability, also constrains the singer to practice "ornamentation" and "expansion" in his composition.[37]

The conditions of performance thus give rise to what Lord has termed "the habit of adjustment" developed in the singer. For what he must learn is not merely a set of lines and phrases from his predecessors; the technique indispensable to his success as an oral artist has to do with "the establishment of various kinds of patterns and rhythms of expression" in the very act of singing.[38] From the practical consideration of how to rest one's voice effectively to the varying of a melodic pattern for the purpose of dramatic emphasis, the singer is learning his craft in transforming received materials into a sung tale of his own making. The response of his audience helps him to acquire an assured sense of rhythm and pace, of how to construct effective beginnings and transitions, of when to lengthen or shorten a certain episode. His final aim is to secure such mastery of his material, such technical control and cultivated spontaneity as will enable him to transcend partially the restrictions of his art. The artistic freedom purchased by his technique is defined by the extent to which the bard can put to use the vast systems of formulaic language with flexibility and expressiveness.

According to Lord's study of the Yugoslavian oral epics, the uses of formulas bear out the observations made by his mentor Parry on the Homeric poems. Though the metrical requisites of the Serbo-Croatian decasyllabic line are less stringent than the Homeric one, the dependence on the repetition of "frequently used and useful phrases" for rapid composition is the same. As in the case of the Homeric songs, "meaning in [the formulas] becomes vestigial, connotative rather than denotative," for the formulas are commodious mediators of essential ideas, not nuanced metaphors of poetic irony.[39]

Perhaps the most important contribution of Lord to the comparative study of oral poetry lies in his extension of Parry's notion of "theme." With his intense concentration on the phenomena of language, Parry had only scattered references to the narrative components of the tale that was being told,[40] though the fact that Homer and other poets of Greek antiquity shared in the presentation of certain common poetic subjects had been observed long ago by Socrates. "Does Homer speak of any other than the very things that all the other poets speak of?" asked Socrates in the *Ion.* "Has he not described war for the most part, and the mutual intercourse of men, good and bad, lay and professional, and the ways of the gods in their intercourse with each other and with men, and happenings in the heavens and in the underworld, and origins of gods and heroes? Are not these the subjects of Homer's poetry?" (531ᶜ).

To be sure, the Socrates of the dialogue was not concerned with oral tradition but with the possibility of artistic judgment and discrimination. It was Lord who defined a theme in oral poetry as "a recurrent element of narration or description," "a grouping of ideas" which forms the constitutive units in the narration of the plot.[41] Though they may vary in length, complexity, and descriptive details, such themes as the assembly or council, the catalog of warriors or ships, the arms and arming of heroes, the birth and childhood of the hero, the long voyage by sailing or journeying, the moments of arrivals and departures, the rites of marriage or funeral, the feasts, the contest of athletic and martial skills, and the battles with supernatural or monstrous beings form the very stuff out of which are made many heroic tales and sagas.[42]

In some instances, an all-encompassing theme like the myth of the Bear-Son may have influenced and inspired two vastly different epics such as the *Beowulf* and the *Odyssey*.[43] And similarly, the theme of the return of Greek warriors from the battle of Troy has created cycles of *Nostoi* stories, the most famous being, of course, the *Odyssey*. But as Lord has argued perceptively, the theme of the hero's return as such may be seen to be operative in both the *Odyssey* and the *Iliad*, for the development of this theme entails in both poems such parallel motifs as the loss of someone dear to the hero, the withdrawal of the hero, the jeopardy of the hero's associates because of his removal, and the hero's return and recognition.[44]

Like the formula, the theme may be located in repeated usage within a single poem (e.g., the arming episodes of the *Iliad*), in identical or modified renditions within different versions of the same poem, or in analogous accounts in poems of divergent cultures and periods. Unlike the formula, however, the theme is not restricted by metrical considerations, but its operative principle is still founded on the singer's skill in building his story within the condition of oral performance. As Lord has described the process,

> usually the singer is carried from one major theme to another by the demands for further action that are brought out in the developing of a theme. Thus the decision of the assembly in "Smailagić Meho" to send Meho to Budapest to obtain his credentials from the vizier leads inevitably to the theme of the journey, which in itself contains preparation and travel. This particular journey theme is distinctive in that Meho meets and rescues a maiden and discovers the treachery of the vizier. The action in this theme leads naturally to the next

large theme of betrothal to the maiden and the return home to gather wedding guests.

And so the poet moves forward.[45]

The noteworthy element in this poetic process is the flexibility with which themes are developed not only within a single poem, but also in different poems. Themes are interchangeable from poem to poem, and what determines their use is not how they contribute to the propriety of structure particularized in a single story, as they would be in a written text, but how they complicate or complement the larger patterns or clusters of ideas accreted through inveterate associations. In different poems, the same themes may be duplicated, conflated, expanded, or transposed to form "conglomerates" of similar or contrasting "configurations."[46] Thus the elements of disguise, deception, and recognition in the Odyssean story of return after long absence of the hero may be detected also in the return songs of Yugoslavia.

The basis of comparing the ancient poems with the modern songs is not derivation or literary imitation, but what James A. Notopoulos has called "oral typology," by which identification one may study the thematic development of oral heroic poetry.[47] The theme of wrath, for example, has been associated with epic heroes ancient and modern, the most grandly dramatized being that of Achilles. This durable convention not only points to the fact that it is a favorite motif in oral poetry, a motif which, though born of the distant past, had itself outgrown historicity to become the recurrent theme; its very popularity, according to Notopoulos, also indicates that "wrath is an inevitable characteristic of highly strung heroes in the epic tradition."[48] How the themes are grouped together is thus controlled by what Lord has characterized as "the logic of the narrative and the force of habitual association."[49] Just as the freezing of metered diction in formulas builds up a *linguistic* tradition which comes to the aid of the poet at his slightest bidding, so the fluidity of thematic deployment evinces a *narrative* tradition which similarly serves the need of oral song.

III

Such, then, are the essential elements in what has come to be known as the Parry-Lord thesis concerning oral poetry. The impact it has had on Homeric scholarship and comparative literary study over the past decades has been enormous, and the far-reaching consequences have been traced with exemplary thoroughness by Adam Parry in his introduction to his father's collected papers. The debate on how this theory affects the Homeric Question is ongoing among classical scholars, and some of its current problems, as enumerated by Lord in a lengthy review essay of the 1966 volume of *Yale Classical Studies* devoted to the subject, have to do with:

1) the effect of writing on a traditional singer, 2) the degree of usefulness of the analogy between Ancient Greek oral epic tradition and Yugoslav oral traditional epic song, 3) the value of quantitative formula analysis, and 4) a return to subjective interpretation and appreciation of the Homeric poems.[50]

As it has been intimated earlier in this essay, the last issue in Lord's statement is the one which requires our attention, for the fundamental question
occasioned by Parry's work is whether criticism, in the traditional meaning
of that term, is still possible for the Homeric poems. In the words of Socrates
to Ion, though with different connotations, is it possible, or even permissible,
to speak of an "art of poetry" in Homer?

The answer to this question, for some critics, has been of necessity a negative one. Wade-Gery's comparison of Parry with Darwin is based on the
seeming impression that Parry's work has "removed the creative poet from
the *Iliad* and the *Odyssey*," just as the biologist's theory of evolution may
seem to have removed "the finger of God from the creation."[51] F. M. Combellack's widely read essay further sharpens the issues in a manner which
deserves to be quoted once more at some length. The regrettable feature of
Parry's research, as Combellack sees the matter,

> is not that Parry has taken the great creative poet out of the *Iliad* and the
> *Odyssey,* but that he has taken from Homeric critics a considerable body of phe-
> nomena which literary critics normally consider a legitimate and significant part
> of their proper study. If Parry's conclusions are sound, it is now hard, or im-
> possible, to find artistry in many places in the Homeric poems where critics
> of the pre-Parry age found beauty and where contemporary critics often still
> find it. . . .
>
> If we accept Parry's view about the traditional formulary nature of the
> Homeric style, his contention that the oral poet chooses a phrase primarily
> because it is convenient, not because of any delicate nuance in its meaning (and
> I should say that in the present state of our knowledge of oral poetry we ought
> to accept this), then we must, in dealing with Homer, renounce a large area of
> normal literary criticism and a vast and varied collection of earlier and con-
> temporary criticism and "appreciations" of Homeric poetry must be thrown
> overboard. . . .
>
> The difficulty is not that Parry's work has proved that there is no artistry
> in these features of Homer's style, but that he has removed all possibility of
> any certitude or even reasonable confidence in the criticism of such features
> of Homeric style and has thus put this side of Homeric criticism into a situ-
> ation wholly different for similar criticism of, say, Sophocles or Shakespeare.
> The hard fact is that in this post-Parry era critics are no longer in a position
> to distinguish the passages in which Homer is merely using a convenient for-
> mula for those in which he has consciously and cunningly chosen *le mot juste.*
> For all that a critic of Homer can now show, the occasional highly appropriate
> word may, like the occasional highly inappropriate one, be purely coincidental—
> part of the law of averages, if you like, in the use of the formulary style.[52]

One result of Parry's investigations, as Combellack seeks to demonstrate,
is that the critic can no longer assign special significance to what seems to
be a striking poetic phrase. A concrete example is cited by him from Book III
(239–44) of the *Iliad,* where Helen referred to the deceased Castor and Pollux
in her description of the Grecian host to Priam. Immediately following her
speech, the poetic narrator comments: "But them, already, the life-giving
earth (φυσίζοος αἶα) possessed, there in Lacedaemon, in the dear fatherland."
John Ruskin, who translated this passage in Book 3 of his *Modern Painters,*

found it to be an instance of "high poetical truth carried to the extreme. The poet has to speak of the earth in sadness, but he will not let that sadness affect or change his thoughts of it. No; though Castor and Pollux be dead, yet the earth is our mother still, fruitful, life-giving."

Though Ruskin's admiration for this line has been echoed by even a modern classicist like C. M. Bowra, Combellack's contention is that the effect of ironical contrast might not have been intended at all by the Homeric poet.[53] When compared with another passage (*Odyssey*. XI. 301) where the phrase appears in almost identical metrical position, "life-giving earth" may suggest no more than a traditional way of conveying the significance of "earth" or "land" with its generic function. This recognition, in fact, confirms Parry's conclusions about the "fixed" noun-epithet formula.

If formulaic language and the recognition of its presence and function force the critic to question or deny the artistry and originality of the poet's diction and style, the knowledge of thematic flexibility in the construction of narratives is no less devastating to the customary conception of poetic unity. Although Lord believes that "the themes lead naturally from one to another to form a song which exists as a whole in the singer's mind with Aristotelian beginning, middle, and end,"[54] Adam Parry and James A. Notopoulos seem less certain about such a possibility. If poems like the *Iliad* and the *Odyssey* have a unity, according to Adam Parry's interpretation of his father's writings, "it is because the use of formulary diction in them is consistent, not because they have a beginning, a middle, and an end, or because they as dramatic narratives reveal any vision, or embody any attitude, which we shall find of value today."[55]

This last statement, of course, has its serious implication, as Adam Parry himself well recognizes, for its logical conclusion even exceeds the older position of the Analyst in denying the poems as artistic wholes by destroying the possibility of any appeal to evidences of "the designing artistic mind." For scholars, however, who are sympathetic with the Parry-Lord thesis, but who are not yet willing to give up entirely the "artist" in Homer, the battle of the books has been over just this very possibility. Even if these poems are regarded as a collection of pastiches, loosely tied together in language and theme, and thus representing finally "the creation of a people,"[56] the question remains as to whether one can discover any quality in them which testifies to the artistic mind, first, in the treatment of particular elements—the smaller units of formulas and individual episodes—and second, in the overall design or structure.

Such a line of investigation has occupied the labor of a multitude of specialists, and one can only indicate here what seems to be the representative approaches to the problem. The crucial element in Parry's argument concerning the Homeric style pertains, of course, to formulas, and especially to the noun-epithet combination which occurs far too frequently and with too great metrical consistency to be considered any particular expression of poetic meaning. As primarily an instrument for the facilitation of versification, the formula may be said to have a function similar to that of any language set to music. W. H. Auden has astutely observed that "the poetic value of the notes may provoke a composer's imagination, but it is their syllabic values which determine the vocal line he writes. In song, poetry is expendable, syllables are not."[57]

This overriding subordination of verbal sense to metrics is, in Parry's judgment, the defining characteristic of the noun-epithet formula. "The fixed epithet," he says, "adds to the combination of substantive and epithet an element of nobility and grandeur, but no more than that. Its sole effect is to form, with its substantive, a heroic expression of the idea of that substantive."[58] Beyond that, there is no "particular reason" for the presence of that epithet; in fact, the particularized meaning of that epithet may stand "in outright contradiction" to the idea of a poetic line or sentence in which it is located. This feature in the Homeric style is, for Parry, the decisive factor distinguishing it from that of any "writing" poet, who, possessing the leisure to search for the *mot juste* for his verse, chooses it "purely for its sense."[59] The "thrift" or "economy" of the formulas, on the other hand, emphasizes their utility in rapid composition, while their complexity and abundance argue for a linguistic tradition too intricate to have been established by a single man.

Critics who have further examined this aspect in Homer have not challenged Parry's conclusions about the linguistic system. D. H. F. Gray's study on the Homeric epithets for helmets, shields, and the sea, for example, confirms the presence of a tradition both in terms of its function and its tendency to preserve archaic elements in diction and thought.[60] Deeper questions, however, persist. How is this tradition put to use in the poems? Is there some explanation, in the words of one recent essay on the subject, "for its power to cast ordinary narration in a transformed medium of art-language?"[61] Is there a complete subjugation of sense to rhythm, of meaning to melody, as some of Parry's statements seem to imply? To answer such questions necessitates additional probings into the Homeric usage of formulas and formulaic language.

William Whallon's careful study of the personal epithets related to several of the prominent Homeric heroes has demonstrated that frequently the descriptions both define and enhance the individual character. In notable occasions, the distinctive epithets of the major heroes may be relevant to the context. An obvious example, for instance, would be the use of "resourceful Odysseus" in *Odyssey*. XIII. 250–55. But even when they are not, "they give the impression of being true to character—not merely because they are tied firmly to their names, but also, and chiefly, because the men denoted by the names really do have, here or there in the *Iliad*, a special claim on the traits and arms that the epithets repeatedly speak of."[62] Such a level of consistency would seem to indicate already that some form of authorial consciousness, whether singular or plural, apparent or submerged, is at work to achieve this kind of aesthetic effect.

The faint traces of calculated or unintentional heightening of character and incident may be discovered even in single words. The celebrated self-revelation of Helen, by her use of "κυνώπιδος (the bitch-eyed one)" in *Iliad*. III. 180, to describe herself, according to one reading of the poem, has at least some claim to uniqueness.[63] Michael Nagler, in his elaborate study of the word κρήδεμνον and its various possible meanings in the Homeric poems ("veil," "battlement," "stopper," and "seal"), has shown that "the oral poet can achieve the same amount of ambiguity, i.e., the same rich density of meanings, as the writing poet."[64] It may be said, of course, that the oral poet's dexterity in exploiting the different shades of meaning in this word is more a sign of habitual skill than conscious design. But other peculiarities of the Homeric style, such as the violent distortion of words or the perversion of traditional formulas, cannot be so simply accounted for. The distinctive manner in which Achilles in the last half of the *Iliad* phrases certain questions, according to Adam Parry's own imaginative interpretation, is symptomatic of something deeper—a sign of Achilles's "basic disillusionment with society and the external world." Homer, to be sure, does not create an entirely new kind of language wherewith to dramatize such a feeling in Achilles. He accomplishes this rather by having Achilles misuse

> the language he disposes of. He asks questions that cannot be answered and makes demands that cannot be met. He uses conventional expressions where we least expect him to, as when he speaks to Patroclus in book 16 of a hope of being offered material gifts by the Greeks, when we know that he has been offered these gifts and that they are meaningless to him; or as when he says that he has won great glory by slaying Hector, when we know that he is really fighting to avenge his comrade, and that he sees no value in the glory that society can confer.[65]

Achilles, Hector, Odysseus, Priam, and all the other Homeric personae must perforce speak within a linguistic tradition which employs the same vocabulary and expressions. But the homogeneity of the formulary language is modified, if not broken up, by the way the formulas are organized, juxtaposed, and joined together in the poetic speeches. This is the salient feature which, in Adam Parry's judgment, contributes to the heroes' individuation as dramatic characters. But to acknowledge such linguistic patterns and their apparent rhetorical effects is to affirm an order of skill and craftsmanship which, while making the fullest use of the tradition, transcends it.[66]

The indicia of Homeric artistry, however, are not confined only to stylistic irregularities and aberrations. There are the developments of character or theme with scrupulous consistency but progressive intensity.[67] There are the masterly uses of digressions which function strategically to call from the past "paradigmatic" significance for present action.[68] There are the episodes of incandescent drama, such as Hector's farewell or Odysseus's reunion with Penelope, where the psychological realism of the moment is reinforced by the subtle interplay of language and symbols.[69] There are the elaborate tapestries of recurrent imageries, and the near mathematical arrangement of thematic sequences has been compared by more than one scholar with ancient Geometric art.[70]

It should be noted that none of these distinctive features of the Homeric poems is considered by contemporary critics to be contrary to the inherent possibilities of oral technique. Indeed, hardly any of them would now deny that the Homeric style is, as Parry has so meticulously and brilliantly demonstrated, an oral style. But it is on the basis of the consistency in the use of this style as well as the consistency in the development of plot and character that G. S. Kirk is led to speak of these two poems as "monumental" compositions and claim for their "overriding unity" the work of a single bard.[71] Whether this last assertion can ever be conclusively proven is dubious, for the matter of the *Iliad* and the *Odyssey*'s authorship involves a number of related issues which still provoke discussion and debate. For one thing, the theory about the circumstances of Homeric composition has not advanced much beyond the level of learned conjectures. For another, the stages of development and transmission of the story until it reaches the fixed textual form are by no means clear. We know with certainty neither the date of "Homer's" performance (or if there ever was a single person who sang either one of these songs in the versions known to us) nor his relationship to the rise of literacy in Greek antiquity.

These perplexities notwithstanding, Kirk is surely right when he declares that "from the aesthetic point of view the *effect* of unity in the *Iliad* and *Odyssey* is what really matters, not the question of whether that effect was achieved by one, two or twenty poets." This remark may sound perilously close to some of the older arguments of the Unitarians and thus verges on the kind of "subjective criticism" deplored by Lord, but Kirk is quick to add that "it is only by understanding how and why the poems were composed that one can hope to penetrate their real meaning and effect for a contemporary Greek audience."[72] Here, I suspect, is the crux of the hermeneutical problem connected with the Homeric poems when they are regarded as oral compositions.

It is the lesson drawn from the modern discussion of hermeneutics that in any process of understanding a literary document, we cannot divorce aesthetic effect from verbal meaning, and we can ascertain verbal meaning only by the determination of intentionality.[73] For this reason, the written text must be accorded a magisterial and regulative role in the attempted act of comprehension, for it is through the indispensable medium of linguistic conventions that the speaker-writer can make known and share his intentions.

An oral performance, by definition and contrast, provides a much more flexible, and, therefore, ambiguous sphere for the transaction of verbal meaning. Whether it is a sung *Lied* of Schubert, a dramatic declamation (Lady Macbeth's famous query of Act I, "We fail?"), or the "improvisatory" creation of a modern oral poet in Greece or Yugoslavia, the nuances of vocal pitch, rhythm, pace, tone, and dynamics, the bodily gestures, and the varied texture of musical accompaniment can, at the very moment of delivery, all convey different levels of intentionality and thus alter verbal meaning—sometimes to a radical extent. In Husserlian terms, we may say that the oral execution of the intentional act can significantly modify the semasiological status of the intended object. But that can be achieved and perceived only if it is a live performance, or a recording of one, during which the performer's technique and the existential intensity of the moment join to illumine or conceal certain aspects of the work that is being rendered.

That such is indeed the nature of our experience may be gathered from the testimony of Notopoulos, who has, in my opinion, written one of the most intelligent discussions concerning the critical principles of an oral poetics. He writes:

Thus one of the most important implications of Parry's work is the need for an aesthetics which emanates from an understanding of the oral technique of composition, the form and mentality of oral poetry. This problem presented itself to me in the following way. When I was recording the heroic oral poetry in Greece I experienced it as part of the audience who was listening to the bard reshape his tradition. The next stage occurred when I replayed the tapes in my study. The last stage was when I transcribed some of the sung poetry into songless text and began studying it with the traditional philological concepts of criticism long ingrained in me. Suddenly the magic was gone—the audience, the bard, the sung tale. I asked myself what had happened, why was my text flat? Why was I one with the audience when I heard the song, completely unaware of contradictions, of bad joints, of the existence of formulae as formulae? The text had lost its magic. This happened again and again. The cause was not to be found in calling it poor poetry, for as soon as I replayed the tape the song got better, and it became better yet when I associated it with my memory of the bard singing it and the audience hearing it. I suddenly realized what happens to oral poetry when it becomes a text. It loses much of its magic; it loses even more when we evaluate it with the principles of literary criticism which ignore the forces at work in oral poetry.[74]

Now, the decisive difference between the modern oral poetry of Greece and Homer, I submit, lies precisely in the fact that the latter loses none of its magic even when it is read as a songless text. Or, to state the matter another way, not having heard the original performances we have no idea as to how much of the magic is lost; Homer is one whose greatness shines through the inscribed text. For all the flaws and inconsistencies in the poems, for all the frequencies of his "nodding," his works are among those which, in the words of T. S. Eliot's tribute to Dante, "one can only just hope to grow up to at the end of life."

This is not to deny that there are vast elements of oral culture and tradition preserved in the Homeric language. It is, however, to take with utmost seriousness the different conditions for the determination of intentionality, meaning, and effect: whereas we have the privilege of hearing viva voce the bards from modern Greece and Novi Pazar, that privilege is forever lost with regard to Homer. To that extent, the criticism of the Homeric epics perhaps can never be based purely on an oral poetics, however it is conceived. In his perceptive rehearsal of the matter, Notopoulos rightly stresses the critical importance of the audience in the poetics of oral poetry. He also points out that the unity of the Homeric as well as other early oral poems of Greece cannot be explained simply by reference to the organic principle of Aristotle; it is rather to be sought in the paratactic style and method of organizing materials, the technique of the "stitching of songs (ῥάψαντες ἀοιδήν)" referred to in one of the Hesiodic fragments.[75] Yet, even in the use of the medias res device in telling his story, a device which according to Notopoulos is familiar to all oral poetry, the Homeric poet displays an order of technical brilliance and mastery that are difficult to surpass.

If Rodney Delasanta's analysis of the *Odyssey* is not far off the mark, then we have in those instances of foreshadowing, flashback, and delegated narrations such scrupulously faithful observation of the changes in point of view that, even by the standards of modern fiction, it must be considered an astonishing feat of narration.[76] And on the surface of the matter, it would seem that such an accomplishment would be hardly possible for the poet or poets in oral performance. But the argument here is not concerned with the question of whether our present Homeric texts are written or oral compositions, but with the fact that the impression Delasanta received is derived solely from the examination of the written text. Since we lack the conditions of actual performance, we cannot demonstrate decisively whether such and such an effect would be in fact possible during the presentation. All that we have, in Homer's case, is the text confronting us, and it must be the determinative guide to our response and to our interpretation.

Again, this assertion is not meant to indicate stubborn obtuseness in the wake of the advances in scholarship. The great legacy and permanent merit of Parry's labor lie in his penetrating elucidation of certain linguistic conventions found in the Homeric poems. By clarifying the nature of its formative and operative principles, he has shown that Homeric language is both formulaic and traditional. In doing so, he has helped to establish norms and limits for the interpretation of intention and meaning, for he enables the reader as audience to perceive what and what not to expect from the Homeric style and diction. That this is a magnificent achievement in historical and philological scholarship needs no further repetition; that it must inform part of the presupposition of every Homeric student is also firmly acknowledged. But the clarification of linguistic conventions, however crucial and important it is, is by itself no more an act of aesthetic judgment than the recognition by the musical historian that the cadence built on the trill over a dominant seventh chord and its resolution is an eighteenth-century musical commonplace favored by Mozart.

To proceed further, criticism must ask how this hackneyed practice has been transformed and assimilated into the magic of Mozart's scores, just as it must ask—as Paolo Vivante has done recently with great eloquence— whether some imaginative principle is at work by which Homeric language and theme are forged into an artistic whole, and what kind of poetic subjectivity is revealed through such uses of language and such representation of reality.[77] In his homage to Dante, St.-John Perse has said that "c'est le destin des grandes forces créatives d'exercer leur pouvoir à travers toutes conventions d'époque." Because of Parry and his successors, we now see with far greater lucidity the conventions of the Homeric epoch, and that should in turn better prepare us to apprehend the poet's destiny as well.

NOTES

1. Susanne K. Langer, *Feeling and Form* (New York, 1953), p.304–5.

2. Cf. Sir John L. Myres's observation in *Homer and His Critics,* ed. by Dorothea Gray (London, 1958), p.214–15: "Our *Iliad* and *Odyssey* survived as they have, because they came into existence at the climax of this [i.e., a traditional] school of literary art. They superseded their forerunners, and they had no successors to supersede them. Of the poems of this epic decline, we know enough to recognize their limitations of scope and style. The reason for their degeneracy is also evident, in the competition of new literary forms— choric, lyric, dithyrambic, tragic; and eventually their place was taken by mere prose extracts and insipid parodies." See also Brooks Otis's chapter, "From Homer to Virgil:

The Obsolescence of Epic," in *Virgil: A Study in Civilized Poetry* (Oxford, Eng., 1964), p.28 and 33–40; Basil Willey, *The Seventeenth Century Background: Studies in the Thought of the Age in Relation to Poetry and Religion* (New York, 1934), p.206–18; J. B. Broadbent, *Some Graver Subject: An Essay on Paradise Lost* (New York, 1960), p.47–65; Douglas Bush, *English Literature in the Earlier Seventeenth Century: 1600–1660*, v. 5 of the *Oxford History of English Literature*, ed. by F. P. Wilson and Bonamy Dobrée (rev. ed., Oxford, Eng., 1960), p.368.

3. Gilbert Murray, *The Rise of the Greek Epic* (4th ed., Oxford, Eng., 1934), p.5.

4. See *Perspectives on Epic*, ed. by Frederick H. Candelaria and William C. Strange (Boston, 1965).

5. See Mark Van Doren, *The Noble Voice: A Study of Ten Great Poems* (New York, 1946).

6. For a succinct summary of the history of criticism on the epic, see Seymour M. Pitcher, "Epic," in *Encyclopedia of Poetry and Poetics*, ed. by Alex Preminger (Princeton, 1965), p.242–47.

7. H. T. Wade-Gery, *The Poet of the Iliad* (Cambridge, Eng., 1952), p.38.

8. The entire collection of Parry's published works together with some unpublished materials is now available in a single volume edition, with translations of his two French theses. See *The Making of Homeric Verse: The Collected Papers of Milman Parry*, ed. by Adam Parry (New York and Oxford, Eng., 1971).

9. For non-Homeric Greek poetry, see James A. Notopoulos, "Homer, Hesiod and the Archaean Heritage of Oral Poetry," *Hesperia* 29:177–97 (1960); also see his "The Homeric Hymns as Oral Poetry: A Study of Post Homeric Oral Tradition," *American Journal of Philology* 82:337–68 (1962); and his "Studies in Early Greek Poetry," *Harvard Studies in Classical Philology* 68:1–77 (1964); T. G. Rosenmeyer, "The Formula in Early Greek Poetry," *Arion* 4:295–311 (1965). For Biblical literature, see R. G. Bolling, "'Synonymous' Parallelism in the Psalms," *Journal of Semitic Studies* 5:221–55 (1960); C. H. Lohr, "Oral Techniques in the Gospel of Matthew," *Catholic Biblical Quarterly* 23:403–55 (1961); Joseph Blenkinsopp, "Structure and Style in Judges 13–16," *Journal of Biblical Literature* 82:65–76 (1963); J. W. Wevers, "Semitic Sound Structures," *Canadian Journal of Linguistics* 7:9–13 (1961); R. C. Culley, "An Approach to the Problem of Oral Tradition," *Vetus Testamentum* 13:113–25 (1963); and his *Oral Formulaic Language in the Biblical Psalms* (Toronto, 1967); William Whallon, "Old Testament Poetry and Homeric Epic," *Comparative Literature* 18:113–31 (1966); and his *Formula, Character, and Context: Studies in Homeric, Old English and Old Testament Poetry* (Cambridge and Washington, D.C., 1969), p.139–210. For medieval literature, see F. P. Magoun, Jr., "Oral-Formulaic Character of Anglo-Saxon Narrative Poetry," *Speculum* 28:446–67 (1953); his "Bede's Story of Caedmon: The Case History of an Anglo-Saxon Oral Singer," *Speculum* 30:49–63 (1955); and his "The Theme of the Beasts of Battle in Anglo-Saxon Poetry," *Neuphilologische Mitteilungen* 56:81–89 (1955); Stanley B. Greenfield, "The Formulaic Expression of the Theme of the 'Exile' in Anglo-Saxon Poetry," *Speculum* 30:200–6 (1955); R. A. Waldron, "Oral-Formulaic Technique and Middle English Alliterative Poetry," *Speculum* 32:792–804 (1957); Andrien Bonjour, "*Beowulf* and the Beasts of Battle," *PMLA* 72:563–73 (1957); Robert Creed, "The *Andswarode*-system in Old English Poetry," *Speculum* 32:523–28 (1957); his "The Making of an Anglo-Saxon Poem," *ELH* 26:445–54 (1959); his "On the Possibility of Criticizing Old English Poetry," *Texas Studies in Literature and Language* 3:97–106 (1961); his "The Singer Looks at His Source," *CL* 14:44–52 (1962); and his "Afterword," in Burton Raffel's translation of *Beowulf* (New York, 1963), p.123–48; Robert E. Diamond, "The Diction of the Signed Poems of Cynewulf," *Philological Quarterly* 38:228–41 (1959); and his "Theme as Ornamentation in Anglo-Saxon Poetry," *PMLA* 76:461–68 (1961); James Ross, "Formulaic Composition in Gaelic Oral Literature," *Modern Philology* 57:1–12 (1959); W. A. O'Neil, "Another Look at Oral Poetry in the *Seafarer*," *Speculum* 35:596–600 (1960); J. Campbell, "Oral Poetry in the *Seafarer*," *Speculum* 35:87–96 (1960); David K. Crowne, "The Hero on the Beach: An Example of Composition by Theme in Anglo-Saxon Poetry," *NM* 61:362–72 (1960); Larry D. Benson, "The Literary Character of Anglo-Saxon Formulaic Poetry," *PMLA* 81:334–41 (1966); R. F. Lawrence, "The Formulaic Theory and Its Application to English Alliterative Poetry," in *Essays on Style and Language*, ed. by Roger Fowler (London, 1966), p.166–83; S. G. Nichols, Jr., *Formulaic Diction and Thematic Composition in*

the *Chanson de Roland* (Chapel Hill, 1961); Ann Chalmers Watts, *The Lyre and the Harp: A Comparative Reconsideration of Oral Tradition in Homer and Old English Epic Poetry* (New Haven, 1969). For non-Western literature, see M. B. Emeneau, "Oral Poets of South India—the Todas," *Journal of American Folklore* 71:312–24 (1951); N. Sen, "Comparative Studies in Oral Epic Poetry and the Valmīkī Rāmāyaṇa: A Report on the Bālākanda," *American Oriental Society Journal* 86:397–409 (1966), and the later reply by J. L. Brockington in *AOSJ* 89:412–14 (1969); K. Kailasapathy, *Tamil Heroic Poetry* (Oxford, 1968), p.135–228; A. T. Hatto, "The Birth of Manas: A Confrontation of Two Branches of Heroic Epic Poetry in Kirgiz," *Asia Major* 14:217–41 (1969), n.s.; Nora K. Chadwick and Victor Zhirmunsky, *Oral Epics of Central Asia* (Cambridge, Eng., 1969); Hans H. Frankel, "The Formulaic Language of the Chinese Ballad 'Southeast Fly the Peacocks'," *Bulletin of the Institute of History and Philology Academia Sinica* 39, pt.2:219–42 (1969); J. L. Brockington, "Stereotyped Expressions in the Rāmāyaṇa," *AOSJ* 90:210–27 (1970); Glen Dudbridge, *The Hsi-yu chi: A Study of Antecedents to the Sixteenth-Century Chinese Novel* (Cambridge, Eng., 1970), p.1–10. For contemporary preaching, see Bruce A. Rosenberg, "Formulaic Quality of Spontaneous Sermons," *JAF* 82:3–20 (1970); and his *The Art of the American Folk Preacher* (New York, 1970).

10. The literature on the Homeric Question is enormous and endless. I refer to works which take account of Parry's contribution: M. P. Nilsson, *Homer and Mycenae* (London, 1933), p.1–55; Myres, *Homer,* esp. Gray's chapters on p.223–93; Rhys Carpenter, *Folk Tale, Fiction and Saga in the Homeric Epics,* Sather Classical Lectures, 20 (Berkeley, 1946); p.1–22; W. C. Greene, "The Spoken and the Written Word," *HSCP* 60:24–31 (1951); C. M. Bowra, *Heroic Poetry* (London, 1952), p.215–329, 404–75, and his *Homer and His Forerunners,* The Andrew Lang Lectures (Edinburgh, 1955); Albin Lesky, *Geschichte der griechischen Literatur* (2d ed., Berne and Munich, 1957–58), p.49–58; Cedric H. Whitman, *Homer and the Heroic Tradition* (Cambridge, 1958), p.1–16; Denys Page, *History and the Homeric Iliad,* Sather Classical Lectures, 31 (Berkeley, 1959, p.218–96; J. A. Davison, "The Homeric Question," in *A Companion to Homer,* ed. by Alan J. B. Wace and Frank H. Stubbings (London, 1962), p.234–65; G. S. Kirk, *The Songs of Homer* (Cambridge, Eng., 1962), p.55–104; G. S. Kirk, ed., *The Language and Background of Homer, Some Recent Studies and Controversies* (Cambridge, Eng., 1964); Charles R. Beye, The Iliad, The Odyssey *and the Epic Tradition* (New York, 1966), p.1–37; E. R. Dodds, "Homer," in *Fifty Years and Twelve of Classical Scholarship,* ed. by Maurice Platnauer (rev. ed., New York, 1968), p.1–16; Watts, *Oral Tradition,* p.6–45; A. Parry, *Collected Papers,* p.ix–lxii.

11. Cf. Whitman, *Heroic Tradition,* p.5; Dodds, "Homer," p.16–17.

12. Kirk, *Songs,* p.101.

13. Cf. Davison, "Homeric Question," p.238–41.

14. See *Conjectures académiques; ou, Dissertation sur l'Iliade,* ed. by Victor Magnien (Paris, 1925).

15. *Remarks upon a Late Discourse of Free Thinking* (published in 1713), quoted by A. Parry in *Collected Papers,* p.xii.

16. This work was reprinted in 1971 by Garland Publishing, Inc., of New York.

17. Cf. Bruce M. Metzger, "Trends in the Textual Criticism of The Iliad, The Mahābhārata, and The New Testament," *JBL,* 65:339–52 (1946).

18. Cf. Ulrich von Wilamowitz-Moellendorff, *Die Heimkehr des Odysseus* (Berlin, 1927), p.172: "Es wird immer Idioten geben, die versichern, der Wundermann Homer hätte Ilias und Odyssee gemacht, der Wundermann Moses den Pentateuch. Aber unsere Wissenschaft hat das Recht, die Abergläubischen so zu behandln wie die Astronomen des Horoskopstellen." See also Murray, *Greek Epic,* chap. 7.

19. Cf. C. M. Bowra's observation in *Tradition and Design in the Iliad* (Oxford, 1930), p.8–9: "The *Iliad* implies a long history before itself, and a long series of poems written in much the same style. . . . But no living tradition is mere tradition. Each poet worthy of the name makes something new of it, even if he is bound by the closest rules and conventions. No matter how strict the form may be or how overmastering the rules, a poet of genius may still impose his personality and create a new thing without contravening the inherited laws of artistry. Just so Villon created masterpieces in the timeworn forms of the *rondeau* and *ballade* when they seemed dead in the hands of Deschamps, so too Homer preserved the properties and created a work of art on which he laid the impressions

of his own great, if elusive, personality. As a man he may elude us, but as a poet we know him and catch his individual utterance. Behind the style there is still the poet." For a qualified view of this relationship between the poet and the poem, see Northrop Frye, *Fables of Identity: Studies in Poetic Mythology* (New York, 1963), p.11.

20. Murray, *Greek Epic*, p.254 and 256.

21. See M. Parry, "A Comparative Study of Diction as One of the Elements of Style in Early Greek Epic Poetry," in *Collected Papers*, p.421.

22. "The Traditional Epithet in Homer," tr. by A. Parry in *Collected Papers*, p.21.

23. Page, *Homeric Iliad*, p.223.

24. See Watts, *Oral Tradition*, p.19–20; *Collected Papers*, p.*xix–xxii*; J. B. Hainsworth, *The Flexibility of the Homeric Formula* (Oxford, Eng., 1968), p.4.

25. Examples are taken from M. Parry, "Traditional Epithet," in *Collected Papers*, p.39 and p.10–11.

26. M. Parry, "Studies in the Epic Technique of Oral Verse-Making. I: Homer and Homeric Style," in *Collected Papers*, p.272.

27. M. Parry, "Traditional Epithet," in *Collected Papers*, p.13.

28. M. Parry, "Homeric Style," in *Collected Papers*, p.275.

29. M. Parry, "Traditional Epithet," in *Collected Papers*, p.19; cf. also "Homeric Style," *ibid*. p.276–77.

30. To support his argument against single authorship, M. Parry in chap. 2 of "Traditional Epithet" sought to demonstrate a single literate poet such as Apollonius or Vergil does not create a vast system of fixed formulas or any formulaic system which can be compared with Homeric "economy." For criticisms of M. Parry on these points, see M. W. M. Pope, "The Parry-Lord Theory of Composition," *Acta Classica* 6:(esp.)7–19 (1963); Arie Hoekstra, *Homeric Modifications of Formulaic Prototypes* (Amsterdam, 1965), p.16–17 and note 1 on p.17; Joseph A. Russo, "The Structural Formula in Homeric Verse," *Yale Classical Studies* 20:226–35 (1966); J. B. Hainsworth, "Structure and Content in Epic Formulae: The Question of the Unique Expression," *Classical Quarterly* 14:158–64 (1964) n.s.; and his *Homeric Formula*, p.9–11. For a recent study of what may seem like formulaic characteristics even in a literate poet, see Carl Conrad, "Word-Order in Latin Epic from Ennius to Vergil," *HSCP* 69:195-258 (1965).

31. "The Homeric Gloss: A Study in Word-Sense," in M. Parry, *Collected Papers*, p.249; cf. also M. Parry, "Traditional Epithet," *ibid*. p.127.

32. M. Parry, "Homeric Style," in *Collected Papers*, p.317.

33. *Ibid.*, p.267.

34. M. Parry, "Whole Formulaic Verses in Greek and South Slavic Heroic Song," in *Collected Papers*, p.377.

35. M. Parry, "Cor Huso: A Study of Southslavic Song," in *Collected Papers*, p.440.

36. Albert B. Lord, *The Singer of Tales* (Cambridge, 1960), p.129 and 137. Cf. also Notopoulos, "Studies," p.14; but G. S. Kirk in "Homer and Modern Oral Poetry: Some Confusions," *CQ* 10:271–81 (1960), (repr. in *Language and Background of Homer*, p.79–89) takes the view that the transmission is done without a text but by verbatim memorization. Lord, of course, has advocated in "Homer's Originality: Oral Dictated Texts," *Transactions and Proceedings of the American Philological Association* 84:124–34 (1953), and in *Singer*, p.152, that our present Homeric texts must have been the result of dictation, but he is strongly disinclined to believe that the idea originated from Homer. For a recent essay supporting the thesis of Lord, see D. M. Gunn, "Narrative Inconsistency and the Oral Dictated Text in the Homeric Epic," *AJP* 91:192–203 (1970).

37. Lord, *Singer*, p.24–25.

38. *Ibid.*, p.37.

39. *Ibid.*, p.65.

40. M. Parry, "Cor Huso," in *Collected Papers*, p.446, 450, and 461.

41. Albert B. Lord, "Composition by Theme in Homer and South Slavic Epos," *TAPhA* 83:73 (1952), and *Singer*, p.69.

42. Lord, *Singer*, chap. 4. Cf. also A. B. Lord, "Homer and Other Heroic Poetry," in *A Companion to Homer*, p.188–93; H. Munro Chadwick and N. Kershaw Chadwick, *The Growth of Literature* (Cambridge, Eng., 1932), v. 1, chaps. 2–4; Bowra, *Heroic Poetry*, chap. 5.

43. See Carpenter, *Folk Tale*, p.112–94.

44. Lord, *Singer,* chap.9. A recent study of other versions of the *Nostoi* theme in the epic cycles may be found in G. L. Huxley, *Greek Epic Poetry* (Cambridge, 1969), p.162–76. For a comparison of different materials, see Victor Zhirmunsky, "The Epic of Alpamysh and the Return of Odysseus," *Proceedings of the British Academy,* p.267–86 (1967).

45. Lord, *Singer,* p. 95.

46. See A. B. Lord, "Tradition and the Oral Poet: Homer, Huso and Avdo Medjedović," in *La poesia epica e la sua formazione,* Problemi attuali di scienza e di cultura, quaderno n.139 (Rome, 1970), p.13–28.

47. Notopoulos, "Studies," p.35.

48. *Ibid.,* p.33.

49. Lord, *Singer,* p.94.

50. Lord, "Homer as Oral Poet," *HSCP* 72:1 (1967).

51. Wade-Gery, *Poet,* p.38.

52. F. M. Combellack, "Milman Parry and Homeric Originality," *CL* 11:196 and 208 (1959).

53. *Ibid.,* 11:203. Cf. Bowra, *Tradition and Design,* p.84, and *Heroic Poetry,* p.240.

54. Lord, *Singer,* p.94.

55. A. Parry, *Collected Papers,* p.*lii.*

56. *Ibid.,* p.*li.*

57. See W. H. Auden, "Some Reflections on Music and Opera," *Partisan Review* 19:10–18 (1952). Susanne K. Langer goes further in *Feeling and Form,* p.150, and asserts that "when words enter into music they are no longer prose or poetry, they are elements of the music. Their office is to help create and develop the primary illusion of music, virtual time, and not that of literature, which is something else; so they give up their literary status and take on purely musical functions. But that does not mean that now they have only sound-value. Here the theory of David Prall, that the 'aesthetic surface' of music is pure sound in orders of pitch, loudness, and timbre, and that in hearing music we perceive designs in the compass of this 'aesthetic surface,' requires a little emendation if it is not to lose its significance in the face of some of the greatest musical endeavors—song, cantata, oratorio and opera. *For what we perceive is not the aesthetic surface.* What we hear is motion, tension, growth, living form—the illusion of a many-dimensional time in passage. . . . The work is, as Prall says, composed of sounds; but everything that gives the sounds a different appearance of motion, conflict, repose, emphasis, etc., is a musical element." That the oral poet in performance is guided more by the shape of his melody and rhythm than by strict metrical considerations has been reported by Notopoulos in "Studies," p.48. Perhaps the question ought to be asked with respect to how the criticism of oral poetry approximates the exegesis of musical texts.

58. M. Parry, "Traditional Epithet," in *Collected Papers,* p.126–27.

59. *Ibid.,* p.133.

60. D. H. F. Gray, "Homeric Epithets for Things," *CQ* 61:109–21 (1947), repr. in Kirk, *Language and Background of Homer,* p.55–67.

61. Michael N. Nagler, "Towards a Generative View of the Oral Formula," *TAPhA* 98:308 (1967).

62. Whallon, *Formula,* p.70.

63. So argued by Watts, *Oral Tradition,* p.40, on the basis that "the meter could dispense with the line; the poetic imagination could not dispense with a deft characterization of Helen of Troy." Cf. also A. Parry, "Have We Homer's 'Iliad'?" in *YCS,* 20:199–200 (1966).

64. Nagler, "Towards a Generative View," *TAPhA* 98:302.

65. Adam Parry, "The Language of Achilles," *TAPhA* 87:6–7 (1956); cf. also Kirk in *Songs,* p.206–7.

66. See, for example, Joseph A. Russo, "Homer Against His Tradition," *Arion* 7:275–95 (1968).

67. See J. I. Armstrong, "The Arming Motif in the 'Iliad'," *AJP* 79:337–54 (1958); M. W. M. Pope, "Athena's Development in Homeric Epic," *AJP* 81:113–35 (1960); William Sale, "Achilles and Heroic Values," *Arion* 2:86–100 (1963).

68. See Norman Austin, "The Function of Digressions in the *Iliad,*" *Greek, Roman and*

Byzantine Studies 7:295–312 (1966). One of the most influential studies of Homeric digression is, of course, Erich Auerbach's "The Scar of Ulysses," first published in *Partisan Review* 17:411–32 (1950), repr. in *Mimesis: The Representation of Reality in Western Literature,* tr. by Willard Trask (Princeton, 1953), p.1–19. For a penetrating criticism of Auerbach's thesis, see Whallon, "Old Testament Poetry and Homeric Epic."

69. See Anne Amory, "The Reunion of Odysseus," in *Essays on the Odyssey: Selected Modern Criticism,* ed. by Charles H. Taylor, Jr. (Bloomington and London, 1963), p.100–36, and her "The Gates of Horn and Ivory," *YCS* 20:3–57 (1966). This last essay drew extensive criticism from Lord in "Homer as Oral Poet," p.34–46. For her rejoinder, see Anne Amory Parry, "Homer as Artist," *CQ* 21:1–15 (1971) n.s.

70. Cf. Whitman, *Heroic Tradition,* chap.11; T. B. L. Webster, *From Mycenae to Homer* (2d. ed., New York, 1964), chaps.7–8; J. A. Notopoulos, "Homer and Geometric Art," *Athena* 61:65–93 (1957); Stephen Bertman, "The *Telemachy* and Structural Symmetry," *TAPhA* 97:15–28 (1966).

71. Kirk, *Songs,* p.253–300.

72. *Ibid.,* p.267.

73. See E. D. Hirsch, *Validity in Interpretation* (New Haven and London, 1967), p.212–35.

74. Notopoulos, "Studies," p.48.

75. *Ibid.,* p.57–59.

76. Rodney Delasanta, *The Epic Voice* (The Hague, 1967), chap. 2.

77. See Paolo Vivante, *The Homeric Imagination: A Study of Homer's Poetic Perception of Reality* (Bloomington and London, 1970).

·II·

DEFINITIONS

C. S. Lewis

PRIMARY EPIC: TECHNIQUE AND SUBJECT

PRIMARY EPIC

Then the first cors come with crakkyng of trumpes,
With mony baner ful bryght that therbi henged;
Newe nakryn noyse with the noble pipes,
Wylde werbles and wyght wakned lote,
That mony hert ful highe hef at her towches.
    Sir Gawayn and the Grene Knyght, 116.

The older critics divided Epic into Primitive and Artificial, which is unsatisfactory, because no surviving ancient poetry is really primitive and all poetry is in some sense artificial. I prefer to divide it into Primary Epic and Secondary Epic—the adjectives being purely chronological and implying no judgements of value. The *secondary* here means not "the second rate," but what comes after, and grows out of, the *primary.*

The Primary Epic will be illustrated from the Homeric poems and from the English *Beowulf,* and our effort here, as throughout the present discussion, will be to discover what sort of thing the Primary Epics were, how they were meant to be used, what expectations they hoped to satisfy. But at the very outset a distinction must be made. Both *Beowulf* and the Homeric poems, besides being poetry themselves, describe poetical performances, at feasts and the like, proceeding in the world which they show us. From these descriptions we can gather what the epic was in a heroic age; but it does not follow that *Beowulf* and the Homeric poems are themselves the same kind of thing. They may or may not *be* what they *describe.* We must therefore distinguish the literary conditions attributed to the heroic age within the surviving poems, which, since they are described, can be studied, from the literary conditions in which the surviving poems were themselves produced, which can only be conjectured. I proceed, then, to some account of the literary conditions which Homer *describes.*

Originally "Primary Epic," "The Technique of Primary Epic" and "The Subject of Primary Epic." From C. S. Lewis, *A Preface to "Paradise Lost"* (London: Oxford University Press, 1961), p.12–31. Reprinted by permission of the publisher.

All poetry is oral, delivered by the voice, not read, and, so far as we are told, not written either. And all poetry is musical. The poet delivers it to the accompaniment of some instrument (*phorminx* and *kithara* are the names given to it—or them). But I think we detect within this oral poetry two kinds —a popular poetry, and a court poetry. We read in one place how "merry boys and girls (at a vintage) carried the sweet fruit in baskets, and amidst them a youth played on the stringed instrument that moves desire and sang the sweet song called *Linos*" (*Il*. XVIII. 569). Or again, we read of a dancing floor where "boys and girls danced hand in hand and amidst them sang the minstrel while two tumblers whirled in the centre" (*Il. ibid.*, 593 *et seq.*). There is no suggestion of the court in either passage. If we now turn to scenes at court we find two things going on, of which the first may or may not be different from the popular poetry, but which are certainly quite different from each other. In the first, the court poet gets up, steps into a central position in the midst of a troupe of expert dancers and sings a short lay which has the three characteristics of being about gods not men, of being comic, and of being indecent. That is the light court poetry. (*Od*. VIII. 256– 65.) The serious court poetry is another matter. The poet has a chair placed for him and an instrument put into his hands. A table is set beside him with wine, that he may drink "when his heart desires." Presently, without orders from the king, he begins his lay when the Muse prompts him; its three characteristics are that it is about men, it is historically true, and it is tragic. (*Od*. VIII. 62–75.)

The important point to notice is that of the three kinds of performance mentioned only the last is epic. Primary Epic is not to be identified with "oral poetry of the heroic age," or even with "oral court poetry." It is *one* of the different kinds of poetry heard in a heroic court. Its sharp distinction from lighter kinds makes less impression on us than it should because we merely read about it. If we had *seen* the poet, first ordered to get up and take his place in a comic and indecent ballet, and then, seated and honoured with wine and spontaneously beginning his tragic lay at the inner prompting of a goddess, we should never again forget the distinction.

Turning to *Beowulf*, we find a slightly different situation. We hear nothing at all in this poem about poetry outside the court. But we can supplement *Beowulf* from other sources. In Bede's account of Caedmon (*Eccl. His*. IV, 24) we get the glimpse of a feast among men apparently of peasant's rank, where each sang in turn as the harp came to him. It is just conceivable that what each sang was a very short heroic lay, but there is no reason to suppose this. Certainly the Anglo-Saxons had songs of a very different type. Alcuin's letter to Hygebald in 797 is always quoted because, in deploring the use of heathen poetry in religious houses, he mentions *Hinieldus* who is probably Hrothgar's son-in-law Ingeld. But it should also be remembered that he asks for "the voice of the reader in the house rather than the laughter of the mob in the streets" (*voces legentium in domibus tuis non ridentium turvam in plateis*). This "laughter" would not be connected with heroic lays. No doubt, Alcuin may be referring to ribald conversation and not to poetry at all. But it seems to me very likely that he means comic poetry, and that comic, or at least light, poems were sung at the feast which Caedmon attended. This is admittedly conjecture; but it would be very odd if the ancestors of Chaucer, Shakespeare, Dickens, and Mr. Jacobs produced no funny stories.

When we turn to *Beowulf's* picture of the court we are on surer ground. In lines 2105 and following we have a performance given by Hrothgar himself. We learn that he sometimes (*hwilum*) produced a *gidd* or lay which was *soþ and sarlic* (true and tragic), sometimes a tale of wonders (*sellic spell*), and sometimes, with the fetters of age heavy upon him, he began to recall his youth, the strength that once was his in battle; his heart swelled within him as he remembered the vanished winters. Professor [J. R.] Tolkien has suggested to me that this is an account of the complete range of court poetry, in which three kinds of poem can be distinguished—the lament for mutability (*hu seo þrag gewat*) now represented by the *Wanderer* and the *Seafarer*, the tale of strange adventures, and the "true and tragic" lay such as the *Finnsburg* poem, which alone is true epic. *Beowulf* itself contains elements of the *sellic spell*, but it is certainly *sarlic* and probably much of it was regarded as *soþ*. Without pressing these distinctions too far, we can certainly conclude from this passage that the author of *Beowulf* is aware of different kinds of court poetry. Here, as in Homer, Epic does not mean simply whatever was sung in hall. It is one of the possible entertainments, marked off from the others, in Homer by the spontaneity and quasi-oracular character of the poet's performance, and in both Homer and *Beowulf* by tragic quality, by supposed historical truth, and by the gravity that goes with "true tragedy."

Such, then, is epic as we first hear of it; the loftiest and gravest among the kinds of court poetry in the oral period, a poetry *about* nobles, made *for* nobles, and performed on occasion, *by* nobles (cf. *Il.* IX. 189). We shall go endlessly astray if we do not get well fixed in our minds at the outset the picture of a venerable figure, a king, a great warrior, or a poet inspired by the Muse, seated and chanting to the harp a poem on high matters before an assembly of nobles in a court, at a time when the court was the common centre of many interests which have since been separated; when it was not only the Windsor Castle, but also the Somerset House, the Horseguards, the Covent Garden, and perhaps even, in certain respects, the Westminster Abbey, of the tribe. But also, it was the place of festivity, the place of brightest hearths and strongest drink, of courtesy, merriment, news, and friendship. All this is a long way from Mr. John Milton printing a book to be sold in seventeenth-century London, but it is not irrelevant. From its early association with the heroic court there comes into Epic Poetry a quality which survives, with strange transformations and enrichments, down to Milton's own time, and it is a quality which moderns find difficult to understand. It has been split up, or dissociated, by recent developments, so that we now have to represent it by piecing together what seem to us quite unconnected ideas, but are really fragments of that old unity.

This quality will be understood by any one who really understands the meaning of the Middle English word *solempne*. This means something different, but not quite different, from modern English *solemn*. Like *solemn* it implies the opposite of what is familiar, free and easy, or ordinary. But unlike *solemn* it does not suggest gloom, oppression, or austerity. The ball in the first act of *Romeo and Juliet* was a "solemnity." The feast at the beginning of *Gawain and the Green Knight* is very much of a solemnity. A great mass by Mozart or Beethoven is as much a solemnity in its hilarious *gloria* as in its poignant *crucifixus est*. Feasts are, in this sense, *more* solemn than fasts. Easter is *solempne*, Good Friday is not. The *solempne* is the festal which is also the stately and the ceremonial, the proper occasion for *pomp*—and the very fact that *pompous* is now used only in a bad sense measures the degree to which we have lost the old idea of "solemnity." To recover it you must think of a court ball, or a coronation, or a victory march, as these things appear to people who *enjoy* them; in an age when every one puts on his oldest clothes to be happy in, you must re-awake the simpler state of mind in which people put on gold and scarlet to be happy in. Above all, you must be rid of the hideous idea, fruit of a widespread inferiority complex, that pomp, on the proper occasions, has any connexion with vanity or self-conceit. A celebrant approaching the altar, a princess led out by a king to dance a minuet, a general officer on a ceremonial parade, a major-domo preceding the boar's head at a Christmas feast—all these wear unusual clothes and move with calculated dignity. This does not mean that they are vain, but that they are obedient; they are obeying the *hoc age* which presides over every solemnity. The modern habit of doing ceremonial things unceremoniously is no proof of humility; rather it proves the offender's inability to forget himself in the rite, and his readiness to spoil for every one else the proper pleasure of ritual.

This is the first fence we must get over. Epic, from the beginning, is *solempne*. You are to expect pomp. You are to "assist," as the French say, at a great festal action. I have stressed the point at this early stage because misunderstandings must be eradicated from the very first. But our history of Epic has so far brought us only to the germ of epic *solemnity*. The Epic does not decline from the lay in the heroic court to the Miltonic level, but rises; it accumulates and enriches *solemnity* as the centuries proceed.

So much for the poems mentioned in Homer and *Beowulf*, but what of Homer and *Beowulf* themselves? Are they also oral court poetry of the kind described?

Whether "Homer" is oral poetry or not is a question that can be answered with great probability. It must not, of course, be confused by identifying "oral" or recited poetry with anonymous poetry, still less with folk poetry. Mr. [M. P.] Nilsson tells us of a modern poet in Sumatra who spent five years on the composition of a single poem, though he could neither read nor write (*Homer and Mycenae* [London, 1933] chap. v). The question whether the *Iliad* is oral poetry is quite separate from the question of authorship. It is even separate from the question whether the author was literate. By oral poetry I mean poetry that reaches its audience through the medium of recitation; a manuscript in the background would not alter its oral character so long as this manuscript was prompt-copy for a reciter and not a book to be sold to the public or given to the patron. The real question is whether the Homeric poems were composed for recitation. Both of them are admittedly too long to be recited as wholes. But we see from the *Odyssey* how that could be got over; a poet, asked for the story of the Trojan Horse, begins "at the point when the Greeks sailed away" (VIII. 500); in other words, he seems to be familiar with the practice of serial or selective recitation from a poem (or body of poetry) too long to recite in its entirety. And we know that Homer was in fact thus serially recited by relays of rhapsodists at the festival of the Panathenaea, in the historical period. There is therefore no evidence that it is *not* oral, and strong probability that it is. About *Beowulf* there is no external evidence either way. It is easily recitable, and would take perhaps three hours; this, with a break in the middle, would not be too long. But about *Beowulf*, and about the Homeric poems, there is internal evidence. They both have the oral *technique,* the repetitions, and stylized diction of oral poetry. If not oral themselves, they are at least closely modelled on work that was. And this is what mainly concerns us.

It remains to ask if they are court poetry. *Beowulf* clearly is. Its preoccupation with honour, its exclusive attention to the life of courts, its interest in etiquette (*duguþe þeaw*) and in genealogy, put the matter beyond doubt. Homer is more doubtful. We have seen that in historical times it was recited not in courts, but at great national festivals, and it is possible that it was also composed for these. In other words, it is either court-poetry or festival poetry. If it is the latter, then epic, since the time of the earliest lays, has moved up, not down. The original *solemnity* of the hall has been replaced by the greater *solemnity* of the temple or the forum. Our first picture of the epic poet needs to be modified by the associations of incense, sacrifice, civic pride, and public holiday; and since this change certainly occurred sooner or later we may as well make the adjustment now. We move a stage *further away* from the solitary, private, and armchair associations which the word "poetry" has for a modern.

Homer and *Beowulf*, then, however or whenever they were actually produced, are in the tradition of Primary epic, and inherit both its oral technique and its festal, aristocratic, public, ceremonial tone. The aesthetic consequences of this now claim our attention.

THE TECHNIQUE OF PRIMARY EPIC

And the words of his mouth were as slaves spreading carpets of glory
Embroidered with names of the Djinns—a miraculous weaving—
But the cool and perspicuous eye overbore unbelieving.

KIPLING.

The most obvious characteristic of an oral technique is its continual use of stock words, phrases, or even whole lines. It is important to realize at the outset that these are not a second-best on which the poets fall back when inspiration fails them: they are as frequent in the great passages as in the low ones. In 103 lines of the parting between Hector and Andromache (justly regarded as one of the peaks of European poetry) phrases, or whole lines, which occur again and again in Homer are twenty-eight times employed (*Il.* VI. 390–493). Roughly speaking, a *quarter* of the whole passage is "stock."

In Beowulf's last speech to Wiglaf (*Beow.* 2794–820) "stock" expressions occur six times in twenty-eight lines—again, they are about a quarter of the whole.

This phenomenon has been explained often enough from the poet's side. "These repetitions," says Mr. Nilsson, "are a great aid for the singer for whilst reciting them mechanically he is subconsciously forming the next verse" (*Homer and Mycenae*, p.203). But all art is made to *face* the audience. Nothing can be left exposed, however useful to the performer, which is not delightful or at least tolerable to *them*. A stage set must be judged from in front. If the poet's ease were the sole consideration, why have a recitation at all? Is he not very well already, with his wine at his elbow and his share in the roast pork? We must therefore consider what these repetitions do for the hearers, not what they do for the poet. And we may observe that this is the only *aesthetic* or critical question. Music means not the noises it is nice to make, but the noises it is nice to hear. Good poetry means not the poetry men like composing, but the poetry men like to listen to or to read.

If any one will make the experiment for a week or two of reading no poetry and hearing a good deal, he will soon find the explanation of the stock phrases. It is a prime necessity of oral poetry that the hearers should not be surprised too often, or too much. The unexpected tires us: it also takes us longer to understand and enjoy than the expected. A line which gives the listener pause is a disaster in oral poetry because it makes him lose the next line. And even if he does not lose the next, the rare and ebullient line is not worth making. In the sweep of recitation *no* individual line is going to count for very much. The pleasure which moderns chiefly desire from printed poetry is ruled out anyway. You cannot ponder over single lines and let them dissolve on the mind like lozenges. That is the wrong way of using this sort of poetry. It is not built up of isolated effects; the poetry is in the paragraph, or the whole episode. To look for single, "good" lines is like looking for single "good" stones in a cathedral.

The language, therefore, must be *familiar* in the sense of being expected. But in Epic which is the highest species of oral court poetry, it must not be *familiar* in the sense of being colloquial or commonplace. The desire for simplicity is a late and sophisticated one. We moderns may like dances which are hardly distinguishable from walking and poetry which sounds as if it might be uttered *ex tempore*. Our ancestors did not. They liked a dance which *was* a dance, and fine clothes which no one could mistake for working clothes, and feasts that no one could mistake for ordinary dinners, and poetry that unblushingly proclaimed itself to be poetry. What is the point of having a poet, inspired by the Muse, if he tells the stories just as you or I would have told them? It will be seen that these two demands, taken together, absolutely necessitate a Poetic Diction; that is, a language which is familiar because it is used in every part of every poem, but unfamiliar because it is not used outside poetry. A parallel, from a different sphere, would be turkey and plum pudding on Christmas day; no one is surprised at the menu, but every one recognizes that it is not *ordinary* fare. Another parallel would be the language of a liturgy. Regular church-goers are not surprised by the service—indeed, they know a good deal of it by rote; but it is a language apart. Epic diction, Christmas fare, and the liturgy, are all examples of ritual— that is, of something set deliberately apart from daily usage, but wholly familiar within its own sphere. The element of ritual which some dislike in Milton's poetry thus comes into epic at the very beginning. . . . Those who dislike ritual in general—ritual in any and every department of life—may be asked most earnestly to reconsider the question. It is a pattern imposed on the mere flux of our feelings by reason and will, which renders pleasures less fugitive and griefs more endurable, which hands over to the power of wise custom the task (to which the individual and his moods are so inadequate) of being festive or sober, gay or reverent, when we choose to be, and not at the bidding of chance.

This is the common ground of all oral poetry. Against it we can now discern differences between one poem and another. The epic diction of Homer is not the same as that of *Beowulf*. It seems to me almost certain, from the language and metre, that the Greek epic was recited more quickly. It therefore needs more, and more complete, repetition.

The actual operation of the Homeric diction is remarkable. The unchanging recurrence of his *wine-dark sea,* his *rosy-fingered dawn,* his ships launched *into the holy brine,* his *Poseidon shaker of earth,* produce an effect which modern poetry, except where it has learned from Homer himself, cannot attain. They emphasize the unchanging human environment. They express a feeling very profound and very frequent in real life, but elsewhere ill represented in literature. What is really in our minds when we first catch sight of the sea after a long absence, or look up, as watchers in a sickroom or as sentries, to see yet another daybreak? Many things, no doubt—all manner of hopes and fears, pain or pleasure, and the beauty or grimness of that particular sea and that particular dawn. Yes; but under all these, like a base so deep as to be scarcely audible, there is something which we might very lamely express by muttering "same old sea" or "same old morning." The permanence, the indifference, the heartrending or consoling fact that whether we laugh or weep the world is what it is, always enters into our experience and plays no small part in that pressure of reality which is one of the differences between life and imagined life. But in Homer the pressure is there. The sonorous syllables, in which he has stereotyped the sea, the gods, the morning, or the mountains, make it appear that we are dealing not with poetry about the things, but almost with the things themselves. It is this that produces what [A. W.] Kinglake (*Eothen* [London, 1844], chap. IV) called "the strong vertical light of Homer's poetry" and made Mr [Owen] Barfield say that in it "not man was creating, but the gods" (*Poetic Diction* [London, 1928], p.96).

The general result of this is that Homer's poetry is, in an unusual degree, believable. There is no use in disputing whether any episode could really have happened. We have seen it happen—and there seemed to be no poet mediating between us and the event. A girl walks on the shore and an unknown lover embraces her, and a darkly shining wave arched over them like a coverlet while they lay; and when he had ended his deeds of love, he told his name,

"Lo, I am Poseidon, shaker of earth" (*Od.* XI. 242–52). Because we have had "shaker of earth" time and again in these poems where no miracle was involved, because those syllables have come to affect us almost as the presence of the unchanging sea in the real world, we are compelled to accept this. Call it nonsense, if you will; we have seen it. The real salt sea itself, and not any pantomime or Ovidian personage living *in* the sea, has got a mortal woman with child. Scientists and theologians must explain it as best they can. The *fact* is not disputable.

The diction also produces the unwearying splendour and ruthless poignancy of the Homeric poems. Miserable or even sordid events may happen; but the brightness of the sun, the "leaf-shaking" largeness of the mountains, the steady strength of rivers, is there all the time, not with any suggestion (as it might be in a romantic poet) of the "consolations of nature" but simply as a fact. Homeric splendour is the splendour of reality. Homeric pathos strikes hard precisely because it seems unintended and inevitable like the pathos of real life. It comes from the clash between human emotions and the large, indifferent background which the conventional epithets represent. Ὣς φάτο, τοὺς δ' ἤδη κάτεχεν φυσίζοος αἶα. (*Il.* III. 243). Thus Helen spoke about her brothers, thinking them alive, but in fact the life-giving earth already covered them, in Lacedaemon, their dear fatherland. Ruskin's comment cannot be improved upon: "Note here the high poetical truth carried to the extreme. The poet has to speak of the earth in sadness, but he will not let that sadness affect or change his thoughts of it. No; though Castor and Pollux be dead, yet the earth is our mother still, fruitful, life-giving. These are the facts of the thing. I see nothing else than these. Make what you will of them" (*Modern Painters*, IV, xiii, *Of the Pathetic Fallacy*). And yet even this does not quite exhaust the passage. In translating we have had to say "their dear fatherland." But *dear* is misleading. The word that Homer uses does not really describe any one's emotions at any particular moment. It is used whenever he mentions anything which is a man's *own*, so that a dull critic might say it was simply the Homeric Greek for *own* the adjective. But it is rather more than that. It is the word for *dear*, but by being always used comes to suggest that unalterable relation, far deeper than fondness and compatible with all changes of mood, which unites a normal man to his wife, his home, or his own body—the tie of a mutual "belonging" which is there even when he dislikes them.

We must avoid an error which Ruskin's words might suggest. We must not think of Homer calculating these effects, line by line, as a modern poet might do. Once the diction has been established it works of itself. Almost anything the poet wants to say has only to be turned into this orthodox and ready-made diction and it becomes poetry. "Whatever Miss T. eats turns into Miss T." The epic diction, as Goethe said, is "a language which does your thinking and your poetizing for you" (*Eine Sprache die für dich dichtet und denkt*). The conscious artistry of the poet is thus set free to devote itself wholly to the large-scale problems—construction, character drawing, invention; his *verbal* poetics have become a habit, like grammar or articulation. I have avoided using such words as *automatic* or *mechanical* which carry a false suggestion. A machine is made out of inorganic materials and exploits some non-human power, such as gravitation, or the force of steam. But every single Homeric phrase was originally invented by a man and is, like all language, a human thing. It is like a machine in so far as the individual poet liberates, by using it, power other than his own; but it is stored human life and human experience which he is liberating—not *his own* life and experience, but none the less human and spiritual. The picture of a Muse—a superpersonal figure, yet anthropomorphically conceived—is therefore really more *accurate* than that of some kind of engine. No doubt all this is very unlike the recipe for poetry which finds favour to-day. But there is no fighting against facts. Make what you can of it, the result of this wholly artificial diction is a degree of objectivity which no other poetry has ever surpassed. Homer accepts artificiality from the outset: but in the result he is something for which "natural" is took weak an epithet. He has no more need to bother about being "natural" than Nature herself.

To a limited extent the technique of *Beowulf* is the same as that of Homer. It, too, has its reiterated expressions, *under wolcnum, in geardum,* and the like, and its "poetical" names for most of the things the author wants to mention. One of its differences from Homer, indeed, is the number of synonymous words which the poet can use for the same thing: Homer has no list of alternatives to compare to the Beowulfian words for man—*beorn, freca, guma, hæleþ, secg, wer.* In the same way, Beowulf is fonder than Homer of partial repetition, of using slightly varied forms of a poetic phrase or compound. Thus, from the passage already mentioned, *Wuldorcyninge* does not, I think, occur elsewhere in the poem, but *wuldres wealdend* and *wuldres hyrde* do. *Wordum secge* is similarly a partial repetition of *wordum bædon, wordum wrixlan,* and *wordum nægde; wyrd forsweop,* of *wyrd fornam, deaþ fornam,* and *guþdeaþ fornam.* In part, this difference of technique goes with a shorter line, a language more full of consonants, and doubtless a slower and more emphatic delivery. It goes with the difference between a quantitative metre and one which uses both quantity and stress accent, demanding their union for that characteristic of alliterative verse which is called weight. One of Homer's great passages is like a cavalry charge; one of *Beowulf's,* like blows from a hammer or the repeated thunder of breakers on the beach. The words flow in Homer; in *Beowulf* they fall apart into massive lumps. The audience has more time to chew on them. Less help is needed from pure reiteration.

All this is not unconnected with a deeper difference of temper. The objectivity of the unchanging background, which is the glory of Homer's poetry, is not equally a characteristic of *Beowulf.* Compared with the *Iliad, Beowulf* is already, in one sense, "romantic." Its landscapes have a spiritual quality. The country which Grendel haunts expresses the same things as Grendel himself: the "visionary dreariness" of Wordsworth is foreshadowed. Poetry has lost by the change, but it has gained, too. The Homeric Cyclops is a mere puppet beside the sad, excluded *ellorgast,* or the jealous and joyless dragon, of the English poem. There is certainly not more suffering behind *Beowulf* than there is behind the *Iliad;* but there is a consciousness of good and evil which Homer lacks.

The "proper" oral technique of the later poem, that which distinguishes it most sharply from Homer, is the variation or parallelism which most of us have first met in the Psalms. "He that dwelleth in heaven shall laugh them to scorn; the Lord shall have them in derision." The rule is that nearly everything must be said more than once. The cold prose about the ship in which Scyld's dead body was sent away (*Beow.* 50) is that nobody knew what became of it. The poetical rendering is that "Men knew not to say for a truth, the talkers in the hall knew not, warriors under the sky knew not, who received that cargo."

THE SUBJECT OF PRIMARY EPIC

> *The gods made a man called Kvásir who was so wise you couldn't ask him any question he hadn't got an answer to. He travelled all over the world teaching men things, until he became the guest of two dwarfs. They got him talking and managed to kill him. Then they mixed honey with his blood and made such a mead of it that anybody who drinks it becomes a poet.*
>
> Abridged from Bragaröþur, LVII.

In the foregoing account of Primary Epic the reader may have noticed that no mention is made of one characteristic which later critics have sometimes thought essential. Nothing has been said about greatness of subject. No doubt, the epics we have been considering do not deal with comic or idyllic matters; but what of the epic theme as later ages have conceived it—the large national or cosmic subject of super-personal interest?

In my opinion the great subject ("the life of Arthur, or Jerusalem's fall") was not a mark of primary epic. It enters the epic with Virgil, whose position in this story is central and who has altered the very notion of epic; so much so that I believe we are now tempted to read the great subject into primary epic where it does not exist. But since this may be disputed, let us consider *Beowulf* and the Homeric poems from this point of view.

The *Odyssey* is clearly out of the running. The mere fact that these adventures happened to Odysseus while he was returning from the Trojan War does not make that war the subject of the poem. Our interest is in the fortunes of an individual. If he is a king, he is the king of a very small country, and there is hardly any attempt to make Ithaca seem important, save as the hero's home and estate are important in any story. There is no pretence, indeed no possibility of pretending, that the world, or even Greece, would have been much altered if Odysseus had never got home at all. The poem is an adventure story. As far as greatness of subject goes, it is much closer to *Tom Jones* or *Ivanhoe* than to the *Aeneid* or the *Gierusalemme Liberata*.

For the *Iliad* a much more plausible case could be made out. It has been treated as an epic about the clash between East and West; and even in ancient times Isocrates praised Homer for celebrating those who fought against the "Barbarian." Professor [Gilbert] Murray to some extent favours this view. It is perhaps presumptuous of me to differ from so great a scholar; and it is certainly disagreeable to differ from one whose books, eagerly read in my teens, are now in my very bones, and whose lectures are still among the most rapturous memories of my undergraduate days. But on this matter I cannot go with him. Professor Murray asks of the *Iliad,* "Is it not the story of the battle of All-Greeks against the barbarian of Asia? 'All-Greeks:' the wonderful word rings out again and again in the poems."[1] This is not the impression I get. If we examine the nine places where the index of the Oxford *Iliad* mentions the word Παναχαιῶν as occurring (and four of them occur in a single book) we find that on eight of the occasions it is preceded by ἀριστῆες or ἀριστῆας—"the champions of the Panachaeoi." There is no contrast suggested between the All-Greeks and the Barbarians; only between the All-Greeks, the Greeks as a whole, and their own best men. In the ninth passage (IX. 301) Odysseus bids Achilles, even if he hates Agamemnon, to pity the other All-Greeks. Here again, the "All" seems to point a contrast between the totality of the Greeks and one member of that totality: there is no idea, so far as I can see, of the Greeks united against the Barbarians. One begins to wonder whether the first syllable of Παναχαιῶν is much more than a metrical convenience.

When I survey the poem as a whole I am even less convinced. The Trojan War is not the subject of the *Iliad.* It is merely the background to a purely personal story—that of Achilles' wrath, suffering, repentance, and killing of Hector. About the fall of Troy, Homer has nothing to say, save incidentally. It has been argued that he does not need to, because the fall of Troy was inevitable after Hector's death; but it is, to me, hardly credible that the climax of a story—and the fall would be the climax if the siege were the theme—should be left to be inferred. At best, it would be an extreme subtlety; the art of Kipling rather than of Homer. Nor do I find any anti-Trojan feeling in the *Iliad.* The noblest character is a Trojan, and nearly all the atrocities are on the Greek side. I find even no hint (except possibly in III. 2–9) that the Trojans are regarded, either for better or for worse, as being a different *kind* of people from the Greeks. No doubt it is possible to suppose an earlier version in which the Trojans *were* hated—just as it is possible to suppose an earlier *Beowulf* free from all the Christian passages, or a "historical" Jesus totally different from the figure in the Synoptic tradition. But that, I confess, is a mode of "research" I heartily distrust. "Entities are not to be feigned without necessity," and there is no necessity here. Parallels from other literatures suggest that Primary Epic simply wants a heroic story and cares nothing about a "great national subject." Professor [H. M.] Chadwick, speaking of the Germanic epics remarks "how singularly free the poems are from anything in the nature of national interest or sentiment."[2] The greatest hero of Icelandic poetry is a Burgundian. In *Beowulf* Professor Chadwick's statement is very well illustrated. The poem is English. The scene is at first laid in Zealand, and the hero comes from Sweden. Hengest, who ought to have been the Aeneas of our epic if the poet had had Virgil's notion of an epic subject, is mentioned only parenthetically.

The truth is that Primary Epic neither had, nor could have, a great subject in the later sense. That kind of greatness arises only when some event can be held to effect a profound and more or less permanent change in the history of the world, as the founding of Rome did, or still more, the fall of man.

Before any event can have that significance, history must have some degree of pattern, some design. The mere endless up and down, the constant aimless alternations of glory and misery, which make up the terrible phenomenon called a Heroic Age, admit to no such design. No one event is really very much more important than another. No achievement can be permanent: to-day we kill and feast, to-morrow we are killed, and our women led away as slaves. Nothing "stays put," nothing has a significance beyond the moment. Heroism and tragedy there are in plenty, therefore good stories in plenty; but no "large design that brings the world out of the good to ill." The total effect is not a pattern, but a kaleidoscope. If Troy falls, woe to the Trojans, no doubt, but what of it? "Zeus has loosened the heads of many cities, and many more will he loosen yet" (*Il.* IX. 25). Heorot has been built nobly, but in the end what of it? From the very outset, "High, horn-gabled, the hall rises, Waits the welter of war's surges, And the fire, its foe" (*Beow.* 81).

Much has been talked of the melancholy of Virgil; but an inch beneath the bright surface of Homer we find not melancholy but despair. "Hell" was the word Goethe used of it. It is all the more terrible because the poet takes it all for granted, makes no complaint. It comes out casually, in similes.

> As when the smoke ascends to the sky from a city afar
> Set in an isle, which foes have compassed round in war,
> And all day long they struggle as hateful Ares bids.
>> (*Il.* XVIII. 207.)

Or again,

> As when a woman upon the body falls
> Of her husband, killed in battle before the city walls . . . .
> She sees him down and listens how he gasps his life away,
> And clings to the body, crying, amid the foes; but they
> Beating her back and shoulders with butts of spears amain
> Pull her away to slavery to learn of toil and pain
>> (*Od.* VIII. 523.)

Notice how different this is from the sack of Troy in *Aeneid* II. This is a mere simile—the sort of thing that happens every day. The fall of Virgil's Troy is a catastrophe, the end of an epoch. *Urbs antiqua ruit*—"an ancient city, empress of long ages, falls." For Homer it is all in the day's work. *Beowulf* strikes the same note. Once the king is dead, we know what is in store for us: that little island of happiness, like many another before it and many another in the years that follow, is submerged, and the great tide of the Heroic Age rolls over it:

> Laughter has left us with our Lord's slaying,
> And mirth and music. Many a spearshaft
> Shall freeze our fingers in frightened dawn,
> As our hands hold it. No harp's delight
> Shall waken warriors. The wan raven
> Keen for carrion, his call sending,
> Shall utter to the eagle how he ate his fill
> At War's banquet; the wolf shared it.
>> (*Beow.* 3020.)

Primary Epic is great, but not with the greatness of the later kind. In Homer, its greatness lies in the human and personal tragedy built up against this background of meaningless flux. It is all the more tragic because there hands over the heroic world a certain futility. "And here I sit in Troy," says Achilles to Priam, "afflicting you and your children." Not "protecting Greece," not even "winning glory," not called by any vocation to afflict Priam, but just doing it because that is the way things come about. We are in a different world here from Virgil's *mens immota manet*. There the suffering has a meaning, and is the price of a high resolve. Here there is just the suffering. Perhaps this was in Goethe's mind when he said, "The lesson of the *Iliad* is that on this earth we must enact Hell." Only the style—the unwearying, unmoved, angelic speech of Homer—makes it endurable. Without that the *Iliad* would be a poem beside which the grimmest modern realism is child's play.

Beowulf is a little different. In Homer the background of accepted, matter-of-fact despair is, after all, a background. In *Beowulf* that fundamental darkness comes out into the foreground and is partly embodied in the monsters. And against those monsters the hero fights. No one in Homer had fought against the darkness. In the English poem we have the characteristic theme of Northern mythology—the gods and men ranged in battle against the giants. To that extent the poem is more cheerful at heart, though not on the surface, and has the first hint of the Great Subject. In this way, as in several others, it stands between the *Iliad* and Virgil. But it does not approach Virgil very closely. The monsters only partly embody the darkness. Their defeat—or its defeat in them—is not permanent or even long lasting. Like every other Primary Epic it leaves matters much as it found them: the Heroic Age is still going on at the end.

NOTES

1. Gilbert Murray, *Rise of the Greek Epic* (Oxford, Eng., 1934), p.21.
2. H. M. Chadwick, *The Heroic Age* (Cambridge, Eng., 1912), p.34.

E. M. W. Tillyard

THE NATURE OF THE EPIC

THE HEROIC POEM

Till recently critics used the terms *epic* and *heroic poem* as names for the same thing; and a safe and good way of treating the subject is to continue this practice while limiting and clarifying it. Certainly you must set limits if you are to avoid confusion. Milton knew that *Paradise Lost* was not heroic in the Homeric sense and proceeded to claim that his own, sacred, subject was more, not less, heroic than Homer's or Virgil's. Today we see that his knowledge was truer than his claim. Thanks (in this country at least) mainly to the Chadwicks, we tend to shift the heroic idea from literature in general and to centre it in a particular, early, stage of man's evolution. In accord with this shift heroic poetry ceases to be poetry with a nominally heroic subject and becomes the narrative verse with a heroic subject belonging to the heroic age, at whatever date or in whatever part of the world that age manifested itself. It is eminently a post-Darwinian conception and it is in its own fashion satisfactory today. On it C. M. Bowra wrote his recent book, *Heroic Poetry*.[1]

But if you use the conception you should play fair and not stretch it beyond its proper bounds. It certainly embraces some things in Homer, it might be stretched to embrace some things in Virgil, it certainly does not embrace *Paradise Lost*. If you want, as I do, to consider the literature, heroic in name, that grew out of the genuine heroic ages but was not of them, you have to seek another entry into the subject.

The great age of this kind of English epic was that of the revival of learning. It knew nothing of heroic ages as such and was little versed in the heroic poetry they produced. It considered Homer not less adult a poet than Virgil. It had great confidence in the epic as a literary form and it had some success in producing actual epic poems. It looks as if there were an initial chance of entering my subject through what people thought of it in the days of its greatness. Let me therefore turn to neo-classic theories of the epic form.

Originally "Introduction: The Nature of the Epic." From E. M. W. Tillyard, *The English Epic and Its Background* (New York: Oxford University Press, 1966), p.1–13. Reprinted by permission of Mr. Stephen Tillyard and Chatto and Windus.

NEO-CLASSIC THEORY

Pernassus *hill, upon whose Airy top*
The Epick *Poets so divinely show,*
And with just pride behold the rest below.
(The Earl of Mulgrave, *An Essay upon Poetry*, 1682)

No one can go far in the history of poetry without recognizing the power of
formal and abstract ideals, especially in the age of the Renaissance. Of the
empty patterns that fascinate the minds of poets there were two pre-eminent:
the Heroic Poem and classical tragedy.

(W. P. Ker)

It is now well known that *Paradise Lost* was no isolated achievement. It represented what many authors, English and foreign, were trying to do. Where it differed from other seventeenth- or early eighteenth-century epics was in its success. Now the aim common to Milton's *Paradise Lost,* Blackmore's *King Arthur,* Courtin's *Chalemagne Pénitent,* or Voltaire's *Henriade* was more than the simple one of writing a successful poem in an acknowledged and valued literary form and of thereby satisfying the motives of ambition or self-expression. It included more and it was more solemn. For several reasons, and particularly through the accepted and unchallenged pre-eminence of Homer and Virgil among the world's poets, the heroic or epic poem was accounted, axiomatically, the noblest literary form. Every particle of all the motives that urged the men of the Renaissance to prize and revere and imitate classical antiquity united in asserting the value, even the sacrosanctity, of the epic form in its strict classical manifestation.

But the sense of that sacrosanctity could not consist in, or at least remain, a timeless and uncircumstantiated adoration of the antique; inevitably it took its colour from contemporary habits of thought. One of those habits was patriotism, another had to do with a taste for abstractions, possibly derived from the Renaissance reverence for Plato. When nations formed and then recognised themselves, they became aware at the same time of their own languages. It would never do to admit that your language, however embryonic at the moment, lacked the highest potentialities. It followed that when an author realised, in a small or a great work of literature, a potentiality of his vernacular, he deserved well of his country. And if the work was an epic on accredited classical lines, he deserved stupendously. It was with this ambition of stupendous national desert that Milton made his plans for a great poem. He decided

> to be an interpreter and relater of the best and sagest things among mine own Citizens throughout this Iland in the mother dialect. That what the greatest and choycest wits of *Athens, Rome,* or modern *Italy,* and those Hebrews of old did for their country, I in my proportion with this over and above of being a Christian, might doe for mine.[2]

About the taste for abstractions it is more dangerous to speak. Perhaps current ideas of kingship furnish an analogy. In earlier times, this or that king had, as the Lord's anointed, been sacred, and so he may have continued to be. But in the seventeenth century the idea of kingship and the awe attached to the abstracted idea reinforced the sanctity of this or that king. Every king embodied the idea, and to embody it worthily was a feat of almost mystical significance. To the thorough-going neo-classic the Rules stood to this or that work in which they were manifested somewhat as the idea of kingship to this or that king. In spite of complaints that the Three Unities forced an author to forgo many cherished beauties, they were principally an *ideal* from whose free and faithful realisation a great good might flow. When Rymer attacked Shakespeare and Fletcher for wrenching their characters away from the type proper to their setting, he believed them to be violating another such ideal. Now the classical form of the epic was yet another. To go against it was sacrilege; to realize it worthily in a work of art an achievement almost superhuman.

Such is part of the setting of *Paradise Lost* or of any other epic or would-be epic written in western Europe in the age of the new learning. It is a strange complex of ideas, some might say perverse, but it is grand. It meant something to its age and it can still strike and entertain us: it is a topic well worth pursuing. But it does nothing to characterize the epic. It tells us that the epic is the noblest form and that to succeed in it is a virtuous act, but it does not tell us the kind of nobility it attains or the conditions of epic success. And when we turn from the high generalisations of the neo-classic critics to their detailed remarks we get less satisfaction. We learn that a noble kind of verse and of language must accompany the nobility of theme and of personages. We hear disputes on supernatural machinery and the propriety of religious subjects. But we do not find any principle to guide us in deciding whether this or that work does or does not make the epic impression. As a matter of history, as a phase of human thought, the general conception of the neo-classic epic is interesting and invites study. But as a help today for finding one's way in the epic writing of the post-heroic ages it is useless.

Now if the neo-classic age cannot help us enter the subject, no other is likely to do so.

What then is to be done? There is still the safe method of defining the epic in external terms alone. I have already indicated how heroic poetry can safely be so defined. (And here the chance of internal congruities also is good.) With equal safety but with less profit one could group together all the strict Renaissance and neo-classical imitations of the classical epic, linking Vida's *Christiad* with the *Lusiad* of Camoens and Blackmore's *Prince Arthur* with *Paradise Lost*. By so doing you bring a lot of incongruous stuff together; but that is not your responsibility, for you have committed yourself to no more than to a community of formal features. But mere safety may be dull; and when you find that the classification by form does not take you far (seeing that the worthless and the excellent are subsumed under it) and if you still believe that there are features, other than formal, that distinguish some literary kinds, you are not likely to rest satisfied or to forbear seeking a different criterion. I do retain such a belief while admitting that the literary forms that embody the distinguishing features are liable to change. If I am to write of the epic at all, in the way I want, I must begin by saying what I think the distinguishing features of the epic spirit to be.

THE EPIC SPIRIT

Tel ouvrage est semblable à ces fecons herbages,
Qui sont fournis de prez et de gras pasturages,
D'une haute fustage, et d'un bocage épais,
Ou courent les ruisseaux, ou sont les ombres frais,
Ou l'on void des estangs, des vallons, des montagnes,
Des vignes, des fruictiers, des forets, des campagnes:
Un Prince en fait son parc, y fait des bastiments. . . .
En l'ouvrage Heroique ainsi chacun se plaist. . . .
C'est un tableau du monde, un miroir qui raporte
Les gestes des mortels en differente sorte.
(Vauquelin de la Fresnaye, *L'Art Poétique*)

But, as a Court or Kings Palace requires other dimensions then a private house:
So the Epick *askes a magnitude, from other Poems.*
(Jonson, *Conversations with Drummond*)

Whether or not the reader likes the ensuing account of the epic, he will have to admit that it squares with a modern practice of going outside the bare form or the bare fact and seeking the essential spirit. A. W. Schlegel used the words *classical* and *romantic* in a very simple sense. *Classical* meant ancient Greek and Roman; *romantic* the Gothic that came after. About a hundred years later Middleton Murry declared that "Romanticism and Classicism are perennial modes of the human spirit."[3] The tragic has now for a long time been allowed to exist outside the limits of strict tragedy; it has been found in *Beowulf, Lycidas,* the *Ancient Mariner,* and *Madame Bovary*: the comic exists in many places outside the comic drama. By such analogy there is warrant enough for refusing to identify epic with the heroic poem and for seeking its *differentia* in matters other than nominal and formal.

To have any value the definition of a literary term must rest on induction; and anyone who has tried to make his own definition and not merely taken one ready made will find that he has been drawing his generalisation from certain (and for the most part unconsciously selected) examples. Experiments with the word *Metaphysical* (in its poetic sense) convinced me that to define it was to generalise on the data of some of Donne's poems. By such a generalisation other metaphysicising poems, whether by Donne or someone else, had been unconsciously measured. Aristotle defined tragedy through the data supplied by a very small number of plays, and in so doing succeeded well enough to invite imitation. The works that first led me to reflect on the spirit of the epic were the *Iliad,* the *Odyssey,* the *Aeneid,* the *Divine Comedy,* the *Lusiad,* and *Paradise Lost*. It was through the conviction of Dante's being as true an epic writer as Virgil that I abandoned any notion of using the heroic subject as a criterion. Finding the *Aeneid* closer in essentials to the *Divine Comedy* than to the *Argonautica* or *Gondibert,* I had to seek a definition of the epic other than the old heroic one. Of course, one must not conceive of the inductive process too simply. It is not a case of drawing conclusions from a limited set of data uninterrupted to the end and then applying those conclusions to works not yet considered. Rather it is a case of passing to and fro between the works you know you will include and those you think doubtful, and allowing each class to influence the other. Thus I soon inclined to include certain novels among the epics. And such inclusion may have affected my general notions. Sometimes the lack of a quality in a work that could not be included might indicate the presence of it (and hence its general desirability) in a work included beyond doubt though not on precisely realised grounds. I did not include the *Book of Job* among the fully authenticated epics because it does not contain enough; nor *Don Quixote,* not because it is in prose but because its construction does not show the human will stretched and sustained to the utmost. And such negative conclusions may have reinforced or even prompted my criteria of wide inclusiveness and sustained will-power. It has therefore been by finding out what works I admit and what reject, and why, that I have gained my conception of the epic.

The first epic requirement is the simple one of high quality and of high seriousness. It is just conceivable, though superlatively improbable, that the other conditions required to give the epic effect could be fulfilled by mediocre means. Hence the need to insist that the writer of epic must use words in a very distinguished way. So to insist excludes from the epic category, as now being characterised, the *King Arthurs* and the *Leonidas's* and all the other inferiorities cast in the traditional form of the heroic poem.

The second epic requirement can be roughed out by vague words like amplitude, breadth, inclusiveness, and so on. Aristotle indicates it with considerable emphasis through his flagrant failure to perceive it in his infamous last chapter of the *Poetics.* Among his reasons for classing the tragic above the epic form is the reason that tragic imitation gains its end in narrower space— τὸ ἐν ἐλάττονι μήκει τὸ τέλος τῆς μιμήσεως εἶναι—and that the concentrated is more pleasurable than the diluted effect. And he asks us to imagine the *Oedipus* of Sophocles expanded to the length of the *Iliad.* Further, he asserts that genuine unity is impossible in an epic, which provides the material for several tragic unities. Taking tragedy, a highly concentrated form, to be the measure of excellence, Aristotle begs the question by calling epic diluted, but, through the very unfairness of so calling it, directs us to that greater amplitude in the epic, that ability to deal with more sides of life, which differentiates it from the tragic drama.

This difference between tragedy and epic, which Aristotle failed to perceive, is simple and fundamental, resting as it does on the physical conditions governing the two forms. A tragedy is limited in length by the physical comfort of a normal audience. Being serious, it will aim at the weightiest effect and it will gain that effect not by crowding everything into a narrow space—that would daze and weary—but by omitting and simplifying. For whatever reason—and the reason is here irrelevant—tragic writers have abbreviated the local and the communal things and have mainly regarded the most general human passions and the individual's concern with his environment, natural, social, or divine: and by presenting experience through the eyes of the individual have been able to turn the limitation of length to the best account. And through that ability acted tragedy has become as it were the home country of certain types of feeling, a home country from which colonies have settled in countries where other types of feeling are characteristic. Thus there is tragic feeling in *Madame Bovary,* but that feeling is not any feeling peculiar to the novel form; it is colonial rather than autochthonous. The peculiar properties of the epic rest, in their turn, on the practical conditions of its performance. Whether a chieftain and his followers in his hall or a band of pilgrims or holidaymakers gathered for some days at a religous festival formed the audience, they wanted or at least tolerated a longer unit than did an audience crowded into the confined space of a theatre. On the side of production mere narrative was less exacting than the complexities of dramatic circumstance and, granted relays of reciters, admitted of great length. And the right retort to the challenge of length is not repetition but variety.

There are different kinds of variety, and not every kind belongs to the epic. An essay by Aldous Huxley, *Tragedy and the Whole Truth,*[4] will help to make the proper distinction. Huxley begins from the passage in the *Odyssey,* Book Twelve, where Odysseus describes how Scylla snatched six of his men from his ship and devoured them at the threshold of her cave as they cried out in terrible struggle,

αὐτοῦ δ' εἰνὶ θύρῃσι κατήσθιε κεκλήγοντας,
χεῖρας ἐμοὶ ὀρέγοντας ἐν αἰνῇ δηιοτῆτι.

Later Odysseus and his men landed in Sicily, ate their supper, and then bewailed their lost fellows. Huxley observes that the intense limited world of tragedy could never have admitted the cool truth to life of the men lamenting only after they satisfied their appetite. Tragedy can exist only through sacrificing what Huxley calls the "Whole Truth." And works that admit the Whole Truth are alien to tragedy.

> Tragedy is an arbitrarily isolated eddy on the surface of a vast river that flows on majestically, irresistibly, around, beneath, and to either side of it. Wholly-Truthful art contrives to imply the existence of the entire river as well as of the eddy. . . . In Wholly-Truthful art the agonies may be just as real, love and the unconquerable mind just as admirable, just as important, as in tragedy. . . . But the agonies and the indomitabilities are placed by the Wholly-Truthful writer in another, wider context, with the result that they came to be the same as the intrinsically identical agonies and indomitabilities of tragedy.[5]

At first Huxley might seem to be thinking of epic in opposition to tragedy; but he ends his essay by finding his "Whole Truth" principally in modern literature, which has become

> more and more acutely conscious . . . of the great oceans of irrelevant things, events and thoughts stretching endlessly away in every direction from whatever island point (a character, a story) the author may choose to contemplate.[6]

And he goes on to cite Proust, D. H. Lawrence, Gide, Kafka, and Hemingway as authors all concerned with the whole truth; thus ending in very different places from his point of departure in the *Odyssey.*

Huxley is quite right in implying that the epic can contain the tragic. Even in the *Odyssey,* usually considered as an epic touching comedy, two at least of the characters who most have our sympathy are subjected to suffering sufficiently acute to rouse their deep passions and to force them like the tragic sufferer to consider their own predicaments in the total world they inhabit. But in another matter Huxley is wrong; and here he can serve us, as Aristotle did, and through his very error point to the truth. His error is to introduce the *Odyssey,* an epic, into his particular modern context, for the epic is alien to the wandering and fortuitous concatenations that Huxley considers typical of recent literature. It will not tolerate amplitude for its own sake; it is not content with an undifferentiated and unorganised display of life's many phenomena. Like tragedy, although its material is ampler, epic must select, arrange, and organise.

But to dwell on this necessity is to leave the present topic for my next; and it is more to the point to consider the five authors Huxley cites as exemplifying his idea of the whole truth as he believes it to be expressed in recent literature. All five—Proust, D. H. Lawrence, Gide, Kafka, Hemingway—are exceptionally introverted, even at times the victims of morbid sensibilities. Anyhow, none of them is near achieving the psychological strength and the healthy balance of mental parts which must mark the writer of epic. (It is in this matter, among others, that tragedy differs from epic. Being narrower and requiring among its first qualities intensity, it is less liable than the epic to be destroyed by the pathological. Swift and Kafka might reasonably ask to be considered tragic writers, but epic writers never.) While at home in large areas of life, the epic writer must be centred in the normal, he must measure the crooked by the straight, he must exemplify that sanity which has been claimed for true genius. No pronounced homosexual, for instance, could succeed in the epic, not so much for being one as for what his being one cuts him off from. Granted the fundamental sanity, the wider the epic poet's mental span, the better. And ideally he should be able to range from the simple sensualities to a susceptibility to the numinous.

The third epic requirement has been hinted already through what I said about fortuitous concatenations. Exuberance, however varied, is not enough in itself; there must be a control commensurate with the amount included. Once again, the clearest illustrations may be from things that fail in the given requirement. The works of Rabelais include a great deal, they may be ample enough. It is their lack of organisation that keeps them remote from the epic. *Don Quixote,* because less remote, illustrates even better. Here at any rate is the true epic range and a superb quality of prose style. And there are passages (and conspicuously the first quarter of the second part) of such weight and density as to bear comparison with those poems I am using unconsciously as criteria. Cervantes must have exerted his will powerfully to have achieved the sustained excellence of these parts. But the work as a whole is not epic because it is governed by no powerful predetermination. Cervantes gathers weight as he writes. Beginning with a pleasant little buccaneering expedition, he insensibly picks up reinforcements on the way until he realises he has collected an army. And he puts that army to fluctuating use. But this is a very different matter from the author's having his strategy settled beforehand and keeping the whole suspended in his mind until composition is complete.

That indeed is the structural ideal: that the whole, however long, should remain fluid and unset till the last word has been written, that the writer should have everything simultaneously in mind and keep it open to modification throughout the process of composition. This must remain an ideal, for no man has possessed the powers of memory and control necessary to fulfil it. Even Dante was inconsistent. And one should not exclude from all possibilities of epic success a work that settles its parts as it goes along, provided it makes one part truly evolve out of the others, provided it retains a general recollection of what has gone before. Such, I conjecture, was the structural method of the *Faerie Queene*.

This insistence on rigorous control and predetermination as necessary in a certain type of poetry is alien to two powerful trends in recent thought. The first is a hostility to the long poem in general: a hostility due partly to theory and partly to the prevalent taste. The theory is that of Poe,[7] which seeks to prove that a long poem is by nature impossible, poetic inspiration being always evanescent and no verse counting as poetry unless written under inspiration. Any so-called long poem, of however high quality, can do no more than consist of a number of short poems connected by verse that is not poetry at all. Poe's theory suited both the French Symbolist poets and those who, like A. E. Housman, had narrowly inspirational theories of poetry. (Housman, in an unpublished paper on Burns, stated that there were six[8] and no more than six lines of poetry in all Burns's works.) And the influence of the theory has extended well into the twentieth century. As to the matter of taste, how should an age which multiplies and abbreviates, which favours many short items in its radio programmes, less time devoted to more subjects in schools, readers' digests, and miniature sermons, take to its heart a long poem calling for sustained concentration?

The other trend is psychological, that towards valuing the spontaneous, unconscious element in art or in life and towards distrusting the exercise of the conscious will. Aldous Huxley's assertion just quoted, that modern literature is concerned with "the great oceans of irrelevant things, events and thoughts stretching endlessly away in every direction," is a good enough illustration.

It is obvious that in writing a long poem or a long highly organised work in prose, the composition of which is perforce extended over years, an author cannot sustain a spontaneous vein of creation. At intervals he will be tempted to break the unity of the original conception and stray after new emotional interests. Spontaneity will not suffice, and the author will have to summon his will to help him abide by the plans he has resolved on. The writing of any poem (except one dictated in dream or trance) needs some effort of the will to control and shape it. But the effort is different in a lyric, a short story, and a play, while only in the most intensely written long works is the will taxed to the utmost. Such sustained writing corresponds to certain phases of the active life. Just as the will may force a man's conduct at a particular time (for instance on an expedition of exploration) to conform to a previously adopted set of resolves, against his present inclinations, so a poet may use his will to suppress new interests and preserve a unity previously resolved on.

Further, in the making of a long poem the will is more than an external driving force; the fact of its exercise and the belief in it become a highly important part of the total experience. Milton speaks of how the Dorian mood of flutes and soft recorders raised

> *To highth of noblest temper Hero's old*
> *Arming to Battel, and in stead of rage*
> *Deliberate valour breath'd.*

But even if Milton had never used the phrase, "deliberate valour" (which describes my meaning so concisely), his belief in the quality of considered courage, aware of issues, which implies the application of the will, would be apparent from the whole trend of his rhetoric. Moreover, in *Paradise Lost*, as in other genuine epics, the very passages which the will has forced into harmony with the more spontaneously composed ones are significant as declaring the value of the quality to which they owe a large part of their being.

This exercise of the will and the belief in it, which are a corollary of our third epic requirement, help to associate epic poetry with the largest human movements and solidest human institutions. In creating what we call civilisation the sheer human will has had a major part.

Although, for my own purposes, I have dissociated epic from the heroic poem, that is the verse narrative of heroic deeds in the heroic age, I want to insist that the true epic creates a "heroic impression." And that impression has to do with, is a by-product of, the present topic: the control of a large material and the exercise of the conscious will. Heroic poetry often concerns actions in which men know exactly what they are doing and rise through deliberate valour to a great height of resolution. And it is natural enough to attribute the heroic impression to a poem's heroic subject matter. But in fact that impression depends also, indeed ultimately, on the temper of treatment. A heroic theme may encourage a writer to treat it in a sustained, "heroic" way, to exercise his will to the utmost; but this does not prevent the treatment's being the decisive element. If this is the case with heroic poetry, it follows that literature lacking a heroic subject is not debarred from making the heroic impression. Here Dante is especially apt. His subject is not at all the old heroic one, though certain of his characters, Farinata and Ulysses for instance, may be of the antique heroic cast. But it is not they that make the heroic impression; it is rather the vast exercise of the will which went to the shaping of the whole poem. The *Faerie Queene* fails of the full heroic impression in spite of its chivalrous setting. And it does so because its organisation is rather loose.

Of course, the epic cannot avoid the defects and the risks of its virtues. The freshness of even its most spontaneous parts cannot share the freshness of certain lyrics. Very long time spent in composition may tax the will more than is healthy and make a man grim. This may explain why in his final version of *Piers Plowman* Langland cut down his prologue and deprived it of some of its most charming touches. Of all the epic poets, Homer alone quite escapes the mode's characteristic dangers. But these dangers are negligible in contrast with the possible majesty. There is nothing so exciting and so awe-inspiring in the world of letters as the spectacle of a great spirit daring to risk everything on one great venture and knowing that in its execution he will be taxed to the limit of what a man can endure.

All the same, I know that some readers will never find the epic congenial. There will always be those who think that it is of the very nature of art to be incomplete and to demonstrate in its action the principles of growth. For them it will be a sin to impose unity on work composed over so long a period of time that the author, if he is alive and moving, cannot feel quite consistently throughout. They will think it more natural for a man to empty his changing self into a series of plays or novels or lyrics, where no one of these is definitive but each grows out of its predecessors into something fresh. And they will find these words of Conrad apt to all great creative writing:

> In the body of Mr Henry James's work there is no suggestion of finality, nowhere a hint of surrender, to his own victorious achievement in that field where he is a master. Happily, he will never be able to claim completeness; and were he to confess to it in a moment of self-ignorance, he would not be believed by the very minds for whom such a confession naturally would be meant. It is impossible to think of Mr Henry James becoming "complete" otherwise than by the brutality of our common fate whose finality is meaningless—in the sense of its logic being of a natural order, the logic of a falling stone.[9]

It is perfectly true that it suits some writers to have their say in instalments; and no reasonable person would compel them to another method. Others dislike the brokenness of the method more than they like its freedom. They desire a single principle of organisation, the all-inclusive work of art. Each method expresses things denied to the other; and to set up the *Divine Comedy* and the plays of Shakespeare as rivals is unnaturally to narrow the bounds of the human spirit.

The fourth requirement can be called choric. The epic writer must express the feelings of a large group of people living in or near his own time. The notion that the epic is primarily patriotic is an unduly narrowed version of this requirement. Should a country command at some time an exceptionally clear ethical temper, that temper may serve an author well enough. Spenser, for instance, does express the Elizabethan temper successfully in the *Faerie Queene*. But the group-feeling need not be national. Dante is medieval rather than Italian. And it is wise not to bring in nationalism at all. Better, with Lascelles Abercrombie,[10] to look on the epic poet as

> accepting, and with his genius transfiguring, the general circumstance of his time . . . symbolizing, in some appropriate form, whatever sense of the significance of life he feels acting as the accepted unconscious metaphysic of the time.

We can simplify even further and say no more than that the epic must communicate the feeling of what it was like to be alive at the time. But that feeling must include the condition that behind the epic author is a big multitude of men of whose most serious convictions and dear habits he is the mouthpiece.

It is in this matter that epic most differs from tragedy. Tragedy cannot lack some imprint of its age, but its nature is to be timeless. It deals with the recurrent human passions and it presents them (having no space to do more) in their bare elements with the least local circumstantiation. It teaches not what it is like to be alive at a certain time but what it is like to be a human being. But though the choric element is necessary to epic and at best adventitious in tragedy, it does not exclude from epic the presentation of those timeless feelings which is tragedy's privilege to isolate and clarify. Indeed, the greatness of epic will partly depend on the inclusion of such feelings. It is when the tragic intensity coexists with the group-consciousness of an age, when the narrowly timeless is combined in a unit with the variegatedly temporal, that epic attains its full growth.

Lascelles Abercrombie postulates that the epic not only should express the "accepted unconscious metaphysic" of its age but do so through a clear and authentic story, a story known and already part of the mythology of the audience. I disagree with this further demand. Certainly, the material of the epic should be largely public, but not necessarily in the form of a narrative where the concatenation of sequent events holds a large proportion of the reader's interest. The "accepted unconscious metaphysic" is the essential starting-point, but the method of conveying it must vary from age to age. When an age holds one kind of opinion on the nature of man, the heroic story may best represent the current metaphysic. But other forms may suit other ages. The Middle Ages regarded man differently and they could not make the heroic story the most serious literary form. Allegory better answered their requirement. In the age of Elizabeth, when the Middle Ages and the new classicism of the Renaissance met, heroic action and allegory combined to express the most serious concerns. In the eighteenth century, prose fiction began potentially to be the best epic medium invading what had been mainly the province of verse. In sum the choric nature of the epic does not dictate any rigidly answering form.

Finally, not every "accepted unconscious metaphysic" can prompt an epic. If for instance it is predominantly elegiac or nostalgic, it cannot serve. Nietzsche believed tragedy to be possible only in an age of optimism. Epic, in similar fashion, must have faith in the system of beliefs or way of life it bears witness to. The reason for this belongs to other qualities of the epic than the choric. Only when people have faith in their own age can they include the maximum of life in their vision and exert their will-power to its utmost capacity.

NOTES

1. C. M. Bowra, *Heroic Poetry* (London, 1952).
2. John Milton, *Reason of Church Government, ii.* Introd., Columbia ed., *iii.* i. 236.
3. [John] Middleton Murry, *To the Unknown God* (London, 1924), p.136.
4. Aldous Huxley, "Tragedy and the Whole Truth," in *Music at Night* (London, 1931), p.3–18.
5. *Ibid.*, p.14–15.
6. *Ibid.*, p.16.
7. In [Poe's] essay, *The Poetic Principle*. Some art criticism shows the same trend: for instance that which cries up Claude's drawings and cries down his elaborate classical landscapes. Of course the drawings are spontaneous in a way the oil-paintings are not; but to make such spontaneity the only test is critical bigotry.
8. I cannot vouch for the exact figure, having to rely on my memory of hearing the paper read.
9. Joseph Conrad, *Notes on Life and Letters* (London, 1921), p.14.
10. Lascelles Abercrombie, *The Epic* (London, 1914), p.39.

Northrop Frye

THE ENCYCLOPAEDIC FORM OF THE EPIC

In every age of literature there tends to be some kind of central encyclopaedic form, which is normally a scripture or sacred book in the mythical mode, and some "analogy of revelation," as we called it, in the other modes. In our culture the central sacred book is the Christian Bible, which is also probably the most systematically constructed sacred book in the world. To say that the Bible is "more" than a work of literature is merely to say that other methods of approaching it are possible. No book could have had its influence on literature without itself having literary qualities, and the Bible is a work of literature as long as it is being examined by a literary critic.

The absence of any genuinely literary criticism of the Bible in modern times (until very recently) has left an enormous gap in our knowledge of literary symbolism as a whole, a gap which all the new knowledge brought to bear on it is quite incompetent to fill. I feel that historical scholarship is without exception "lower" or analytic criticism, and that "higher" criticism would be a quite different activity. The latter seems to me to be a purely literary criticism which would see the Bible, not as the scrapbook of corruptions, glosses, redactions, insertions, conflations, misplacings, and misunderstandings revealed by the analytic critic, but as the typological unity which all these things were originally intended to help construct. The tremendous cultural influence of the Bible is inexplicable by any criticism of it which stops where it begins to look like something with the literary form of a specialist's stamp collection. A genuine higher criticism of the Bible, therefore, would be a synthetizing process which would start with the assumption that the Bible is a definitive myth, a single archetypal structure extending from creation to apocalypse. Its heuristic principle would be St. Augustine's axiom that the Old Testament is revealed in the New and the New concealed in the Old: that the two testaments are not so much allegories of one another as metaphorical identifications of one another. We cannot trace the Bible back, even historically, to a time when its materials were not being shaped into a typological unity, and if the Bible is to be regarded as inspired in any sense, sacred or secular, its editorial and redacting processes must be regarded as inspired too.

Originally "Specific Encyclopaedic Forms." From Northrop Frye, *Anatomy of Criticism* (copyright © 1957 by Princeton University Press; Princeton Paperback, 1971), p.315–326. Reprinted by permission of Princeton University Press.

This is the only way in which we can deal with the Bible as the major informing influence on literary symbolism which it actually has been. Such an approach would be a conservative criticism recovering and re-establishing the traditional typologies based on the assumption of its figurative unity. The historical critic of the Song of Songs, for instance, is largely concerned with fertility cults and village festivals: the cultural criticism of it would concern itself mainly with the developments of its symbolism in Dante, Bernard of Clairvaux and other mystics and poets, for whom it represented the love of Christ for his Church. This latter is not an allegory inappropriately stuck on to the poem, but the larger archetypal or cultural context of interpretation into which it has been fitted. There is no need to choose between the two types of criticism; no need to regard the book's literary career as the result of a prudish distortion or over-imaginative mistake; no need to treat the view of it as a voluptuous *orientale* as a modern and an ironic discovery.

Once our view of the Bible comes into proper focus, a great mass of literary symbols from *The Dream of the Rood* to *Little Gidding* begins to take on meaning. We are concerned at present with the heroic quest of the central figure called the Messiah, who is associated with various royal figures in the Old Testament and identified with Christ in the New. The stages and symbols of this quest have been dealt with under the *mythos* of romance. A mysterious birth is followed by an epiphany or recognition as God's son; symbols of humiliation, betrayal, and martyrdom, the so-called suffering servant complex, follow, and in their turn are succeeded by symbols of the Messiah as bridegroom, as conqueror of a monster, and as the leader of his people into their rightful home. The oracles of the original prophets appear to have been mainly if not entirely denunciatory, but they have been furnished with "postexilic" sequels which help to infuse the whole Bible with the rhythm of the total cyclical *mythos* in which disaster is followed by restoration, humiliation by prosperity, and which we find in epitome in the stories of Job and the prodigal son.

The Bible as a whole, therefore, presents a gigantic cycle from creation to apocalypse, within which is the heroic quest of the Messiah from incarnation to apotheosis. Within this again are three other cyclical movements, expressed or implied: individual from birth to salvation; sexual from Adam and Eve to the apocalyptic wedding; social from the giving of the law to the established kingdom of the law, the rebuilt Zion of the Old Testament and the millennium of the New. These are all completed or dialectic cycles, where the movement is first down and then up to a permanently redeemed world. In addition there is the ironic or "all too human" cycle, the *mere* cycle of human life without redemptive assistance, which goes recurrently through the "same dull round," in Blake's phrase, from birth to death. Here the final cadence is one of bondage, exile, continuing war, or destruction by fire (Sodom, Babylon) or water (the flood). These two forms of cyclical movement supply us with two epic frameworks: the epic of return and the epic of wrath. The fact that the cycle of life and death and rebirth is closely analogous in its symbolism to the Messianic cycle of pre-existence, life-in-death and resurrection gives us a third type of analogical epic. A fourth type is the contrast-epic, where one pole is the ironic human situation and the other the origin or continuation of a divine society.

Even in myth the full apocalyptic cadence is rare, though it occurs in Northern mythology, in the Eddas and the Muspilli, and the last book of the *Mahabharata* is an entry into heaven. There are myths of apotheosis, as in the legend of Hercules, and of salvation, as in the Osiris symbolism of the Book of the Dead, but the main concern of most sacred books is to lay down the law, chiefly of course the ceremonial law. The resulting shape is an embryonic form of contrast-epic: myths accounting for the origin of law, including creation myths, are at one pole and human society under the law is at the other. The antiquity of the contrast-epic is indicated by the epic of Gilgamesh, where the hero's search for immortality leads him only to hear about the end of the natural cycle, symbolized here, as in the Bible, by a flood. The collections of myth made by Hesiod and Ovid are based on the same form: here the poet himself, a victim of injustice or exile, has a prominent place at the human pole. The same structure is carried on through Boethius, where the two poles are the lost golden age and the poet in prison falsely accused, into medieval times.

Romantic encyclopaedic forms use human or sacramental imitations of the Messianic myth, like the quest of Dante in the *Commedia*, of St. George in Spenser, and of the knights of the Holy Grail. The *Commedia* reverses the usual structure of the contrast-epic, as it starts with the ironic human situation and ends with divine vision. The human nature of Dante's quest is established by the fact that he is unable to overcome or even to face the monsters who confront him at the beginning: his quest thus begins in a retreat from the conventional knight-errant role. In Langland's great vision we have the first major English treatment of the contrast-epic. At one pole is the risen Christ and the salvation of Piers: at the other is the somber vision of human life which presents at the end of the poem something very like a triumph of Antichrist. *The Faerie Queene* was to have ended with an epithalamium, which would probably have been filled with Biblical bridegroom imagery, but as we have it the poem ends with the Blatant Beast of calumny still at large and the poet a victim of it.

In the high mimetic we reach the structure that we think of as typically epic, the form represented by Homer, Virgil, and Milton. The epic differs from the narrative in the encyclopaedic range of its theme, from heaven to the underworld, and over an enormous mass of traditional knowledge. A narrative poet, a Southey or a Lydgate, may write any number of narratives, but an epic poet normally completes only one epic structure, the moment when he decides on his theme being the crisis of his life.

The cyclical form of the Classical epic is based on the natural cycle, a mediterranean known world in the middle of a boundlessness (*apeiron*) and between the upper and the lower gods. The cycle has two main rhythms: the life and death of the individual, and the slower social rhythm which, in the course of years (*periplomenon eniauton* in Homer, *volvibus* or *labentibus annis* in Virgil), brings cities and empires to their rise and fall. The steady vision of the latter movement is possible only to gods. The convention of beginning the action *in medias res* ties a knot in time, so to speak. The total action in the background of the *Iliad* moves from the cities of Greece through the ten-year siege of Troy back to Greece again; the total action of the *Odyssey* is a specialized example of the same thing, moving from Ithaca back to Ithaca. The *Aeneid* moves with the household gods of Priam, from Troy to New Troy.

The foreground action begins at a point described in the *Odyssey* as *hamothen*, "somewhere": actually, it is far more carefully chosen. All three epics begin at a kind of nadir of the total cyclical action: the *Iliad*, at a moment of despair in the Greek camp; the *Odyssey*, with Odysseus and Penelope furthest from one another, both wooed by importunate suitors; the *Aeneid*, with its hero shipwrecked on the shores of Carthage, citadel of Juno and enemy of Rome. From there, the action moves both backward and forward far enough to indicate the general shape of the historical cycle. The discovery of the epic action is the sense of the end of the total action as like the beginning, and hence of a consistent order and balance running through the whole. This consistent order is not a divine fiat or fatalistic causation, but a stability in nature controlled by the gods, and extended to human beings if they accept it. The sense of this stability is not necessarily tragic, but it is the kind of sense that makes tragedy possible.

It does so in the *Iliad*, for example. The number of valid reasons for praising the *Iliad* would fill a bigger book than this, but the relevant reason for us here is the fact that its theme is *menis*, a song of wrath. It is hardly possible to overestimate the importance for Western literature of the *Iliad's* demonstration that the fall of an enemy, no less than of a friend or leader, is tragic and not comic. With the *Iliad*, once for all, an objective and disinterested element enters into the poet's vision of human life. Without this element, poetry is merely instrumental to various social aims, to propaganda, to amusement, to devotion, to instruction: with it, it acquires the authority that since the *Iliad* it has never lost, an authority based, like the authority of science, on the vision of nature as an impersonal order.

The *Odyssey* begins the other tradition of the epic of return. The story is a romance of a hero escaping safely from incredible perils and arriving in the nick of time to claim his bride and baffle the villains, but our central feeling about it is a much more prudent sense, rooted in all our acceptance of nature, society, and law, of the proper master of the house coming to reclaim his own. The *Aeneid* develops the theme of return into one of rebirth, the end in New Troy being the starting-point renewed and transformed by the hero's quest. The Christian epic carries the same themes into a wider archetypal context. The action of the Bible, from the poetic point of view, includes the themes of the three great epics: the theme of the destruction and captivity of the city in the *Iliad*, the theme of the *nostos* or return home in the *Odyssey*, and the theme of the building of the new city in the *Aeneid*. Adam is, like Odysseus, a man of wrath, exiled from home because he angered God by going *hyper moron*, beyond his limit as a man. In both stories the provoking act is symbolized by the eating of food reserved for deity. As with Odysseus, Adam's return home is contingent on the appeasing of divine wrath by divine wisdom

(Poseidon and Athene reconciled by the will of Zeus in Homer; the Father reconciled with man in the Christian atonement). Israel carries its ark from Egypt to the Promised Land just as Aeneas carries his household goods from the fallen Troy to the eternally established one.

Hence there is, as we go from the Classical to the Christian epic, a progress in completeness of theme (not in any kind of value), as Milton indicates in such phrases as "Beyond the Aonian mount." In Milton the foreground action of the epic is again the nadir of the total cyclical action, the fall of Satan and Adam. From there the action works backward through the speech of Raphael, and forward through the speech of Michael, to the beginning and end of the total action. The beginning is God's presence among the angels before the Son is manifested to them; the end comes after the apocalypse when God again is "all in all," but the beginning and end are the same point, the presence of God, renewed and transformed by the heroic quest of Christ. As a Christian, Milton has to reconsider the epic theme of heroic action, to decide what in Christian terms a hero is and what an act is. Heroism for him consists in obedience, fidelity and perseverance through ridicule or persecution, and is exemplified by Abdiel, the faithful angel. Action for him means positive or creative act, exemplified by Christ in the creation of the world and the recreation of man. Satan thus takes over the traditional qualities of martial heroism: he is the wrathful Achilles, the cunning Ulysses, the knight-errant who achieves the perilous quest of chaos; but he is from God's point of view a mock-hero, what man in his fallen state naturally turns to with admiration as the idolatrous form of the kingdom, the power, and the glory.

In the low mimetic period the encyclopaedic structure tends to become either subjective and mythological, or objective and historical. The former is usually expressed in *epos* and the latter in prose fiction. The main attempts to combine the two were made, somewhat unexpectedly, in France, and extend from the fragments left by Chenier to Victor Hugo's *Légendes des Siècles*. Here the theme of heroic action is transferred, consistently with low mimetic conventions, from the leader to humanity as a whole. Hence the fulfilment of the action is conceived mainly as social improvement in the future.

In the traditional epic the gods affect the action from a continuous present: Athene and Venus appear epiphanically, on definite occasions, to illuminate or cheer the hero at that moment. To gain information about the future, or what is "ahead" in terms of the lower cycle of life, it is normally necessary to descend to a lower world of the dead, as is done in the nekyia, or katabasis, in the eleventh book of the *Odyssey* and the sixth of the *Aeneid*. Similarly in Dante the damned know the future but not the present, and in Milton the forbidden knowledge which "brought death into the world" is actualized in the form of Michael's prophecy of the future. We are thus not surprised to find a great increase, in the low mimetic period of future hopes, of a sense of Messianic powers as coming from "underneath" or through esoteric and hermetic traditions. *Prometheus Unbound* is the most familiar English example: the attempt to insert a katabasis into the second part of *Faust*, first as the descent to the "mothers" and then as the Classical Walpurgis Night, was evidently one of the most baffling structural problems in that work. Sometimes, however, the katabasis is combined with and complemented by the more traditional point of epiphany. Keats's Endymion goes "down" in search of truth and "up" in search of beauty, discovering, not surprisingly for Keats, that truth and beauty are the same. In Hyperion some alignment between a Dionysian "below" and an Apollonian "above" was clearly on the agenda. Eliot's Burnt Norton is founded on the principle that "the way up and the way down are the same," which resolves this dichotomy in Christian terms. Time in this world is a horizontal line, and God's timeless presence is a vertical one crossing it at right angles, the crossing point being the Incarnation. The rose garden and subway episodes outline the two semi-circles of the cycle of nature, the upper one the romantic mythopoeic fantasy world of innocence and the lower the world of experience. But if we go further up than the rose garden and further down than the subway we reach the same point.

Comedy and irony supply us with parody-symbolism, of which the relation of the bound Gulliver in Lilliput to Prometheus, of the staggering hod-carrier in Finnegans Wake to Adam, of the madeleine cake in Proust to the Eucharist, are examples on varying levels of seriousness. Here too belongs the kind of use of archetypal structure made in Absalom and Achitophel, where the resemblance between the story and its Old Testament model is treated as a series of witty coincidences. The theme of encyclopaedic parody is endemic in satire, and in prose fiction is chiefly to be found in the anatomy, the tradition of Apuleius and Rabelais and Swift. Satires and novels show a relation corresponding to that of epics and narratives: the more novels a novelist writes the more successful he is, but Rabelais, Burton, and Sterne build their creative lives around one supreme effort. Hence it is in satire and irony that we should look for the continuing encyclopaedic tradition, and we should expect that the containing form of the ironic or satiric epic would be the pure cycle, in which every quest, however successful or heroic, has sooner or later to be made over again.

In Blake's poem The Mental Traveller we have a vision of the cycle of human life, from birth to death to rebirth. The two characters of the poem are a male and a female figure, moving in opposite directions, one growing old as the other grows young, and vice versa. The cyclical relation between them runs through four cardinal points: a son-mother phase, a husband-wife phase, a father-daughter phase, and a fourth phase of what Blake calls spectre and emanation, terms corresponding roughly to Shelley's alastor and epipsyche. None of these phases is quite true: the mother is only a nurse, the wife merely "bound down" for the male's delight, the daughter a changeling, and the emanation does not "emanate," but remains elusive. The male figure represents humanity and therefore includes women—the "female will" in Blake becomes associated with women only when women dramatize or mimic the above relation in human life, as they do in the Courtly Love convention. The female figure represents the natural environment which man partially but never wholly subdues. The controlling symbolism of the poem, as the four phases suggest, is lunar.

To the extent that the encyclopaedic form concerns itself with the cycle of human life, an ambivalent female archetype appears in it, sometimes benevolent, sometimes sinister, but usually presiding over and confirming the cyclical movement. One pole of her is represented by an Isis figure, a Penelope or Solveig who is the fixed point on which the action ends. The goddess who frequently begins and ends the cyclical action is closely related. This figure is Athene in the *Odyssey* and Venus in the *Aeneid;* in Elizabethan literature, for political reasons, usually some variant of Diana, like the Faerie Queen in Spenser. The *alma Venus* who suffuses Lucretius' great vision of life balanced in the order of nature is another version. Beatrice in Dante presides over not a cycle but a sacramental spiral leading up to deity, as does, in a far less concrete way, the *Ewig-Weibliche* of *Faust.* At the opposite pole is a figure— Calypso or Circe in Homer, Dido in Virgil, Cleopatra in Shakespeare, Duessa in Spenser, sometimes a "terrible mother" but often sympathetically treated— who represents the opposite direction from the heroic quest. Eve in Milton, who spirals man downward into the Fall, is the contrasting figure to Beatrice.

In the ironic age there are naturally a good many visions of a cycle of experience, often presided over by a female figure with lunar and femme fatale affiliations. Yeats's *Vision,* which Yeats was quite right in associating with *The Mental Traveller,* is based on this symbolism, and more recently Mr. Robert Graves' *The White Goddess* has expounded it with even greater learning and ingenuity. In Eliot's *Waste Land* the figure in the background is less "the lady of situations" than the androgynous Teiresias, and although there is a fire sermon and a thunder sermon, both with apocalyptic overtones, the natural cycle of water, the Thames flowing into the sea and returning through death by water in the spring rains, is the containing form of the poem. In Joyce's *Ulysses* a female figure at once maternal, marital, and meretricious, a Penelope who embraces all her suitors, merges in her sleep with the drowsy spinning earth, constantly affirming but never forming, and taking the whole book with her.

But it is *Finnegans Wake* which is the chief ironic epic of our time. Here again the containing structure is cyclical, as the end of the book swings us around to the beginning again. Finnegan never really wakes up, because HCE fails to establish any continuity between his dreaming and waking worlds. The central figure is ALP, but we notice that ALP, although she has very little of the Beatrice or Virgin Mary about her, has even less of the femme fatale. She is a harried but endlessly patient and solicitous wife and mother: she runs through her natural cycle and achieves no quest herself, but she is clearly the kind of being who makes a quest possible. Who then is the hero who achieves the permanent quest in *Finnegans Wake?* No character in the book itself seems a likely candidate; yet one feels that this book gives us something more than the merely irresponsible irony of a turning cycle. Eventually it dawns on us that it is the *reader* who achieves the quest, the reader who, to the extent that he masters the book of Doublends Jined, is able to look down on its rotation, and see its form as something more than rotation.

In encyclopaedic forms, such as the epic and its congeners, we see how the conventional themes, around which lyrics cluster, reappear as *episodes* of a longer story. Thus the panegyric reappears in the *klea andron* or heroic contests, the poem of community action in the convention of the games, the elegy in heroic death, and so on. The reverse development occurs when a lyric on a conventional theme achieves a concentration that expands it into a miniature epic: if not the historical "little epic" or epyllion, something very like it generically. Thus *Lycidas* is a miniature scriptural epic extending over the whole range covered by *Paradise Lost*, the death of man and his redemption by Christ. Spenser's *Epithalamion* also probably contains in miniature as much symbolic range as the unwritten conclusion to his epic would have had. In modern times the miniature epic becomes a very common form: the later poems of Eliot, of Edith Sitwell, and many cantos of Pound belong to it.

Often too, in illustration of our general principle, a miniature epic actually forms part of a bigger one. The prophecy of Michael in *Paradise Lost* presents the whole Bible as a miniature contrast-epic, with one pole at the apocalypse and the other at the flood. The Bible itself contains the Book of Job, which is a kind of microcosm of its total theme, and is cited by Milton as the model for the "brief" epic.

Similarly, oratorical prose develops into the more continuous forms of prose fiction, and similarly too the growing points of prose, so to speak, which we called the commandment, parable, aphorism, and oracle, reappear as the kernels of scriptural forms. In many types of prose romance verse or characteristics of verse are prominent: the old Irish epics, euphuism in Elizabethan romance, the rhyming prose of the Arabian Nights, the use of poems for cultivated dialogue in the Japanese *Tale of Genji*, are random examples showing how universal the tendency is. But as *epos* grows into epic, it conventionalizes and unifies its metre, while prose goes its own way in separate forms. In the low mimetic period the gap between the subjective mythological epic and the objective historical one is increased by the fact that the former seems to belong by its decorum to verse and the latter to prose. In prose satire, however, we notice a strong tendency on the part of prose to reabsorb verse. We have mentioned the frequency of the verse interlude in the anatomy tradition, and in the *melos* of Rabelais, Sterne and Joyce the tendency is carried much farther. In scriptural forms, we have seen, the gap between prose and verse is very narrow, and sometimes hardly exists at all.

We come back to where we started this section, then, to the Bible, the only form which unites the architectonics of Dante with the disintegration of Rabelais. From one point of view, the Bible presents an epic structure of unsurpassed range, consistency and completeness; from another, it presents a seamy side of bits and pieces which makes the *Tale of a Tub, Tristram Shandy*, and *Sartor Resartus* look as homogeneous as a cloudless sky. Some mystery is here which literary criticism might find it instructive to look into.

When we do look into it, we find that the sense of unified continuity is what the Bible has as a work of fiction, as a definitive myth extending over time and space, over invisible and visible orders of reality, and with a parabolic dramatic structure of which the five acts are creation, fall, exile, redemption, and restoration. The more we study this myth, the more its descriptive or sigmatic aspect seems to fall into the background. For most readers, myth, legend, historical reminiscence, and actual history are inseparable in the Bible; and even what is historical fact is not there because it is "true" but because it is mythically significant. The begats in Chronicles may be authentic history; the Book of Job is clearly an imaginative drama, but the Book of Job is more important, and closer to Christ's practice of revelation through parable. The priority of myth to fact is religious as well as literary; in both contexts the significance of the flood story is in its imaginative status as an archetype, a status which no layer of mud on top of Sumeria will ever account for. When we apply this principle to the gospels, with all the variations in their narratives, the descriptive aspect of them too dissolves. The basis of their form is something other than biography, just as the basis of the Exodus story is something other than history.

At this point the analytic view of the Bible begins to come into focus as the thematic aspect of it. In proportion as the continuous fictional myth begins to look illusory, as the text breaks down into smaller and smaller fragments, it takes on the appearance of a sequence of epiphanies, a discontinuous but rightly ordered series of significant moments of apprehension or vision. The Bible may thus be examined from an aesthetic or Aristotelian point of view as a single form, as a story in which pity and terror, which in this context are the knowledge of good and evil, are raised and cast out. Or it may be examined from a Longinian point of view as a series of ecstatic moments or points of expanding apprehension—this approach is in fact the assumption on which every selection of a text for a sermon is based. Here we have a critical principle which we can take back to literature and apply to anything we like, a principle in which the "holism," as it has been called, of Coleridge and the discontinuous theories of Poe, Hulme, and Pound are reconciled.

Albert B. Lord

HOMER
AND ORAL POETRY

The practice of oral narrative poetry makes a certain form necessary; the way in which oral epic songs are composed and transmitted leaves its unmistakable mark on the songs. That mark is apparent in the formulas and in the themes. It is visible in the structure of the songs themselves. In the living laboratory of Yugoslav epic the elements have emerged and they have been segregated. We have watched singers in the process of learning songs, we have seen them change songs, and we have seen them build long songs from short ones. A panorama of individual singers, some of them true artists, has passed before us, and the details of their art no longer mystify us. With this new understanding, which further research will eventually deepen, we must turn again to the songs that we have inherited from the past in precious manuscripts. Do they also show the marks of oral composition as we have come to know them? . . .

At last we find ourselves in a position to answer the question as to whether the author of the Homeric poems was an "oral poet," and whether the poems themselves are "oral poems." We now know exactly what is meant by these terms, at least insofar as manner of composition is concerned. We have cleared away and discarded some false notions of "oral tradition," "oral composition," and "oral transmassion," and installed in their stead knowledge gained from observation and analysis of oral tradition in action.

We realize that what is called oral tradition is as intricate and meaningful an art form as its derivative "literary tradition." In the extended sense of the word, oral tradition is as "literary" as literary tradition. It is not simply a less polished, more haphazard, or cruder second cousin twice removed, to literature. By the time the written techniques come onto the stage, the art forms have been long set and are already highly developed and ancient.

There is now no doubt that the composer of the Homeric poems was an oral poet. The proof is to be found in the poems themselves; and it is proper, logical, and necessary that this should be so. The necessity of oral form and style has been discussed; their characteristic marks have been noted. What

Originally "Homer," p. 141–57 and 291–94. Reprinted by permission of the publishers from Albert B. Lord, *The Singer of Tales,* Cambridge, Mass.: Harvard University Press, Copyright, 1960, by the President and Fellows of Harvard College.

marks of formulaic technique and of thematic structure does examination of the Homeric poems reveal?

Parry's analyses have, I believe, answered the first part of this question.[1] His discovery of the intricate schematization of formulas in the Homeric poems has never been challenged; though there have been critics who have not been willing to accept his interpretation of the meaning and implication of the phenomenon of formula structure. It is highly important to emphasize the fact that the formulas are not limited to the familiar epithets and oft-repeated lines, but that the formulas are all pervasive. In [the accompanying] chart it will be noted that about 90 per cent of the 15 lines analyzed are formulas or formulaic. Considering the limited amount of material available for analysis—only two poems, approximately 27,000 lines—the percentage of demonstrably formulaic lines or part lines is truly amazing. It is even more to be wondered at because of the subtlety and intricacy of the Greek hexameter. The task before the ancient Greek bards was not easy, and one should have the most profound respect for their accomplishment in creating a formulaic technique so perfect and rich in expressive possibilities. It is a complex and delicately balanced artistic instrument.

The Greek hexameter is probably the best known meter in all literature, and for this study of formulas it needs no further elucidation than has already been given it. But something must be said about formula length so that the divisions in [the] Chart may be understood. In the Yugoslav poems there are formulas of four, six, and ten syllables in length. The structure of the Yugoslav line, with its strict break after the fourth syllable, is comparatively simple. The Greek hexameter allows for greater variety, because the line may be broken at more than one place by a caesura. It is probably correct to say that this flexibility is closely allied to the musical pattern in which the poetry was sung or chanted, but since we know nothing of this music, any such statement is speculative. The caesura can occur in any one of the following points in the line: (a) after the first syllable of the third foot, (b) after the second syllable of the third foot if it is a dactyl, and (c) after the first syllable of the fourth foot. To these should be added (d) the bucolic diaeresis (after the fourth foot) and (e) the pause after a run-over word at the beginning of the line, which occurs most frequently after the first syllable of the second foot. One can, therefore, expect to find formulas of one foot and a half, two feet and a half, two feet and three quarters, three feet and a half, four feet, and six feet in length measured from the beginning of the line, and complementary lengths measured from the pause to the end of the line.

The only satisfactory way to analyze formulaic structure is the one which Parry used. . . : to select a number of lines (in our case fifteen), and to analyze each of them for its formulaic content. I shall use the first fifteen lines of the *Iliad* for [the] chart, and since my divisions differ slightly from Parry's, I invite comparison with his table. As in the analysis of the Yugoslav poetry, an unbroken line indicates a formula, and a broken line a formulaic expression. A list of the supporting passages from the Homeric corpus is given in the notes to the chart.[2]

CHART[2]

ΙΛΙΑΔΟΣ Α

Μῆνιν ἄειδε, θεά, Πηληϊάδεω ᾽Αχιλῆος

‒ ‒ ‒ ‒ ‒ ‒ ‒ ‒ ‒ ‒ ‒ ‒ ‒ ‒ [1]

‒ ‒ ‒ ‒ ‒ ‒ [2] ———————————[3]

οὐλομένην, ἥ μυρί᾽ ᾽Αχαιοῖς ἄλγε᾽ ἔθηκε,

‒ ‒ ‒ ‒ ‒ ‒ ‒ ‒ ‒ ‒ ‒ ‒ ‒ ‒ [4]

————[5]‒ ‒ ‒ ‒ ‒ ‒ —————[6]

πολλὰς δ᾽ ἰφθίμους ψυχὰς ᾽Αϊδι προΐαψεν

‒ ‒ ‒ ‒ ‒ ‒ ‒ ‒ ‒ ‒ ‒ ‒ ‒ ‒ ‒[7]

‒ ‒ ‒ ‒ ‒ ‒ ‒ ‒ ‒ [8]————————[9]

ἡρώων, αὐτοὺς δὲ ἑλώρια τεῦχε κύνεσσιν[10]

———— , ‒ ‒ ‒ ‒[11]   [12]

5 οἰωνοῖσί τε πᾶσι, Διὸς δ᾽ ἐτελείετο βουλή,[13]

‒ ‒ ‒ ‒ ‒ ‒ ‒ [14]————————[15]

ἐξ οὗ δὴ τὰ πρῶτα διαστήτην ἐρίσαντε

‒ ‒ ‒ ‒ ‒ ‒ ‒ ‒ ‒ ‒ ‒ ‒ [16]

——————————[17]‒ ‒ ‒ ‒ ‒ [18]

᾽Ατρείδης τε ἄναξ ἀνδρῶν καὶ δῖος ᾽Αχιλλεύς.

‒ ‒ ‒ ‒ ‒ ‒ ‒ ‒ ‒ ‒ ‒ ‒ ‒ ‒[19]

————[20]————[21]————————[22]

Τίς τ᾽ ἄρ σφωε θεῶν ἔριδι ξυνέηκε μάχεσθαι ;

‒ ‒ ‒ ‒ ‒ ‒ ‒[23] ———————————[24]

————[25]

Λητοῦς καὶ Διὸς υἱός· ὁ γὰρ βασιλῆϊ χολωθεὶς

‒ ‒ ‒ [26] ‒ ‒ ‒ ‒ ‒ ‒ ‒ ‒ ‒ ‒[27]

10 νοῦσον ἀνὰ στρατὸν ὦρσε κακήν, ὀλέκοντο δὲ λαοί,

‒ ‒ ‒ ‒ ‒ ‒ ‒ ————[28]‒ ‒ ‒ ‒ ————[29]

οὕνεκα τὸν Χρύσην ἠτίμασεν ἀρητῆρα

‒ ‒ ‒ ‒ ‒ ‒ ‒ ‒ ‒ ‒ ‒ ‒ ‒[30]

———— ‒ ‒ ‒ ‒ ‒[31]   [32]

᾽Ατρείδης· ὁ γὰρ ἦλθε θοὰς ἐπὶ νῆας ᾽Αχαιῶν

————[33]‒ ‒ ———————————[34]

‒ ‒ ‒ ‒ ‒ ‒ ‒ ‒ ‒ ‒

λυσόμενός τε θύγατρα φέρων τ᾽ ἀπερείσι᾽ ἄποινα,

———————————————————[35]

———— ‒ ‒ ‒ ‒ ‒[36]——————[37]

στέμματ᾽ ἔχων ἐν χερσὶν ἑκηβόλου ᾽Απόλλωνος[38]

——————
——————

‒ ‒ ‒ ‒ ————————[39]————[40]

15 χρυσέῳ ἀνὰ σκήπτρῳ, καὶ λίσσετο πάντας ᾽Αχαιούς,

——————————————————[41]

‒ ‒ ‒ ‒ ‒ ‒ [42]‒ ‒ ‒ ‒ ‒ ————[43]

The divisions of the lines do not always agree with those of Parry, and it is very likely that someone else would divide them in still another way. Without dwelling on these details, but considering the chart as a whole, we notice that well over 90 per cent of the sample is covered by either an unbroken line or a broken one. In the case of the two half lines which are labelled as non-formulaic, I believe that I have erred on the side of being overcautious, and this is probably true for the six whole lines which are put in the same category. The concordances do not furnish any examples of the patterns under the key words of these passages. But it is almost certain that a line-by-line search of the two poems would reveal other instances of these rhythmic and syntactic patterns. It is not necessary to do this, however, because the formula structure is clear enough from what has been underlined.

The formula technique in the Homeric poems is, indeed, so perfect, the system of formulas, as Parry showed, is so "thrifty," so lacking in identical alternative expressions, that one marvels that this perfection could be reached without the aid of writing.[3] We have already shown that the thrift of the Yugoslav poetry is greater than was previously believed. To determine the thrift of a poetry, one should confine oneself to the work of a single singer . . . and one should take into consideration all the poetic elements in a formula, including its acoustic pattern. The misunderstanding of Yugoslav thrift has come about by reading hastily through collections from many different singers from different regions and from different times. This method is not precise enough to yield reliable results. Moreover, even were one to limit oneself to a single singer and make use of only sung texts, one would still not arrive at a just picture of the situation for comparison with the Homeric poems. One must always make allowances and adjustments for sung texts and their deviations which arise from the pressure of rapid composition. Dictated texts of a carefully controlled type must be used for the comparison. When this was done, we saw that we had statistics comparable to those for the Homeric poems, which must of necessity be dictated and not sung texts. By making one's methods more exact, by considering the nature of the texts chosen in the Yugoslav experiment, and by understanding the type of text represented in the Homeric poems, one sees that the discrepancies between the statistics for the two traditions disappear.

The formulaic techniques, therefore, in the Greek and South Slavic poetries are generically identical and operate on the same principles. This is the surest proof now known of oral composition, and on the basis of it alone we should be justified in the conclusion that the Homeric poems are oral compositions. But there are other characteristics which can corroborate this conclusion.

In his study of enjambement in the Homeric poems Parry indicated that necessary enjambement is much less common in the epics of Homer than in Virgil or Apollonius.[4] The line is a metrical unit in itself. In Yugoslav song necessary enjambement is practically nonexistent. The length of the hexameter is one of the important causes of the discrepancy between the two poetries. It is long enough to allow for the expression of a complete idea within its limits, and on occasion it is too long. Then a new idea is started before the end of the line. But since there is not enough space before the end to complete the idea it must be continued in the next line. This accounts for systems of formulas that have been evolved to fill the space from the bucolic diaeresis to the end of the line, with complementary systems to take care of the run-over words in the following line.

Parry pointed out the situation in the Homeric poems, and I have already compared this with statistics from the Yugoslav poetry in a separate article.[5] Here, too, it was necessary, as always, to be aware of the differences of language, length of line, and possible influence of a different type of musical accompaniment in order to understand the discrepancy between the Greek and Yugoslav poetries in the higher instance of end-stop lines in the latter than in the former. Again, by paying particular attention to matters of method, one was able to arrive at an understanding of this basic stylistic feature. The test of enjambement analysis is, as a matter of fact, an easily applied rule of thumb that can be used on first approaching a new text to determine the possibility of oral composition. It should be done, however, with a knowledge of the musical background, if such information is available, and with an awareness of differences that may be brought about by length of line and peculiarities of the languages involved.

Another corroborating test for oral composition is less easily applied— though just as decisive—because it requires a greater amount of material for analysis than is usually available from the poetries of the past. This is the investigation of thematic structure.[6]

The Homeric poems have probably been analyzed more often and more variously than any other poems in world literature. It would be a brave man who would undertake another analysis of them, unless he were convinced that there are really new and significant grounds for so doing, and that the analysis would bring decisive results.

The first step in thematic analysis must be to prove the existence of themes in the poem under consideration. In other words we must find, either in the poem under scrutiny or in other poems by the same singer or otherwise belonging to the same tradition, the same situations repeated at least once. The method is the same used for formula analysis; but the units are larger and exact word-for-word correspondence is not necessary. In fact, exact word-for-word correspondence, as we have seen, is not to be expected.

One of the more readily isolated themes in the Homeric poems, indeed in all epic literature, is that of the assembly. It is easily isolated because it has an obvious beginning and an obvious end. Let us observe this theme in Books I and II of the *Iliad*. The first assembly in the *Iliad* is an informal and unofficial one, and it is brief. Chryses comes to the Achaean fleet, and makes his petition to the people in general and to the Atridae in particular. The people applaud, but Agamemnon sends the priest away with harsh words. This form of the theme of the assembly is a hybrid. It is halfway between the general theme of interchange of words between two characters and the general theme of the formal assembly, because it takes place in the presence of the people, yet it lacks the calling and dismissing of an assembly.

The next assembly in the poem is a full-dress affair, called by Achilles at the instigation of Hera, complete with the risings and sittings of the speakers and with the dismissal of the assembly. This assembly can serve as a model for the full use of the theme.

The third assembly in Book I, and the final scene in the book, is that of the gods, where Hera and Zeus bandy words and Hephaestus takes his mother's part. Here again is a special form of the general theme, because this group of gods is usually always together except for individuals away on a mission. It needs to be called into formal council only when there is special and important business. It is like a family scene, or like the aghas of the Border in the Yugoslav Moslem songs, who are always gathered together in the green bower in Udbina. There is no need usually to call an assembly, hence no need to dismiss one. It is not unlike the first assembly described above, except that in that case the conversation was started by a newly arrived stranger, and in this instance it is confined to the family group.

The relationship between these three examples of the assembly theme in Book I could be expressed as A (the assembly called by Achilles), B_1 (the assembly of the gods), and B_2 (the quarrel between Chryses and Agamemnon).

Book II furnishes a number of instructive cases of this theme. First comes the council of elders called by Agamemnon as a result of the deceptive dream. It is a formal affair and belongs in the A category. If we designate the full assembly of the people as A_1, we may call the council of elders A_2, although structurally there is no difference between them. In the example under consideration in Book II, however, the council of elders is introduced within the framework of the full assembly. Heralds are sent out to summon an assembly of the people, and while the men are gathering together a council of elders is held. A_2 is here included in A_1. This popular assembly is not formally dismissed for some time; it is broken up by the men themselves, who have to be brought back by the efforts of Odysseus. We might term this interrupted and reconvened assembly of the people A_{1a}.

There are two more examples of our theme in Book II. The first may be considered as a special variety of A_2, the council of elders. Agamemnon calls together the elders and chief men; there is a sacrifice and dinner (both of which are themselves themes, of course), followed by a brief speech of instruction and command by Nestor. We might call this A_{2a}. Although I am including this theme with the assembly themes, it might perhaps more properly belong with feasting and sacrifice themes. This ambiguity emphasizes the overlapping of themes, or, more precisely, the way in which minor themes are useful in more than one major theme. The summoning of the elders is a minor theme in point, as is also the speech of Nestor. This can be seen again in the lines that immediately follow the speech and tell of the sounding of the call to battle and the assembling of the army. The lesser theme of summoning is itself useful in numerous situations: in this case in the larger theme of summoning an army, which is the prelude to the theme of the catalogue. The architectonics of thematic structure are wondrous to observe.

The final assembly in Book II is one already in progress on the Trojan side. It is a popular assembly, and hence a form of A_1. It has been addressed by Iris and will be dismissed by Hector. We see only the end of the assembly.

Thus, in the first two books of the *Iliad* we find some seven examples of the theme of the assembly. The second example in Book I provides a good model. The rest seem to be variations in different tonalities on this theme. We have already become aware in this analysis of the interweaving and over-lapping of major themes; we have begun to glimpse the complexity of thematic structure in the *Iliad*.

We have now applied the three sets of tests that we recognize as valid in determining whether any given poem is oral or not. The Homeric poems have met each of these tests. We now realize fully that Homer is an oral poet. Some of the implications of that fact have already been apparent from our thematic analysis. But we cannot leave it at that.

First, this knowledge places Homer inside an oral tradition of epic song. He is not an outsider approaching the tradition with only a superficial grasp of it, using a bit here and a bit there, or trying to present a "flavor" of the traditional, yet ever thinking in terms essentially different from it. He is not a split personality with half of his understanding and technique in the tradition and the other half in a parnassus of literate methods. No, he is not even "immersed" in the tradition. He *is* the tradition; he is one of the integral parts of that complex; for us, as undoubtedly for his own audiences, he is the most gifted and fascinating part of that tradition. His vividness and immediacy arise from the fact that he is a practicing oral poet. Those who would make of Homer a "literary" poet, do not understand his "literariness"; he has none of the artificiality of those who use traditional themes or traditional devices for nontraditional purposes. From ancient times until the present we have been misled about the true nature of Homer's art and greatness. And the reason has been that we have tried to read him in our own terms, which we have labelled "universal terms of art."

We have exercised our imaginations and ingenuity in finding a kind of unity, individuality, and originality in the Homeric poems that are irrelevant. Had Homer been interested in Aristotelian ideas of unity, he would not have been Homer, nor would he have composed the *Iliad* or *Odyssey*. An oral poet spins out a tale; he likes to ornament, if he has the ability to do so, as Homer, of course, did. It is on the story itself, and even more on the grand scale of ornamentation, that we must concentrate, not on any alien concept of close-knit unity. The story is there and Homer tells it to the end. He tells it fully and with a leisurely tempo, ever willing to linger and to tell another story that comes to his mind. And if the stories are apt, it is not because of a preconceived idea of structural unity which the singer is self-consciously and laboriously working out, but because at the moment when they occur to the poet in the telling of his tale he is so filled with his subject that the natural processes of association have brought to his mind a relevant tale. If the incidental tale or ornament be, by any chance, irrelevant to the main story or to the poem as a whole, this is no great matter; for the ornament has a value of its own, and this value is understood and appreciated by the poet's audience.

Each theme, small or large—one might even say, each formula—has around it an aura of meaning which has been put there by all the contexts in which it has occurred in the past. It is the meaning that has been given it by the tradition in its creativeness. To any given poet at any given time, this meaning involves all the occasions on which he has used the theme, especially those contexts in which he uses it most frequently; it involves also all the occasions on which he has heard it used by others, particularly by those singers whom he first heard in his youth, or by great singers later by whom he was impressed. To the audience the meaning of the theme involves its own experience of it as well. The communication of this supra-meaning is possible because of the community of experience of poet and audience. At our distance of time and space we can approach an understanding of the supra-meaning only by steeping ourselves in as much material in traditional poetry or in a given tradition as is available.

But we are getting ahead of our story. Having determined that the method of composition of the Homeric poems is that of oral poetry, we must next decide what degree of oral composition they represent. What degrees can we distinguish? First, there is the *actual performance*.

Let us make one thing clear at this point. An interested audience, with time and desire to listen for a long period and from one day to another, coupled with a singer of talent in a rich tradition might produce songs as long as the Homeric poems. But our texts as we have shown in a previous chapter could not have been written down during performance. Actual performance is too rapid for a scribe. One might possibly suggest that the scribe might write as much as he could at one performance, correct it at the next, and so on until he had taken down the text of the whole from several singings. I mention this because Parry had an assistant in the field at the beginning who thought that he could do this, but the variations from one singing to another were so great that he very soon gave up trying to note them down. It should be clear by now that such a suggestion makes sense only when there is a fixed text being repeated. In oral epic performance this is not the case. Without recording apparatus, it is impossible to obtain an exact text of actual performance, and hence we cannot say that our texts of the Homeric songs represent oral poetry in the first degree.

The second degree is close to the first in matter of composition. This degree is the dictated text. This is the nearest one can get to an actual performance without the use of a recording machine, but there are important differences. In the hands of a good singer and competent scribe this method produces a longer and technically better text than actual performance, for reasons that we have already analyzed. It seems to me that this is where we should most logically place the Homeric poems. They are *oral dictated texts*. Within this class of texts, we can differentiate between those skillfully and those ineptly done. The first will have regular lines and fullness of telling. The second will have many irregularities in lines and the general structure will be apocopated. Even allowing for later editing, we must see in the Homeric texts models of the dictating and scribal technique.

The third degree of oral composition is when the oral poet is literate and himself writes down a poem. At best the result may be the same as in the second degree described above, except that the pen is in the hand of the singer, and there is no scribe involved. This may be attractive to those who must have a literate Homer writing. Theoretically, it makes little difference, if any, in the results at this stage. Yet it is not a normal situation, and the experience which we have of such cases would indicate that texts thus produced (which we have termed *oral autograph texts*) are inferior in all respects to oral dictated texts. There seems to be little sense in grasping at this solution for purely sentimental reasons. In putting a pen into Homer's hand, one runs the danger of making a bad poet of him. The singer not only has a perfectly satisfactory method of composition already in the highly developed oral technique of composition, but is actually hampered and restricted by writing. The method he knows came into being for the very purpose of rapid composition before a live audience, as we have said. Writing is a slow process even at best, and the oral poet would find it annoying, indeed, not worth the bother.[7] I cannot accept Homer as semi-literate, whatever that may mean. His skill demands that he be either the best of oral poets or the best of literary poets, not a nondescript hybrid. Anyone actually acquainted with "semiliterate" texts would, I believe, strongly resist any pressure to place Homer in such a category.

Those who wish may seek to find comfort and corroboration in the discovery of pre-Homeric literacy as shown by Linear B. They will be prone to "discount" and ignore the wise caution of Professor Sterling Dow,[8] who has pointed out the limited use of Linear B and the disappearance of the script on the mainland perhaps around 1200 B.C. He writes (p.128):

> Four or five hundred years the Greeks had lived in Greece before they learned to write. In other skills and arts, including those of power, they had advanced tremendously. In literacy—the very nerve of Classical civilization—the Mykenaian Greeks, after they once got it, made no advance at all. . . . Literacy arrived tightly associated with practical day-by-day bread and butter purposes. Created for these purposes, it was all too adequate for them. . . . The origin was in government and commerce, not in *belles lettres*. When, with the coming of the Dorians and the Dark Ages, the purposes which writing served—commerce and elaborate government—were choked off, writing ended; whereas literature— oral, that is—went on. . . .
>
> Europe's first taste of literacy was comparatively brief, meager, and unpromising. However severe the cataclysm that caused it, the loss of that literacy was not itself an unqualified disaster. The oral tradition which gave us the Homeric poems may well have been saved at an early stage (i.e. before the twelfth century) by the restricted nature of Mainland literacy, which doubtless excluded it from the field of heroic poetry; and heroic poetry remained oral, i.e. unthreatened, during its great period of growth, because in that period literacy, instead of expanding, perished.

And in the same article (p.108) Professor Dow has indicated our tendency to naïveté concerning literacy:

> Literacy is usually spoken of, for instance, as a simple indivisible essence (so that we say "the Mykenaians were literate"), whereas in reality literacy is a complex skill applicable to a wide variety of purposes, in fact, to practically all the purposes of human communication. It would obviously be hazardous to assume that as soon as a person—child, barbarian, or Minoan—learns to write, he will use writing for the full range of purposes familiar to us.

But even were we to assume that writing flourished in the service of literature in Homer's day, it does not follow that we must also assume that Homer wrote. We have already seen that oral literature can and does exist side by side with written literature. The discovery of an entire literature, including written epics, in Linear B would not in any way alter the fact that the Homeric poems are oral.

And so we see Homer as the men of his own time saw him, a poet singer among poet singers. That there was a Greek tradition of oral epic we have abundant reason to believe. The *Odyssey* gives us a picture of the practice, and what we know of the Cyclic epics gives us some idea of what kind of stories were told in this tradition. Homer was one of many singers in his own day; he was preceded by generations of singers like him; and certainly, scanty though our evidence may be here, the tradition of oral epic in Greece scarcely stopped with Homer. It would be the height of naïveté to conceive of Homer as the inventor of epic poetry in Greece or in our Western culture. The tradition in which he belonged was a rich one. He heard many good singers, and he himself had great talent, so that he was well known wherever songs were sung.

The singer who performed the *Iliad* and the *Odyssey* was obviously no novice in the art. Both poems are too well done, show too great a mastery of technique (and by this I mean oral technique) to be by a young man in the stages of learning. To attain such mastery, Homer must have been a singer with a large repertory of songs. He must also have performed his songs, and especially the tale of Achilles and that of Odysseus, many times. He was not a two-song man; nor was he one who sang but once a year at a festival. He sang these two songs often. It is normal to assume that he learned them from other singers. The songs were current in the tradition; Homer did not make them up. We do not have to depend on the analogy with Yugoslav epic or with any single Yugoslav singer to come to this conclusion. The songs themselves betray the fact that they have been long in the tradition. If Separatist scholarship has taught us nothing more, if it has not proved the kind of multiple authorship which it had ever in its mind, it has brought to our attention the mingling of themes, which is an indication of a long period of existence in the traditional repertory. It should be understood, however, that we are speaking about the songs, the tales of Achilles and of Odysseus, and not about the *Iliad* and the *Odyssey*, which are fixed texts (at a given period) by a given singer whom we call Homer. We shall consider that moment and those texts shortly, but it is necessary first to see what can be said about the two songs before they became the *Iliad* and the *Odyssey*.

We shall never be able to determine who first sang these songs, nor when they were first sung, nor where, nor what form they had. We can only be sure that it was a long time before Homer's day; for, as I have said, the songs themselves show that they have had a long history. We can with some certainty assume that their original form, their first singing, was crude as compared with our texts and only in basic story similar.[9] And it is only fair to recognize that the generic tales and many of the themes were already formed and in Greek tradition long before they were applied to Achilles and to Odysseus. Our *Iliad* and *Odyssey* were many centuries in the making.

The poet who first sang these songs changed them in the second singing in the manner which we have already demonstrated in the Yugoslav tradition, and this change continued in each successive singing. He never thought of his song as being at any time fixed either as to content or as to wording. He was the author of each singing. And those singers who learned from him the song of Achilles or that of Odysseus continued the changes of oral tradition in their performances; and each of them was author of each of his own singings. The songs were ever in flux and were crystallized by each singer only when he sat before an audience and told them the tale. It was an old tale that he had heard from others but that telling was his own. He did not claim it, yet all could see that it was his; for he was there before them.

This is the way of oral tradition. To call it multiple authorship is to belittle the role not only of Homer but of all the singers in an oral tradition. It is based upon a false premise, namely, that at one time someone created a fixed original for each song in the tradition and that thereafter whatever happened to the tales was a change of something that had been formed from a marble monolith. As long as scholars felt that they were dealing with firm entities, they could speak of multiple authorship and of interpolation. A part of one monolith could be chiseled away and set upon another. But it should be clear from our investigation of oral tradition in the field in Yugoslavia that one is not dealing with monoliths but with a pliable protean substance. When the same or similar ideas are properly useful in many tales, they belong to none, or perhaps even better, they belong to all of them. Interpolation implies, I believe, that an element belonging to only one song is moved consciously into another. In the flux of oral tradition where a theme is fitting in many tales, the term interpolation is misapplied. And the same may be said for multiple authorship. Once Homer's texts of a particular performance of our two songs were set in the *Iliad* and in the *Odyssey*, interpolations were possible; for here for the first time probably in Greek epic tradition were two definite monoliths. But that belongs to the story of what happened to the manuscripts of the Homeric poems after Homer had sired them.

He must have sung them many times before and many times after those momentous occasions that gave us the *Iliad* and the *Odyssey*. And then came one of the greatest events in the cultural history of the West, the writing down of the *Iliad* and the *Odyssey* of Homer. We know the results of that moment of history, but other than the poems themselves we know nothing about the actual moment. We are in the dark about why the poems were written down. We may be fairly certain, however, that it was not Homer's idea. He would have no need for a written text; he would not know what to do with it. Surely, as master of the oral technique, he needed no mnemonic device. That he might wish to see his songs preserved may seem a valid reason for us, but no oral poet thinks even for a moment that the songs he sings and which others have learned from him will be lost. Nor has he a concept of a single version which is so good that it must be written down to be kept. In suggesting such reasons we are putting into the mind of an oral poet something logical for us but foreign to him. I feel sure that the impetus to write down the *Iliad* and the *Odyssey* did not come from Homer himself but from some outside source.

One reads such statements as "Homer composed the *Iliad* and the *Odyssey* for performance at a festival."[10] Homer did not need a written text. He indeed may have and probably did sing the tales of Achilles and of Odysseus at festivals. At a much later period, once the poems were written down, there were singers who memorized the written text and performed them at festivals. But these were not oral poets. A festival might give an oral poet an opportunity to sing a song over several days and thus to sing a long song. Homer might have sung these songs long at such a festival. But I am afraid that even here we are straining to explain the length of the *Iliad* and the *Odyssey*. In some ways it seems to me that a festival would be the least likely circumstance to afford opportunity for a long song. There is too much going on at a festival. The audience is constantly distracted and is constantly moving about. A long song seriously delivered to an appreciative audience can be produced only in peace and quiet.

Our texts of Homer can have come only from an ideal condition of dictating, inasmuch as there were no recording apparatuses in ancient Greece! Since there is only one way in which the *Iliad* and the *Odyssey* could have been taken down from our oral epic singer, Homer, the problem of the festival lasting several days to allow time for Homer to sing his songs becomes irrelevant. I have already suggested that such festivals or circumstances which would allow for the singing of moderately long songs are important only for the development of a rich tradition; hence they would have only an indirect influence on the actual texts of the poems we have. It is more likely that epics were sung in brief or in moderately long versions on such occasions. What we can be sure of is that in the course of Greek oral tradition there must have been opportunity for the singing of epics of several thousand lines. A tradition does not become as rich in ornamental themes as the ancient Greek tradition if singers have opportunity to perform songs of only a few hundred lines. Yet the length of the *Iliad* and of the *Odyssey* must have been exceptional.

The length of the songs in the Epic Cycle may provide a rough measurement of the length of the ordinary songs in the tradition in ancient Greece. They seem to belong to a collection that someone made from various singers, or possibly from a compilation of several manuscript collections of various dates.[11] We are told that the *Oidipodeia* had 6,600 verses, the *Thebaid* (ascribed to Homer), 7,000 verses, and the *Epigonoi* (also ascribed to him), 7,000 verses. Other indications of length are in terms of books. If we compare them with the Homeric poems, then the *Cypria,* with its eleven books, was a little less than half the length of those poems; and so proportionately with the five books of the *Aithiopis* and the *Nostoi,* the four books of the *Ilias Mikra,* and the two books of the *Sack of Ilium* and of the *Telegonia.* In other words the longest of the poems in the Epic Cycle were not more than half as long as the *Iliad* and *Odyssey*. To Homer belongs the distinction of having composed the longest and best of all oral narrative songs. Their unusual length predicates exceptional circumstances of performance. If I be not mistaken, dictation to a scribe provides this opportunity. Would not the fact

that Homer was the man who dictated the "long songs" account for the reputation which both he and the songs came to enjoy? Would not the city-states
have vied with one another for the credit of having nurtured this unusual
man?

Yet we still have no answer to the question of why someone chose to ask
Homer to dictate 27,000 Greek hexameters to him. The most recent conjecture is found in Cedric Whitman's *Homer and the Heroic Tradition*.[12] After
recognizing the fact that "Homer's mode of composition seems to be, from
beginning to end, strictly that of the oral poet" (p.79), Whitman continues
by excluding the possibility that Homer himself wrote down his songs. Whitman then points to an example noted by J. Notopoulos[13] previously, of a
Greek revolutionary who from being an oral singer became a writer of his
own memoirs, as an indication of "a dissatisfaction with the improvised
accounts in verse which he had formerly sung to his companions. In an age
when the art of writing has gone far toward thrusting back the boundaries of
illiteracy, it can hardly fail to strike a creative artist sooner or later that the
medium of pen and paper has something new to offer. One might even say
that, with writing, a new idea of permanence is born; oral communication
is shown for what it is—inaccurate and shifting. Writing has a godlike stability, and to anyone with an eye for the future, its significance is scarcely
to be mistaken. . . . If one seeks the motivation for the transference of oral
verse to written form it must lie in the disseminated knowledge of writing
itself, in its disintegration of the belief that unwritten songs never change,
and in the promise of real fixity. One ought, therefore, to associate the great
epic, in contrast to the short epic song, not only with festal audiences, but
also with writing, not because writing is necessary for its creation, but because
the monumental purpose of the large epic is profoundly served by anything
which bestows fixity of form. In the century which saw the rise of the city-
state, the festivals, and the first flowering of the great colonial movement, the
Greek mind cannot have failed to recognize that written characters have a
peculiar permanence, whatever had been commonly believed about the im-
mutability of oral tradition" (p.80–81). I have quoted Whitman at some
length for convenience in analyzing his thinking on this subject.

First, the example of the Greek revolutionary is not really apt for Homer,
unless we assume much more writing in Greece in Homer's time, and that of
a literary sort, than there is evidence of, at the moment at least. Revolutionary Greece had a rich tradition of written literature, and Makriyannis' progress from illiteracy to literacy was a progress from a more backward, peasant
social group to a more advanced, and more privileged social stratum. It is
to be doubted that his dissatisfaction with the older oral songs (which was
probably very real) sprang at all from any recognition of the possibilities of
a fixed text as against the lack of them in an oral text. It is far more likely
that he was dissatisfied with them because they belonged to the peasant society and he had now graduated into the company of the elite. Are we to
assume that there was such a literate and elite group of littérateurs in Homer's
day? If so, where is the evidence for it? Makriyannis moved into a milieu
with a long-established tradition not only of writing (we might even say from

Homer's day), but of fine writing in the form of literature. "The boundaries of illiteracy" were of a different kind in modern Greece from what they were in ancient, more specifically, late eighth century B.C. Greece, and the gulf between the oral singer and "the creative artist" was both broad and deep in Makriyannis' time. In Homer's day, on the contrary, the oral singer was a creative artist; in fact there was no distinction—I believe that the idea of the "creative artist," the "inspired poet," and so forth, is derived from the mantic and sacred function of the singer. In assessing the situation in Homer's day in Greece, we must reckon with the fact that we have no other literary texts from that time, no written literary tradition. Yet suddenly 27,000 Greek hexameters appear! Are we supposed to believe that Homer, or someone else, saw the lists of chattels and, realizing what this meant for epic, sat down to record the *Iliad* and *Odyssey?* Makriyannis had much more than jar labels to read when he learned his ABC's. A slow progress with small written beginnings in the field of literature, recording short pieces, over a long period of time is believable, and Whitman allows for some possibility of this later when he says, "For all we know, some of his [Homer's] predecessors may have committed their work to paper somehow." Without interference from outside of Greece, this is the only way one could have arrived at the point of writing down so many lines of verse.

The trouble with Whitman's "creative artist" is that, in spite of the fact that he is said to compose entirely as an oral poet, he is not in the tradition; he is not an oral *traditional* poet. *And oral poets who are not traditional do not exist.* With this in mind, if one should substitute "the best oral traditional singer" for "creative artist" in Whitman's statement, it would read, "it can hardly fail to strike the best oral traditional singer sooner or later that the medium of pen and paper has something new to offer." I cannot help, when the statement reads this way, but ask *why* the idea of "something new" is so inevitable for the oral poet, even the greatest and best of them. Why should permanence and fixity be so attractive to an oral poet? And how does he come to recognize and to distrust oral communication as "inaccurate and shifting?" Remember that the man with whom we are dealing is an oral poet in a society with writing, but no extensive writing in literature, if any at all. Whitman has tacitly and naturally assumed that the oral poet has the same sense of propriety for the "form" of his song, even for "his song" that the written poet has. He hears the "creative artist" saying, "This is *my* song, *my* masterpiece, every word of it"; but the oral poet does not say this because he is in the tradition. What he says is, "I learned this song from someone else, and I sing it as he sang it." Does this man with his sense of the tradition see permanency so readily, if at all, for the tradition's song? It is not in the psychology of the oral poet to concern himself with stability of form, since stability of meaning and story already exist for him. Oral communication is not "inaccurate and shifting" until you have the idea that a given *form, one* given performance, is worth fixing. And this idea may come readily to the "creative artist" who is self-consciously creating something which he is accustomed to think of as his very own, but it is a large order for the oral poet who is intent upon preserving a meaningful traditional song. We must not suddenly endow the oral poet with the mentality of the developed literary artist in a written tradition, with his sense of ownership.

Perhaps we shall never have a certain solution to the riddle of the writing down of the Homeric poems, but we can hypothesize on what is most likely. We have already seen that the idea would not have come from Homer, and it is logical that the group to which he belonged and which regularly listened to him would not have had any reason (other than what we might project backward from our own thinking) for wanting these two songs, or any songs, written down. We should do well, therefore, to look about in the world of ancient Greece, before, let us say, 700 B.C., if perchance we might discover people who were recording or had already recorded in writing their literature, people with whom the Greeks may well have come into contact.

In the ninth century in Palestine the oldest of the documents of the Old Testament seems to have been written, namely, the J Document, and in the following century the E Document came into being.[14] These writings or records told of the creation of the world and of the history of the founders of the Jewish people or of man in general. They contained the epics and myths of these people. In the eighth century Sargon II (722–705) established the library at Nineveh and under him the Assyrian Empire was at its greatest extent. His library contained tablets inscribed with epic, mythic, magic, and historical material in several languages, including Sumerian, and dating from as early as 2000 B.C. Here were to be found the Epic of Creation and the Epic of Gilgamesh, among other texts.[15] Two bodies of recorded lore, one already ancient in ancient times, the other new and exciting in its serious intensity, were thus available to any Greeks who might turn in their direction. And it seems that it would be normal for them to look to the East during these centuries; for it was in the East that the cultural center was then located.

Hence, I should like to suggest that the idea of recording the Homeric poems, and the Cyclic epics, and the works of Hesiod, came from observation of or from hearing about similar activity going on further to the East. The list of works on Sumerian tablets given by [S. N.] Kramer in his *Sumerian Mythology*[16] reminds one of the kind of literature recorded at the earliest period in both Palestine and Greece: "epics and myths, hymns and lamentations, proverbs and 'wisdom' compositions." And the wisdom compositions consist of "a large number of brief, pithy, and pointed proverbs and aphorisms; of various fables, such as 'The Bird and the Fish,' 'The Tree and the Reed,' 'The Pickax and the Plow,' 'Silver and Bronze'; and finally of a group of didactic compositions, long and short, several of which are devoted to a description of the process of learning the scribal art and of the advantages which flow from it." The Greeks and the Hebrews were reliving in their own terms the cultural experiences of older civilizations. The scribe who wrote down the Homeric poems was doing for the Greeks what the scribes of Sumer had done for their people many centuries before.

NOTES

1. For Parry's analyses see "Studies in the Epic Technique of Oral Verse-Making. I: Homer and Homeric Style," *HSCP* 41:118 ff. (1930).

2. Notes to Chart follow:

[1] Cf. μῆνιν ἀλευάμενος ἑκατηβόλου 'Απόλλωνος (Ε444, Π711) and μῆνιν ἀπειπόντος μεγαθύμου Πηλεΐωνος (Τ75).

[2] Cf.

$$
μῆνιν \begin{cases} ἀλευάμενος & (Ε444, Π711) \\ ἀποειπών & (Τ35) \\ ἀπειπόντος & (Τ75) \end{cases}
$$

$$
\left. \begin{array}{l} οἶτον \; (α350, \; θ489) \\ νόστον \; (α326) \end{array} \right\} \begin{array}{l} ἀείδειν \; (α350) \; ἀείδεις \; (θ489) \\ ἄειδεν \; (α326) \end{array}
$$

$$
\begin{array}{ll}
γιγνώσκω \; σε & (Ε815) \\
σὺν \; σοί, \; δῖα & (Κ290) \\
τῶν \; ἀμόθεν \; γε & (α10) \\
ἄλλο \; τι \; δὴ \; σύ & (ε173) \\
ἀργαλέον \; σε & (ν312) \\
σὺν \; σοί, \; πότνα & (ν391) \\
"Αρτεμι \; πότνα & (υ61) \\
"Ηρη \; πρέσβα & (Ε721, \\
& Θ383, \; Ξ194, \; 243)
\end{array}
$$

[3] Α322, Ι166, Π269, 653, Ω406, λ467, ω15.
[4] Cf. ὦ πόποι, ἦ δὴ μυρί' 'Οδυσσεὺς ἐσθλὰ ἔοργε (Β272).
[5] Ε876, ρ287, 474.
[6] See note [4]. For ἄλγε' ἔθηκε see Χ422.
[7] Cf. πολλὰς δ' ἰφθίμους κεφαλὰς "Αϊδι προΐαψειν (Λ55).
[8] See note [7].
[9] Ζ487 (προϊάψει).
[10] Nonformulaic, but see note [12].
[11] Cf. ἡρώων τοῖσίν τε (Ε747 οἷσίν τε, Θ391, α101). For ἡρώων see Ι525, Ε747, Θ391, α101, and ω88. For αὐτοὺς δέ cf. Ε747, Θ391, α101 (τοῖσίν τε), etc.
[12] Nonformulaic, but cf. καλλείψω, μή πώς μοι ἔλωρ ἄλλοισι γένηται (ν208).
[13] Nonformulaic.
[14] Cf. ἀντιβίοις ἐπέεσσιν (Β378), and προβλῆτι σκοπέλῳ (Β396) and the related system:

$$
ἀνδράσι \begin{cases} πυγμαίοισι & (Γ6) \\ παυροτέροισι & (Β122) \\ δυσμενέεσσι & (Ε488, Ρ158, Τ168) \\ γε \; θνητοῖσι & (Κ403, Ρ77, Υ266) \end{cases}
$$

[15] λ297.
[16] Cf. αὐτὰρ ἐπεὶ τὰ ἔκαστα διαρρήδην ἐρίδαινον (Η. Merc. 313).
[17] For ἐξ οὗ δή see ξ379. For τὰ πρῶτα see Δ424, Ν679, Ρ612, Ψ275, 523, 538, and cf. Ζ489, Μ420, α257, and θ268, and 553.
[18] See note [16].
[19] Cf. "Ατρεΐδη, κύδιστε, ἄναξ ἀνδρῶν, 'Αγάμεμνον (Β434, Ι96, 677, 697, Κ103, Τ146, and 199). Cf. also Ρ12 'Ατρεΐδη, Μενέλαε, Διοτρεφές, ὄρχαμε λαῶν.
[20] Γ271, 361, Ι89, Ν610, Τ252, δ304.
[21] There are twenty-two instances listed by Parry, q.v.
[22] α7, Υ160. For instances of δῖος 'Αχιλλεύς see Parry, who lists fifty-three.
[23] For τίς τ' ἄρ in this position see Β761, and Γ226. For θεῶν in this position see Γ269, Ε442, Λ74, Ν55, 632, Τ96, Ξ201, 302, 342, Ο290, Σ107, Φ443, α338, γ147, δ364, η247, κ157, φ28.
[24] Cf. μένεϊ ξυνέηκε μάχεσθαι (Η210).
[25] Υ66.
[26] Cf. Ζηνί τε καὶ Διὸς υἷι (Χ302).
[27] Cf. ὁ δ' ἤϊε νυκτὶ ἐοικώς (Α47), παλαιῷ φωτὶ ἐοικώς (Ξ136)
   ὁ γὰρ πολὺ φέρτατός ἐστιν (Α581, Β769 ἦεν)
and ὁ γὰρ προγενέστερος ἦεν (Β555), etc.

[28] Cf. πάντῃ ἀνὰ στρατὸν εὐρὺν 'Αχαιῶν (A384),
αἶψα μάλ' ἐς στρατὸν ἐλθέ (Δ70), and
ἀνὰ στρατόν εἰσι (K66). For κακήν in this position, see the system:

νύκτα φυλασσομένοισι (K188)
ἤ τ' ἂν ὑπέκφυγε κῆρα (Π687)
σχέτλιος, ὅ's ῥ' ἔριν ὦρσε (γ161)
φύζαν ἐμοῖς ἑτάροισι (ξ269, ρ438)

[29] Cf. ἀρετῶσι δὲ λαοί (τ114), δαινῦτό τε λαός (Ω665).
[30] Cf. οὔνεκ' ἐγὼ φίλον υἱὸν ὑπεξέφερον πολέμοιο (E377).
[31] See note [30]. ''Ουνεκα is found in this position 13 times in the first 12 books: A111, 291, B580, Γ403, 405, Δ477, E342, 377, Z334, H140, I159, 442, and Λ79.
[32] Nonformulaic.
[33] B577, 614, I339, 516, 648, Π59, Λ130, 169, P71, etc.
[34] For ὁ γὰρ ἦλθε cf. ὁ δ' ἀρ' ἦλθε (H416), δέ οἱ ἦλθε (B408, and Δ529), πρὸ γὰρ ἦκε (A195), etc. For θοὰς ἐπὶ νῆας 'Αχαιῶν cf. B8, 17, 168, Z52, K450, 514, Λ3, Ω564, etc. For ἐπὶ νῆας 'Αχαιῶν cf. H78, Θ98, K525, O116, P691, X417, 465, Ω118, 146, 195, etc. For ἦλθε θοὰς ἐπὶ νῆας 'Αχαιῶν cf. A371. For θοὰς ἐπὶ νῆας cf. B263, Λ568, Π247, Ω1, etc.
[35] A372.
[36] Cf. λυσόμενος παρὰ σεῖο (Ω502). For the position of λυσόμενος cf. also ἀξόμενοι Διὸς υἱόν (A21).
[37] Ω502. For ἀπερείσι' ἄποινα cf. A372, 249, 427, I120, K380, Λ134, T138, Ω276, 502, 579.
[38] A373.
[39] Cf. the following system:

τόξον (O443)
ἔγχος (P604)
κάπρον (T251) } ἔχων ἐν χειρί
ὀξύν (γ443)
οἶνον (o148)
φᾶρος (Θ221)

For ἔχων ἐν χερσίν cf. Ξ385 (χειρί),. and for στέμματ' ἔχων cf. the following system:

σκῆπτρον (Σ557)
τεύχε' (H137)
αἰγίδ' (O361) } ἔχων
χεῖρας (Σ33)
ἕλκος (T52)

[40] A438, Π513, Ψ872 (ἐκηβόλῳ 'Απόλλωνι)
[41] A374.
[42] Cf. χρυσέῳ ἐν δαπέδῳ (Δ2), and
χρυσέῳ ἐν δέπαϊ (Ω285).
[43] Cf. μάλα δὲ χρέω πάντας 'Αχαιούς (I75)
κέκαστο δὲ πάντας 'Αχαιούς (Ξ124)
θάμβος δ' ἔχε πάντας 'Αχαιούς (Ψ815)
ἐφάμην ἥρωας 'Αχαιούς (M165)
κτεῖναι δ' ἥρωας 'Αχαιούς (N629)
φοβέειν ἥρωας 'Αχαιούς (O230)

For πάντας 'Αχαιούς cf. A374, Γ68, 88, H49, Θ498, I75, Ξ124, Ψ815, γ137, 141, δ288, ω49, and 438.

3. See C. M. Bowra, *Heroic Poetry* (London, 1952), p.233 ff.
4. Milman Parry, "The Distinctive Character of Enjambement in Homeric Verse," *TAPhA* 60:200–20 (1929). For the term "necessary enjambement" see A. B. Lord, "Homer and Huso III: Enjambement in Greek and Southslavic Heroic Song," *TAPhA*, 79:113–24 (1948). . . . I follow the definition of enjambement given by Parry, *ibid.*, p.203–4: "Broadly there are three ways in which the sense at the end of one verse can stand to that at the beginning of another. First, the verse end can fall at the end of a sentence

and the new verse begin a new sentence. In this case there is no enjambement. Second, the verse can end with a word group in such a way that the sentence, at the verse end, already gives a complete thought, although it goes on in the next verse, adding free ideas by new word groups. To this type of enjambement we may apply Denis' term *unperiodic*. Third, the verse end can fall at the end of a word group where there is not yet a whole thought, or it can fall in the middle of a word group; in both of these cases enjambement is *necessary*. . . . To know where there is no enjambement we must gauge the sentence. The varying punctuation of our texts, usually troublesome, will not do. I define the sentence as any independent clause or group of clauses introduced by a coordinate conjunction or by asyndeton; and by way of showing that this definition is fitting I would point out that the rhetoricians paid little heed to the sentence as we understand it: for them the unit of style was the clause, and the only group of clauses of which Aristotle speaks is the period." The statement of Jakobson, following perhaps a more widely known definition of enjambement, that there is no enjambement in Serbocroatian epic, is correct, although rare exceptions can be found.

5. Lord, "Homer and Huso III: Enjambement in Greek and Southslavic Heroic Song," *TAPhA* 79:113–24 (1948).

6. See Lord, "Composition by Theme in Homer and Southslavic Epos," *TAPhA* 82: 71–80 (1951).

7. There is an excellent treatment of the slowness of reading and writing in medieval times in *From Script to Print* (Cambridge, Eng., 1945) by H. J. Chaytor, Master of St. Catherine's College, Cambridge. He writes:

> The medieval reader, with few exceptions, did not read as we do; he was in the stage of our muttering childhood learner; each word was for him a separate entity and at times a problem, which he whispered to himself when he had found the solution [p.10] . . . the history of the progress from script to print is a history of the gradual substitution of visual for auditory methods of communicating and receiving ideas [p.4].

The task, yes, the very physical task of writing down the *Iliad* and the *Odyssey* is a tremendous one.

8. Sterling Dow, "Minoan Writing," *American Journal of Archeology* 58:77–129 (1954).

9. As an example of a song that has not been perfected by much singing and is close in frequency of performance, if not in time, to its first singing, see Salih Ugljanin's song of the Greek War (Parry and Lord, *Serbocroatian Heroic Songs* [Cambridge and Belgrade, 1954], vs. 1 and 2, no. 10. [For further discussion of this point,] see note. 3 to chap. 5 [in *The Singer of Tales*]).

10. See especially H. T. Wade-Gery, *The Poet of the Iliad* (Cambridge, Eng., 1952).

11. *Hesiod, the Homeric Hymns and Homerica,* ed. by H. G. Evelyn-White, Loeb Classical Library (Cambridge and London, 1943), p.480 ff.

12. Cedric W. Whitman, *Homer and the Heroic Tradition* (Cambridge, 1958), p.79 ff.

13. J. A. Notopoulos, "The Warrior As an Oral Poet: A Case History," *Classical Weekly* 46:17–19 (1952).

14. See Robert H. Pfeiffer, *Introduction to the Old Testament* (New York, 1941; rev. ed., 1948), p.282 ff.

15. For these texts see James B. Pritchard, ed. *Ancient Near Eastern Texts Relating to the Old Testament* (Princeton, 1950).

16. S. N. Kramer, *Sumerian Mythology* (Philadelphia, 1944), p.13 ff.

·III·

THE NARRATOR AND NARRATIVE TECHNIQUE

Rodney Delasanta

THE CLASSICAL EXEMPLUM

Any responsible criticism of the Greek epic must be prefaced with a discussion of certain assumptions that have not yet been universally accepted by the world of scholarship. These assumptions are: 1) The *Iliad* and the *Odyssey* were written each by a single poet. The author of the *Iliad* may not have been the same man as the author of the *Odyssey,* but each work is the product of a single artist. This kind of unitarian assumption absolutely precludes the possibility that the poems, in the form in which they have survived, represent a kind of catalogue of epic lays. 2) The *Iliad* and the *Odyssey* are the products of an oral formulaic system of epic composition that makes possible a unitarian theory of authorship. To agree with [Friedrich August] Wolf —that the extraordinary length of these poems would have made oral composition by a single poet impossible—would render literary criticism of these poems meaningless. But now that the field work of men like Milman Parry and Albert Lord has restored scholarly confidence in the theory of unitarian composition,[1] literary criticism of Homer becomes possible again. 3) The genius of Homer is not incompatible with the oral formulaic system of epic composition. Rather the oral formulaic poet must be judged within the limitations of his own medium. The oral tradition does, in some ways, limit the narrative art of an epic singer, but in many ways it offers him larger stylistic building blocks with which to proceed. As [Cedrick] Whitman points out:

> Oral poetry is neither primitive nor mechanical, nor does its traditional nature preclude the play of genius. Its methods may differ to a degree from those of written literature, and therefore Homer's greatness will not be found in imagined departures from oral technique, any more than Shakespeare's can be discovered by trying to envision those moments when he threw away his quill and chanted his verses aloud. A poet's native medium is his best artistic device. In seeking Homer's original genius, we must not seek the newly turned phrase, the non-formulaic line, or even the character who . . . did not exist in previous tradition. It is not outside tradition that Homer has triumphed, but within it.[2]

With these assumptions removed from the arena of dispute and with the single authorship of the *Iliad* and *Odyssey* back in favor, literary criticism of Homer becomes possible again. Two considerations will be paramount in the following analysis. . . . The first is that the breadth of omniscient voice in an epic is determined by the particular species of epic that the voice is "subject

"The Classical Exemplum." From Rodney Delasanta, *The Epic Voice* (The Hague and Paris: Mouton, 1967), p.37–56. Reprinted by permission of the publisher.

to." Conditioned by the exigencies of oral recitation, for example, the omniscient voice of the heroic poem refrains from the kind of incidental, extra-narrative activity common to the literary and romantic epic. One finds few philosophical digressions, lyrical interludes, and political and teleological prophecies in the heroic poem. The second consideration, more important and of central significance throughout the rest of this study, is that in epics of *in medias res* structure the omniscient voice delegates to another, restricted voice that part of the total narrative that precedes in time the events of the *in medias res* beginning and delegates it in a way that indicates the poet's real awareness of the narrative artistry of restricted voice. Happily, the classical epic affords excellent examples of both considerations, especially the latter.

Schiller in his famous definition of epic—that it is "in style objective . . . [narrating] habitually without interposition by images visual, auditory, motor," that its "method is to suggest heroic life by its physical sensations, to make the characters, as Aristotle says, reveal themselves"[3]—misunderstands to a certain extent the function of the omniscient voice. Certainly his insistence that Homer and Shakespeare are as invisible behind their material as the Creator behind his universe applies to Shakespeare with more accuracy than it does to Homer. The careful reader of the Homeric poems is constantly aware of the existence of the author: by his reference to the Muses, by subjective explanation of events or causes that cannot be related with complete objectivity, by the poet's explicit reaction, favorable or unfavorable, to an event he is narrating, at times even by the poet's direct address to the character in the story who is at the moment dramatically important. As [Samuel] Bassett points out:

> We must remember the difference between the epic poem and the simple account of facts. The child or the primitive savage is purely objective in his report of a highly emotional incident. It is only by repeated questioning that he yields the details from which the scene may be reconstructed in the imagination. The oral epic poet must anticipate such questions in the mind of his audience; he must furnish the details along with the facts, and he must do this in such a way as both to facilitate the imaginative construction of the scene and to heighten its emotional effect. Hence any tale worthy of the name cannot be by any means purely objective.[4]

What part of the narrative in Homer transcends the limitations of the "purely objective"? Or in terms to which this study is addressed, where does the main impact of the omniscient narration make itself felt in Homer? The most obvious answer, of course, is present in Homer's panoramic vision of his own world. When he is not delegating omniscience to a narrating character, his point of view leads from a position that makes everything in time and place open to himself, from the splendor of Zeus's court to the squalor of Eumaeus's cave, from the recesses of Hera's Zeus-seducing mind to the erratic behavior of Eurycleia's memory. Apart from the panoramic view peculiar to this kind of narration, however, Homer's omniscience reveals itself precisely in those subjective areas where Schiller insisted the "naive" epic author never moved, in the area of interposition, intrusion, non-dramatic value-judgment. Bassett has pointed to slight but significant examples of this.[5] More obvious examples would include: 1) the poet's open revelation of the outcome of some encounter (at Patroclus's request to Achilles that his chief allow him to enter the battle, the poet interrupts with: "He knew not what he was asking, nor that he was suing for his own destruction")[6]; 2) the poet's prayer to the Muses that they supply the correct details of historical information that he is about to relate ("Tell me now, O Muses . . . who was the first of the Argives to bear away blood-stained spoils after Neptune . . . had turned the fortune of war?"); 3) the poet's undramatic appraisal of a situation wedged into his otherwise objective account of the action (about the exchange of armor that took place at the Glaucus-Diomede truce, the poet says: "But the son of Saturn made Glaucus take leave of his wits, for he exchanged golden armour for bronze, the worth of a hundred head of cattle for the worth of nine"[7]; 4) the poet's direct second-person address to a character at the moment involved in the action (Menelaus, Melanippus, Patroclus and Appolo are so addressed in the *Iliad*, Eumaeus in the *Odyssey*).

Yet, when one compares Homer to Virgil by testing in their epics the ratio of objective to subjective elements, one finds a quality of omniscience in the former that is remarkably more confined. Partially, perhaps chiefly, this limitation is due to the medium, to the species of epic poem that each was composing. In the oral epic, the poet's tone is *literally* present: in his, or the rhapsode's, voice, his delivery, his very physical presence. The degree of explicitness necessary to the audience's appreciation of the story does not always need to be supplied by the narrated word. Approbation or disapprobation, tonal subtlety, irony can be supplied by a gesture, a vocal inflection, even a raised eyebrow. The literary poet has no such "on-the-spot" advantage. He is totally cut off from his audience and, as C. S. Lewis points out, must simulate the ritualistic occasion of the recited epic by means of a heightened style. In the literary epic "there are no external aids to solemnity which the Primary [heroic] poem enjoyed. . . . The Virgilian and Miltonic style is there to compensate for—to counteract—the privacy and informality of silent reading in a man's study."[8]

How does this heightened style affect the degree of omniscience in an epic? If the above thesis is correct in stating that the literary poet must compensate tonally for his physical absence from the audience, then more of him*self* —by intrusions if necessary—must find its way into the poem. With three poetic manners operating in any epic—the objective narration proper, the dramatically imitative (dialogue), and the subjectively explanatory—any proportionate increase in the latter will necessarily result in a decrease of the first two. But any decrease in dialogue and in objective narration—the agents of restriction in an omniscient structure—will extend the breadth of omniscience considerably. Bassett has estimated that the Homeric poems contain one-fifth objective narration, three-fifths dialogue or speeches, and one-fifth subjective explanation. Although statistics are not available for the *Aeneid*, a close reading should reveal considerably fewer speeches and considerably less inclination to use direct discourse. A comparison of the first books of the *Odyssey* and the *Aeneid*, for example, tends to indicate the general ratio of direct discourse to narrative. Of the 440 lines in the first book of the *Odyssey,* 298 represent direct discourse. Of the 756 lines in the first book of the *Aeneid,* only 319 represent direct discourse. Sixty-seven percent of the lines of the *Odyssey* (assuming these proportions could be extended throughout the epic) is utilized for direct dramatic imitation; only 42 percent of the *Aeneid,* however, is so utilized.

But the number of speeches is only as significant as their quality and function. From Homer's extensive use of speeches that by themselves reveal the character of the speaker we recognize a self-imposed limitation on his omniscient voice. Examples can be multiplied, but one will suffice here. The omniscient characterization of Nestor as an old man, wise in council, is corroborated in Nestor's own speeches, but in a way that brings more truth and more of the human being to his character than any series of epithets could ever hope to accomplish. For from Nestor's speeches we learn not only that he is an old man, wise in council, but also that he is a garrulous old man who often reminisces about his youth and former glory at most improbable times. In Book XI of the *Iliad,* when Achilles sends Patroclus in the heat of battle to inquire of Nestor the identity of the wounded man removed from the field, Nestor, stung by the thought of Achilles' refusal to fight, answers peevishly: "Why should Achilles care . . . ? Our most valiant chieftains lie disabled"; whereupon he lists those who have been wounded in battle and ends with a lament for his own lack of strength. If the speech had ended there, it would have characterized Nestor closely, but not precisely enough. Instead, Homer allows Nestor to continue speaking, and what he relates, considering the circumstances, turns out to be an absurdly lengthy and unnecessarily detailed story of an incident in his own youth when he battled the men of Elis. Whitman suggests that speeches of this kind objectify the inner state of a character whose creator had not yet the opportunity to use the "stream-of-consciousness" technique,[9] and that the seeming incongruity of a speech like Eurycleia's in the *Odyssey,* flashing back 76 lines between her recognition of Ulysses' scar and her gesture of joyous surprise, is simply a dramatization of her mental image. Be that as it may, whether we interpret Nestor's utterances as an example of mental image or an actual speech (and I would incline to the latter in Nestor's case), the result of characterization by the technique of personal exposure is the same. We know more about Nestor because Homer has allowed Nestor to speak of himself in a peculiarly revealing way than we could have known by a detached, omniscient characterization or by a different kind of speech, one that merely tends to put quotes around lines which, with a change of the personal pronoun, could just as easily have been spoken by the poet himself.

Homer's self-imposed limitation on his omniscient narration reveals itself in still another way in the *Iliad.* It is common, as I have just pointed out, for Homer's heroes to reveal details about their characters that the omniscient voice simply could not reach. A less common, but perhaps more skillful method of restricted characterization, is Homer's way of revealing the character of his heroes by what *other* people say. The most impressive example occurs in Book III of the *Iliad* just before the single combat between Paris and Menelaus. At this point in the poem, the Greek *dramatis personae* had not been "formally" introduced. Except for Agamemnon and Achilles in their quarrel, Homer had merely scattered hints about the other characters. As Helen is summoned to the wall to view the battle, Priam calls her to his side to tell him the names of those heroes who by their noble bearing seem to stand out from the rest. Helen then names Agamemnon, Ulysses, Ajax, and Idomeneus, drawing a short character sketch of each. What Homer has done here, it seems, is to allow some of his heroes to be formally introduced without offending by familiarity his Greek audience, who obviously would have been as familiar with their heroes as an American audience would be with George Washington. To have introduced them omnisciently would have involved with no real purpose the repetition of epithets like "crafty" Ulysses. The Greek audience knew all about "crafty" Ulysses. But to allow Helen, whose fate is ironically entangled with the heroes she describes, to introduce them to Priam, who has never met them but who will suffer much from them in the near future, is to succeed in setting up a *dramatis personae* of ironic anticipation.

Two fairly lengthy interpolated stories, one told by Glaucus to Diomede in Book VI and the other by Phoenix to Achilles in Book IX further suggest Homer's self-imposed limitation on his omniscient voice and, precociously, his awareness of the function of a narrating character. At first glance, the Phoenix story seems to be more closely related to the main action, paralleling in its account of the recalcitrant Meleager, who refuses out of anger to do battle with Auretes, Achilles' own refusal to do battle against the Trojans. But the parallel is not subtle, Phoenix himself pointing out the relationship as a moral exemplum for Achilles. The other story serves no parallel function but rather identifies the families of Glaucus and Diomede as closely related in ancient friendships and, as Whitman points out, "illustrates the maintenance of contact between the Achaeans overseas [at Troy] and the old families at home."[10] As such the story functions as a peace maker for two warriors who refuse to fight each other when they hear it, as a kind of ironic reminder that the war in which thousands of their compatriots are similarly involved and to some extent related by blood is totally futile. Homer's hatred for war, despite its heroic celebration in the *Iliad*, reveals itself dramatically, and not declamatorily, here.

It is not the purpose of this chapter to determine the extent to which Virgil places a self-imposed limitation on his omniscient voice in the *Aeneid;* but one cannot help feeling that in contrast to Homer's incipient sense of restricted characterization in the *Iliad* Virgil remains fixed on the level of omniscient characterization. The impression often gained is that when Virgil's characters are speaking the omniscient voice has not relinquished its control over them but uses them as a mouthpiece, rhetorical and declamatory. And in Virgil's peculiar use of the Muse this impression is strengthened. Not only is Virgil's invocation to the Muse more frequent than Homer's, but it is also more indiscriminate. That is, whenever Virgil recognizes the need for a solemn heightening of style, whether the need should come at a moment of extended description, of historical exposition, or of a causal connection between events, he does not hesitate to call upon her. Moreover, his invocation pleads that the Muse employ the poet as her mouthpiece, in the Heliconian sense. "Come, Muse of Love," Virgil writes (at a moment of particularly undramatic exposition in Book VII), "let me rehearse the kings, the phase of History, and the conditions that reigned in antique Latium/ When first that expedition arrived upon the beaches of Italy. . . . *Speak through me, then, Spirit of Song!*"[11] Whether Virgil uses this kind of invocation as a genuine heart-felt prayer or as a heightened rhetorical device to simulate the occasion of the Homeric epic matters not at all. If the poet thinks he is the human instrument of the divine singer, then he has at least convinced himself that the divine view is his view. If, on the other hand, the poet is merely affecting inspiration, he has at least committed himself dramatically to the omniscient view of the divine inspirer. The final effect of either possibility remains the same. The breadth of omniscience becomes necessarily extended.

In Homer, the invocation to the Muse is not Heliconian, but Olympian. "Homer's Muses do not dwell in the Pierian valley, but on Olympus. They are in no wise chthonian; their power is not mysterious and their gift is not transcendental. The Muse is the daughter of Zeus, whose voice is authority. . . . the authentic Voice of the Past."[12] Contrary to the common assumption that in Homer the poet is the spokesman of the Muse, then, it would seem that he is more of a "Pelagian" poet, that he calls for divine help only to validate historically his version of the past:

> The poet's own tale of the long-vanished past has the supreme sanction for its veracity. The brief appeal to the Muse in the proems makes the audience hear, as it were, the voice of one who was present, the daughter of Zeus, "who above all others bringeth true tidings to men." How better could the hearer be made to feel—all unconsciously—that he was to view with the eye of the imagination the reincarnation of great human lives?[13]

Lest the preceding discussion (whose purpose it was to indicate the significant differences between omniscient voice in the literary epic and omniscient voice in the heroic poem) suggest that the *Iliad* and the *Odyssey* utilize equally the narrative advantages of restricted voice, I must make clear now that the quality of restriction in the *Iliad* is different in kind from the quality of restriction in the *Odyssey* and that the differences are intimately related to the structural problem of *in medias res*. To point to both the *Iliad* and the *Odyssey* as examples of poems beginning *in medias res* is to misunderstand the essential meaning of the term by confusing the total occasion of an epic with its actual narrative boundaries. The *total* setting of the *Iliad* can be considered to be the Trojan War, which began with Paris's abduction of Helen and ended with the sack of Troy. When the reader keeps this *terminus a quo* and *terminus ad quem* in mind, and he remembers that the first book of the *Iliad* begins with the disastrous quarrel between Achilles and Agamemnon, he assumes that the poet has plunged in *medias res* by beginning his story late in the war. The actual *terminus a quo* and *terminus ad quem* of the *Iliad*, the setting dictated by the plot of the narrative itself, is much more limited however. Although the reader may interpret the quarrel, in the larger context of the war, as coming *in medias res*, he must recognize that in the limited context of the poem the quarrel occurs precisely at the beginning. What the reader and careless critic have done, therefore, is to confuse the term *in medias res* with *in media belli*. The two terms are certainly not synonymous. One may disagree with C. S. Lewis that the Trojan War is not the subject of the *Iliad*, that it is "merely the background of a purely personal story—that of Achilles' wrath, suffering, repentance and killing of Hector,"[14] but one cannot disagree about the temporal confines of the work. The killing of Hector may well symbolize the eventual destruction of Troy, but in point of actual chronology in the *Iliad* the topless towers have not yet begun to burn. If one were to label temporally the order of incidents in the *Iliad*, he would discover a perfectly untampered chronology proceeding from the beginning— the quarrel—to the end—Hector's funeral.

The *terminus a quo* of the *Odyssey*—Ulysses' departure from Troy— does not, however, come at the actual beginning. The departure itself is not spoken of until Book III in Nestor's story, and its details are not explored until Book IX where Ulysses begins his great narration. The epic begins, in terms of *narrated* beginning, where Telemachus decides to make search for his father, who, as we discover in Book V, is imprisoned on Calypso's island. (I discount here, of course, the "argument" of Book I which reveals all this information before the action commences.) The interim details from the *terminus a quo* of the poem to the narrated beginning of the poem thus are supplied later by one major and two minor narrating characters to whom the poet delegates his story.

Homer's entirely different commitments to temporal structure in the *Iliad* and the *Odyssey*, as I have briefly pointed out already, are responsible for the entirely different kinds of voice operating in the two poems. Voice in the *Iliad* may be described as a modified omniscience working with the structure of temporal contiguity; voice in the *Odyssey* may be described as an omniscience which, for purposes of narrating the prerequisite action, delegates its function to one or more restricted voices.

Whitman, in his enlightening discussion of structural design in the *Iliad*, has offered an architectonic theory that can be utilized here both as a point of reference and a point of departure. Suggesting that the structure of the *Iliad* can be seen as a literary counterpart of Greek geometric vase design and proving that the age of geometric vase design coincided with the time of Homer, Whitman proceeds to see the *Iliad* as an incredibly balanced poem, "a schematicized pattern rationally worked out and altogether consistent with the observable artistic practices of the Geometric Age."[15]

> The principles of circularity, including concentricity, or framing by balanced similarity and antithesis, is one of the chief dynamic forces underlying the symmetry of Geometric vase design. In the Iliad, the old device of hysteron proteron has been expanded into a vast scheme far transcending any mere mnemonic purpose, a scheme purely and even abstractly architectonic. Not only are certain whole books of the poem arranged in self-reversing or balancing designs, but the poem as a whole is, in a way, an enormous hysteron proteron, in which books balance books and scenes balance scenes by similarity or antithesis, with amazing virtuosity.[16]

To do justice to Whitman's theory, I shall reproduce here one example of what he means by structural hysteron proteron. Bowra had recognized the antithetical relationships of the first book with the last, the epic beginning "with an uncontrolled scene of wrath and [ending] with the appeasing of wrath in reconciliation."[17] But Whitman's critical contribution is in seeing the antithesis working within the incidents of the books themselves.[18]

BOOK I

1. Plague and funerals
2. Quarrel and seizure of Briseis
3. Thetis and Achilles (appeal to Zeus)
   Journey to Chrysa
4. Thetis and Zeus (adoption of Achilles' cause)
5. Quarrel on Olympus

BOOK XXIV

5. Quarrel on Olympus
4. Thetis and Zeus (modification of hero's cause)
3. Thetis and Achilles (message from Zeus)
   Journey of Priam
2. Reconciliation and restitution (of Hector's body)
1. Funeral of Hector

Such a geometric design makes impossible, and this is my point in dwelling on Whitman's theory, any manipulation of normal temporal pattern. That is to say, if Books I, II, III, IV function in reverse balance to Books XXIV, XXIII, XXII, XXI, the reversal can only make sense in terms of temporal *order*. And because the contiguous chronology of the *Iliad* needs no significant exposition (the *terminus a quo* coinciding with the narrated beginning), the poem contains no inherent obstacles to a geometric ordering of its large structure. Moreover, there exists a natural, almost ineffable, affinity between the omniscient voice and this kind of structural pattern. Because the omniscient voice in the *Iliad* never delegates or "gives away" its function, its control over the structure is first-hand and proximate, foreseeing the end while it describes the beginning. It is true that when the omniscient voice yields its function to a restricted voice it is in fact *assuming* limited narration while all the time controlling and ordering as it did in an exclusively omniscient narration. But, at the same time, by delegating a significant segment of the narration, as in the *Odyssey,* the omniscient voice foresakes the immediate, geometric control that it wields while functioning alone. If one can believe with Keats and Hazlitt that the great artist becomes the thing he creates, that his negative capability must necessarily result in a sympathetic identification with his creation, then in a very real sense, the omniscient voice, having once delegated its authority, can no longer control in quite the same way. Having passed its function to another, it must honor for the moment the autonomous voice of the subordinate.

Thus, what becomes possible by way of geometric structure with a work controlled entirely by an omniscient voice is not possible in a work controlled by both omniscient and restricted voices. And thus, the kind of geometric balance one finds in the *Iliad* cannot, because of the very nature of the narrating voices, be repeated in the *Odyssey*. Furthermore, the kind of balance intended in the *Odyssey* is not the balance of geometric structure but rather the balance of tones—an ironic counterpointing of attitudes. And since irony works best when functioning within the range of restricted narration (when the voice, that is, is not directly conscious of the irony), the *Odyssey* with its restricted voice exploits irony to the fullest. A discussion of these ironic balances will occupy the next section. Suffice it to repeat here that whereas Homer in the *Iliad* exhibited an artistry of geometric architectonics made possible by his exclusive use of the omniscient voice (albeit a modified one), in the *Odyssey* his artistic experimentation with restricted voice led him away from formal geometric design and resulted in an entirely different kind of balance.

The *Odyssey* is without a doubt the best example in classical literature of the omniscient voice delegating artistically to subordinate voices large areas of the narration. Unlike Virgil, who awkwardly uses the device of the delegated narrator for only two books early in his epic (II and III) and then proceeds to an uninterrupted, completely omniscient and chronological narration of Aeneas's adventures, Homer in the *Odyssey* uses the restricted voice fully in four books and partially in two more, manipulating the elements of time and space with infinitely more skill than his Roman imitator.

Most commentators have paid little *critical* attention to the fact that the account of Ulysses' wanderings are never related by the omniscient voice but are narrated exclusively by Ulysses himself. Certainly, every critic has recognized that the entire length of Books IX, X, XI and XII is enclosed in editorial quotation marks, but most have neglected to relate this fact to the intention of the whole.

That Homer was acutely sensitive to the demands and to the dramatic advantages of the restricted voice (never allowing the restricted narration to become a mere mouthpiece for the omniscient but respecting always the former's autonomy) can be proved by a close reading of the poem. In the first place, the restricted voice is always faithful to the limitations of its restricted knowledge, never reporting events that it could not itself have known, never assuming for a moment an omniscient timbre. Examples of this kind of narrative "epistemology" are numerous, but three will suffice. When Ulysses relates his Circe adventure to the Phaeacians in Book X, he explains that a company of his men led by Eurylochus was chosen to explore Circe's island, his own company having been left behind to guard the ships. The next lines describe the "porcine" fate of the men when they reached Circe's house, an event that Ulysses, back at the ships, could not have known. However, by including in Ulysses' account of the adventure, the simple detail of Eurylochus suspecting mischief, staying outside and reporting back to Ulysses the sad fate of his comrades, Homer succeeds in scrupulously respecting the limitations of the restricted voice. Again, at the end of Book XII when Ulysses describes the divine anger at his crew's slaying of the sun cattle, the account includes what Lampetie reported to Hyperion, what Hyperion complained of to Jove, and finally how Jove promised divine punishment for the sin. Obviously, Ulysses' knowledge could not have extended to the divine councils, and for the moment this episode reads like a restricted narration in which the limitations of knowledge in restricted voice have been forgotten. But a few lines later, Ulysses reports: "I was told all this by Calypso, who said she heard it from the mouth of Mercury."[19]

The most sophisticated example of this kind of awareness occurs in the voyage-to-the-underworld episode in Book XI. Ulysses meets, among others, his old chieftain Agamemnon, who after much lamentation reveals the circumstances of his death at the hands of Aegisthus and inquires solicitously after his own son, Orestes. Ulysses' reply—"why do you ask me? I do not know whether your son is alive or dead, and it is not right to talk when one does not know"—is not only faithful to the obvious limitations of his own knowledge under the circumstances, but also observes an extraordinary respect for the fact of manipulated time in the poem. By Ulysses' own calculations, he spent the last seven years of his ten-year voyage imprisoned on Calypso's island. His wanderings, reported in Books IX through XII, would necessarily have taken place in the first three years. From Nestor's account of the voyage back from Troy we learn that Menelaus returned home eight years after his departure from the sacked city: and his return coincided exactly with the day that Orestes was celebrating the funerals of Aegisthus and Clytemnestra. Therefore, although Orestes' vengeance in the manipulated chronology of the narrative had already been reported *before* Ulysses' encounter with Agamemnon,[20] in point of *real* time Ulysses in Book XI could not in fact have known of Orestes' vengeance, first because he had no opportunity to know, but, more significantly, because the event had not yet taken place. At the point, of course, at which Ulysses is *telling* the story—presumably the tenth year of his voyages—Orestes' vengeance had already been two years old, but because Ulysses, detained as he was on Calypso's island at the time of the vengeance, could not have known of Orestes' act, he does not report it to the Phaeacians even in what might have been an aside.

The real chronology would look like this: a) second year—Ulysses meets Agamemnon in Hades, does not know the fate of Orestes; b) eighth year—Orestes avenges his father's murder by killing Aegisthus and Clytemnestra; c) tenth year—Ulysses tells his version of the meeting in Hades to the Phaeacians. The manipulated order of narration, however, is: b, c, a—with b narrated twice, once by Nestor in Book III and again by Menelaus in Book IV. Ulysses's expression of his ignorance, therefore, both circumstantially and chronologically true, is remarkable when one realizes that the occasion for chronological error in an oral epic complicated by manipulated time would have been more than likely.

But the poet's fidelity to the knowledge of his restricted voice is not the only indication of artistic awareness of the restricted narration. It would be folly, of course, to expect that Homer would tailor the style of his restricted narration to the character of his narrator. The physical limitations of an oral formulaic style would have made such a modern narrative device almost im-

possible. Yet, if we examine certain characteristics of the style of the omniscient voice and that of the restricted, we find at least one significant difference—the use of epic simile. Such a device would function as the natural
tool of the omniscient narration. With its complex parallelism and formal
syntax, with its recognition of artificial resemblances between often dissimilar
things, the epic simile is well suited to the timbre of the omniscient voice.
Such a device used repeatedly either in dialogue or in the delegated narration,
however, would militate against the more limited observation of the restricted
voice.

Bowra has pointed out that the *Odyssey* has far fewer similes than the *Iliad*
because it is Homer's practice to use the simile more often in battle scenes
which, unrelieved by variation, would tend to become monotonous.[21] As correct as this insight may be, he neglects to mention that Homer uses the full-
blown epic simile almost exclusively when he is speaking in his own voice
with omniscient formality. When on those few occasions that the simile is used
within dialogue, he usually modifies its formal syntax to suit the exigencies
of speech. Of the 144 fully developed similes in the *Iliad*, for example, three
are spoken by characters and the rest by the omniscient author. Of the eleven
similes in the *Odyssey* used in dialogue, only four make use of the formal
syntax of the epic simile. The other seven are clearly modified and shortened
syntactically to fit into the more regular patterns of normal speech. Moreover, the proportion of formal epic similes from the *Iliad* to the *Odyssey*—
144 in the former, 23 in the latter—suggests more than the poet's predilection
for similes in the battle scenes. It suggests too that because the *Iliad* contains
no significant restricted narration, the epic simile would fit more naturally
into its omnisciently narrated style. And because the frequency of epic simile
seems to occur in inverse proportion to the amount of restricted narration,
the *Odyssey* would logically show a more limited use of the device.

Homer's artistic awareness of the function of restricted voice in the *Odyssey*
extends beyond his fidelity to the epistemology of his narrator and his judi-
cious use of the epic simile. It takes into account the very obvious but the
very often neglected fact that the audience of an internal narrator is quite
different from the audience whom the omniscient voice is addressing, and that
this internal audience must function as an integral part of the total work. One
is immediately reminded of Marlow's audience in Conrad's *Heart of Darkness*.
The shipmates whom that story teller is addressing may very well symbolize
the totality of the outside world, but in the literal confines of the story they
function as little more than auditors, allowing Marlow simply an occasion to
tell his story of Kurtz. Except for the psychological verisimilitude of Marlow
telling his story to someone, one wonders why Conrad bothered to enclose the
Marlow narration within the boundaries of a larger setting and why so much
time was spent introducing the reader to an internal audience whose function,
if it can be defended at all, remains indefinable. The internal audience of
Ulysses' narration in the *Odyssey*, however, represents more than a mechanical function. . . . It is the Phaeacians listening to their *aidos* Demodocus who
conveniently and convincingly set up the Ulysses story. Moreover, once they
have heard him, "all [holding] their peace throughout the covered cloister,

enthralled by the charm of his story," they are now completely sure that this man is the great hero they suspected him to be, and they confirm with rich gifts their offer of safe convoy back to Ithaca.

As there exists a dramatic relationship between story teller and auditor, so does there exist an equally dramatic relationship between auditor and his effect on the story teller. It is interesting to note that the parts of the *Odyssey* which have come under heaviest critical censure through the centuries have been the fabulous episodes of Ulysses' wanderings. As Ker points out, the romantic elements in the *Odyssey* were probably not believed even by the auditors in its own day, whereas "many of them must have had their grand- mothers' testimony for things like the portents before the death of the suitors."[22] Considering what we know of crafty Ulysses as a story teller in less spectacular parts of the *Odyssey* and remembering that all the fabulous episodes occur during *his* narration, one would hardly be accused of idle speculation in wondering how much of Ulysses' story can be interpreted as a device by which to impress the Phaeacians rather than simply as a story for its own sake. It is true that in both of his earlier accounts of the ship- wreck, the first spoken to Nausicaa and the second to King Alcinous and Queen Arete in Book VI, Ulysses tells the whole story truthfully. But this kind of truthfulness is an exception in Ulysses' other experiences. Danger has taught him to appraise the situation and tell the kind of story that would cause him the least harm or the most good. The first example of this craftiness we see in the *Iliad* where, in reporting Agamemnon's "peace" offering to the recalcitrant Achilles, Ulysses conveniently excises the part that he feels would cause Achilles to refuse—Agamemnon's insistence on his rights of seniority and royalty.[23] We see again in the *Odyssey* how in each of his encounters with the people on Ithaca—Minerva in disguise, Eumaeus, Antinous, Penelope and Laertes—Ulysses rejoices not only in confirming his disguise with an appropriate story but also in embellishing the story with a multitude of un- necessary details. He is "glad" when he hears Penelope in Book XVIII "trying to get presents out of the suitors, and flattering them with fair words which he knew she did not mean." He is almost sadistic in teasing Laertes about his own identity after all danger from the suitors had disappeared, fabri- cating a wild story about his coming from Alybas, the son of King Apheidas, to meet Ulysses and exchange presents.[24]

Would it to too ingenious to suggest that the fabulous elements in Ulysses' narrative are fabulous only because Ulysses is narrating them? Certainly it is clear from the introductory lines that modulate into his large narration that Ulysses is crafty enough to tell the Phaeacians stories they *want* to hear. The account of his voyages, after all, is related not only in answer to Alcinous's question: "Where have you been wandering?" but also in answer to his com- mand: "Tell us of the people themselves, and of their cities—*who were hostile, savage, and uncivilized and who, on the other hand hospitable and humane.*"[25] Alcinous earlier had pointed with understandable pride to the hospitality of the Phaeacians, to their advanced civilization (now almost become soft), and to their charitable habit of escorting ship-wrecked foreigners back to their homes. His question, then, seems as much a subtle invitation for Ulysses' praise by contrasting his people with the barbarousness of other civilizations as it is an open invitation for Ulysses to tell of his wanderings. And Ulysses, sensitive always to the demands of his safety and his total dependence on the good will of his guests, complies.

Of the ten different episodes he narrates, Ulysses in effect categorizes various kinds of *in*hospitality, in direct and almost unsubtle contrast to the treatment he is at the moment receiving. Of violent, barbarous inhospitality, he cites two examples: the Cyclops and the Laestrygonians. And those details about the Cyclops that he stresses are arranged in diametric opposition to the attributes of the Phaeacians that Alcinous had earlier boasted of. Whereas the Phaeacians welcome with open arms all wanderers and suppliants, feasting, dressing and convoying them back home, the Cyclops devours his "guests." Whereas the Phaeacians enjoy the comforts of cleanliness—warm baths and frequent changes of linen—the Cyclops leaves his dung in unholy heaps all around the cave. The royal palace of the Phaeacians is surrounded by a "large garden of . . . four acres with a wall around it . . . full of beautiful trees" cultivated and irrigated; the natural habitat of the Cyclops is wild and completely uncultivated, his only palace a cave.[26] The Phaeacians are master mariners; the Cyclops can only stand on the shore and throw huge boulders at the sea-nimble Ulysses. The smaller details might be multiplied, but the effect is the same. Ulysses deliberately ingratiates himself by praising the hospitality of his guests. And his praise is not an explicit commendation of their civilization. Such a gesture would have offended against the dictum which insists that a suppliant is entitled by divine command to hospitality. Rather its oblique praise for the Phaeacians is arrived at by describing with gruesome details the suffering that results from *in*hospitality.

The Laestrygonian episode, though much shorter than the Cyclops episode, is similar in its series of contrasts. Ulysses, however, makes added use of the wicked queen whom his men discover to be "a giantess as huge as a mountain" and who calls her husband to kill the visitors. She functions clearly, of course, as foil to Queen Arete.

Of inhospitality disguised as a good, Ulysses tells the story of Circe who functions, presumably, as foil to Nausicaa. Whereas Homer takes great pains to characterize the Phaeacian princess as a maiden pure in heart and in body, a saviour of the ship-wrecked Ulysses, Circe is characterized as an erotic goddess, whose eroticism is perhaps allegorically related to her transforming of men into pigs. Mercury's offering to Ulysses of an antidote that would counteract Circe's porcine drug and his suggestion that she will indiscriminately offer any man her body if he is able to resist her magic add to the picture of her as a divine nymphomaniac. Nausicaa, on the other hand, is described as a beautiful maiden innocent of sexual impurity. Homer's almost unsubtle attempt at characterizing her purity by way of image interplay—the long description of her washing clothes scrupulously clean at the riverside followed by an epic simile comparing her beauties to those of Diana—interacts successfully with his description of her innocent refusal to run away from the half-drowned Ulysses and her prudent wish to avoid scandal by suggesting that he follow behind the waggons on their return to court. Alcinous's desire, later expressed, to keep Ulysses at Phaeacia as a husband for Nausicaa contributes further to characterizing her as a type of "Britomartian" chastity. Ulysses' subsequent description of the eroticism of Circe, therefore, would be recognized by the Phaeacians as a tribute to the purity of their princess.

The episode of the lotus eaters, the shortest adventure of the ten episodes, also exemplifies a type of inhospitality—that of euphoric imprisonment. Alcinous's request to Ulysses that he remain on the island as husband to Nausicaa is qualified by his explanation that "no one (heaven forbid) shall keep you here against your own wish"; whereupon he immediately arranges for Ulysses' safe convoy back to Ithaca. Again, the contrast is functional. Like the land of the lotus eaters, Phaeacia offers Ulysses every conceivable happiness: an advanced civilization, a lovely wife, a royal position, heroic fame. But the Phaeacian offer is gratuitous and unconditional. The euphoria offered not only by the lotus eaters but by Calypso and Circe as well can only be purchased at the price of freedom. For Ulysses, an uncertain and dangerous future in freedom is preferable to a euphoric present in slavery, and his dramatization of this preference in the episodes narrated to the Phaeacians pays tribute to their own gratuitousness.

Except for the episodes of the Sirens and of Scylla and Charybdis—which can be dismissed here as examples of destruction by surprise and chicanery (one destroying its victims by attraction and the other by repulsion)—the episodes remaining can be characterized not by the host's offense against hospitality but by the "indiscretions" of guests. Although Ulysses in his great narrative would have the Phaeacians see him as a suffering hero, buffeted unmercifully by the gods and by the inhumanity of other men, he recognizes at the same time that offense against hospitality is not always one-sided. Naturally in the three episodes so functioning it is the crew who commit this offense against Ulysses' orders. The first example with the Ciconians describes Ulysses' men loth to leave Ciconia after the sack, foolishly gorging themselves on wine and allowing the conquered to reorganize and drive the invaders out. The second example of the crew's folly is described in the Aeolus incident in which, after the god of the winds has feasted the Greeks for a month, he ties up the winds in a sack in order to assure Ulysses a safe voyage home. The crew, envious of what they think are gifts awarded to Ulysses alone, foolishly untie the sack and thereby unloose the winds, driving the ships far off course. The final episode of guests' offense against hosts dooms the men to Jove's anger and they perish. Against the explicit command of Ulysses, the men slaughter and eat the sacred cattle of Hyperion. Having been warned against such an act both by Circe and Tiresias, their punishment is eminently just.

The episode of Ulysses' voyage to the underworld at first glance seems to deviate from the pattern of story with which Ulysses answers Alcinous's question. But despite the fact that it reads like a short sequel to the *Iliad*, each of the famous heroic warriors of that poem making his appearance and by his or Ulysses' account bringing the reader up to date on his post-*Iliad* experiences, the center of the episode is in reality closely concerned with the pattern of answer that Ulysses had been rehearsing. In Agamemnon's lament for his fate at the hands of Aegisthus and Clytemnestra, Ulysses dramatizes the most infamous kind of inhospitality—a man murdered in his own house by one who has already cuckolded him. And in his mother's and Tiresias's account of the present situation in Ithaca, Ulysses is able to parallel the generous hospitality of his own household with what the Phaeacians are at the moment showing him—with the ironic difference that the guests at his home have offended against all canons of behavior and have violated by their excesses the sacred relationship between host and guest. The Hades episode, therefore, not only works, as did all the others, as a foil to the treatment Ulysses is at the moment enjoying, but it functions too as an introduction for Ulysses' return to Ithaca. In this respect, it bridges the first half of the epic with the second by dramatizing that what *is* at the moment in Ithaca scarcely resembles what *is* at the moment in Phaeacia, that the actual and the ideal are disturbingly, almost tragically, disparate, and that the principle of order must by violence be restored.

NOTES

1. For a review of this whole controversy, see Cedric H. Whitman, *Homer and the Heroic Tradition* (Cambridge, 1958), chap. 1.
2. Whitman, p.6.
3. Quoted in Samuel E. Bassett, *The Poetry of Homer* (Berkeley, 1938), p.81.
4. Bassett, p.83.
5. Bassett, p.87.
6. *The Iliad of Homer and the Odyssey,* tr. by Samuel Butler, Great Books of the Western World, v. 4 (Chicago, 1948) Book XVI, 46, p.112. All future references to the *Iliad* and *Odyssey* will be to this volume.
7. VI. 232.
8. C. S. Lewis, *A Preface to Paradise Lost* (London, 1942), p.40–41.
9. Whitman, p.119.
10. Whitman, p.39.
11. *The Aeneid of Virgil,* tr. by C. Day Lewis (New York, 1953), p.157 (italics mine).
12. Bassett, p.31.
13. Bassett, p.32.
14. Lewis, p.28.
15. Whitman, p.250.
16. Whitman, p.255.
17. C. M. Bowra, *Tradition and Design in the Iliad* (Oxford, 1930), p.16.
18. Whitman charts the entire plot in the pull-out sheet in the back cover.
19. XII. 389.
20. Nestor had informed Telemachus of this fact in Book III.
21. Bowra, p.123. Thomas Greene's explanation is more "geographical." For him, the circumscribed locale of Troy required the "contrast of another plane," whereas the landscape of the *Odyssey,* obviously less confined than that of Troy, does not require so frequently the expansiveness of the epic simile (p.55).
22. W. P. Ker, *Epic and Romance* (London, 1931), p.15.
23. IX. 162.
24. XXIV. 302 ff.
25. VIII. 572 ff.
26. "Now the Cyclops neither plant nor plough . . . and live on such wheat, barley and grapes as grow wild without any kind of tilage." (IX. 105 ff.)

Kenneth Quinn

THE TEMPO
OF VIRGILIAN EPIC

We expect of epic a loose-knit style and a leisurely tempo. In Homer we find them. The dimensions of the form, the poet's emotional attachment to a departed gentlemanly age that subordinated efficiency to good manners, the genesis itself very likely of Homeric epic (to venture on conjectural ground)[1] —all made for a mellifluous fullness.

Virgil is different. The tempo of the *Aeneid* seems by comparison curt, swift-moving, matter-of-fact. The difference lies in the narrator's manner rather than in his story. His plot can hardly be said to be crowded with action. The *Aeneid* is shorter, admittedly, than the *Iliad* or the *Odyssey;* all the same, 10,000 lines—almost—are ample for the story told.[2] Virgil tells it, however, with an urgent economy that makes us feel every word counts. Naturally the pressure varies. Virgil's own narrative is terser and tighter than the speeches he assigns his characters. Within the narrative the sustained similes are fuller and richer in style; but in them a cohering density, likewise alien to old Greek epic, is substituted for brevity. In the narrative proper the tempo changes constantly. But take a couple of hundred lines of narrative at random and compare them with a similar sample from Homer: your impression will be that, however much Virgil appears to vary the speed of his narrative, his closepacked lines maintain a tempo consistently faster than Homer's.

Some of the pruning has a structural purpose: to reduce the poem to proportions compatible with real artistic form and give it clear lines. But Virgil has another, more important object: to create a new style, one whose distinctive quality shall be terse excitement rather than the charm of leisurely fullness. What he is attempting is not pastiche, but a style founded on the resources of expression of his own day, refined by the craftsman in verse and raised to a new level by the poet's genius. We sense the influence of contemporary prose as often as that of contemporary verse. In prose the orator and the historian had each since Homer's day contributed much to the art of telling a story efficiently. As for verse influences, Virgil owes a lot to the Roman tradition since Catullus and the emphasis that tradition placed on a manner that was closely woven and allusive and yet light, and so shorn of unproductive adornment as to make it deceptively plain.

"The Tempo of Virgilian Epic." From Kenneth Quinn, *Latin Explorations: Critical Studies in Roman Literature* (London: Routledge & Kegan Paul, 1963), p.198–299. Reprinted by permission of Routledge & Kegan Paul and Humanities Press.

The drive for conciseness is easiest seen in Virgil's manipulation of the mechanics of syntax. The devices he employs form part of the repertoire of poetic syntax and are familiar enough to the student of Latin. But, though they are regularly pointed out and labelled in annotated editions, their purpose is seldom clearly stated or appreciated. Among them are the extensive use of an infinitive after a finite verb instead of a subordinate clause; the frequent excision of *est, sunt*, etc., in the perfect passive—leaving the past participle to act unsupported as a finite verb; a preference for simple verbs where compound forms of the same verbs are usual in contemporary prose; a considerable reduction in the incidence of prepositions—using the dative case instead of *ad* and the accusative, or leaving out the preposition that normally accompanies certain ablative forms.

Many of the devices are commonly written off as archaisms, as though it were enough for poetry, or enough for poetry of the quality that Virgil wished to write, to be old-fashioned. Virgil takes from older Latin poetry those features which help him to achieve simplicity and directness and a purity of diction that can predispose us to being moved in the ways in which it is poetry's function to move us, without recourse to the ostentatious sublimity of the grand manner. But above all Virgil concentrates on cutting down the incidence of the small, fussy, unproductive word, often reducing his hexameter to five or six solid, massy words, all pulling their weight.[3] The words, moreover, especially when the narrative is unusually elaborate or allusive, often cohere, linked together by patterns of syntactical ambiguity (the units mutually interlocking) to a degree that almost defies analysis.[4] For he wishes, as well as moving us by an austere simplicity of diction, to excite us (when excitement is appropriate) and to sustain our interest (when things less exciting must be dealt with expeditiously) by a style that will suggest a tight, urgent complexity of thought.

We shall see better how economy makes for speed by considering passages of some extent than by detailing the minutiae of poetic syntax. Take, for example, these lines from Book IV; it is the moment near the end when Anna reaches the pyre and takes her dying sister in her arms:

> sic fata gradus euaserat altos   685
> semianimemque sinu germanam amplexa fouebat
> cum gemitu atque atros siccabat ueste cruores.
> illa grauis oculos conata attollere rursus
> deficit; infixum stridit sub pectore uulnus.
> ter sese attollens cubitoque adnixa leuauit,
> ter reuoluta toro est oculisque errantibus alto   690
> quaesiuit caelo lucem ingemuitque reperta.

A prose translation that preserves the grammatical structure of the Latin is necessary to bring out the point I wish to make:

Speaking thus, she had emerged from the high stairway, and having taken in her arms her sister now near death, she was caressing her in the midst of her grief and was stanching the dark blood with her dress. Dido, attempting to raise again her eyes, lacked the strength. There was a sharp sound from the wound inflicted deep in her chest. Three times, straining and leaning on an elbow for

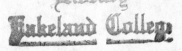

support, she raised herself; three times she rolled back onto the couch, and with her wandering eyes looked to high heaven for the light of day, and groaned on discovering it.

There is not one subordinate clause in these eight lines—something much more unusual in Latin than it would be in English. Confronted with so much action to describe, the Latin writer's problem is this: if he subordinates, the sense of urgency is lost; a series of simple sentences on the other hand is liable (in Latin) to result in a jerkiness that will break up the flow of the writing and destroy its dignity; a succession of *and*'s may prove equally disastrous. Virgil has attained the effect he desires by a construction normal enough in prose, but in prose much less common than a subordinate clause: the deponent past participle. There are four here (*reperta* is passive): *fata* ("speaking"), *amplexa* ("having taken in her arms"), *conata* ("attempting"), *adnixa* ("leaning"). Only one sentence is left as a single statement, the terrible *infixum stridit sub pectore uulnus,* and it stands out starkly in this smoothly articulated context.[5]

So concentrated an employment of the deponent past participle must naturally be reserved for special occasions if it is not to degenerate into mannerism. More frequent is the well-known Virgilian use of an accusative noun after a past participle, a simple, distinctive construction that usually obviates a subordinate clause.[6] Virgil naturally by no means denies himself the subordinate clause in setting out the steps in a complicated piece of narrative. It is striking, however, that nowhere in the poem does he use *cum* with the pluperfect subjunctive—perhaps the most characteristic subordinate clause of contemporary prose narrative. Clearly the construction seemed to him, somehow, irredeemably prosy—or insufficiently supported by tradition (it is not used in early Latin).[7] His favourite temporal conjunction is *ut.* But instead of using it to state a simple temporal relationship ("When X happened, A did so-and-so"), he is fond of using it as a kind of comment on motive, combining *ut* with a verb of perceiving (i.e., *ut uidit* . . . , "When A *saw* that X had happened . . .")—looking at the action from inside his character, as it were, instead of as an impersonal, remote observer.[8]

ELLIPTICAL NARRATIVE

But the drive for conciseness is seen also in the way the story is shaped for telling. The method of selecting events dictates the tempo of the narrative, no less than the techniques Virgil exploits for presenting these events once selected and fitted into the pattern of his story. All skilful writers do this to some extent. But not all take the trouble Virgil takes to sustain an impression of urgency and variety.

The procedure has an interesting and important consequence. The illusion is created of a story with an existence of its own, independent of Virgil's telling of it. This is something different from the knowledge the reader may or may not possess of earlier differing versions, say, of the Aeneas or Dido legends. Quite apart from the aid it receives from any resources of allusion, Virgil's narrative itself makes us feel continually that his story neither begins nor ends with what he tells us. We seem all the time to catch hints of things left out. We sense explanations the poet might have given if he had had time.

At first sight Virgil's technique seems the opposite of that of the realist writer and his wealth of detail painstakingly recorded. The difference is more, however, that in Virgil the details are *suggested,* often, as much as they are recorded. The true opposite of realism is the story so clear-cut that the writer is able to present in his narrative everything the reader needs for the story to proceed. A story so simple that it elicits no curiosity for fuller information, no puzzlement about the causal relationships between events.

But Virgil expects of his readers this curiosity and this puzzlement, the realization that steps have been omitted, explanations not given. He relies on them to conjecture half-consciously about what is missing, but needed if they are to grasp the story properly.[9] Virgil in fact transfers to epic the evocative economy of Hellenistic epigram and Horatian ode. It is another instance of his reliance upon the reader's active collaboration. . . . For example, . . . in *Aeneid* IV Virgil tells us practically nothing about the events at Dido's palace between the day of the hunt and the day of Aeneas' decision to depart. At the same time he makes us feel that time has gone by, that much has passed between Aeneas and Dido to complicate their relationship. Yet we haven't any feeling that something is missing. On the contrary, Virgil's story somehow acquires the solidity and depth of real life, where there is no limit to the data relevant to an episode, but only limits to our knowledge. A story that does not elicit the curiosity and puzzlement that real life elicits cannot ring true.

Let us look at some simpler examples with more care. In the story of the boxing-match in *Aeneid* V Virgil passes on from the braggard display of Dares (who looks like taking the prize without having to fight because no opponent comes forward) with the words (V. 387–88):

> hic grauis Entellum dictis castigat Acestes,
> proximus ut uiridante toro consederat herbae.

> *Here, Acestes, speaking sternly to Entellus, upbraided him,*
> *after he had sat down close beside him on the grass.*

Two words—*grauis, consederat*—draw the reader out and set him putting together the details of the story the way Virgil intends. Why should Acestes speak "sternly"? Why are we told so precisely that Entellus "had sat down" —not merely that he "was sitting"? The reader, sensitive to the precision of Virgil's narrative text, hardly needs to ask these questions consciously. The form of the verb *consederat* (the pluperfect tense, the pre-verb *con-*) bring action into what *sedebat* would have left as description of scene. Entellus, the recognized local champion (our filling-out begins) had come along expecting to compete. That is why he has his great gloves with him. But he is an old man; seeing the visiting champion brings second thoughts and he sits down. This action explains *grauis:* Acestes is not merely urging Entellus to fight, but upbraiding him for his decision not to fight (revealed by the action of sitting down).

Expansion like this of Virgil's text may seem high-handed until we realize how constantly his technique of elliptical narrative requires it. It illuminates, too, the conclusion of the boxing match, where obscurity has been felt:

"nate dea, uosque haec" inquit "cognoscite, Teucri,
et mihi quae fuerint iuuenali in corpore uires   475
et qua seruetis reuocatum a morte Dareta."
dixit, et aduersi contra stetit ora iuuenci
qui donum astabat pugnae, durosque reducta
librauit dextra media inter cornua caestus
arduus, effractoque inlisit in ossa cerebro: 480
sternitur exanimisque tremens procumbit humi bos.
ille super talis effundit pectore uoces:
"hanc tibi, Eryx, meliorem animam pro morte Daretis
persoluo; hic uictor caestus artemque repono."

"Just you look, goddess' son," he said, "you Trojans, too:
you'll see what strength my body had when I was young—
and the death your intervention saved your Dares from."
With that he planted himself right before the bull—
there it stood, the winning fighter's prize—drew right hand
back, balanced the cruel gloves evenly between the horns, and
from his full height drove them through the splintering skull.
The bull fell to the ground to sprawl a twitching lifeless mass.
Standing over it, his voice lifting from his chest, he said:
"Here, instead of Dares' death, a better life I offer
to you, Eryx: my gloves, my craft, I the winner now renounce."

What actually does Entellus do? The picture is far from clear on a first reading. A double hint is given by *duros . . . caestus* in lines 478–79. First the
plural: how more than one glove on one hand (*dextra*)?[10] Then why *duros?*
Is the epithet distinguishing or ornamental? An eye cast back over the preceding lines shows us how Virigil expects us to fill out his narrative. Clearly
they are the gloves of Eryx, not the ordinary gloves Entellus wore in the fight.
There is a distinct interval after the fight stops—the time needed for Dares'
friends to carry him back to the ships and then return to recover the loser's
prize. More than enough time for Entellus to remove his gloves and take up
the gloves of Eryx which he had brought with him in the first place.

Virgil makes more than one use of these gloves of Eryx. If he had used
them only for Entellus' gesture in accepting the challenge, it would have been
a little flat to have them thrown aside when the fight began—though we could
admire Virgil's taste in avoiding undue brutality. They are needed as well,
however, in the last line of the episode: it is the gloves he has used throughout
his career that Entellus dedicates to Eryx in his declaration of retirement,
not the substitute gloves. A less compact writer might have included some
specific statement of Entellus' resumption of the gloves of Eryx for the ceremony of dedication. Virgil, however, prefers to work by suggestion. The
reader who wants to visualize the scene, instead of reading the passage quickly
for its superficial excitement, is expected to look for the clues the poet has
taken care to leave him. It is not Virgil's aim to provide a clear-cut image.
He leaves it to the reader, aroused to responsiveness by his puzzlement, to
assemble his own.

Next to be decided is the meaning to attach to *librauit* (line 479). If
Entellus is carrying both gloves in one hand, they must be brought down on
the bullock's skull with a swing, not a punch; *librauit* then is the preliminary

calculation of the swing, not the poising of the clenched fist for a punch. A detail in Entellus' words before he struck the blow that ought to have puzzled us is now explained. How can Entellus show the strength of body he had as a *young* man now he is *old?* By some superhuman effort? No, really by a sort of trick. A theatrical gesture (a calculated swing with two gloves) demonstrates what he could have done once, he claims, with a normal punch. Today he has to resort to a trick to crack open the tough skull of a bullock. But Dares' skull he could still manage, he asserts, even with an ordinary glove and an ordinary punch.

Commentators on Virgil tend to be resentful at the lack of clarity which results from his technique of elliptical narrative. The fifth book, because of the wealth of complicated incident related, provides many examples of the sort of thing that annoys them. Details that seem important are left obscure. What use, if any, for instance is made of sail in the boat-race?[11] Details not mentioned at what one would take to be the proper time crop up afterwards. Mnestheus presents himself for the archery contest wearing an olive garland awarded in the boat-race, though we were not told in the narrative of the prize ceremony after the boat-race that he had won one.[12] Ascanius, before speaking to the women who had set the fleet on fire, throws down his helmet; but in the parade he was not wearing a helmet.[13] Even in an unfinished poem, the commentators feel, Virgil should not nod as often as this.

The questions they ask can hardly be dismissed as irrelevant or wrong-headed, like Professor [L. C.] Knights' model of the sort of question not to put to the text of Shakespeare: "How many children had Lady Macbeth?"[14] At the same time it is obvious that, if Virgil had attempted to forestall all possible relevant questions, his narrative would have become intolerably crowded and slow-moving. Most of the apparent slips complained of are the results of omissions, not inconsistencies, and most details the sensible reader can supply for himself.

Sometimes, however, Virgil's method imposes omissions beyond the needs of economy. It is then as though he wished to observe on our behalf only what the actual spectators might have observed. For often *they* would be left unsure what exactly has happened even though they had been watching; often they would only realize afterwards that things they missed at the time must have occurred. Why shouldn't then the reader, too, be left to worry details out of the text on a second, a third and a fourth reading and still, here and there, be left unsure what happened?

But Virgil's narrative has more to it than the story. He wants us to understand the sort of people his characters are, how they are affected by the decisions they take, the rightness or wrongness of those decisions. None of this can be made clear-cut and remain convincing. Even the evidence for our judgments—what actually happened—must not be too neatly presented. Often, too, he wishes us to sense the symbolic significance of an episode. But we must no more than sense it. If the symbolism is too expressly implanted, it will lose its power to move us.

In *Aeneid* II, while the Greeks are pouring out of the wooden horse into the streets of the sleeping city, Hector appears to Aeneas in a dream, to warn him of Troy's impending destruction and to tell him what he must do:

"heu fuge, nate dea, teque his" ait "eripe flammis.   290
hostis habet muros; ruit alto a culmine Troia.
sat patriae Priamoque datum: si Pergama dextra
defendi possent, etiam hac defensa fuissent.
sacre suosque tibi commendat Troia penatis;
hos cape fatorum comites, his moenia quaere
magna, pererrato statues quae denique ponto."   295

"Ah! flee, goddess' son," he said, "snatch yourself from these flames.
The enemy has the walls; Troy is crashing headlong down.
There's no more to do for country or for Priam. If Troy's defence
had lain in strength of hand, mine had so defended it.
To you Troy entrusts her holy things, her city's gods.
Take them to share your destiny, seek for them the fabric of
a mighty city you shall found, your ocean journeys ended."

The symbolism is as plain as Virgil dare make it. Aeneas is to replace Hector as the protector of the Trojans. But he is to be their protector in exile, and their religious as much as their military champion. Aeneas rushes to a vantage point and Hector's opening words are confirmed by the scene before his eyes: Troy is in flames. His natural instinct is to spring to the defence of the doomed city:

arma amens capio; nec sat rationis in armis,
sed glomerare manum bello et concurrere in arcem   315
cum sociis ardent animi; furor iraque mentem
praecipitat, pulchrumque mori succurrit in armis.

Distraught I snatch up arms, though there's little sense in arms;
but to build a band for battle, to rush with comrades to the
citadel—thus the hot impulse; a mad anger tumbles over
reason, and the quick thought comes: how fine a fighting death!

The stress Virgil lays on the folly of Aeneas' reaction should warn the sensitive reader he has in mind something other than the nobility of hopeless resistance. A moment later appears

Panthus Othryades, arcis Phoebique sacerdos,
sacra manu uictosque deos paruumque nepotem   320
ipse trahit cursuque amens ad limina tendit.

Panthus Othryades, arcis Phoebique sacerdos,
the holy things, the vanquished gods, his little grandson,
these he clasps as he runs distraught toward my house.

It is as though Hector's words were once again confirmed, as though the same power that sent Hector to Aeneas in vision is now sending Panthus to him in reality.

It is clear Virgil wishes us to understand that Panthus is bringing to Aeneas the gods that Aeneas must take with him into exile—the gods he eventually does take with him when he sets out at the beginning of Book III:

feror exsul in altum   11
cum sociis natoque penatibus et megnis dis.

An exile I put to sea;
with me comrades, son, ancestral gods, mighty powers.

It is equally clear Virgil cannot say so in as many words: the hand of fate must not appear too mechanical. And any identification of the images of the gods with the gods themselves must be no more than discreetly implied.[15]

But, though the reader senses the hand of fate when Panthus appears with the city's gods, Aeneas does not.[16] He assumes Panthus' appearance carrying the gods means that the citadel where they were kept (Panthus is carefully described as *arcis Phoebique sacerdos*) is being evacuated and another established:

> "quo res summa loco, Panthu? quam prendimus arcem?"   322

> *"Where's the last stand, Panthus, what take we for our citadel?"*

It is clear from Panthus' despondent reply that there is no question of an organized stand. But Aeneas does not seem to grasp the hopelessness of resistance. Panthus, for his part, either does not know he is to commit the gods to Aeneas' care, or forgets. Both he and Aeneas are described as *amens*—"distraught," "not thinking." The impulse to fight is so strong that, despite Hector's charge, Aeneas joins the battle. So does Panthus, but, with characteristic economy of detail. Virgil does not say so. Only when Panthus is killed (lines 429–30) are we told he had fought till then by Aeneas' side. For the moment the tempo of events is too fast for them, or us, to grasp clearly all that happens.

The battle scenes follow (lines 336–587), lit up by the flames that join with the Greeks in destroying Troy. Before the end of this central and longest section of the three which comprise the book, we see Priam brutally murdering Helen. The writing is magnificently vivid and moving; yet all the time, though we, like Aeneas, have forgotten it, Aeneas is out of step with destiny. He is neglecting what Hector told him he must do. Virgil has the courage to imply in his epic of Rome's greatness that death in battle is the easy way out. The implication underlies all the time the glamour of the battle scenes. It pervades the first words Aeneas speaks in the poem (I. 94–96):

> "o terque quaterque beati,
> quis ante ora patrum Troiae sub moenibus altis
> contigit oppetere!"

> *"O three times blessed and more they*
> *that before their fathers' eyes, by Troy's towering walls,*
> *were granted death!"*

But the easy way out is denied Aeneas. His mission, as Hector told him, was to save his people and their gods, not to fight for the doomed city. At the very moment when his hand is raised to murder Helen, his divine mother Venus intervenes, makes him realize at last that Troy is doomed, and restores him to his destined mission:[17]

> "eripe, nate, fugam finemque impone labori"   619

> *"Clutch your chance of escape, my son, end your struggle."*

Throughout the epic heroics of the night of fighting, Virgil intends us to preserve this sense, not merely of the futility of fighting, but of its misguidedness. He has gone as far as he dares. A lesser poet might have imperilled our acceptance of his message by reintroducing the images of the gods at this point. That would make it all just too contrived. Virgil instead sets Aeneas about preparations for exile and keeps the gods back until the moment of departure. Aeneas' words then to his father

"tu, genitor, cape sacra manu patriosque penatis"   717

"You, father, clasp the holy things, our ancestral gods!"

echo Hector's words[18]

"sacra suosque tibi commendat Troia penatis;
hos cape fatorum comites, his moenia quaere
magna."   295

*"To you Troy entrusts her holy things, her city's gods.
Take them to share your destiny, seek for them the fabric of
a mighty city."*

And in the next book we have the final reminder (III. 11–12):

feror exsul in altum
cum sociis natoque penatibus et magnis dis.

*An exile I put to sea;
with me comrades, son, ancestral gods, mighty powers.*

INTERWEAVING

Another device for suggesting ramifications of the story beyond the framework of the actual narrative is a technique we shall call *interweaving*. Its function is to prepare for the main appearance of an important secondary character by an anticipatory glimpse of him in action—sometimes a whole series of glimpses. When his main scene comes, we feel that, though the tempo of the action has not given the opportunity for more than an occasional glance, he has been there all the time.

Virgil makes use of this technique in building up the character of Mezentius. Mezentius does not come into the foreground until Book X, but the pattern of reference to him and glimpses of him taking part in the fighting begins as far back as Book VII. His name occurs first in the list of princes opposing Aeneas (VII. 647–48):

primus init bellum Tyrrhenis asper ab oris
contemptor diuum Mezentius . . .

*First into battle goes a formidable Etruscan,
god-despising Mezentius. . . .*

Nothing is said of him here beyond the arresting comment *contemptor diuum*. Instead Virgil tells us about his son Lausus, who gets six lines to his father's two: a short panegyric ending with the remark that he deserved a better father. The reader's interest in this striking and vaguely sinister character is economically aroused—and then no more is said of him until the beginning of the next book.

This time we have a brief glimpse of him in action, marshalling his forces with other princes (VIII. 6–8),

> ductores primi Messapus et Vfens
> contemptorque deum Mezentius undique cogunt
> auxilia et latos uastant cultoribus agros.

> *First the leaders Messapus, Ufens, and*
> *god-despising Mezentius comb the countryside for*
> *troops, stripping fields far and wide of husbandmen.*

—the reference again vague but menacing and an echo of the same intriguing phrase. Then no more about him for nearly five hundred lines. His name now crops up while Evander is talking to Aeneas (VIII. 481 ff.), and at last we learn something about this cruel, bizarre prince living in exile from his own people. Evander, in bidding farewell to his son Pallas, who is going to fight with Aeneas, mentions Mezentius again (VIII, 569–71) and again it is his cruelty and barbarity that are stressed.

The name Mezentius is becoming familiar. We start to feel we know something about the man. In Book IX Virgil is content to remind us that Mezentius is present, taking part in the fighting. We catch sight of him a couple of times, both action shots (IX. 521–22 and 586–89). In the first he stands out among a group attempting to set fire to the ramparts. In the second we see him kill a man with a spectacular sling shot. Book X brings in his name again by yet another device. A glimpse of Aeneas journeying through the night to rejoin his men is followed by a recapitulatory passage telling us of his negotiations with the present Etruscan prince. Once more the name of Mezentius crops up. We are made to feel, not only that he is there all the time fighting, but also that he is present in the thoughts of the other characters—a man to be reckoned with.

We glimpse him again for a moment at X. 204. Then, at X. 689, he comes at last into the foreground to take a major part in the fighting during the absence from the battle of Turnus. He is mentioned again at X. 714. Then for the first time he is allotted a scene of some importance at X. 729–46: the dying Orodes predicts to his assailant standing over him that death will seek him out, too, before long. Mezentius despatches him with a smile— though irritated by Orodes' words, he is still sufficiently master of himself to treat the Jupiter he despises with heavy irony, addressing the god by his full traditional title:

> ad quae subridens mixta Mezentius ira: 742
> "nunc morere. ast de me diuum pater atque hominum rex
> uiderit."

> *Smiling and angry, too, Mezentius replied,*
> *"Now die: as for me, the king of gods and men will give*
> *the matter his attention."*

Virgil's touch is subtle. We begin to understand why Mezentius is known as *contemptor diuum*. And when god-despising Mezentius, with a gesture of uneasy bravado, invites the wrath of Jupiter upon his own head, the thrill of presentiment we feel is accompanied by a fresh insight into the much talked of cruelty of Mezentius. This is no unfeeling brute, we sense, but a man made ruthless by embitterment.

Virgil has now prepared us for Mezentius' main scene, his first fight with Aeneas, in which he is wounded and saved from death by the intervention of his son Lausus—the son who deserved a better father. Aeneas kills the boy and his body is brought to where his father is resting by a stream, urgently asking for news of the duel. Shamed beyond endurance, Mezentius calls for his horse (for whom he feels an affection shown no human companion), determined to face Aeneas in a fight he does not hope to win.[19] After a fierce encounter, he meets death with the hard, realistic courage we expect of him, no more willing to beg quarter from Aeneas than he was willing to extend it to Orodes.

Our concern, however, is not with the main episode, which is magnificent and moving, but with the way Virgil has woven it into his story. Nor is Mezentius forgotten about as soon as his big scene is over. We hear of him again during the burial of the dead at the beginning of Book XI in a final pathetic echo: Mezentius, who had boasted he would array his son as a living trophy with the arms of Aeneas (X. 775), is now himself offered as a trophy to the god of war (XI. 7). The whole pattern of interweaving repays the closest study, not only as an example of economical presentation of a fully rounded and highly individual secondary character, but also as a sustained illustration of an important narrative device.

The same device on a more limited scale is used many times. Nisus and Euryalus, for example, are first presented to us in a minor episode during the games in Sicily as contestants in the sprint (V. 294 ff.), so that, when their major scene comes four books later (IX. 230 ff.), two things will have been achieved. First, we shall see them come forward, not as characters suddenly created, but as people we have seen before, whose presence all along among Aeneas' men we can believe in, and into whose characters we feel we already possess some insight. Second, the two episodes four books apart provide one of the bonds that hold together the main structure of the narrative.

The two Palinurus episodes are closer together, standing at either end of Book V. Their main function is to underline, by a clear piece of symbolism, the progress of the rehabilitation of Aeneas in the eyes of his men. The opening lines of Book V show clearly how their misgivings about the rights and wrongs of their commander's quarrel with Dido have imperilled Aeneas' moral ascendancy. . . . In the crisis of the storm immediately following, Palinurus assumes the initiative and Aeneas merely acquiesces. At the end of the book the Trojans are at sea once more. But it is a calm night, not a night of storm (a further piece of symbolism). The eventual happy outcome of events in Book V has restored Aeneas' confidence in himself. When the crisis comes now, he springs to assume control of the situation (lines 867–88).

But symbolism apart, the second Palinurus episode relies for its vividness on the reader's memory of the first. It becomes unnecessary to burden the second with a delineation of Palinurus' character: we feel we know the man already. And, knowing him as a seaman of resource and authority, we can appreciate the importance of his loss to Aeneas. These are facts the reader needs, to grasp the magnitude of the crisis when Palinurus is lost. But they are facts he feels he can supply from his own knowledge, not facts suddenly created and asserted by the poet.

This is not the end of Palinurus. We meet him again in Book VI. Nor is this by any means a full account of the patterns of interweaving in the poem. The more one comes to know the poem, the clearer the more subtle patterns stand out. The patterns do not always work forward to a main scene. For example, the description of the *Lusus Troiae* in Book V breaks off a description of the leaders with a short apostrophe to the father of one of them, Polites (V. 563–65):

> una acies iuuenum, ducit quam paruus ouantem
> nomen aui referens Priamus, tua clara, Polite,
> progenies, auctura Italos!

> *One column of exulting youngsters is led by a little*
> *Priam (named after his grandfather)—your stock, Polites,*
> *famous now, to have Italian descendants soon!*

The touch is characteristic enough of Virgil's manner. But it helps as well to draw out on this happy occasion our recollection of the brutal murder, described so vividly in Book II, of the boy's father, followed by the murder of his grandfather, King Priam.[20] The grandfather's name comes in almost casually because it is also the boy's name. But in a sense the whole story of the poem (murder and destruction in Troy, a new bright future in Italy) echoes through these two and a half lines.

ALLUSION

Another of Priam's sons who died the night Troy fell is Deiphobus. His role in the story illustrates, not so much interweaving, as a narrative technique which we may call *allusion*. In Virgil's own story Deiphobus occurs only twice. Indeed the first time hardly ranks as an occurrence. His name is mentioned to localize one detail in the panorama of destruction that Aeneas surveys from his roof-top before his meeting with Panthus. While he watches, the house of Deiphobus crashes to the ground, engulfed in the fire destined that night to consume Troy (II. 310–11):

> iam Deiphobi dedit ampla ruinam
> Volcano superante domus.

But the reader who knows his Homer catches an echo here that others miss. In *Odyssey* VIII Odysseus, at the banquet given by King Alcinous, asks the Phaeacian minstrel Demodocus to relate to him the destruction of Troy. Demodocus provides in fact no more than an excerpt from the story. As reported by Homer, his lay occupies a mere twenty lines (*Odyssey* VIII, 499–520). A paraphrase of the episode of the wooden horse occupies nearly the whole. One detail only of the ensuing destruction is highlighted: how Odysseus himself, Menelaus with him, made for the house of Deiphobus and there fought courageously a particularly bloody battle.

Virgil says nothing of this, relying on his readers to catch the echo of Homer and feel they know what has happened to Deiphobus. In Book VI, however (lines 494–534) Aeneas meets Deiphobus among the shades of the dead, his body cruelly mutilated, and is told the story of how the brutal Ulysses and Menelaus burst in that night upon Deiphobus and Helen.[21] The second reference picks up the first, by the normal process of interweaving— except that the first really only exists as the result of the process we have called allusion. Moreover, the information Virgil expected his readers to draw from Homer is now corrected: what Homer had presented as a heroic deed is now shown to have another, less attractive side. The correction is the more effective for being delayed: instead of retelling the story his way at the time (which might have tempted us to dismiss his version as partial, or an attempt to rewrite Homer), Virgil allows allusion to implant the Homeric version, and the truer version, we feel, of what happened to come out later.

Basically it is one more device for making Virgil's story sound real by implying the endless ramifications of reality. Set against an implied pattern of endless, conflicting detail, Virgil's own narrative sounds urgently selective. Allusion is, of course, an aspect of Virgil's constant imitation of Homer; but it represents a considerable refinement on the more normal techniques. Episodes, similes, tricks of language and style borrowed from Homer may pass undetected without much harm to our enjoyment. Something usually is lost if we miss Homer's words behind Virgil's; but success does not depend on recognition of the borrowing. Allusion, however, deliberately challenges our memory of Homer. Details are incorporated often that are dependent on our knowledge of Homer's story. When, for example, in recounting his vision of Hector the exclamation is wrung from Aeneas (II. 274–75),

> ei mihi, qualis erat, quantum mutatus ab illo
> Hectore qui redit exuuias indutus Achilli!
>
> *Alas! how he looked! He was not the Hector now*
> *that returned wearing the captured armour of Achilles!*

a detail is built in to arouse our active collaboration with the poet. We are challenged to remember it was not Achilles whom Hector killed, but Patroclus, who was wearing the armour of Achilles. Stimulated by our perception of this detail, we feel the whole story of Hector's own death flooding back with a fullness and a pressure that Virgil could not achieve by any explicit statement without destroying the narrative tempo.

Or take Priam's words to Neoptolemus, who has just killed Priam's son before his eyes (II. 540–43):

> "at non ille, satum quo te mentiris, Achilles
> talis in hoste fuit Priamo. sed iura fidemque
> supplicis erubuit corpusque exsangue sepulcro
> reddidit Hectoreum meque in mea regna remisit."
>
> *"You lie when you claim Achilles was your father: he did*
> *not treat his enemy Priam so. Shamed, he acknowledged*
> *my suppliant's right to claim for burial Hector's body;*
> *restored it, life poured from it, sent the royal father home."*

Our recollection is summoned of the compassion with which Achilles at the end of the *Iliad* received the grief-stricken Priam when he came to beg for the body of his son. Neoptolemus has shown, by his brutal disregard for Priam's feelings, that he is no son of such a father. Virgil's second sentence does not so much retell the story (retold so briefly it has little emotional impact on us) as guide us back to the reminiscence, so that allusion can do its work.

The most interesting type is that in which the new context implies a reversal of attitude, a correction of Homer. In the *Odyssey* the killing of Deiphobus is recounted with brief gusto as one of the manly exploits of Odysseus. In *Aeneid* VI, it is set against the initial picture of Deiphobus' mangled body as yet another instance of the barbarous brutality of the Greeks, and the role of Odysseus reduced to that of the contemptible accomplice (*comes additus una hortator scelerum*, VI, 528–29) of Menelaus. Naturally the story is seen from the Trojan side, but there is more to it than that: we feel in these passages the contrast between Virgil's melancholy revulsion at violence in an age that was sick of violence and Homer's neutral acceptance of it.

Another type uses allusion to create a fresh emotional context. When Dares comes forward as challenger in the boxing-match in *Aeneid* V, his name elicits two allusive touches (V. 370–74):

> solus qui Paridem solitus contendere contra,
> idemque ad tumulum quo maximus occubat Hector
> uictorem Buten immani corpore, qui se
> Bebrycia ueniens Amyci de gente ferebat,
> perculit et fulua moribundum extendit harena.

> *He was the only man who would take on Paris in a fight,*
> *and it was he, by the grave where mighty Hector sleeps,*
> *knocked out giant champion Butes (who had come, passing*
> *himself off as descended from Amycus of Bebrycia), and*
> *sent him sprawling on the yellow sand, as good as dead.*

After the quick implicit correction of Homer in the first line (we see a more manly Paris), the allusion to the grave of Hector at this point in Virgil's story is aimed less at stirring our memories of Homer than at making us understand how the Trojan exiles who are watching Dares must feel. On this festive day in Sicily they have temporarily forgotten their past. The sight of Dares with gloves again on his fists brings it all back. And then comes the thought that mighty Hector sleeps now outside a city that does not exist, linked only by memories with Aeneas' men and their present fate.

Finally, allusion may aim (apart from its central purpose of adding solidity to the story) at conciliating the reader by the fullness of his response. The real winner of the archery contest in *Aeneid* V, for example, Eurytion, is introduced as the brother of Pandarus (V. 495–97):

> . . . tuus, o clarissime, frater,
> Pandare, qui quondam iussus confundere foedus
> in medios telum torsisti primus Achiuos.

> *. . . your brother, famous Pandarus*
> *(you they told that time to wreck the truce, when*
> *you fired first shot slap into the Achaeans).*

The reader who catches none of the allusions simply feels that Eurytion's prestige is somehow enhanced. The reader who remembers the role of Pandarus in breaking the truce in the *Iliad* (IV, 85 ff.) is likely to appreciate, too, the rather Alexandrian way in which the build-up is underplayed. The words *telum torsisti* do not even make it clear that Pandarus was an archer, but in Homer there is an elaborate description of Pandarus' bow and the shot he fired to break the truce. And *iussus,* too, underplays the allusion—"ordered" is mysteriously vague: it was the goddess Athene, disguised as a comrade, who persuaded Pandarus to take a sniping shot at Menelaus. This is the sort of pleasure recognizing an Homeric simile behind one of Virgil's offers. At the same time Virgil's story acquires depth, without sacrifice of the narrative tempo.

THE NARRATIVE SENTENCE: TENSES

Despite his reliance upon the techniques of allusion, suggestion and implication, Virgil's story is still very long. In the actual telling of it devices are needed to maintain and vary the tempo, so that it neither flags nor becomes monotonous. Virgil's narrative sentence ranges constantly from staccato statement of essentials, notes for a sentence, almost, rather than a rounded sentence, to sustained, flowing narrative period. The middle and commonest course is a series of simple narrative statements linked by co-ordinating *and*'s. In the longer sentence he favours certain distinctive patterns in the arrangement of the steps in a narrative.

One of the major problems of the longer narrative sentence is to secure freshness in the temporal clause. Virgil, as we have seen, avoids the *cum* and pluperfect subjunctive of contemporary prose. He prefers *ut* for the lightly sketched-in recapitulation of preliminaries to the main action of his sentence. The rather grander *postquam* is used for the more significant step forward, or the more complete break with what went before. The opening lines of Book III are an example:

> Postquam res Asiae Priamique euertere gentem
> immeritam uisum superis, ceciditque superbum
> Ilium et omnis humo fumat Neptunia Troia,
> diuersa exsilia et desertas quaerere terras
> auguriis agimur diuum.   5

> *After the overthrow of Asia and Priam's undeserving house*
> *by decision of the gods above, after proud Ilium's*
> *fall when Neptune's Troy was all a smoking ruin,*
> *a life of exile in all manner of distant, empty lands*
> *the gods to us in prophecy commended.*

He is fond of "inverted" *cum* and an emphatic *donec* "until" clause (usually with the perfect indicative) to round off a longish narrative sentence.[22]

Virgil's use of the narrative tenses to vary and enliven the tempo of his story is an aspect of his technique that has not received the attention it deserves.[23] He has four tenses at his disposal: the perfect indicative, the historic present indicative, the imperfect indicative, and the historic infinitive—leaving out of account the pluperfect indicative. Two of the four call for little comment. The historic infinitive serves as no more than an occasional variation by comparison with the other tenses—three or four examples (perhaps all together) per book.[24] In force it resembles the imperfect, denoting a process or state of affairs consequent upon action rather than action. The imperfect indicative represents a rather more frequent departure from the basic narrative tempo, which is built upon variation and contrast between the two main narrative tenses, the perfect and the historic present.

The commonest narrative tense is the historic present, though it does not preponderate in Virgil's narrative to the extent implied by some reference grammars. The overall proportion of historic present to perfect in the actual narrative fabric of the poem (excluding dialogue, similes, flash-backs and other interpolations, but including description strictly within the narrative) is about three to one. The incidence of perfects rises markedly, however, with an increase in the excitement or the complexity of the narrative.[25]

We see this clearly if we take as an example the three sections of *Aeneid* II. In the first section, the story of the wooden horse and the preliminaries to disaster, the narrative moves quickest and quietest, mainly in the present tense. In the central section, the story of the night of fighting, where the variation in tempo is much more marked, the proportion of perfects rises to the normal level for sustained narrative, about three to one. In the final section the proportion of perfects is even higher, in keeping with the greater structural complexity of this section. There are more imperfects, too.

Virgil's use of the two main narrative tenses shows a marked and individual refinement on the practice of his predecessors. The historic present is not used at all by Homer (as a literary device it appears have been invented by Herodotus) and it remained unexploited in Greek epic.[26] On the other hand, Homer makes freer use of the aspectual contrast between aorist and imperfect than the nature of the Latin tenses permitted. Variation is also possible in Homer between augmented and unaugmented past tenses. Latin epic, however, uses the historic present from the beginning, though it is hard to tell from the fragments that survive what principles guided the practice of the first epic poets. Catullus in his hexameter epyllion, Poem 64, is clearly conscious of the stylistic possibilities of a variation in the narrative tenses, but his practice differs completely from Virgil's.[27] The main structure of the narrative has perfect verbs.[28] Only in one short passage do we find anything approaching Virgil's alternation of tenses within a single piece of narrative.[29]

The effect of the historic present is to represent past action as actually taking place before the narrator's eyes—a description of action rather than action reported. It represents, of course, the literary use of a very common device of conversational narrative. The perfect has more than one use—at least three in Virgil. The relationship between the different uses is elusive, to be accounted for in part perhaps by the double origin of the form, which morphologically, is both a true perfect and an aorist.

In a narrative otherwise uniformly conducted in the historic present we find, not uncommonly, an isolated verb in the perfect, apparently with the force of a genuine perfect—for example (II. 252–53):

> fusi per moenia Teucri
> conticuere; sopor fessos complectitur artus.

> *Sprawled in their fortress the Trojans*
> *have fallen silent; sleep clasps their tired limbs.*[30]

Much more frequent is the *instantaneous* use of the perfect: a perfect breaking into a series of presents (occasionally imperfects) to denote sudden, abrupt action.[31] The present being a descriptive tense, expressing, as we have said, what is going on before the narrator's eyes, and the imperfect the past equivalent of this, neither is suited to the expression of an action begun and completed in an instant. Such instantaneous perfects in Virgil are common, but usually occur in isolation, or in groups of two or three perfects at most. The effect may be very vivid. For example, the battle scene in *Aeneid* XII, 289–310, is conducted throughout in historic presents (eighteen of them)— except for a sentence in the middle, describing how Corynaeus dashed a smouldering brand from the altar in Ebysus' face:

> olli ingens barba reluxit   300
> nidoremque ambusta dedit.

> *His great beard burst into*
> *flame with a sudden stench of burning.*

The inherent aptness of the perfect *reluxit* for expressing a sudden flash of flame is increased by the unexpected change of tense; the perfect *nidorem . . . dedit* expresses the sudden odour of singeing.[32]

Most examples of the instantaneous perfect are of this kind. It is the tense used, for example, of Laocoon abruptly hurling a spear at the wooden horse and the sinister noises produced when it struck (II. 50–53). Or the tense used when the wooden horse stuck in the gateway as the happy Trojans were drawing it into the doomed city (II. 243). More interesting is the description of the beginning of the boat-race in *Aeneid* V, and the simile of a chariot-race that supports it:

> inde ubi clara dedit sonitum tuba, finibus omnes,
> haud mora, prosiluere suis; ferit aethera clamor   140
> nauticus, adductis spumant freta uersa lacertis.
> infindunt pariter sulcos, totumque dehiscit
> conuulsum remis rostrisque tridentibus aequor.
> non tam praecipites biiugo certamine campum
> corripuere ruuntque effusi carcere currus,   145
> nec sic immissis aurigae undantia lora
> concussere iugis pronique in uerbera pendent.

> *Then when the clear trumpet sounded, from their starting-point*
> *all bounded straightway forward. An uproar of sailors strikes*
> *the air, arms strain in a stroke that turns water to foam.*
> *In line they plough forward, the whole stretch of water*

yawns, churned by oars and three-pronged prows.
Not like this the sudden bound onto the track of the racing
chariots that stream along once poured out of the starting pen.
Not like this the charioteers' sudden jerk of the snaking reins
over teams that then, stretched forward, they belabour with whip.

Virgil's purpose is to stress in both scene and simile the contrast between the abrupt springing into action of the contestants and the continuity of the action that follows. There is the sudden trumpet-peal (*dedit sonitum*), the sudden surge forward from the·starting-line (*prosiluere*); then the protracted uproar (*ferit clamor*), the continuous disturbance in the water (*spumant, infindunt, dehiscit*). Likewise the charioteers hurl themselves on the track from the starting pens (*corripuere*), then race on along the track (*ruunt*); there is the sudden slap of the reins on the horses' backs to get them under way (*concussere*), and then the continuous urging on (*in uerbera pendent*).[33]

The instantaneous perfect produces a momentary marked change in the narrative tempo. It seems probable it was the effectiveness of this device that led Virgil to experiment with the use of the perfect on a more sustained scale —not for the single isolated action, but for a whole section of the narrative where he wished to vary the tempo. The section in perfects no longer necessarily relates actions more abrupt than those surrounding them. The narrative simply acquires a greater rapidity of movement, the object of which may be to increase excitement or to produce the opposite effect: a break in the excitement while details of minor importance are run through quickly.

For example, in the narrative of the first encounter between Aeneas and Mezentius (*Aeneid* X. 762–802) the main line of narrative runs again in historic presents. But at 783–86 we have three perfects, relating how Aeneas' spear pierced Mezentius' shield and inflicted a minor wound. The three perfects do not describe things that happen with especial speed. Indeed the action in both the preceding sentence and that following is more quick-moving. The effect of the perfects is rather to create a parenthesis on a different emotional level. The narrator's voice drops, as it were, for a moment from a level of excited description to tell us quickly and tersely the effects of the blow, and then the tone of excited description is resumed.

The device enables Virgil to break up a long narrative section into blocks. The change of tense represents the kind of change in tempo and emotional level that an experienced reader makes in reading sustained narrative, in order to avoid monotony. We have a good simple example in the description of the Troy game in Sicily (V. 553–602). After twenty-four lines of precise description in the historic present of the opening march-past, ending with the round of applause with which the riders are greeted, comes a short block of six lines containing six perfects. This section, at a quicker tempo and a more restrained emotional level, briefly recounts the complicated manœuvres with which the performance begins—a respite in the excitement before the description of the actual battle-game, for which the historic present is resumed.

The imperfect indicative may also be used to vary the tempo of the narrative. It can, for example, mark the change from detailed narrative, where much is related as happening within a short space of time, to more slow-moving narrative. A good example is the story of the settlement Aeneas and his men established in Crete and the pestilence which eventually forced them to leave (III. 132–46). The opening lines are full of action, the *preparations* for construction. The tenses are historic presents. A change comes at line 137. The *process* of construction is about to get under way. This is marked by a single imperfect. Then abruptly the work is suspended by the sudden outbreak of a mysterious disease (instantaneous perfect):

> subito cum tabida membris 137
> corrupto caeli tractu miserandaque uenit
> arboribusque satisque lues et letifer annus.

> *Suddenly to waste our limbs*
> *from a corrupt quarter of the sky there came to trees*
> *and crops a hideous disease and a year of death.*

Then come three lines describing the months of pestilence (*letifer annus*): the narrative occupies only three lines, but the tempo is retarded by four imperfects and an historic infinitive. After that the tempo quickens again: the decision is taken that something must be done. A single historic present (*hortatur pater*) cuts this section off from what precedes. The change of tense makes it clear, without further comment, that what Virgil means is not that Anchises "kept on urging" Aeneas to act, but that he "finally urged" him to act. With it thus established that a single occasion is meant, the imperfect *nox erat,* "it was night," which begins the next sentence (line 147) is also defined without need of further explanation: it is the night after Anchises advised Aeneas to do something to stop the pestilence that the Penates appeared to Aeneas in his sleep. Often, as here, the change in tempo produced by the change in tense fixes the meaning as much as any inherent force of the tense itself.

The other main use of the imperfect is to set the background to action. The contrast here may be between imperfect and perfect, or between imperfect and historic present. Virgil often uses these narrative resources with great delicacy within the space of a few lines, sometimes within a single sentence. Here are the opening lines of *Aeneid* V:

> Interea medium Aeneas iam classe tenebat
> certus iter fluctusque atros Aquilone secabat
> moenia respiciens, quae iam infelicis Elissae
> conlucent flammis. quae tantum accenderit ignem
> causa latet; duri magno sed amore dolores 5
> polluto, notumque furens quid femina possit,
> triste per augurium Teucrorum pectora ducunt.
> ut pelagus tenuere rates nec iam amplius ulla
> occurrit tellus, maria undique et undique caelum,
> olli caeruleus supra caput astitit imber 10
> noctem hiememque ferens et inhorruit unda tenebris.

> *Meanwhile Aeneas was holding his fleet, now well under way,*
> *upon its course, resolutely biting into waves blackened by the northerly,*
> *gazing back at walls on which the fire unhappy Dido lit*

sheds flickering flames. What caused so great a conflagration
remains obscure; but, aware how harsh the grief when great
love is poisoned, and what a frenzied woman may essay,
the Trojans feel foreboding of disaster pervade their hearts.
When the ships reached the open sea and land no more coursed up
at their approach—everywhere the ocean, everywhere the sky—
a sombre blue squall took up position just above his head,
bringing night and storm, and the water shuddered at the dark.

The book begins quietly: an evening scene viewed from a distance. A fleet in movement (imperfects *tenebat, secabat*). In line 3 the present participle *respiciens* picks out the figure of Aeneas whose presence as commander we no more than sensed in the first two lines (*tenebat* and *secabat* imply no particular action on his part). The historic present *conlucent* in line 4 almost startles us. We have that feeling which we get in a film when the camera, after steadily tracking closer to a scene, suddenly is close enough for us to feel we are not viewing the scene from a distance, but are present in it. The second sentence of the book (two historic presents) studies Aeneas and his men and their feelings as though from close up. Then the third sentence switches to perfects and fast-moving narrative:[34] they reach the open sea, the remainder of the day passes, and with evening comes storm.

NOTES

1. See C. M. Bowra, *From Virgil to Milton* (London, 1945), p.3–5.
2. On the length of various epic poems, see J. W. Mackail, *The Aeneid* (London, 1930), p.*xxxviii–xxxix*.
3. Though he does not strain after this effect as hard as Catullus does in Poem 64. Occasionally there are only four words in a Virgilian hexameter. The most striking of these is *Aeneid* II. 549, a line that conveys the splendid bravura with which the arrogant young Neoptolemus taunts old Priam (who has reproached him for letting down his father):

"degeneremque Neoptolemum narrare memento!"

4. See Kenneth Quinn, "Syntactical ambiguity in Horace and Virgil," *Aumla* 14:36–46 (1960). Since writing this article I find my arguments are lent considerable detailed support by R. S. Conway's commentary on *Aeneid* I (*P. Vergili Maronis Aeneidos liber primus* [Cambridge, Eng., 1935]), *passim*. E.g., his comment on I. 75:

to ask which of two possible constructions must be chosen for any one word is often like enquiring whether a particular figure in a picture is to be regarded as belonging to the left- or the right-hand side.

5. Even here the past participle *infixum* introduces a second verbal idea, binding the words tightly together and introducing a daring and effective ambiguity. Taking the words at their surface meaning *infixum uulnus* is the wound "inflicted" by the sword Dido has just plunged into her breast. But behind the surface meaning lies the suggestion of a different kind of wound: the wound of passion, described in the opening lines of the book, and brought back to the reader's memory now by the echo here of Virgil's words in line 67: *tacitum uiuit sub pectore uulnus*. To this new meaning of *uulnus* a new meaning of *infixum* ("deep-seated") is appropriate. (Nor should we overlook the symbolism of the sword. The psychical wound was inflicted by Aeneas, the physical wound by his sword.) For *stridit*, see Mackail, p.162 (approved by Austin, [*CQ* 11:185–198 (1961),] p.198:

stridit (a word over which commentators have bungled strangely) accurately expresses the whistling sound with which breath escapes from a pierced lung.

But with the breath escapes, of course, life itself, and with life the metaphorical wound that had "been living deep-seated" within her.

6. E.g., IV. 589–91:

> terque quaterque manu pectus percussa decorum
> flauentisque abscissa comas "pro Iuppiter! ibit
> hic," ait . . .

> *Three times, four times she struck her fair breast with her hand,*
> *and tore at her golden hair, "In Jove's name! shall*
> *he go," she said . . .*

Three statements in one sentence, but no subordinate clause. On this construction see Quinn, pp.66–67.

7. He uses *cum* freely enough with the imperfect subjunctive. In more dramatic contexts he has a fondness (beyond prose usage) for the inverted-*cum* construction with the indicative.

8. Of 53 examples of temporal *ut* in the *Aeneid*, 18 are of the type *ut uidet,* and 14 more involve equivalents of *uidet.* The usage seems peculiar to Virgil.

9. We should remember, of course, we are reading an unfinished poem. What we are discussing, however, is something different from unintentional slips or oversights.

10. R. D. Williams's suggestion (*Aeneidos liber quintus* [New York and Oxford, 1960]), p.134, that *caestus* is a poetic plural is implausible: (1) It falls too far outside the normal range of poetic plurals (see the discussion in Einar Löfstedt, *Syntactica,* (2d ed., Lund, Sweden, 1942), v. 1, p.35–38; (2) It throws away the hint provided by *duros.* Mackail's explanation, p.188, of the passage undoubtedly builds up the picture Virgil intended.

11. See the commentators on V. 211–12.

12. See the commentators on V. 494.

13. See the commentators on V. 673.

14. L. C. Knights, "How Many Children Had Lady Macbeth?," in *Explorations* (London, 1946), p.1–39.

15. While he naturally avoids making things too specific, Virgil does imply a distinction between (1) the physical images of the gods which can be carried from place to place; (2) the divinities themselves with whom contact is made and whose protection is secured by the worship of the physical images. E.g., in III. 148–55 the Penates appear to Aeneas in a dream in Crete. What he sees are the physical objects,

> effigies sacrae diuum Phrygiique penates,
> quos mecum ab Troia mediisque ex ignibus urbis
> extuleram.

But when the Penates address him, their words make it clear the actual divinities are speaking, sent to Aeneas by Apollo: *tua nos en ultro ad limina mittit.* Often there is initial ambiguity and we should not press for its resolution, e.g., III. 11–12, and VIII. 679.

16. The hand of fate has been missed, too, by more than one modern editor without Aeneas' justification that his mind was distraught by the turmoil of disaster. They assume Panthus' own domestic Penates must be meant. Yet Richard Heinze put the matter beyond inadvertence by his admirably clear analysis of Virgil's elliptical narrative, *Virgils Epische Technik* (3d ed., Leipzig and Berlin, 1914), p.35.

> Panthus rettet diese *sacra* von der Burg herab zu Aeneas . . .: so bestätigt sich unverzüglich der Traum. . . . dass [Panthus] die Heiligtümer . . . nicht mit sich genommen, sondern bei Aeneas zurückgelassen hat, brauchte wohl nicht besonders gesagt zu werden. Somit geht dann auf Aeneas die priesterliche Pflicht über. . . .

17. Needless doubts about the authenticity of the Helen episode have been finally dispelled by R. G. Austin, *CQ* 11:185–98 (1961).

18. The verbal echoes make it clear it is Troy's Penates and not Aeneas' domestic Penates (or even Priam's domestic Penates, as some have oddly supposed from II. 514) that are meant. For Roman domestic Penates in historical times, see Cyril Bailey, *Religion in Virgil* (New York, 1935), p.31 ff.; for the city's Penates, ibid., p.91 ff.

19. Mezentius' affection for his horse (858–66) stresses his isolation. Toward his son he recognizes obligation and is humiliated by his failure to discharge it; but his words (846–56) show no affection for Lausus.

20. The murderer Pyrrhus, we learn, met a like fate at the hands of Orestes (III. 332), who

excipit incautum patriasque obtruncat ad aras

—another example of interweaving. Later in the same book (III. 469) his name occurs once more when, as a final act of retribution, his armour is given to Aeneas by Helenus.

21. Deiphobus' marriage to Helen after the death of Paris is un-Homeric, but justified by Homer's reference to the two in *Odyssey* IV. 276 ff.

22. We saw in chapter 5 [*Latin Explorations*] that Tacitus imitates this.

23. The variation between historic present and perfect is seldom noticed by commentators, most often neglected in reference grammars, or at best made the subject of inaccurate generalization. The only systematic attempt to deal with the historic present known to me is that in Raphael Kühner and Carl Stegmann, *Ausführliche Grammatik der lateinischen Sprache, Satzlehre* (3d. ed., Leverkusen, 1955), v. 1, p.111–17: they remark that in verse the historic present is the normal narrative tense and the perfect used mainly for convenience, but add the perceptive observation:

aber es lässt sich auch nicht verkennen, dass die Dichter (besonders Vergil) das Perfekt als ungewöhnliches tempus gern zur Hervorhebung bedeutsamer Momente eintreten lassen.

The examples given, however, do not probe the question at all deeply. Cf. the brief remarks of Edward Norden, *Vergilius, Aeneis VI* (2d. ed., Leipzig, 1915), p.113 on 3 ff.

24. See Williams, p.166.

25. A count of the narrative tenses in Book V gives 308 presents to 108 perfects; in Book II there are 243 presents to 82 perfects. The figures are necessarily rather arbitrary. Forms which, out of context, could be either present or perfect (*soluit*, etc.) can usually be assigned the tense of other verbs in the immediate context. A breakdown of the three past tenses in the narrative section of Book II, arranged according to the three sections of the book, looks like this:

		Present:	Perfect:	Imperfect:
Section I	(to 267)	76	11	5
Section II	(to 633)	122	44	13
Section III	(to 804)	45	27	19
		243	82	37

26. See Jean Humbert, *Syntaxe grecque* (2d. ed., Paris, 1954), p.137–38.

27. Catullus makes much freer use of imperfects and of reported action: e.g., the section preceding Ariadne's speech, 124–31, is all infinitives and participles.

28. Except for one section, the bridge passage between the first wedding-day scene and a description of the picture of Ariadne on the beach (31–67). These 37 lines contain 29 historic presents, 2 perfects and a concluding imperfect.

29. The infinitives of 124–31: perfect, present, present, perfect.

30. Another example probably is to be found in V. 680–82:

sed non idcirco flammae atque incendia uiris
indomitas *posuere;* udo sub robore *uiuit*
stuppa uomens tardum fumum, etc.

31. In II. 1–2,

Conticuere omnes intentique ora tenebant.
inde toro pater Aeneas sic orsus ab alto,

conticuere, followed by *tenebant* (imperfect) and *orsus* (= perfect), is *instantaneous:* "all fell silent," i.e. there was a sudden hush as Aeneas began to speak. Both here and in

II. 252 (just quoted) the preverb *con*-denotes the *action* of falling silent (as opposed to the *state* of silence, denoted by the simple verb *tacere*) ; in II, 252 the force of the perfect is what grammarians sometimes call *resultative* (silence reached), here *ingressive* (silence beginning).

32. Some see in these instantaneous perfects the influence of the Greek instantaneous aorist. They can equally well be regarded as true perfects—just as in English in an animated commentary on a race, say, ("they're coming fast up the straight," etc.) the commentator may lapse into a perfect tense to describe something sudden or unexpected ("X has fallen").

33. The use of the perfect tense in the simile seems strange to us in English, because the chariot-race is not, like the boat-race, a past event. It depends, perhaps, on the *gnomic* use of the perfect in such cases, though its force here is clearly instantaneous.

34. Reckoning *occurrit* as perfect.

Erich Auerbach

DANTE'S ADDRESSES
TO THE READER

There are some twenty passages in the *Commedia*[1] where Dante, interrupting the narrative, addresses his reader: urging him either to share in the poet's experiences and feelings, or to give credence to some miraculous occurrence, or to understand some peculiarity of content or style, or to intensify his attention in order to get the true meaning, or even to discontinue his reading if he is not duly prepared to follow. Most of the passages concerned are highly dramatic, expressing, toward the reader, at the same time the intimacy of a brother and the superiority of a teaching prophet. Professor Hermann Gmelin, who has listed and discussed them in a recently published paper,[2] is certainly right in saying that the addresses to the reader are one of Dante's most significant style patterns, and that they show a new relationship between reader and poet.

Indeed, it is difficult to find anything similar in earlier European literature. Formal address to the reader was never used in classical epic poetry, such as Vergil's or Lucan's. Elsewhere, it was not unknown, but almost never reached the level of dignity and intensity present in Dante. Ovid addresses his reader fairly often, mostly in the *Tristia*,[3] apologizing, asking for pity, or thanking the reader for his favor which promises the poet eternal glory. These addresses are still more frequent in Martial's *Epigrams;*[4] Martial creates an atmosphere of witty and polite intimacy between the public and himself. There are, indeed, a few passages on his literary fame which have an accent of earnestness and solemnity;[5] but everywhere he considers the reader as his patron, and his attitude is that of a man whose main object is to win the reader's favor. There are some casual addresses in Apuleius' *Metamorphoses*[6] and in Phaedrus;[7] that is all, as far as I know. One may perhaps add certain funeral inscriptions such as the famous epitaph of a housewife: "hospes quod deico, paullum est, asta et pellege. . . ."[8] All these examples have little in common with Dante's style.

In the Middle Ages, addresses to the reader, or to the listener, were rather frequent in poetry, both Latin and vernacular. But there, too, the form was mostly used somewhat casually and without much emphasis: asking for attention, announcing the content, apologizing for deficiencies, sometimes moralizing or asking the reader to pray for the writer. Examples from medieval Latin poetry can easily be found in the anthologies or in Raby's *History of Secular Latin Poetry in the Middle Ages.*[9] As for vernacular poetry, Gmelin has quoted (p. 130–31) some introductory passages from Chrétien de Troyes' *Cligès* and *Ivain,* and from the *Chanson d'Aspremont* ("Plaist vos oïr bone cançun vallant . . ."). Such addresses are very frequent in the Chansons de geste,[10] as they are in ancient Germanic poetry. One may add the beginning of the *Passion* of Clermont-Ferrand, or of *Aucassin et Nicolette.* In this latter poem, there is also the recurrent formula *si com vos avés oï et entendu.* Observe, finally, that the first chronicler in vernacular prose, Villehardouin, constantly addresses his narrative to the reader, using phrases such as: *Or oiez . . .* or *Lor veïssiez. . . .* Most of these forms are not very emphatic; they help give to Villehardouin's prose that air of solemn story-telling which is one of its charms. The tradition continued with many later chroniclers in the vernacular; it may have some importance for our problem, since Villehardouin was, like Dante, a man who tells the story of a journey to those who have remained at home.[11]

There appears in the Middle Ages another type of address to the reader, less casual and more urgent: the religious appeal. It is, obviously, nearer to Dante's style than anything we have hitherto encountered. For if Dante's sublimity is Vergilian, his urgency is Augustinian.[12] Most of the medieval examples are not addressed to the reader as such, but to mankind in general, or to the hearers of a sermon. They are very numerous; typical specimens are Bernard of Morlaix's *De contemptu mundi* or Alexander Neckham's *De vita monachorum.* Similar forms occur also in the vernaculars. One may recall the beginning of Marcabru's crusade-song, basically nothing but the usual call for attention; however, the subject confers upon it much greater intensity:

> Pax in nomine Domini!
> Fetz Marcabrus lo vers e'l so.
> Auiatz que di!

Before ending this rapid inventory, let me say a few words regarding ancient and medieval theories of rhetoric. The theorists have never described or listed the address to the reader as a special figure of speech. That is quite understandable. Since the ancient orator always addresses a definite public—either a political body or the judges in a trial—the problem arises only in certain special cases, if with an extraordinary rhetorical movement, he should address someone else, *a persona iudicis auersus,* as Quintilian says. He may, in such a moment, call on somebody who is present, e.g., on his opponent, as did Demosthenes with Aeschines, or Cicero with Catiline—or on someone absent, e.g., the gods, or any person, living or dead—or even an object, an allegorical personification—anything suitable to create an emotional effect. This rhetorical figure is called apostrophe,[13] and it very often has the character of a solemn and dramatic invocation,[14] which interrupts a comparatively calmer exposition of the facts. The classical apostrophe no doubt exercised a deep influence on Dante's style; it was in his mind and in his ears. But it is not identical with the address to the reader; this address constitutes a special and independent development of the apostrophe.

Nor did the medieval theorists mention the address to the reader as a special figure of speech, for they did nothing but imitate or adapt their precursors in Antiquity to their needs and to their horizon. They do describe the apostrophe; one of the most important, Geoffroi de Vinsauf, devoted some two hundred verses to such a description.[15] He considers the apostrophe as a means of amplification and uses it for moral purposes: his examples are meant to serve as an admonition against pride and insolence, as an encouragement in adversity, as a caution against the instability of fortune, etc. They are highly, indeed pedantically, rhetorical; the purpose of "amplification" is unpleasantly evident throughout. But they are put in the second person, and thus directly addressed to the persons or groups or countries which are supposed to invite criticism or admonition (Geoffroi uses the word *castigare*). In this respect they closely resemble "addresses to the reader."

Dante's address to the reader is a new creation, although some of its features appear in earlier texts. For its level of style, i.e., its dignity and intensity, it is nearest to the apostrophe of the ancients—which, however, was seldom addressed to the reader. The compositional schema of Dante's addresses recalls the classical apostrophe, especially the apostrophe of prayer and invocation ("Musa, mihi causas memora . . ."). In both cases the basic elements are a vocative and an imperative (*Ricorditi, lettor,* or *Aguzza qui, lettor*). Both may be paraphrased and, in some instances, replaced by other forms. The most frequent paraphrase of the vocative is the solemn invocation known from classical poetry: *O voi che . . .* , or its humbler variant, the simple relative clause: (*Immagini*) *chi bene intender cupe* (much as in the Old French introductions *Qui vorroit bons vers oïr*). The vocative is an essential element of the address to the reader as well as of the apostrophe in general; the imperative is not essential. The ancient invocational apostrophe can be complete without any verbal addition (μὰ τοὺς Μαραθῶνι προκινδυνεύσαντας . . .). The address to the reader may be introduced into any discourse or statement whatsoever. There are passages in Dante where the imperative is paraphrased by a rhetorical question or by some other expression of the poet's intention, as in the following verses from the *Vita Nuova:*

> Donne ch'avete intelletto d'amore,
> i' vo' con voi de la mia donna dire, . . .

Others are even without any imperative intention at all (*Inf.* XXV. 46: "Se tu se' or, lettore, a creder lento"; *Purg.* XXXIII. 136: "S'io avessi, lettor, più lungo spazio . . ."; *Par.* XXII. 106 ff.: "S'io torni mai, lettor . . ."). But these passages too possess the specific intensity of Dante's addresses.

There are two passages in the *Commedia* where Dante uses the noblest and most suggestive pattern, the *O voi che* form with the imperative: one in *Inf.* IX: "O voi ch'avete li intelletti sani," and the other in *Par.* II: "O voi che siete in piccioletta barca . . . / Voi altri pochi che drizzaste il collo. . . ." It is definitely a classical pattern; Dante knew many passages (apostrophes, not addresses to the reader) from classical Latin poets which may have inspired him. There are frequent examples in earlier medieval Latin poetry also (see fn. 9), but Dante's Italian verses have much more of the antique flavor and of what was then called "the sublime" than any medieval Latin passage I happen to know. Dante had used this form long before he wrote the *Commedia*, at the time of his youthful Florentine poetry. The earliest example seems to be the second sonnet of the *Vita Nuova* (7). It is not addressed to the reader (no readers are mentioned in the *Vita Nuova;* the corresponding addresses in this work are either the *Donne amorose* or, more generally, the *fedeli d'amore*, and, on one occasion, the pilgrims who pass through the city of Florence). This second sonnet begins as follows:

> *O voi che per la via d'Amor passate,*
> *attendete e guardate*
> *s' elli è dolore alcun, quanto 'l mio, grave.*

This is, obviously, not a classical inspiration, but a paraphrase, or even a translation, of a passage from the *Lamentations of Jeremiah* (1: 12): "O vos omnes qui transitis per viam, attendite et videte, si est dolor sicut dolor meus." Indeed, Dante has in some way diverted its meaning from the prophet's original intention; he does not address everyone who happens to pass, but only those who pass by the rather esoteric way of love: the *fedeli d'amore*. But a little later, in the final chapters after the death of Beatrice (29 and ff.), when he again quotes the *Lamentations* ("Quomodo sedet sola civitas. . . ."), the development leads to a new address and apostrophe, this time directed to a much larger group of persons: "Deh peregrini che pensosi andate . . ." (Sonnet 24, chap. xli). And after many years, or even decades, he again several times chose to quote the motives of the first chapter of the *Lamentations:* in the apostrophe to Italy, *Purg.* VI. 78 ff. ("non donna di provincie, ma bordello"), and in the Latin *Epistola VIII* written in 1314 to the Italian cardinals. In the meantime, his horizon had widened; he had long since ceased to address his verses to an esoteric minority. The range of his ideas now comprehended the whole world, physical, moral, and political; and he addressed himself to all Christians. The "lettore" in the *Commedia* is every Christian who happens to read his poem, just as the passage in the *Lamentations* was addressed to everyone who happened to pass through the streets of Jerusalem. Dante had reached a point where he conceived his own function much more as that of a *vas d'elezione*, a chosen vessel, than as that of a writer soliciting the favor of a literary public. Indeed, from the very beginning, he never had the attitude of such a writer. Although he expects glory and immortality, he does not strive for it by trying consciously to please the reader; he is too sure of his poetic power, too full of the revelations embodied in his message. Already in the *Vita Nuova*, his charm is a kind of magic coercion; even though much of this work is an expression of grief and lamentation, his voice very often sounds no less commanding than imploring; calling up those who have *intelletto d'amore*, and ordering them into the magic circle of his verses (recall also the Casella episode in *Purg.* I).

But only in the *Commedia* does the accent of authoritative leadership and urgency reach its full strength—and it is there linked to the expression of brotherly solidarity with the reader. The *Fauete linguis* of Horace, the "musarum sacerdos" (*Carm.* I. 3), may be comparable to Dante's addresses for its authoritative sublimity—still, it remains quite different. It lacks Dante's actual urgency; Dante is much nearer to the reader; his appeal is that of a brother urging his fellow brother, the reader, to use his own spontaneous effort in order to share the poet's experience and to *prender frutto* of the poet's teaching. "O voi ch'avete li intelletti sani, / mirate. . . ." It is as sublime as any ancient apostrophe, but has a distinctly more active function: incisive, straightforward, upon occasion almost violent, yet inspired by charity; a mobilization of the reader's forces. To be sure, the imperative echoes Vergilian apostrophes, but these were not addressed to the reader; Vergil did not, as Dante does, interrupt an extremely tense situation by an adjuration, the content of which, in spite of its urgency, is an act of teaching. Inciting emotions and teaching were separated in ancient theory and very seldom combined in practice.[16] Dante's *mirate* presupposes the Christian *uigilate;* it presupposes a doctrine centered around the memory and the expectation of events. It occurs at a moment of present danger, immediately before the intervention of Grace—just as another passage, comparable in many respects, though lacking the figure *O vos qui:* "Aguzza qui, lettor, ben li occhi al vero" (*Purg.* VIII).[17]

Other addresses to the reader are less dramatic, but almost all contain an appeal to his own activity. Very often, the imperative is *pensa* ("pensa per te stesso"; "pensa oramai per te, s'hai fior d'ingegno");[18] in other passages it is *ricorditi, leggi, immagini chi bene intender cupe, per te ti ciba,* and so on. The pedagogical urgency is sometimes very strong, as in one passage just mentioned (*Inf.* XX. 19 ff.):

> Reader, so God grant thee to take profit of thy reading, now think for thyself. . . .

or in the following encouragement to the reader confronted by an example of very severe and deterrent punishment in the *Purgatorio* (X. 106 ff.):

> I would not, reader, that thou be scared from a good purpose through hearing how God wills that the debt be paid.
> Heed not the form of the pain; think what followeth, think that at worst beyond the great judgment it cannot go.

The most telling example of the pedagogical attitude is probably the passage on the movement of the celestial spheres, *Par.* X. 7 ff.:

> Then, reader, raise with me thy sight to the exalted wheels, . . .[19]

with its continuation:

> Now stay thee, reader, on thy bench, back thinking on this foretaste, wouldst thou have good joyance ere that thou be weary.
> I have set before thee; now feed thou thyself. . . .

There is, of course, a great variety of style in the addresses. They include the levels of horrible sublimity, of gloomy humor ("O tu che leggi, udirai nuovo ludo," *Inf.* XXII. 118), of invocation (*Inf.* XVI. 127 ff.; *Par.* XXII. 106 ff.), of friendly advice, and many other intonations. Note one passage, among the most charming, possibly involving a shade of playful humor (though I have my doubts; friendly irony is a very infrequent phenomenon in Dante). It occurs in *Par.* V, 100 ff., when in the heaven of Mercury the souls gather around Beatrice and Dante, just as fishes in a quiet and limpid pond gather around something which may be food—exclaiming: "Here is someone who will increase our fervor." At this juncture Dante interrupts:

> Think, reader, if what I now begin proceeded not, how thou would'st feel an anguished dearth of knowing more, and by thyself thou shall perceive . . .

Obviously, the originality of Dante's addresses to the reader is a symptom of a new relationship between both, one which is based on Dante's conception of his own role and function as a poet. With the utmost explicitness and consistency, he maintains the attitude of a man who, by special grace, after Aeneas and Paul, has been admitted to see the other world, and has been entrusted with a mission as important as theirs: to reveal to mankind God's eternal order and, accordingly, to teach his fellow men what is wrong in the structure of human life at this special moment of history. The imperial power, ordained to unite and to govern human society, is despised and almost destroyed; the papacy has forgotten its spiritual function; by transgressing its boundaries, by pursuing worldly ambitions and world avarice, it has ruined itself and has corrupted the entire human family. Dante goes so far as to describe this disorder as a second fall of man. True, such ideas were not unheard of: similar motifs had occurred at least since the time of the Investiture conflict.[20] Yet a great poem in the vernacular with such a content and such an attitude of the writer was entirely new. It implied, indeed, it necessitated a kind of relation to the reader similar to a prophet's to his hearers: authoritative, urgent, and, at the same time, inspired by Christian charity; trying, at every moment, to keep his hold upon the reader, and to let him share, as concretely and intensely as possible, in the whole experience reported in the poem. The form of the addresses, indeed, is often similar to that of classical apostrophes; but whenever Dante adapted such a classical form in addressing his reader, he would Christianize it.

Yet there is a limit to Dante's attempt to carry the reader along with him on the journey: the reader of the poem never becomes an actual companion of the journey. Dante alone, among the living, has been in Hell, in Purgatory, and in Heaven. One passage, an address to the reader, may seem to cast doubt on this claim. It is the most sublime of all, the beginning of *Par.* II. 1–15: "O voi che siete in piccioletta barca. . . ." It is extremely tempting to interpret this apostrophe as addressed not to readers of a book, but to actual followers on a journey. If one isolates these fifteen verses from the remainder of the poem, such an interpretation would not be difficult. It would imply the explanation of *qui* (vs. 11–12: ". . . al pan de li angeli, del quale / vivesi qui ma non sen vien satollo") not as "here on earth," but as "here in heaven." That makes sense since many authoritative texts, from Augustine to Peter Damiani and Richard of St. Victor,[21] describe the beatitude of the blessed as an *insatiabilis satietas*, where the celestial manna is given *ad plenitudinem, sed numquam ad satietatem.* One could even go on to demonstrate that only in

Heaven one lives really on the bread of Divine Wisdom which is *per se uiuifi-catiuus*. . . .²² Yet all this would be misleading. The traditional explanation of *qui* as "here on earth" is correct; Dante's readers are summoned to interrupt (or to continue) the reading of a book, not a journey through Heaven. For it is not even certain whether, at the moment of this address, Beatrice and Dante have already entered Heaven. Furthermore, Dante, as the narrator, invariably uses *qui* for "here on earth."²³ Finally, just a short time ago (in Canto I. 4 ff.) he has said that he has been in Heaven ("nel ciel . . . fu io") and is now going to report his experiences:

> Whatever of the holy realm I had the power to treasure in my memory, shall now be matter of my song.

At this point, as always, he remains the man who has returned from the other world and records what he has seen, so that others may read it.

Dante was the writer of a book, and the *vas d'elezione* of a revelation which he had to report in that book. Hence, the book had to combine didactics and poetic fascination; a forceful charming of the soul which particularly suited his revelation, since this was shaped as a sequence of events, as a journey through the other world, highly emotional in all its parts, and linked at every moment to the most urgent problems of contemporary life. The *Commedia* is a special development of the tradition of the Gospels, which also were a revelation of a doctrine centered around an historical event. As the announcer of a revelation, the poet surpasses his readers: he knows something of the highest importance which they have to learn from him. In spite of the charity that he exercises toward his fellow men, by imparting his knowledge, and of the fact that, as a human being, he is their equal before God, Divine Grace, by electing him for this special revelation, has raised him above all other mortals. The reader is not his equal. He may well repudiate Dante's message, accuse him as a liar, a false prophet, an emissary of Hell, yet he cannot argue with him on a level of equality, he must "take it or leave it." These last sentences, of course, are exaggerated; the contemporary reader already knew that all this: mission, journey, and actual revelation in Purgatory and Heaven, was poetical fiction. But a fiction so fused with reality that one easily forgets where its realm begins; and Dante's narrative is so dense, so invariably consistent in its linking of true events that some of its realistic suggestion survives, at least temporarily, in many minds. At any rate, his relation to the reader, as expressed in the addresses, is inspired by this "poetic fiction": Dante addresses the reader as if everything that he has to report were not only factual truth, but truth containing Divine Revelation. The reader, as envisioned by Dante (and in point of fact, Dante creates his reader), is a disciple. He is not expected to discuss or to judge, but to follow; using his own forces, but the way Dante orders him to do.

I know of, at least, one classical apostrophe, linked with an address to the hearer, which seems comparable to Dante's loftiest addresses as regards its sublimity and its urgency. It is due to a man who is himself comparable to Dante—both had the same psychagogical power, the same partiality, the same vindictiveness and cruelty toward their enemies; also, both experienced an utter failure of all their political aspirations. I am thinking of Demosthenes.

In 330 B.C., when Philip of Macedon was dead and his son Alexander far advanced in the conquest of Persia, Demosthenes had to defend his policy of resisting Philip's power in the past. At the time when he made his famous speech on the Crown, everyone, including himself, knew that the policy of resistance had failed. The battle of Chaironeia (338) had decided against Greek independence and against the course of Demosthenes. In a certain passage of the speech (199 ff.), he raised the question whether a policy worthy of the Athenian tradition of defending Greek independence should be condemned because fate had denied it victory. His answer was, no.

> Even had we been able, he says, to foresee what was to happen, we should have acted as we did. You followed my advice at that time. That is your glory as it is mine. If you now condemn this policy, as my opponent [Aeschines] requires you to do, that would rob you of the enduring praises of posterity; you would appear not as men who suffer the blows of insensible fate, but as men who have done wrongly.[24] But it cannot be, no, men of Athens, it cannot be that you have acted wrong, in encountering danger bravely, for the liberty and the safety of all Greece. No! by those generous souls of ancient times who were exposed at Marathon, by those who stood arrayed at Plataeae, by those who encountered the Persian fleet at Salamis, who fought at Artemisium; by all the brave men whose remains lie deposited in the public monuments. All of whom received the same honorable interment from their country, Aeschines: not those only who prevailed, not those alone who were victorious. And with reason. What was the part of gallant men they all performed; their success was such as the deity dispensed to each.

This apostrophe of §208: μὰ τοὺς Μαραθῶνι προκινδυνεύσαντας was the most famous passage of oratory in Graeco-Roman history. In modern times, as long as Greek was an essential part of higher education, many generations of students read and admired it. Read after more than twenty-two centuries, in a private study (not, as it once was, delivered in a stormy political assembly by an incomparable master of rhetoric), it still has the power to make the reader's heart beat faster. It represents the most magnanimous, and also the most violent, attempt to win the support of the audience which classical literature has bequeathed to us. Still, there can be no doubt that Demosthenes is arguing a cause, and that he awaits the decision of his hearers. He is not supported by the infallible judgment of the Divinity. On the contrary, this lack of an unerring ally becomes his strongest argument. He argues against the Divinity. For his divinity, Fate, decides only what happens; it cannot decide what is right or wrong. This decision belongs to the men of Athens, to their conscience, guided by the traditions of their city. Demosthenes, a man of Athens, appeals to the judgment of his equals, the citizens of a community proud of having been, since the days of Marathon, the champion and protector of Greek independence. He does not know the future; the object of his interpretation is the past; and his opponent, Aeschines, has the same right as he to submit another interpretation of that past to the decision of their fellow citizens.

Dante's position is quite different. The Christian God is not only the ruler who governs the universe, he is also the sole source and the sole arbiter of justice. Therefore, whoever advocates a cause on earth, has to present it as the will of God. Now, God has disclosed his will; his revelation, linked through the Incarnation to human history, involves a providential plan of this history. But the revelation—the Holy Scriptures as well as earthly events taken as expressions of Divine Providence—may be interpreted in many different ways, especially if practical issues are at stake. The ambiguity of God's revelation creates an uncertainty even greater than that facing Demosthenes and his contemporaries. Their criterion (i.e., their conscience as citizens of a "polis") has lost its decisive authority; and the new criterion, God's will, is inscrutable. Demosthenes' argument, that one must not judge by the event, has not lost its strength. The argument stands, only its basis has changed. God does not reveal his decision on a particular earthly issue by bestowing victory upon the righteous. The victory of the righteous will be manifest only at the last judgement. On earth, evil will always play its part, and will very often prevail, since it has an essential function in the drama of human redemption.

The struggle over political issues (I use the word "political" in its widest sense) had thus become a struggle over the interpretation of the will of God; Dante was not the first to present his interpretation as an authentic one. The appeal to divine authority was the natural and normal way to express strong political convictions in medieval civilization, as it had been at the time of Jewish prophecy. Indeed, very few of Dante's medieval predecessors had gone so far as to claim that a special revelation had been granted them; and never before had this claim been asserted with such an encyclopedic unity of vision and with such a power of poetic expression. Politically, it was a failure. Dante's idea, the re-establishment of the Roman Empire as the providential form of united human and Christian society on earth, was a lost cause long before the *Commedia* became known. The life which the great poem won "tra coloro che questo tempo chiameranno antico" (*Par.* XVII. 110–20) is not due to its political doctrine, but to its poetic power. Yet Dante's poetic power would not have reached its highest perfection, had it not been inspired by a visionary truth transcending the immediate and actual meaning. The Christian revival of the Imperium Romanum is the first conception of political unity on earth, and the Christian interpretation of human life as fall and redemption is at the root of all dialectical understanding of history. Dante, in his vision, combined both. He reached conceptions far beyond the horizon of Demosthenes' Athenian democracy. Thus it may well be legitimate that he spoke to his readers, as he still speaks to us, with the authority and the urgency of a prophet.

NOTES

1. *Inf.* VIII. 94–96; IX. 61–63; XVI. 137–42; XX. 19–24; XXII. 118; XXV. 46–48; XXXIV. 22–27; *Purg.* VIII. 19–22; IX. 70–72; X. 106–11; XVII. 1–19; XIX. 98–103; XXXI. 124–26; XXXIII. 136–39; *Par.* II. 1–18; V. 109–14; X. 7–27; XXII. 106–11. Gmelin adds *Par.* IX. 10–12, and XIII. 1–12.

2. Hermann Gmelin, *Deutsches Dante-Jahrbuch*, 29–30 (Weimar, 1951), p.130–40.

3. E.g., I. 7, 32; I. 11, 35; IV. 1, 2; IV. 10, 131; V. 1, 66.

4. Examples: I. 1; I. 113; II. 1; IV. 55, 27; IX. pr., 5; X. 2; XI. 16; XI. 108.

5. E.g., x. 2.

6. *Metam.* I. 1, 16; x. 2, 12; xi. 23, 19.

7. Lib. II, Prol.; IV. 7, 21. Horace's *fauete linguis* will be mentioned later. The editorial office of the *Thesaurus Linguae Latinae* (W. Ehlers) kindly sent me, at my request, a list of passages where *lector* is used as a vocative. Apart from the passages mentioned above, it includes Avienus (*Orb. terr.* 257 ff.), *Ausonius* (118, 15 [p.421] and 159, 15 [p.29], ed. by Peiper), Rutilius Namatianus (1, 1), several inscriptions and *carmina epigraphica,* and Christian authors, some of whom I quote in n. 11.

8. *Corpus inscriptionem Latinarum* I, 1007 and VI 15346; also in many anthologies, e. g., W. M. Lindsay, *Handbook of Latin Inscriptions* (Boston, 1897), p.79, or Ernst Diehl, *Altlateinische Inschriften* (2d. ed., Bonn, 1911), no. 494.

9. Let me quote a few texts. Nigel Wireker, at the beginning of a collection of his poems (quoted by F. J. E. Raby [Oxford, 1934], v. 2, p.99, cf. J. H. Mozley in *Speculum* 7:398 ff.):

> In quascunque manus peruenerit iste libellus
> dicat, in eterna requiescat pace Nigellus.
> si quid in hoc modico quod te iuuet esse libello
> contigerit, dicas: sit lux eterna Nigello.
> huius quisquis eris conspector forte libelli,
> dic ita: Christe Ihesu, miseri miserere Nigelli.
> factoris memor esto tui: sic parue libelle
> sepius et dicas: uiuas sine fine Nigelle.

Gottfried of Viterbo, *Pantheon* (Raby, v. 2, p.165, cf. *Monumenta Germaniae Historica, Scriptores,* v. 2, p.135:

> O uos qui me legitis, uiri literati,
> super hoc uolumine iudices uocati,
> si non satis fuerint uersus elimati,
> indulgeri competit mee paruitati.

Note a rather amusing example at the end of a poem (early 13th cent.) against sacerdotal celibacy (Raby, v. 2, p.225, cf. Thomas Wright, ed., *The Latin Poems Commonly Attributed to Walter Mapes* [London, 1841], p.171–73):

> ecce iam pro clericis multum allegaui,
> necnon pro presbyteris multa comprobaui:
> paternoster nunc pro me, quoniam peccaui,
> dicat quisque presbyter cum sua suaui.

10. The oldest Italian example I know is the beginning of the *Ritmo Cassinese:* "Eo, siniuri, s'eo fabello, lo bostro audire compello. . . ." (quoted after Ernesto Monaci, *Crestomazia italiana dei primi secoli,* p.17).—For Spain, see Ramón Menéndez Pidal, *La España del Cid* (2d ed., Buenos Aires, 1943), p.422 f. My colleague Stephen Reckert has kindly drawn my attention to the great number of analogous addresses in the poems of Berceo.— See also Werner Hövelmann, *Die Eingangsformel in germanischer Dichtung* (Diss., Bonn, 1936).

11. In the same way, the Arabic story of the journey of Mahomet to the other world (*al Mi'rāŷ*) is addressed to the reader. Cf. *La Escala de Mahoma,* ed. by José Muñoz Sendino (Madrid, 1949), p.265 ff. See also Miguel Asin Palacios, *La escatologia musulmana en la Divina Comedia* (2d ed., Madrid and Granada, 1943), p.37. I am indebted for this information to Da Maria Rosa Lida de Malkiel.

12. For Augustine, cf. his "vide si potes" (*De Trinitate,* VIII, 3; commented upon by me in "Sermo humilis," *Romanische Forschungen* 64:329–31 [1952]). Other patristic addresses to the reader:

Jerome, *In Matth.* 10, 29 (Migne, XXVI, 66); "Prudens lector, caue semper superstitiosam intelligentiam, ut non tuo sensui attemperes Scripturas, sed Scripturis iungas sensum tuum . . ."; Prudentius, *Hamartigenia* 624, with a movement of interruption: "Sanctum lector percense uolumen. . . ." Vercundus, *In Cant. Ionae* 8, 14 (Pitra, *Spicilegium Solesmense,* IV): "Excita, lector, auditum; rimare secreta prudentissimi regis; et ultro reperies quod debes, admirari. . . ."

13. Quintilian, *Inst. orat.* IV, 1, 63; IX, 2, 38, and 3, 24; cf. also the figura called *communicatio, ibid.* IX, 2, 20–22 and the author Περὶ ὕψους, XXVI, on the figure called τῶν προσώπων ἀντιμετάθεσις.

14. Demosthenes: μὰ τοὺς Μαραθῶνι προκινδυνεύσαντας... Cicero; "Quousque tandem, Catalina," or "O leges Porciae legesque Semproniae" (*Verr.* V. LXIII, 163) or Horace: O quae fontibus integris gaudes. . . ." (*Carm.* I, 26).

15. *Poetria nove,* written in the first decades of the 13th century, vv. 264–460; Edmond Faral, *Les Arts poetiques* (Paris, 1921), p.205 ff.

16. One may here remember Lucretius who says *tu* rather frequently, if not to the general reader, at least to C. Memmius.

17. Dante liked the image *acuere oculos;* cf. "aguzzavan le ciglia" (*Inf.* XV. 20). In spite of the meaning of *acies (oculorum)* there are no examples of Dante's image in the *Thesaurus Linguae Latinae.*

18. *Inf.* VIII. 94; XX. 20; XXXIV. 26; *Purg.* X. 110; XXXI. 124; *Par.* V. 109.

19. The movement *Leva* may well be inspired by biblical and liturgical passages, just as *ciba* in the following verses.

20. See e.g., the letter of Anselm of Lucca to Bishop Hermann of Metz, written probably in 1085, in *Briefsammlungen der Zeit Heinriche IV,* ed. by Carl Erdmann and Norbert Fickermann, *Monumenta Germaniae Historica, Die Briefe der deutschen Kaiserzeit* (Weimar, 1950), v. 5, p.50 ff. Cf. Carl Erdmann, *Die Entstehung des Kreuzzugsgedankens* (Stuttgart, 1935), p.224, n. 56.

21. Augustine, *Sermo* 362, 29; Petrus Damiani, *Hymnus de gloria Paradisi,* Migne, CXLV, 862 and in many anthologies; Richard of St. Victor, *De gradibus charitatis,* chap. ii, Migne CXCVI, 1198–1200 (on our subject col. 1200).

22. See Thomas Aquinas, *Commentum in Johannem,* chap. vi, lectio 4. For the meaning of *pan degli angeli* see Bruno Nardi in *Studi Danteschi* 25:131–36 (1940).

23. I owe this observation, and some other useful suggestions, to my colleague Thomas G. Bergin.

24. Up to here, I have given a summary, rather than a translation, of Demosthenes' text. In the next sentences (208), I follow Thomas Leland's translation (*The Orations of Demosthenes* [London, 1802], v. 2, p.349 ff.), with slight changes.

Anne D. Ferry

POINT OF VIEW AND COMMENT

The "World/ Of woe and sorrow" (VIII. 332–33), the world of storms and shadows, of change and loss, of variety and abundance, to which Adam and Eve are banished at the end of the poem, is the world in which the narrator and the reader of *Paradise Lost* now live. The tone of the speaker is controlled by his personal experience of this mortal world and his inspired vision of its contrast with the true pastoral world of Eden before the Fall and of the Paradise to come. The response of the reader to that tone is controlled by his awareness that he can *only* share the narrator's vision by contrasting the world that is lost with the only world he has ever known, the world that is gained by Adam and Eve through the paradox of the fortunate Fall.

The role of the narrator as interpreter to the fallen reader of the unfallen world, the world "invisible to mortal sight," determines the distinctive style of *Paradise Lost*. Truths which, according to Milton's outline in the Cambridge manuscript, were to be bodied forth in the allegorical "shapes" or "mask" of *Adam unparadiz'd*, are expressed in the epic poem by the narrator's elaborately sustained pattern of contrasts between the "invisible" world and our own. The bird's song, the blind bard's vision are of these contrasts and the style created for the narrative voice is designed to express these contrasts. The bird transcends the earth in his circular flight and the blind bard turns inward for heavenly illumination, while the reader remains in the mortal world, which is always the ground from which he looks back at the world which he lost in Adam's Fall. We know that we are continually meant to view the events of the poem from this lower world of chance and change because from the first lines the narrative voice repeatedly reminds us of our experience in this world. The reminders are made explicitly, in direct comments by the narrative voice, and implicitly, in many and varied devices which characterize Milton's style in *Paradise Lost*.

The epic introductions to Books I, III, VII, and IX are essential to the pattern of Milton's epic because . . . they create an identity for the narrative voice, and establish relations between the narrator and his characters and readers. This narrator, pictured as bird and especially as blind bard, is present without exception throughout the poem. Sometimes he directly addresses the Muse, or the characters, or the reader as mankind. Sometimes he narrates, describes, or explains, assuming mankind as his audience without directly identifying us. In other scenes he is himself the immediate audience or witness, endowed by his celestial patroness with a vision of Hell or Heaven or Eden, of events which occurred before the creation of the world and time, or of happenings to come when the world and time shall be no more. Nothing takes place in the poem which is not first spoken, or heard and retold by the narrative voice. Mood and meaning are consequently controlled by his tone, and unless the reader remains aware of the distinctive role of the narrative voice, he is liable to misinterpret mood and meaning from his own position in the fallen world. To keep the narrator in the center of his epic, Milton therefore devised a large number of stylistic devices which give the language of *Paradise Lost* its unique character.

The most simple of these devices is the speaker's practice of explicitly distinguishing his own situation in space and time from the experience of the readers of his poem or its characters.[1] This device is particularly useful in the introduction of a new scene, which is almost inevitably in the poem the entrance into another world. The action of the epic begins in Hell, which existed before the creation of the world, or time, or men, and which in the theology of the poem provided the reason for the creation of that world and of man. The narrative voice must therefore interpret his vision of Hell to us, who know only our own world, and it is essential to Milton's design that we recognize the speaker's role. The description of Hell begins then with a reminder:

> Nine times the Space that measures Day and Night
> To mortal men, he with his horrid crew
> Lay vanquisht, rowling in the fiery Gulfe
> Confounded though immortal . . .   (I. 50–53)

From the opening invocation of the epic, we, its audience, have been prepared to include ourselves among "men." We therefore recognize this elaborate way of phrasing "a long time" or "as long as nine whole days" to be more than a means of giving epic dignity to the style. It is a reminder that we, the readers, have lost the unfallen ways of knowing, that we are condemned to understand only in the dimension of time what the blind bard can conceive by other categories, by "Space" or some nontemporal scheme analogous to the unity of divine vision which encompasses all things simultaneously. Our identification not only as "men" but as "mortal" further reminds us that we are both limited and fallen, corrupted by the "mortal tast" which was the consequence of Satan's Fall. The sign of our mortality is that we must measure all experience by the passing of time, the diurnal course which to us means change and loss. We are meant to remember that the events of the poem have already occurred, to us and to the poet, and that it is because of what happens in the poem, because we and all men were corrupted by the Fall, that we stand in need of a guide to correct our reading of it. The narrative voice is our guide.

When the narrator reminds us of his complex relation to us, he usually at the same time places us in relation to his story and its characters. The description of Satan's host, for example, begins:

> . . . For never since created man,
> Met such imbodied force . . .   (I. 573–74)

Here it is not our "mortal" condition, but our "created" nature which we remember. We are God's creatures, like Satan, and our creation is as much a result of his fall as is our mortality; both are contained by God's will. In the beginning of the catalogue of devils we are told:

> Nor had they yet among the Sons of *Eve*
> Got them new Names . . .   (I. 364–65)

We are the "Sons of *Eve*." We are looking *back* with the speaker on our own history, to the time when we gave the devils the names of false gods, and the narrator is interpreting for us that history before time which as "Sons of *Eve*" we cannot see. We are also looking *forward* to our own history, for to be "Sons of *Eve*" is to be redeemed as well as fallen, and the inspired speaker is reminding us of events which he can foresee and which we will share with him in the fullness of time.

With equal explicitness the narrator distinguishes his situation and therefore his vision from the situation and point of view of his characters. The first description of Hell, which contrasts the narrator's vision with the understanding of "mortal men," also sets him apart from Satan:

> At once as far as Angels kenn he views
> The dismal Situation waste and wilde . . .   (I. 59–60)

"Angels kenn" is by implication more extensive than that of unaided "men," since without help Satan can survey Hell, but more limited than the narrator's, whose Muse is omniscient:

> . . . for Heav'n hides nothing from thy view
> Nor the deep Tract of Hell . . .   (I. 27–28)

Unlike Satan, the speaker knows not only what is past, but what will be "Long after known in *Palestine*" (I. 80), the future outcome of the events in which Satan is involved, by which he is bound. To give one final illustration, the speaker describes the vision of the angels descending to banish man to the fallen world as "A glorious Apparition, had not doubt/ And carnal fear that day dimm'd *Adams* eye" (XI. 211–12). The contrast between the narrator's view and Adam's asserts that the speaker was in some sense present at the scene to see and judge for himself, that his sight and judgment are truer than our fallen vision or Adam's and are therefore the measure of meaning in the epic.

The voice which throughout the poem so often by a phrase distinguishes itself from reader and characters at times speaks out directly, even at length, to comment upon the action, to extend it into the past or future, or to interpret the motives of characters. These passages of "author-comment" have been isolated by critics as if they were detachable—didactic, nondramatic, undemonstrated statements in a work which otherwise convincingly acts out its meanings in the manner of dramatic literature. A further assumption commonly associated with this attitude is that these comments are made personally by Milton, at moments when his private enthusiasms moved him to speak, as in the hymn to wedded love, or at other times when he felt the dramatic life of his poem might of its own accord dim his intention to justify God's ways, or threaten the rightness of his theological propositions.[2] These critical notions involve a number of misconceptions which must be examined if we are to see the way the narrative voice in Milton's epic controls its mood and meaning.

It is, as we have seen, misleading to call the speaker in *Paradise Lost* "Milton." In any narrative the author must find some sort of voice in which to speak; yet this voice, however much it may echo his private manner of talking, can never be equated with his total personality. Wordsworth in *The Prelude* invents a voice which he identifies as himself and he endows that speaker with a biography and attitudes and feelings selected from his own experience; yet if we call that voice "Wordsworth," we must remind ourselves that it is a sustained invention, the poet's conscious artistic creation. To call the narrator of *Paradise Lost* "Milton" is to violate his intention even more drastically. For it is part of Wordsworth's artistry to suggest the qualities of "speech," to deny art, to be "natural" rather than literary. The opening lines of *The Prelude* echo Milton's epic in part in order to point out Wordsworth's avoidance of its "poetical" qualities, its formality, its literary conventions. Milton's intention, on the other hand, is to exploit literary tradition, to intensify formality, to remind the reader continually of the elaborateness of his artistry. His poem is not talk but "song," not autobiography but inspired "vision." His narrator is not "himself" but a bird, or a bard who shares prophetic powers with Moses and Isaiah and Tiresias, who shares blindness with Milton himself, but also with Homer, with Samson, with the man cured by Jesus in the Gospel of John. To be sure, Milton's selection of images to portray the narrative voice must have been influenced by his own experience, and just as surely his private enthusiasms are often expressed by the speaker in the epic. But those images create an objectified voice with a distinct identity, tone, and manner, and the attitudes which the voice expresses are in keeping with that identity.

The other misconceptions involved in much critical discussion of the didactic comments in the epic are that these are the only occasions when we are made aware of a narrator and that his intention is to check the drift of the poem's dramatic life. Yet the speaker who utters the hymn to wedded love, the sermon on riches in Hell, the lecture against hypocrisy, the criticisms of corrupt clergy—these "preachier" passages in the epic—is the same speaker who describes Hell and Eden, who witnesses the council in Heaven, hears the love speeches of Adam and Eve, retells the fables of mortal poets. The direct addresses by this voice are not nervous attempts to correct the dramatic direction of the poem. They are reminders of the speaker's identity, that the reader may never lose his awareness of that distinctive voice in its unique situation. The explicit comments by the narrative voice are part of the total pattern, are essential to the expression of the speaker's vision, which directs the reader's interpretation by controlling the mood and meaning of every scene in the poem.

The description of Satan's entrance into Eden, again our introduction to a new and unknown world, provides a number of illustrations of how our interpretation is controlled by the narrator through direct comments working organically with all the other devices of narration.

We see the earthly Paradise for the first time on the occasion of Satan's entrance into it, but we do not see it as he does. The assertion often repeated by critics that we see Eden through Satan's eyes illustrates again the dangers of ignoring Milton's special narrator. These critics have, I believe, recognized in the tone that the observer of Eden is fallen, but have identified that tone with the character rather than with the speaker, whose presence they tend to discount or forget.[3] We are told what sights confront Satan, but those sights are described for us in the language of the narrator, not the language of the fallen Archangel, so that our interpretation of the scene we are made to imagine is the speaker's. His interpretation depends in part upon his knowledge that Satan did in fact enter the Garden, but he sees it independently of Satan's point of view and describes it so that we will feel what Satan cannot feel. For example, as Satan stands outside the Garden looking up at the trees which encircle and guard its wall, we are told that this wall "to our general Sire gave prospect large/ Into his neather Empire neighbouring round" (IV. 144–45). We are therefore taken into the scene while Satan is still excluded from it. We are included in its physical bounds and in its moral history; Adam is the "general Sire" of reader and narrator but not of Satan. The Garden can therefore never mean to Satan what it means to us because it was never his to lose. Next the speaker places us at a geographical distance from the character and his setting by showing us the outlines of the mountain Satan wishes to climb (IV. 172). This is not the way the hill looks to Satan "Now" trying to ascend it but how it is envisioned by the narrator. Then we are given an account of the undergrowth obstructing Satan's path:

> . . . so thick entwin'd,
> As one continu'd brake, the undergrowth
> Of shrubs and tangling bushes had perplext
> All path of Man and Beast that past that way . . .
> (IV. 174–77)

This is not the baffled report of the character himself, but an explanation in the voice of one who knows the nature of the obstacle and its history, knows that already on other occasions the tangled growths "had perplext" man and animals.

These distinctions in point of view are expressed in part by complicated alternations of tense. To Satan the setting is physically present; the events are happening to him in the present time, or belong to his immediate past or future. To the reader Eden and all the events of the story are long past (our final redemption is not a part of the action of the poem but the subject of a prediction made in the past about our future). The speaker as fallen man shares our previous history, but as a blind bard inspired with supernatural vision, he miraculously experiences the events and places of prehistory in the present and miraculously sees into the future. His manipulations of tenses therefore transcend our experiences of time, logic, grammar. Satan's entrance into Eden begins, "So on he fares" (IV. 131); we watch as he "comes" in the present "Now nearer" (IV. 133) (Milton's equivalent in English for the Latin "historical present"); but then we are told of the obstacle which "deni'd" him access to the Garden (IV. 137), and the description continues in the past tense until the "now purer aire/ Meets his approach" (IV. 153–54). When later in the scene Satan as cormorant descends from his perch in the Tree of Life, his actions are described first in the present tense. He "alights" (IV. 396), but that verb is modified by the previous word "Then." Next we are told as if it were past action how he assumed whatever disguises "servd" his ends (IV. 398), but this action is modified by repetitions of "now." In this first description of Eden and throughout the poem, by such shifts in tense we are introduced as to a scene in a dramatic work without being allowed to forget the voice which interprets to us all the meanings of the scene by its contrast with our own present.

Once we are told that "th' arch-fellon" has lawlessly entered the Garden (and the use of the epithet reminds us again of the epic poet's presence), we are then given two similes which elaborate that action, as the preceding pair of similes had elaborated the sense impressions created by the scene:

> As when a prowling Wolfe,
> Whom hunger drives to seek new haunt for prey,
> Watching where Shepherds pen their Flocks at eeve
> In hurdl'd Cotes amid the field secure,
> Leaps o're fence with ease into thee Fould:
> Or as a Thief bent to unhoord the cash
> Of some rich Burgher, whose substantial dores,
> Cross-barrd and bolted fast, fear no assault,
> In at the window climbes, or o're the tiles;
> So clomb this first grand Thief into Gods Fould . . .
>   (IV. 183–92)

. . . Similes are one of the most important marks of the speaker's style. Here it is enough to recognize their self-consciousness. The speaker seems to be calling attention to his deliberate artistry by using a conventional rhetorical device. The similes do tell us more about Satan, or more accurately, give us ways of feeling for Satan and his victims. He is like a wolf or a thief or a bad priest—dangerous, malevolent, greedy, furtive; man is like an innocent lamb or a guarded but all the more naive and vulnerable citizen. But the extended similes also make us more aware of the narrator. They remind us that he is a poet familiar with the literary conventions of epic and a man familiar with a life infinitely remote from the vision he is presenting. He knows the fallen world of innocence destroyed, of petty viciousness, of corruption even in God's Church. Yet his familiarity with mortal verse and his experience of mortal vice do not destroy his understanding of the archetypal world. He can penetrate Satan's disguise (the ambiguity of "Sat like a Cormorant" in line 196 suggests either that Satan has assumed the form of the bird or that the narrator is describing him by comparing him to a shape more familiar to the reader). He knows what Satan is thinking, knows what Satan does not know (IV. 197–98). Because he can penetrate beyond our perception of surfaces, this speaker can interpret for us the moral meaning of the action:

> So little knows
> Any, but God alone, to value right
> The good before him, but perverts best things
> To worst abuse, or to thir meanest use.
>
> (IV. 201–4)

This is not "Milton" suddenly intervening between Satan's point of view and the reader in order to speak out on his favorite theme, misused freedom. This is the same narrator who has described the hill, the undergrowth, and Satan's actions, who has uncovered his dissembling and told us his hidden schemes. It is the same narrator who will describe to us what "To all delight of human sense" (IV. 206)—his, our own, and Adam's—is exposed but not to Satan's, who "Saw undelighted all delight" (IV. 286). It is the same voice who will predict "Our Death" (IV. 221) in which, with that phrase, he acknowledges and laments his share.

These didactic comments remind us of the narrator's presence and his special vision in order that we may accept his moral interpretation of the story. They are intended to remind us that what we see and feel differs from Satan's experience of the Garden as it will differ from unfallen Adam's. They are not *opposed* to the action of the poem, but are part of the total pattern of that action, not checks upon our immediate responses to drama, but a means of expressing the speaker's double point of view, his fallen knowledge and his inspired vision. To detach the moral comments as the sole expressions of the narrator's attitude is to oversimplify and flatten it, to make the speaker an unauthorized judge who lectures us like a prig just when we are most involved in the story.

NOTES

1. This and similar devices are mentioned but not discussed in detail by Frank Kermode, "Adam Unparadised," in *Living Milton* (London, 1960), p.85–123.
2. See, for example, A. J. Waldock, *Paradise Lost and Its Critics* (Cambridge, Eng., 1947), p.49, 78, 81.
3. See, for example, D. C. Allen, *The Harmonious Vision* (Baltimore, 1954), p.104; William Empson, *Some Versions of Pastoral* (London, 1935), p.189; Kermode, "Adam Unparadised," p.106.

·IV·

THE EPIC HERO

James Redfield

THE MAKING OF
THE *ODYSSEY*

The *epos* is a *techne* and therefore has a technical history, a history of innovation and obsolescence. Here I will discuss the *Odyssey*'s place in that technical history. I think we will read the *Odyssey* best if we understand that it was composed at a special moment in the history of poetry.

I am thus, of course, involved in the Homeric Question. I will avoid that question by answering it, by stating eight dogmatic hypotheses which I will assume in further argument. Any reader who finds these hypotheses offensive may of course stop reading at this point. I do not, however, expect my hypotheses to offend many. Two hundred years of controversy, while inconclusive, have not been fruitless, and no student of the issues will find the following either eccentric or original.

1) Circa 750 B.C. a single man, the so-called "monumental composer of the *Iliad*," composed a poem which was substantially, but not exactly, the *Iliad* we now possess.

2) That *Iliad* was considerably longer and more complex—perhaps by a factor of ten—than any poem that preceded it.

3) The monumental composer of the *Iliad* had been trained in an ancient and living tradition of improvising heroic song.

4) In this tradition song had two kinds of existence. The theme or *oimē* endured in the tradition by transmission from poet to poet. The *oimē*, however, was only, as it were, a song in *potentio*, the outline or idea of a song. The *aoidē*, the rendering of the *oimē* in hexameters, was evanescent, newly created in each performance.

5) The monumental composer of the *Iliad*, in contrast, intended the hexameters he composed to endure as he composed them. The *Iliad* was therefore at the time of its composition a novelty: lasting *aoidē*.

6) Some time after the composition of the *Iliad* another poet, who knew the *Iliad* well, composed the *Odyssey*.

"The Making of the *Odyssey*," by James Redfield. From Leon Botstein and Ellen Karofsky, eds., *Essays in Western Civilization in Honor of Christian W. Mackauer* (Chicago: The College of the University of Chicago, 1967), p.1–17. Reprinted by permission of the author and the College of the University of Chicago. Internal notes have been moved to the end of the essay for this edition.

7) This second poet had also been trained in the tradition of improvised heroic song, but less thoroughly.

8) He also intended an enduring poem, and the *Odyssey* he composed was substantially, but not exactly, the poem we now possess.

Most of these points have been ably defended by G. S. Kirk in his recent book *The Songs of Homer* (Cambridge, 1962); I need not go over the arguments here. Kirk particularly stresses the originality of Homer:

> The monumental poem . . . by the normal canons of heroic song . . . is an aberration. . . . The chief factor in the making of this new literary form was not function or occasion but . . . the special aims, imagination, and reputation of a particular singer; the singer who in fact compounded the first large-scale *Iliad* and who was known as Homer. . . . The crucial factor was the creative imagination, the singer of outstanding brilliance and an exceptionally large Trojan repertoire who suddenly saw that many of its songs could be interlocked to make a complete and universal Trojan song. This was not like the evolution of tragedy, for instance, in which each stage may have seemed a logical development from the last; it was more like the evolution of the monumental Geometric amphora or crater. The evidence of archaeology does not suggest that pots became systematically larger and larger until eventually one was made that was seven feet tall, but rather that there was a leap from a largish pot to a perfectly colossal one, a leap which must have been made for the first time by a particular potter who suddenly had a flash of ambition and the inspiration of sheer size, and at the same time realized that he had the necessary materials and technique.[1]

The poet of the *Iliad* created a work of art on a grand scale; we know that because we possess the poem. We cannot be equally sure that he intended his work to survive, but it seems unlikely that any poet would create a work of art monumental in the one sense if he did not also intend it to be monumental in the other. Indeed we may go further and suppose that a poet with the strength of will to create the *Iliad* intended nothing less than the definitive Trojan poem, perhaps the definitive epic.

Any serious attempt to explain "definitive" would make this an essay on the *Iliad*. The *Iliad* is definitive in structure and in theme: Homer built a unified poem in which, at the same time, he could find place for any heroic story he chose to include. The whole poem is the story of one heroic action, yet for much of the time the hero is not on the scene, yet the poem does not stop being about him. The *Iliad* is a poem of the private, of duels and friendship, and of the public, of politics and war. At the same time it is a poem of the domestic, of parent and child, husband and wife. It is a poem of war which is also a poem of peace; through memory and anticipation, through the shield and especially through the similes the poem reaches out to a wider world; by a trick of artistic inversion the wider world is included in the narrower. The *Iliad* is a complete poem. Many who have lived with it a while think it the greatest work of literature in any European language.

It is hard to imagine the effect of this poem on the first audiences to hear it. They would have found the language natural and the themes familiar; the originality of the conception must have left them the more astonished. Certainly the *Iliad* spoiled their taste for the improvising bards; the *Iliad* must have put out the bards as the full sun puts out a table set with candles. H. T. Wade-Gery put this very well in *The Poet of the Iliad* (Cambridge, 1952):

> Few people are outstandingly creative in (for example) language or morals: most people appear to follow, with varying fidelity and skill, some kind of norm. Protagoras maintained that we learn our notions of right and wrong in the same way we learn the language we speak, from the usage of our fellow men. Societies need both these things, a conventional morality and a language: both are compounded of tradition and a constant creative element; the vitality of both lies in that tension. But the creative element is normally small, and societies are preserved by the not-too-creative norm: few moralists are creative on Socrates' scale, and societies sometimes founder beneath them. The minstrels' tradition, centuries old in Greece, foundered beneath the *Iliad*.[2]

The *Iliad* was the first monumental poem in Greek; the monumental poem, like any grand technical innovation, was the construction of something and the destruction of something. As the *Iliad* became part of the repertoire of singers other than its author, as the poem became famous and captured its audience, the demands of the audience shifted. People stopped asking for "the story of such-and-such" and began asking for "this or that part of the *Iliad*." They stopped asking the bard to compose a poem and began to ask for the poem which had already been composed. So bardic singing stopped being an art of composition and became a performing art; the *aoidos* was transformed into the *rhapsodos,* the spinner of heroic song into the stitcher of bits from Homer.

With this transformation the spring of heroic poetry began to run dry; the creation of the *Iliad* made it harder for others to learn to write epic. Bardic improvisation is a kind of poetry and also a school of poets; the bardic composer as he sings is a teacher of composition. As the young men emulate the old the tradition of composition is kept alive. A. B. Lord has described this process as it occurs in modern Yugoslavia:

> The oral poet has no idea of a fixed model text to serve as his guide. He has models enough, but they are not fixed and he has no idea of memorizing them in a fixed form. Every time he hears a song sung it is different. . .
>
> Over many generations there have been developed many phrases which express in the several rhythmic patterns the ideas most common in the poetry. . . . The young singer must learn enough of these formulas to sing a song. He learns them by repeated use of them in singing, by repeatedly facing the need to express the idea in song and repeatedly satisfying that need, until the resulting formula which he has heard from others becomes a part of his poetic thought. . .
>
> Learning . . . is a process of imitation, both in regard to playing the instrument and to learning the formulas and themes of the tradition. It may truthfully be said that the singer imitates the techniques of composition of his master or masters rather than particular songs. For this reason the singer is not very clear about the details of how he learned his art. . . . He will say that he was interested in the old songs, had a passion for them, listened to singers, and then "work, work, work" and little by little he learned to sing. . .
>
> He has arrived at a definite turning point when he can sit in front of an audience and finish a song to his satisfaction and that of the audience. . . .

Whether his first song is fully developed or not, it is complete in its story from beginning to end and will tend to follow the story as he learned it from his master. If, however, and this is important, he has not learned it from one singer in particular, and if the stories of the song differ in the various versions he has heard, he may make a composite of them. . .

When he has sufficient command of the formula technique to sing any song that he hears, and enough thematic material at hand to lengthen or shorten a song according to his own desires and to create a new song if he sees fit, then he is an accomplished singer and worthy of his art. . .

The singer never stops in the process of accumulating, recombining, and remodeling formulas and themes, thus perfecting his singing and enriching his art. He proceeds in two directions: he moves toward refining what he already knows and toward learning new songs. The latter process has become for him one of learning proper names and of knowing what themes make up the new song. The story is all that he needs; so in this stage he can hear a song once and repeat it immediately afterwards—not word for word of course—but he can tell the same story again in his own words.[3]

As the singer learns the *oimai* and the formulas he is learning his tradition. As he learns to turn an *oimē* into *aoidē* he is learning to be a poet. He learns the joints in his story, how to introduce characters, convey information, shift a scene. He watches his audience and learns what is too long and too short, what is exciting, amusing, moving. He learns how to make a series of events into a story, and how to make a story that means something.

None of these things can be learned by reciting the *Iliad,* any more than one can learn to write a play by acting Lear. The accomplished rhapsodes were no doubt marvellous artists, but they were not poets, and if Plato's Ion is any sample they possessed the stupidity which is often found among, and even recommended for, actors. The performer is not a creator; he responds to another's creation; sometimes it seems that the less he understands what he does the better he does it.

The composition of the *Iliad* therefore initiated the decline of epic poetry; that decline can be traced through the Hymns, the Hesiodic corpus, and the Cycle. The period between Homer and the fifth century is, in fact, an undistinguished one for literature, a period in which the best work was done for a small audience and on a small scale. The next large-scale masterpieces performed before crowds, the works of Aeschylus and Pindar, spring from a new and rather unexpected source: choral lyric. From the middle of the archaic period the epic was a lost art, which could be reconstructed only as a literary artifice.

The *Odyssey* belongs already to the period of decadence, although early in it; we can, I think, see signs of the decline of the *aoidoi* in the decay of the epic language in the *Odyssey*. Kirk describes the difference between the two poems well:

> The language of the *Odyssey* is smoother and flatter than that of the earlier poem. It is more polished, less stark and angular, yet more diffuse and much less lively. . . . The language is in a way less stereotyped, and I conjecture that the proportion of more or less free composition to strictly formular composition

is higher in the *Odyssey* than in the *Iliad*, in certain respects the main poet of the later poem is technically superior to the singer of the monumental *Iliad*. The main trouble with this smoother and less angular language is . . . that it is plethoric, redundant, and over-digested.[4]

The *Odyssey*, long before Samuel Butler, had the name of a woman's poem, and there is something feminine about it; it can charm us to any degree, it can, now and then, stir us to the depths, but it has not those endless resources of power, half used and half concealed, which animate the *Iliad*.

However, since I am here concerned with the technical history of poetry I am not concerned with the relative greatness of the two poems, but with their relative originality. The originality of the *Iliad* is evident. The *Odyssey* looks much less original, if only because it is clearly a sequel. Since Longinus, most readers (Denys Page is an unaccountable exception) have seen that the *Odyssey* presupposes the *Iliad* while the reverse is not the case. The dependence of the *Odyssey* on the *Iliad*, in fact, is the chief proof that the *Odyssey* is the later poem. No story told in the *Iliad* is told again in the *Odyssey;* at the same time the *Odyssey* completes the *Iliad* by bringing to a conclusion the stories of all the major heroes, living and dead. As Longinus says:

> He included in the *Odyssey*, as subordinate incidents taken from the Trojan war, many left-overs from the disasters of the *Iliad;* indeed he goes on to allot the heroes the pity and lamentations which are their right, treating these as matters long known in advance. For the *Odyssey* is nothing other than the emotional peroration of the *Iliad:*
>
> > There lies the valiant Ajax, there Achilles,
> > There lies Patroclus, god-like counsellor;
> > There my dear son.
> > (Longinus IX [slightly altered from
> > Einarson's translation])

The *Odyssey* develops themes which are hardly touched in the *Iliad;* Odysseus' travels take him out of the heroic world proper and into the rich unexpected world of Indo-European folk-tales, what Longinus calls "fabulous and incredible tales of wonder." Odysseus' return takes him back to the most ordinary world, the world of the similes of the *Iliad*. "Of this type," says Longinus, "are the passages about the household of Odysseus, told with truth to ordinary life . . .—a sort of comedy of manners." So the *Odyssey* is partly a poem of what lies beyond the limits of the *Iliad*, partly a poem of what the *Iliad* takes for granted.

To say so much, however, is only to say that the *Odyssey* is a poem of the Cycle, that its poet has been resourceful in writing a poem that is not the *Iliad*. I wish to go further and suggest that the *Odyssey* is a new kind of poem, a creative response to the new situation created for poetry by the composition of the *Iliad*.

The poet of the *Odyssey* was self-consciously an epigonid; he thought of the *Iliad* much as we do, as The Poem. The *Iliad*, to put it a bit fancifully, is the song the sirens sing:

> We know all things that in the plain of Troy
> Greek and Trojan by gods' will endured;
> We know what comes to be on the fertile earth.
>   (XII. 189–91)

The man who hears this song "thinks no more of return to his wife and innocent children" (XII. 42–43)—so great is its power. Such power must be resisted by the man who wants to make something of his own. The poet of the *Odyssey* confronted an obstacle unknown to the poet of the *Iliad:* he was writing in a literary universe already inhabited by a masterpiece.

The great creative act of the poet of the *Iliad* was the conception of the monumental form; once he had defined this project to himself the tradition lay before him where to choose. He did not aim to make a poem of this or that kind, but simply the most epic possible epic. He inherited the poetry and of it made The Poem. In the somewhat extravagant words of Cedric Whitman:

> There is no evidence that the poet of the *Iliad* invented a single character or episode in his whole poem. He may not even have invented a single phrase. His invention was the *Iliad*.[5]

The author of the *Odyssey* was faced with a problem which had never faced a great Greek poet before: he had to be original about the sort of poem he made. Confronted by the *Iliad* he had to ask what other sort of poem might exist. So we know one thing about the *Odyssey* which distinguishes it from the *Iliad:* its making was accompanied by a certain kind of reflection on the proprieties of poetry.

Song in the *Iliad* always accompanies something else: dancing (XVIII. 604) or feasting (I. 603–4), weddings (XVIII. 495; XXIV. 63) or funerals (XXIV. 720–22 cf. XXIV. 60–62) or harvest (XVIII. 569–72). There is no narrative poet in the *Iliad*—except perhaps for Achilles himself; we catch one glimpse of him singing the *klea andrōn* (IX. 186–89). Achilles, who alone among the heroes comprehends his own fate, can be his own poet, but we do not hear his song; it is private. The other persons of the *Iliad* act and suffer, knowing that the song is to come, that they "will be a theme for song for men who are yet to be" (VI. 358) as Helen says. Epic is the story lesser men tell of the heroes; therefore there is no epic in the heroic world.

When Helen's phrase recurs in the *Odyssey,* in the mouth of King Alcinoos (VIII. 580) it means something different; we are now among the "men who are yet to be." The poet of the *Odyssey* dramatized his sense of himself as epigonid by filling his poem with epic; in Phaeacia and Ithaca the persons of his poem look back to the Trojan war, and look back to it not directly but through the medium of bardic song. In the *Odyssey* as in the *Iliad* the bards sing for dancing (I. 150–55; I. 421; VIII. 256–65; XVII. 605; XVIII. 304; XXIII. 129–52) and once for tumblers (IV. 15–19) but song in the *Odyssey* is primarily the sung story, the vehicle for history's judgement. Agamemnon's statement in the last book may not have been part of the original poem, but I quote it as a summary of this view of song:

> Blessed son of Laertes, crafty Odysseus,
> Excellent indeed the way you got you a wife,

> So fine the spirit of prudent Penelope,
> Icarius' daughter. So well she remembered Odysseus,
> The man she married. Therefore the fame will fail not
> Of her excellence; the immortals will make for men
> A lovely song of Prudent Penelope.
> Not she like Tyndarus' child contrived at evil,
> Killing her wedded husband. A fearful song
> That will be among men, and a hard name given
> To woman-kind, to even the decent housewife.
>   (XXIV. 192–202)

The event passes but the song endures, and the enduring song is itself part of the world the characters inhabit. When Odysseus hears his own story sung (VIII. 62–103; 499–520) he meets an experience unknown to Achilles: in his own time he has become a character in literature.

Odysseus weeps to hear his story told, yet he asks the bard to continue (VIII. 487–98). He knows the value of poetry and he values the bards:

> Then he addressed the herald, did wise Odysseus,
> Carving from the joint where the meat was still thickest
> Of the white-fanged boar, and the fat shone on it.
> "Herald, here, take this meat, for him to eat,
> To Demodocus. I'll embrace him, for all my grief.
> Among all men living on earth the bards
> Share in respect and honor, for to them
> The muse taught *oimai;* she loves the race of bards."
>   (VIII. 474–81)

The bards are important figures on the *Odyssey*'s human landscape, escorted by heralds and cosseted by kings. We are a little surprised to hear from Nestor that Agamemnon left his wife in the charge of his bard when leaving for Troy (III. 267–71) but after all why not? The bard is not an aristocrat but neither is he a serf or retainer; he is a free agent whose irreplaceable skill gives him the run of society. As Eumaius says:

> Who invites any guest and himself goes to him
> Unless he is one of the public craftsmen:
> Seer or physician or worker in wood
> Or the sacred bard, who delights with his singing?
> These alone are sought out among mortals.
>   (XVII. 382–86)

The bard receives honor, *timē,* because with his skill he delights the hearts of men; he receives respect, *aidōs,* because his skill is more than human. There is something uncanny about the inspired bard who can make anything happen, who can create and uncreate worlds. Odysseus feels this, and his feeling saves Phemius' life in the Slaying.

> Then he jumped forward and took Odysseus' knees
> And supplicating spoke to him winged words:
> "I pray you, Odysseus, respect me and pity me.
> You'll be sorry for it yourself later on, if you kill
> A bard like me, who sings for gods and men.

> I am self-taught; god made grow in my wits
> The *oimai,* all sorts. Perhaps I could sing for you
> As for a god. Don't be eager to cut my throat.
> (XXII. 342–49)

Song is god's gift to the bard, and each song grows from an inspiration (VIII. 47, 63–64). The bard as he sings becomes godlike (I. 371; IX. 4); therefore his person, like the herald's, is sacrosanct. And the listener too is, in a way, transported; he is touched by the divine light of song.

The bards of the *Odyssey* are like Pindar's recurrent celebration of song in the Odes: a reflexive element within the work of art. The poet of the *Odyssey* as he sings makes us aware of the nature of song, so that we respond at one and the same time to the tale and to the modality of its telling.

Odysseus is himself a poet, an inventive and persuasive liar who is never at a loss for a tale. He tells four books of his own story, and we have only his word for the most marvellous adventures. Eumaius says of him:

> Whatever he tells you, he would beguile your heart.
> Three nights I had him, three days kept him close
> In my hut, for he came to me first when he left his ship,
> But not even so did he finish his tale of misfortune.
> As when a man watches a bard, who with gods' gift
> Sings, knowing the words that are lovely to mortals,
> And they want to hear him forever, as long as he'll sing,
> So he beguiled my heart as he sat in my house.
> (XVII. 514–21)

Odysseus is a poet in the bardic style; he works by thematic variation. In disguise on Ithaca he tells three stories of his life; each is a lie, each is quite different, but the same elements recur. In each he announces himself as a man from Crete (XIII. 256; XIV. 199; XIX. 172); each narrative involves at some point the Trojan war (XIII. 263; XIV. 238; XIX. 182) and the Phenicians appear in two (XIII. 272; XIV. 289). Idomeneus appears in all three stories, once as the father of the man he has murdered (XIII. 259), once as his co-commander at Troy (XIV. 237), once as his brother (XIX. 181). More general themes are repeated. We can leave out of account Odysseus' explanations of his present poverty; those are required by the situation. There is perhaps no significance in the recurrent theme of the giving of gifts; it seems that no travel story is ever complete without them. But we note that in each story Odysseus describes himself as somehow marginal: he refused to serve as *therapōn* to his superior (XIII. 265); he is illegitimate (XIV. 202); he is the younger and lesser son (XIX. 184). In each story he describes a voyage spoilt by contrary winds (XIII. 276; XIV. 292; XIX. 186) and each story includes a journey homeward in the company of strangers. First it was Phenicians who tried to take him home and could not (XIII. 278); then it was Thesprotians who promised to take him home but cheated him (XIV. 340); in the last story Thesprotians faithfully took him on his way as far as Doulichion. In the first two stories there is a common theme of deprivation: Idomeneus' son tried to cheat him of his share of the spoils at Troy (XIII.

262); his half-brothers refused him a share of the inheritance (XIV. 210). Odysseus has a command of the *oimai:* by manipulating his stock he can make of an endless stream of novel lying tales.

Odysseus' Cretan tales differ in length and quality according to the circumstances of their telling. The first (XIII. 256–86) is composed impromptu on the beach, in response to an unexpected question. It is quite short, clear and to the point, with no elaboration. The second (XIV. 192–359) is told at leisure in Eumaius' hut; Odysseus begins by remarking that if he had time and an audience he could talk for a year. The story he then tells is more than six times as long as the first, complex, coherent, and full of incident. The third story (XIX. 165–202) is told to Penelope under adverse conditions. Odysseus finds his disguise so painful, he is so filled with the desire to tell the truth, that he asks to be spared another lie.

> Ask me now anything else in your house
> But not my race and my home-land.
> Lest you the more should fill my heart with sorrow
> Remembering.   (XIX. 115–18)

When Penelope presses him, he tells a brief story with little in it about his fictional self; it is mostly an account of how he happened to meet Odysseus. The force of Penelope's response then incites him to describe the clothes Odysseus was wearing when he left for Troy and the herald he had with him (XIX. 221–48). Finally he tells again, in much the same words, the end of his story to Eumaius, but garbles it badly in the re-telling (XIX. 262–307); he leaves out the explanation of Odysseus' absence, that he is consulting the oracle at Dodona, and must put it in at the end. Here under the stress of emotion Odysseus' poetic gifts fail him. So by adapting each of these stories to its dramatic setting the poet of the *Odyssey* has sketched the conditions of the creative process.

Odysseus "speaks many lies that are like to truth" (XIX. 203). They are like the truth because they are a retelling of the truth under color of lying. In the second Cretan tale, for example, Odysseus describes himself as a warrior and ship-captain, proud of his wife but deprived of his property by insolent young men (XIV. 209–11). He gives a brief straightforward account of the expedition to Troy and the disastrous return of the heroes (XIV. 240–42), themes treated at length in the first four books. After Troy this fictional Odysseus goes to Egypt, and as in Book IX the north wind is the beginning of all his troubles; one line is even repeated (IX. 78 = XIV. 256). In Egypt he sends out scouts, as in the adventure of the lotos-eaters; the result, the foolish violence of the scouts and the vengeance of the local inhabitants, is a kind of conflation of the cattle of the sun and the Kikones.

The Egyptian king and the Phenician trader seem to be completely fictional characters, but the storm which overtakes the Phenician ship is the same storm that Helios sent against Odysseus' ship in Book XII; seven lines are repeated (XII. 403–6 = XIV. 301–4; XII. 418–19 = XIV. 308–9; XII. 447 = XIV. 314), and many details are the same. Thesprotia is a pseudo-Phaeacia; the hero, worn with cold and the sea, is saved by the mercy of the king's son (in this case). And finally, the journey to Dodona where Odysseus asks how he can return to Ithaca and whether he should come openly or secretly, is a brief version of the nekuia, with Tiresias and Agamemnon combined.

Like Conrad's Marlow or Stephen Daedalus, Odysseus is both hero and poet; he lives his experience twice, once as he endures it, again as he recreates it into art. Odysseus is both doer and knower; he sees and describes everything, even his own house:

> Eumaius, this must be the beautiful palace of Odysseus.
> It is easily recognized; one could pick it out among many.
> Part rises beyond part, the courtyard is joined together
> With wall and turret, there are well-made doors
> Double-hung; no man could despise it.
> I notice that many men have set out here a feast
> For the smoke rises on high, and within the lyre
> Resounds, which Zeus has made a companion for feasting.
> (XVII. 264–71)

Odysseus' narrative of Books IX through XII is enthralling partly because of the extraordinary adventures he tells, and partly because Odysseus with his poet's eye and ear can make vivid quite ordinary things—the island covered with goats off the Cyclops' land (IX. 116–51), the stag he kills in Circe's woods (X. 156–73), Circe singing at her loom (X. 221–23), the crash of the Cyclops' firewood (IX. 233–35). The material richness of the *Odyssey*, the sharp sense of sensual detail, belongs as much to the hero as to the poet; they are one in their feeling for the actual.

The poet/hero of the *Odyssey* is another reflexive element within the work of art. As Odysseus meets himself in the songs of Demodocus, so the poet of the *Odyssey* has dramatized himself as knower and maker in the hero he has made.

The notion of a poet/hero is in epic terms a paradox. The heroic life is a life of action; the arts are relaxations from action. Paris plays the lyre and dances; such talents go with his long hair and his pretty manners, all signs of weakness (III. 54–55). Priam speaks with contempt of the poor scum that's left to him, "dancers and liars and foot-tappers in the chorus" (XXIV. 261). Menelaus, exhausted by heroic battle, thinks of the pleasures of rest, "sleep and love and sweet singing and blameless dancing" (XIII. 636–37). The most artistic folk in the *Odyssey* are the frivolous Phaeacians:

> Ever to us the feast is dear, the lyre and the chorus,
> Change of clothes, warm baths, and bed.
> (VIII. 248–49)

Poetry is not serious because it does not have to be true; it is a kind of purposeless lying, and therefore playful. Therein lies its charm to Athena, for instance, who claps Odysseus on the back after the first of his Cretan tales:

> He would be a cunning man and a real deceiver
> Who could get the better of you in trickery

> Even if a god should meet you. You rascal,
>   with intricate mind
> Full of tricks, you certainly wouldn't give up
> Even in your own country cheating and deceiving words
> Which suit you down to the ground.
>   (XIII. 291–95)

But any poet knows there is a difference between poetry and lying; the poet of the *Odyssey,* with his concern for the poets, is concerned to tell us something about that difference. Even King Alcinoos has some sense of the distinction, although he is not sure why; Odysseus' tale of the underworld stretches his credulity to the limit, but the king knows that he is not hearing plain lies:

> Odysseus, when we look at you you don't have the look
> Of a man who lies or a cheat; there are a lot of them
> Who live on the black earth, scattered about among men,
> Constructing lies so well that no one can see through them.
> But yours is the skill of speech, and your wits are good;
> It's like a story told by a bard who knows how.
>   (XI. 363–68)

The distinction between poetry and lying, or between poetry as frivolous and poetry as serious, has something to do with the attitude of the audience. The *Odyssey* shows us a difference between mature and immature responses to poetry, establishes this difference at the very beginning, when Phemius sings of the return of the heroes from Troy:

> In the upper story she caught in her wits the song,
> Icarius' daughter, prudent Penelope,
> And she came down the high stair of her house
> . . .
> And weeping addressed the divine bard:
> "Phemius, you know many other sorrows of men,
> Acts of gods and of men, that the bards celebrate;
> Keep your place and sing one of those for them, and they
>   in silence
> Can drink their wine. But stop this song,
> This miserable song, which wears at my heart,
> Since there comes upon me a sorrow I can't forget.
> For such was the man I desire, and remember him always;
> His fame was great through Greece and middle Argos."
>
> Her Telemachus taking breath addressed in reply:
> "My mother, why should you be annoyed at the faithful bard
> If he gives pleasure in whatever way the spirit moves him?
> The bards are not at fault, Zeus did it, Zeus who gives
> To grain-eating men whatever he wants, each by each.
> It's no blame to him to sing the fate of the Danae.
> People always rather praise that song
> Which newly comes to the ears of its audience—
> So let your heart and spirit endure to hear it.
>   (I. 328–53)

For Penelope, song is memory, and the poet revives the grief that memory brings her. For Telemachus with his child's impatience with grief the song is mere song; once the event has been transformed into poetry it ceases to be serious, ceases to be history, and becomes an amusement like any other.

Odysseus also weeps at song; when Demodocus sings of the strife between Odysseus and Achilles he "covers his head and cries" (VIII. 92). Alcinoos observes Odysseus' tears and stops the bard; as a good host he is distressed by his guest's distress (VIII. 97–103). The next time Demodocus sings he sings of Ares and Aphrodite and "Odysseus rejoiced in his heart as he listened" (VIII. 367–68). But when it falls to Odysseus to ask the bard for an *oimē* he does not ask for one of those pleasant songs; he asks him for the story of the Trojan horse.

> These things the famous bard sang. But Odysseus
> Melted, and the tears made damp the cheeks beneath
> > his lids.
> As a woman mourns her dear husband and clings to him,
> A husband who fell before the city and the folk
> For his place and his children warding off the day
> > of destruction
> And she, when she sees him quivering and dead
> Throws her arms around him with shrill keening. Others
> Beside her slash with their spears her back and shoulders
> To drag her to slavery, to endure the toil and the sorrow,
> And with the piteous grief her cheeks are wasted—
> So Odysseus poured the piteous tears under his brows.
> > (VIII. 521–31)

Again Alcinoos tells the bard to stop, "for he does not sing in a way which is pleasant to us all" (VIII. 538).

> Let him hold his tongue, so we may all rejoice together,
> Guest and hosts, for it is better thus.
> > (VIII. 542–43)

Alcinoos takes song as an after-dinner amusement, like the ball-dance and the footraces; a song which draws tears is ill-chosen. But Odysseus himself chose the song which brought him to the greatest transports of grief. Odysseus has a different notion of art.

The whole of Book VIII is a kind of introduction to Odysseus' tale; Demodocus' three songs give us a standard for judging Odysseus'. In the little preface to his tale Odysseus makes the point explicit:

> Noble Alcinoos, exalted among the people,
> Surely it is a fine thing to hear the voice of the bard
> A bard like this one, with a voice like the gods.
> I at least can say no higher perfection of delight
> Than when gladness of heart takes hold of all the folk
> And the banqueters in the hall listen to the bard
> Seated in rows, and beside them the tables are full
> Of bread and meat, and the wine splashes from the bowl
> As the cupbearer passes, pouring it from the cups.
> This I know is loveliest for the heart.

> But my mournful troubles to you my heart has moved me
> That I tell them, so that still more I may cry for sorrow.
> What first then, what last shall I tell over?
> The sorrows are many that the gods of Olympus gave me
> First I will tell you my name. . . .
>
> (IX. 2–16)

Making poetry of his own experience Odysseus must somehow settle the proper relation between poetry and fact. In so doing he becomes serious. Alcinoos, all the Phaeacians, are dilettantes; they value in poetry the delight, the elegance and charm. But for Odysseus the poem is good in that it revives his sorrow. Poetry is a kind of mourning.

Mourning and delight are woven together in the epic, even compacted in a fixed line:

> She, once she had taken delight in tearful mourning . . .
> (XIX. 213 = XIX. 251 = XXI. 57)

Mourning is not sorrow but a constructive response to sorrow, a mastery of experience. The unendurable memory is made endurable as it is translated into the outward signs of grief.

> I'll find no fault
> With weeping for a man who dies and meets his fate.
> This is the sole privilege of unfortunate mortals;
> To shear the hair and let run the cheeks with tears.
> (IV. 195–98)

From mourning rises song, as Penelope says:

> For me the *daimōn* contrived pain without measure.
> All day I take delight in sorrow, in mourning,
> Seeing to my work and the servants about my house
> But when the night comes, and sleep overcomes them all
> I lie in my bed, and thick around my heart
> The sharp cares trouble me in my sorrow.
> Its like the daughter of Pandarus, the nightingale
> Who sweetly sings when the spring is first beginning;
> She sits in the close-set leaves of the trees
> And often changing her note pours out her echoing voice,
> Mourning her dear child Itylus, whom with the bronze
> She killed in her folly, the son of King Zetheus,
> So in me the spirit is carred this way and that. . .
> (XIX. 512–24)

And for Eumaius the thing mourned becomes a story:

> For us in the hut as we eat and we drink
> Let us delight in one another's sorrows
> Remembering. For later a man takes pleasure
> Even in sorrow, when he has suffered and wandered much.
> (XV. 398–401)

As the past is put into words, as it becomes an external fact shared with someone else, the memory loses its mastery over the present. Eumaius accepts his fate, bad and good together; the mark of his acceptance is his ability to tell the story. So Odysseus masters his experience, not only in action, but in memory, in song.

The poet of the *Odyssey* knew the difference a great story can make; he had the *Iliad* before him. The *Odyssey* takes account of that difference as the *Iliad* could not. In the *Iliad* experience is immediate; the heroes speak, act and endure the consequences. In the *Odyssey* action is set about with memory; experience is mediated, reflected upon, transformed. The more thorough the transformation the more memory approaches poetry; in the poem all things are set in order, *kata moiran* (VIII. 496). So poetry becomes for the persons of the *Odyssey* one model of that order toward which the human enterprise aspires.

Poetry is at the moral center of the *Odyssey*. In making poetry a theme of his poem the poet of the *Odyssey* achieved something both enduring and original; he set a new kind of model for the poetry to come. The *Odyssey* is a classic of poetic response. Odysseus, like the epic heroes before him, is a hero of action, of courage and craft; he is also, as the earlier heroes were not, a knower and a maker, a craftsman and a poet. In the silence before the great moment of action in the poem all these qualities are drawn together in a single metaphor:

> Then he handled the bow
> Turning it each way, trying it this way and that
> Lest worm had eaten the horn while its king was gone.
> And a man who watched him might say to another beside him:
> "Surely this is some skillful student of bows.
> Perhaps he has another such in his house
> Or he's moved to make one, seeing that thus in his hands
> He handles it this way and that, this traveller acquainted
> with evils."

. . . .

> Then crafty Odysseus
> When he had worked the great bow and tried it each way
> As when a man who's knowing in lyre-play and song
> Easily stretches the string to a new peg
> Joining to both ends the twisted gut of the sheep,
> So without trouble was the great bow strung by Odysseus.
> In his right hand he took it and tested the string,
> And the string in response sweetly sang. . .
> (XXI. 393–411)

NOTES

1. G. S. Kirk, *The Songs of Homer* (Cambridge, Eng., 1962), p.280–81.
2. H. T. Wade-Gery, *The Poet of the Iliad* (Cambridge, Eng., 1952), p.32.
3. Albert B. Lord, *The Singer of Tales* (Cambridge, 1960), p.22–26.
4. *Singer*, p.361.
5. Cedric Whitman, *Homer and the Heroic Tradition* (Cambridge, 1963), p.14.

Peter F. Fisher

THE TRIALS OF THE EPIC HERO IN *BEOWULF*

The unity of *Beowulf* is at least secure in the person of the hero whose character and actions provide the basis for any critical examination of structure and theme. According to some, this is all that holds the epic together.[1] Others see more than a sequence of disconnected episodes related to one person. In their view, the fights with Grendel and his dam are united to the dragon fight in the opposition of hero and king, youth and age, the beginning and ending of a life of achievement.[2] It is in their spirit that I have attempted to take a fresh view of the subject with special reference to unity of theme and treatment. The suggestion is that this unity is to be found in the theme of redemption and judgment treated in a way which skilfully blends the Germanic hero with the Christian saint. The symbolism is not regarded as contrived or studied, but rather as of that kind which is the usual result of an author's finding an apt subject to illustrate his theme. A symbolic interpretation does not, after all, exclude a literal interpretation; it contains it. The dragon, for instance, can be both a universal symbol and a very literal and particular monster. We have surely become too literal-minded if we suppose that the audience of *Beowulf* could see no universal significance in the epic story because they accepted the literal truth of the narrative. The many symbolical interpretations of the Biblical narrative during the period which followed bear witness to the improbability of this view. Once the underlying theme of redemption and judgment is adopted and is seen to be the epic theme par excellence, the process of selection from myth and legend becomes somewhat clearer, and there is no longer the necessity to account for a gap between the Grendel fights and the dragon fight. The details in the fifty-year reign of the hero would have been irrelevant. An epic is surely not a biography nor a chronicle nor a mythology, although it draws upon all these.[3]

More selective than the corpus of mythology itself, the epic was still concerned with the same traditional records, the same searching questions, and the same supernatural background which extended beyond ordinary life. In its complete form, the matter of a mythology went beyond the natural cycle of birth and death to the larger theme of the creation of man and his world

"The Trials of the Epic Hero in *Beowulf*," by Peter F. Fisher. Reprinted by permission of the Modern Language Association of America from *PMLA* 73: 171–83 (1958).

along with the problem of his redemption and final judgment. Even the most primitive mythology was a mutual penetration of the historical and the religious, since it was the best available answer to the spiritual needs of its people. There was no fundamental distinction between the sensible and the intelligible worlds, for racial myth provided a bridge between action and aspiration, between men and their gods. The matter of the epic had, therefore, a completed mythology in the background, and in the foreground, the figure of the human hero embodying in his own person the struggles and trials of his people. The hero did not merely "symbolize" the trials of the race; he was the actual incarnation of those trials, hence the "historical" elements which made the heroic career both authentic and real.

The bard sang or declaimed the story of the human hero much in the same style as he delivered the ancient legends of the gods. In Homer, the word from which the term *epic* is derived meant a speech given in the public assembly, and the style of the epic is revealed to be—in both the *Iliad* and the *Odyssey*—rhetorically correct and formally within the grasp of an audience in a reasonable period of time. It was also the opinion of Aristotle that it should be possible for the beginning and the end of the work to be viewed as a whole;[4] but it is not sufficient to consider the formal characteristics solely in terms of the Greek and Roman models which obviously did not provide the standard for the author of *Beowulf*. The fact that Homer and his successors began their works in the middle did not alter the completeness of the cycle of heroic adventure or series of trials which distinguished the form here called "epic," but emphasized the economy and selectivity of the form itself. The author of *Beowulf* made use of the same economy in a different way—by omitting the irrelevant account of the hero's fifty-year reign. Within this epic form, the trials of the hero concerned him as an individual, as a tribal or culture hero, and as the demigod or universal hero closing the gulf between the actions of life and its meaning in the midst of a frequently hostile environment. It is also possible to classify the different kinds of epic according to the way the trials of the hero are presented. The first kind of epic has scarcely emerged from the collections of myths and legends from which it is derived, and it represents the universal trials of the race or tribe. Such are the Hebraic writings from the Mosaic books to the later prophets, and such are the Northern *Eddas* which give a complete description of human experience from the creation to the apocalyptic destruction and renewal of all things.[5] The second kind of epic includes the trials of the hero as the incarnation of his race or tribe, and is, therefore, tribal or national in its emphasis. The *Mahabharata*, the *Aeneid*, and the *Volsungasaga* or *Nibelungenlied* are perhaps most representative of this type. In the third category are to be found the individualistic epics in which the emphasis is placed on the trials of the hero with the hero as the central and dominating figure—the *Ramayana*, the *Iliad*, and the *Beowulf*. In all of these, there is a basic struggle between the divine, the natural, and the demonic within the field of the hero's experience. In *Beowulf*, the natural is made to serve the purpose of redemption, while the demonic is resisted and uprooted. The natural field of experience which is first represented by Heorot is cleansed, while the demonic Grendel and Grendel's dam are destroyed. The cleansing is itself a preparation for rule over this field of experience which is later represented by the realm of the Geats and the fifty-year reign of the heroic king—the successor in epic myth to the original "divine king."

The hero of the epic might be a particular incarnation of divinity, like Rāma, boast immediate descent from the gods, like Aeneas and Achilles, or at least be extraordinarily gifted, like Ulysses, Sigurd and Beowulf. The conception of the hero derived from classical antiquity is that of a man who transcends the ordinary scope of human actions, and who aspires to divine honors. He is, in a manner of speaking, the athlete of the gods. The impact of his life which has enriched the traditions of his people exalts his struggle into a universal myth of the conflict which man wages in the field of his earthly environment to realize and assert his humanity. In the pursuit of this goal, the hero, unlike his fellows, goes beyond social convention and ordinary rewards. According to the legend, Hercules, after the successful completion of his twelve labors, was said to have been caught up to the stars, signifying his attainment of the immortal life of the gods. The universal appeal of the hero's victories over uncommon foes, and finally over death itself, becomes clearer when it is realized that his achievement involves the fullest expression of that life which generations of his people have chosen as their ultimate goal. His labors are a vicarious atonement, and his final achievement preserves the hope of salvation for all. It is therefore entirely likely that the story of the hero will combine the most honorable vocation of his people with their religious conceptions of divinity and redemption. In the Old English epic saga of Beowulf,[6] the hero combines the role of the warrior with that of the savior of those with whom he comes in contact. The mode of redemption is not always clearly Christian, and it is obvious that the epic embodies a deep strain of the old Northern religion. This does not in any way obscure the fundamental pattern of the heroic adventure but rather reveals the roots of the Anglo-Saxon conception of the warrior as hero and redeemer.

The theme of the *Beowulf* is not as easily designated as, for example, that of the *Iliad*. In the Homeric epic, we are told at the very beginning that the subject which the author has chosen is "the wrath of Achilles" and that the story is one of famous men and events related to the one main episode. The *Beowulf* begins in a similar epic vein with the allusion to mighty deeds and a description of those told specifically of Scyld Scēfing. The importance of his illustrious ancestry is emphasized, making of him a figure of heroic stature and lineage; but more important is the account of his mysterious arrival and departure, suggesting a divine origin. In this way, it is indicated that a hero is not merely mortal in the power and scope of his actions, but is possessed in some way of the divine destiny. It is that much more fitting, therefore, that such actions should be remembered by men and be made the subject of a narrative. This is the attitude which the reader is asked to take at the outset, and he would do well to pay at least as much attention to the implied request as to a search for historical sources. The story of Scyld, however, although it sets the temper of the poem, does not designate the theme in the manner of the *Iliad*, nor does it serve to introduce the main character, Beowulf the Geat, who is not to be confused with his earlier Danish namesake, the ancestor of Hrothgar. Perhaps the spirit of the theme is suggested by the opening reference to the glory of the Danish kings (*þēodcyninga þrym*)[7] which is the tribute to their greatness, and at the same time the judgment of their actions. By recounting the story of the "wrath of Achilles," Homer suggests, without actually formulating, a judgment of his main character. Similarly, the author of the *Beowulf* appraises his hero's actions in harmony with the Germanic outlook. As an introduction to the second episode, Beowulf, in his speech to Hrothgar, says that he who is able should achieve greatness before death. Since it is the fate of the noble warrior to await death, what can be rescued from life is the measure of his fame.

> Ūre æghwylc sceal ende gebīdan
> worolde lifes; wyrce sē þe mōte
> dōmes ǣr dēaþe; þæt bi∂ drihtguman
> unlifigendum æfter sēlest.   (1386–89)

> (Each of us must await the end of life in
> the world; let him who can achieve fame
> before death.   That is best for the warrior
> when life is over.)

The word *dōm* carries with it the threefold meaning of 'judgment,' 'choice,' and 'glory'—indicating surely the significance which was attached to the life of the hero regarding his future, both as it affected himself and his descendants for whose benefit it would be recounted. The theme, then, of the epic may be stated as the "doom of Beowulf."

The three episodes comprising the narrative are held together by the peculiar mission of the hero who is represented as engaging in three fights with fabulous monsters. The first of these is quickly dealt with; the second is described with greater elaboration; and the last, separated from the other two by a lapse of many years, brings the specifically heroic career of Beowulf to a close. As Klaeber suggests (*Beowulf*, p.*lii*), the incidents are structurally parallel, and the action moves through the stages of "the exciting cause," the preliminaries, the fight, and the aftermath. There is first a call to adventure, and to answer this call the hero is required to leave the protecting confines of his family that he may encounter and overcome the initial trials of his task. He defeats or conciliates the power barring his passage or preventing him from successfully completing his mission. Such is Beowulf's fight with Grendel. Beyond the threshold, the hero journeys through an unfamiliar and frequently subterranean realm in search of the maternal root of the earthly power which he has already encountered. This is clearly a description of Beowulf's fight with Grendel's dam. He acquires a boon in the form of the sword hilts of the giants, and returns to gain recognition by the initiator of his quest in the person of Hrothgar. Finally, after fulfilling the role of king and father of his people to whom he has returned, Beowulf enters the stage of apotheosis in his battle with the Fire-Dragon.[8] There is also a kind of progression in the attitude of the protagonist. In the first episode, he is defending Heorot for the aged king, Hrothgar, against the ravages of the monster who has invaded it. In the second, he is more aggressive and actually goes in search of his antagonist, penetrating into the depths of the monster's lair. In the third encounter, he seeks the enemy who has been provoked by another and engages in battle with a resolution unmodified by age.

Beowulf, as he is introduced to the reader, is already a man of renown— the young adventurer who seeks to establish his prowess abroad by coming to the assistance of Hrothgar. As more details are added, he appears in the role of the hero whose exploits are connected with the slaughter of sea-monsters. He boasts that he is the protector of mariners and the destroyer of evil-doers. The possible connection of the Beowulfian legend with the *Bear's Son Tale* adds little, for present purposes, to the general picture. It might be used, however, to emphasize the high destiny of the hero; but the parallel with the *Grettissaga* is more striking and more pertinent to the present treatment of the subject. Beowulf, then, before his encounter with Grendel, is represented as the typical young adventurer whose peculiar traits admirably fit him to be the protector of Heorot. Hrothgar in assessing his qualifications mentions first that he is of noble blood and then remembers that he is said to have the strength of thirty men in his handgrip (379–81). Nobility, strength, an adventurous spirit, and the hope of divine aid make Hrothgar feel confident of his abilities and his mission. The dwelling which he is to defend, or rather to *cleanse* of its defilement, is the centre of tribal fellowship suitably adorned in turn by each group of blood-relatives throughout this world (*geond þisne middangeard*) (75), as distinct from the hell-world of Grendel. In this hall was heard the sound of the minstrel singing the song of Creation, and it was this, along with the revelry of the companions, that tormented the spirit of darkness. This part of the poem skilfully suggests the immediacy with which the minstrel's audience heard and understood the story of Creation (90–114). Within the context of the adventures of this particular hero, reference is made to the universal adventure of humanity, and there is no sense of remoteness in the way the story is told as an introduction to the visits of Grendel. The juxtaposition of earth and hell is graphically indicated, and the "exciting case" of the first episode is seen to be a malignant incursion from the hell-world into the "earthly paradise" of Heorot.

In one variant of the *Bear's Son Tale* mentioned by Grimm, the enemy whom the hero overcomes but does not kill is called *dat Erdmänneken*—the Earth-man.[9] Grendel might be considered the lineal descendant in folklore of some kind of Germanic Caliban, but the author of the *Beowulf* gives him a much more sinister ancestry. He is not merely represented as coming from the earth but from the underworld—the land of monsters descended from Cain. It may be that this Christian interpretation of the status of Grendel came late to the author of the epic, but it would seem that such an idea had gained a considerable hold on the contemporary imagination by the very fact of the elaboration and detail with which it was described. The tradition in its Christianized form had become established. There is another reference to monsters in the poem which connects them with the sea in Beowulf's answer to Unferth. Unferth charged Beowulf with being such a man as he was himself—a man in whom cunning and craft had not only taken the place of courage, but were used to disguise the lack of it.[10] The charge is answered by Beowulf's account of his fights with the monsters of earth and sea—struggles which reach their culmination in the fight with Grendel and his dam. Grendel is himself a combination of sea- and earth-monster who has been metamorphosed into a descendant of Cain (574–75, 1258–68). The act of accommodation to the Hebraic myth was not difficult. A denizen of the moors and deserted places, Grendel could easily be transformed into an offspring of the exile from Eden wandering in the land of Nod. For the Christian poet, Cain and his descendants had come to represent not only the reprobate who was eternally condemned but also the positive forces of evil inhabiting the land of monsters (*fīfelcynnes eard*) (104) or a purgatorial realm not easily distinguished from hell itself. In Hebrew legend,[11] Adam is said to have been banished to such a place after he had forfeited Eden, and this could be more readily applied to Cain.

The evidence presented in the *Beowulf* suggests the strong connection between the conception of the archfiend and that of the human reprobate; one had become identified with the other. Apart from a passage which would seem to give Scriptural authority to the tradition that Cain was of the devil,[12] early legends existed which claimed that he was born between the transgression of Adam and Eve and their repentance. According to some rabbis, a dualism was established, using the symbolism of Cain and Abel, the good souls descending from Abel and the evil ones from Cain whose body had been derived from Eve but whose spirit had come from Samael. It was not surprising that such a tradition founded on dualism became a part of the Manichaean heresy. The early Fathers used the story in a metaphorical sense and thereby probably added the weight of their authority to the popular belief.[13] In Italian folklore, the legend was given a lunar significance and Cain was associated with the man in the moon whose "thorns" were "the fruit of the ground"— the burnt offering rejected by God. Dante uses the phrase "Caïno e le spine" (*Inferno* XX. 126) as a synonym for the moon, and it was popularly believed that Cain might be seen in the moon, going with a bundle of thorns to sacrifice. The *Cursor Mundi* records the belief that the offering was not accepted because it was given with an evil will.

> For Caym gaf him with ivel will.
> Ur Loverd loked noght þartill.[14]

Chaucer, in the *Parson's Tale,* joins Cain and Judas in a condemnation without the hope of mercy: "and that a man ne be nat despeired of the mercy of Jhesu Crist, as Caym or Judas."[15]

The author of the *Beowulf* describes the descendants of Cain as monsters (*untȳdras*), giants joyless as that of the land of monsters. The scene which forms the background for the coming of Grendel suggests the burden of darkness which he brings with him to add to the accumulated gloom which his invasions have already caused. Beowulf in his "boast" before the battle shows himself to be confident but not overconfident. He displays the characteristic traits of the hero: confidence balanced by magnanimity in discarding his weapons, and a readiness to accept the outcome whatever it may be.[16] During the course of the struggle, he gains the advantage over his enemy and holds him from flight. He is completely in command of the situation, and the first fight is quickly won. The monster leaves Heorot which is thereby cleansed of its defilement in the form of this threat from the underworld of the mere. Beowulf escapes from the battle apparently unscathed, in direct contrast to the aftermath of Grettir's fight with the troll-wife (*Grettissaga*, chap. lxv). The gift hall is restored as the place of assembly of the warriors, and they examine the mere into which the monster has disappeared, doomed to die and fugitive (*fǣge ond geflȳmed*) (846). Grendel is represented as surrendering his life to the powers of Hell, Beowulf, with the aid of divine Providence, has conquered not only his own fate in the form of this heathen soul (*hǣþene sāwle*), but that of Hrothgar's retainers as well. The author seems to regard his hero as in some sense the servant of Providence without surrendering completely the Germanic outlook towards *Wyrd* or Fate to which Beowulf is still subject as a mortal. He may be, to a certain extent, under the power of Fate, but he˙ is not under the condemnation of the reprobate like Grendel. The apparent conflict between the two conceptions of Fate (*wyrd*) and Providence (*metod*)[17] forms the background and also indicates the meaning of each battle. Whether Fate be regarded as that inescapable pattern of events which the hero must encounter and by means of which he is judged or whether it is the mythological expression of a hard and rigorous environment, it still remains the circumscribed mortality of the hero who, while he plays his part with courage, may wrest from it a favorable judgment. In this context Fate is best described as the whole "virtue" of the hero —all his developed possibilities—when it is brought to bear on a crisis in his life and the constituted conditions of his environment.

> Wyrd oft nereð
> unfǣgne eorl, þonne his ellen dēah!
> (572–73)
>
> (Fate often succours the warrior who is
> not fated to die when his valor is strong!)

In the first contest, Beowulf is confident of his fate and places his trust in the providential Lord of Fate. In the second battle, he trusts too much, perhaps, in Fate, and only escapes at the last moment by the aid of providential grace.

This time Beowulf invades the precincts of Grendel's lair and, following the pattern of the *Bear's Son Tale*, makes a descent into the underworld. The passage in which the poet describes the haunted mere forms a contrast to the description of Heorot (1358–76).[18] The immediately unknown and, for that reason, malignant forces which are outside the scope and control of man are represented. Again the emphasis is placed on the alien nature of the monsters: they are alien spirits (*ellorgǣstas*). They inhabit the moors as exiles and possess mysterious land (*dȳgel lond*). Every phrase is intended to suggest the dark side of nature in its most forbidding aspect. The knowledge of the monsters is remote and vague. Grendel's dam is in the likeness of a woman, but further knowledge of her appearance or her son's is uncertain.

The position of the mere and the mention of an underground flood indicate a connection with the sea. The mountain stream (*fyrgen-strēam*) surely signifies more than an inland lake, but the high cliffs and mountain trees which surround the waterfall seem to preclude this interpretation. Perhaps the description is intended to be suggestive rather than geographically accurate. To the imagination of a seafaring people, the power of the sea would be connected with a force not under human control, yet interwoven completely with the pattern of their lives. The blending of the waters of the fall with the surrounding atmosphere to darken the air gives the effect of some uncanny vapor produced by elemental nature which rises from the abode of the monsters and is blown about over the windy headlands. Mist and darkness are associated in a way which conjures up the Land of Darkness, the Northern Hades called Niflheimr—from Old Norse *nifl* meaning 'mist' or 'darkness.' The approaches to this world are also forbidding. The path is both narrow and steep; the fen is placed in the midst of precipitous mountains, and each night there appears a sinister and mysterious light on the flood suggesting the horrible light (*lēoht unfæger*) (727) which gleamed from the eyes of Grendel on the night of his last assault. This is apparently a picture of the hell-world combining the darkest features of both land and sea. Not only is the mere represented as inaccessible but its confines are deliberately avoided by men, and the knowledge of its depths is hidden even from the wise.

The description in the *Grettissaga* is neither as elaborate nor as suggestive as that of the *Beowulf*. Grettir, examining the tracks of the troll-wife, leads the priest to the waterfall where they see a cave under the rock. Grettir descends, holding the rope which has been fastened to a stake driven into the ground. He is armed only with a short sword. Beowulf, however, puts on his war corslet and helmet and takes his sword with him to the bottom of the mere. Grettir leaves the priest to watch the rope. Hrothgar and his wise men await the outcome of Beowulf's venture. The two stories are parallel in plot and incident but the author of the *Beowulf* takes more trouble to describe the details and to recreate the background. In doing this, he expresses more fully the inner significance of the action. Beowulf, as the waters close over his head, is entering the domain of the unknown and is seized by the sea-wolf and borne off to her hall. The act of aggression is balanced by the initiative of Grendel's dam. The hero notices that *he,* this time, is in a hostile hall (*nīðsele*) (1513). He has passed out of the power of the flood with which he had wrestled heretofore and entered upon a completely new experience in the underworld. The author of the epic skilfully suggests this utter separation from human haunts by having Beowulf recognize the source of the infernal gleam on the waters as observed by men.

> fȳrlēoht geseah
> blācne lēoman beorhte scīnan. (1516–17)
>
> (He saw the fire-light, a gleaming radiance
> shining brightly.)

The reader is led to infer from all this that whatever may have been his successes in the past, this will be a more difficult victory to achieve. All his resources will be needed and some, if not all, may prove to be of no avail. He has come fully armed, as if expecting to be put to the test.

Grettir uses his sword to good effect in his battle with the giant but Beowulf is not so fortunate. The weapon which has proved its worth in contests with human foes is found to be useless. In the preliminaries to the first contest, he had discarded the man-made weapon and had trusted to his own valor and the help of Providence. Now he is *forced* to discard it and rely on the strength of his handgrip which proves to be insufficient, and he is on the point of despairing of life. Here the poet introduces providential aid which, we are led to suppose, had not been granted until this moment. In his "boast" before the second encounter, Beowulf makes no direct reference to his faith in the divine power, and his attitude is apparently fatalistic. He seems to be concerned with practical matters such as the distribution of his wealth after death. He is neither as unconcerned nor as devout as in his former "boast" (cf. 686 ff.). Yet it is not quite true to call his attitude fatalistic; for Beowulf is no mere "primitive" bowing to an inevitable Fate. He is closer to being a Christian Stoic, and the author of the epic goes to some pains to show that his "boasts" are in the nature of an effort to master fate rather than to submit to it. As Augustine said, the Stoics held that there were three emotions which were contrary to the perturbations or disturbances of the soul: instead of covetousness, desire or will; instead of mirth, joy; instead of fear, caution. Although the Stoics would not allow that sorrow could be in the soul of the wise man, Augustine admitted the sorrow which is the result of repentance; and it is significant that Beowulf appears to have surrendered to a penitent sorrow only before his *last* battle.[19] Fatalism is, after all, the outlook of the mere child of nature who recognizes the supremacy of the powers of the natural environment. In this second encounter, however, Beowulf experiences the intervention of divine grace which makes him a participant in the powers of the Lord of Fate. Before this battle, he is simply the confident warrior who hopes, most of the time, that he will be lucky.

Before the second trial, the protagonist seems to be very concerned about his possessions, and the requests he makes regarding the future of his followers may be an indication of the beginning of the change from the triumphant warrior to the reigning monarch. The reward for the successful completion of the labors of the hero is undoubtedly suggested. Beowulf is about to prove himself or fail utterly; and yet, he seems to be unprepared for the decisive intervention which realizes his victory over the demonic power within the underworld of Grendel's cave. The author probably intended that the intervention of Providence should emphasize the nature of the contest and the powers for which each of the contestants stood. Beowulf sees an old sword of the giants, and succeeds in overcoming his opponent with its aid. The size of the weapon is mentioned as a further indication of the hero's superior strength. It is a victorious blade (*sigeēadig bil*) (1557) suitable to do battle against the remnants of the race which produced it. Ornamented with serpents and runes, its hilt might suggest the old theme of the magic sword, but the occult properties of the weapon, if any, are not recorded. It is simply a larger sword than his own, Hrunting, and it eventually melts—all but the hilt—in the blood shed by the antagonist. The gold hilt is given by the victor to Hrothgar, and is pronounced to be the work of smiths of wondrous art (*wundorsmiþa geweorc*)[20]—possibly a reference to the Biblical story of Tubal-cain, "instructor of every artificer in brass and iron."

The melting of the sword which anticipates an incident in the last battle with the dragon also serves to emphasize the infernal nature of the mere-woman and her race. Beowulf's second victory represents a greater struggle than the first, for it is undertaken within the confines of the enemy's lair—the enemy, not only of man, but of God (*Godes andsaca*) (1682). Evidence of the fray reaches the upper world in the form of water stained with blood. The wise men, after a consultation, decide that the prince has been slain. They wait until the ninth hour of the day and then depart.[21] The strangers, the companions of the hero, remain, sick at heart, staring at the mere. They wish and dare not hope.

> wīston ond ne wēndon, þæt hīe heora winedrihten
> selfne gesāwon. (1604–5)
>
> (They wished and did not expect that they would
> see their friendly lord himself.)

In the *Grettissaga*, the priest, seeing the entrails of the giant floating downstream, is seized with panic, and runs off home to report the death of Grettir. Beowulf, however, is not abandoned by his comrades but they have surrendered to despair. In the first instance, they endeavor to assist him in his struggle and their assistance is ineffectual; in the second, they wait for him but give up all hope of his success; in the third encounter, they promise their aid but finally take refuge in flight. The sequence is striking. Throughout the epic narrative, the emphasis is placed on the solitary nature of the hero's task. Beowulf appears to live and fight alone. His three battles emerge as three distinct judgments wrested from Fate by an intrepid and completely individual mind.

The descent into the underworld on the part of the hero may be described as a universal myth—whether the underworld is called Niflheimr, Hades, or Amenti. Its purpose is always the expulsion of embodied evils from the individual, the community, and the race which they seem to afflict both mentally and physically. Beowulf's task of cleansing Heorot is not completed in the first battle. He must venture into the abode of the evil spirit and kill it—an ordeal closely connected with the discovery of an enchanted treasure. In this way the hero seeks to gain a boon of final, enduring value. In the context of *Beowulf*, the second fight with Grendel's dam points significantly and directly to the final dragon fight. As recorded in the *Volsungasaga* (chap. xix), Sigurd, after overcoming the dragon, Fafnir, finds a great store of gold along with the sword, Hrotti, and takes all of it. Grettir, however, after killing the giant, is supposed to have found some treasure in the cave along with the bones of two men. He carries away the bones of the two men and leaves the treasure, having succeeded in his purpose and cleared the valley of monsters and night spirits. After his victory in Grendel's cave, Beowulf, like Grettir, takes with him only the sword hilts and the head of the antagonist as a token of victory. In the description of his ascent to the upper world, the poet indicates that he has achieved his end; the surging waters are cleansed. Earlier, the surge of waves (*ȳ̃ðgebland*) (1373, 1593, 1620) formed the mist and darkness surrounding the haunted mere. Later on, the wave-surges were seen, mixed with blood, by Hrothgar's thanes and the companions. Now, they are cleansed along with the haunts of the monsters.

> wǣron ȳ̃ðgebland   eal gefǣlsod,
> ēacne eardas,   þā se ellorgāst
> oflēt līfdagas   ond þās lǣnan gesceaft.
> (1620–22)

(The wave-surges were all cleansed, the mighty
haunts where the alien spirit relinquished
his life and this transitory world.)

What has been going on has been a process of purgation. In the minds of the bard's contemporaries, the world was full of elves, giants, and evil spirits which harassed and tormented them in mind and body. The consciousness of their presence was insistent, wearisome, and exasperating. Hence their conception of the hero was intimately connected with the desire for a deliverer from these contingencies of existence. Beowulf, in this sense, has not merely performed an act of deliverance and revenge but also of atonement. If there is any indication that his role is that of the savior, he must surely be both victim and deliverer. In the first fight with Grendel, he is ostensibly the deliverer. In the second battle with the mere-woman, he is more forcibly represented as the victim sacrificed for the good of the people—a role which is completely realized in his fight with the dragon.

Beowulf is no tragic hero; he delivers and is delivered. The Germanic gloom which darkens the background of human life with its mortal fate discloses more clearly the splendor of heroic achievement in the face of the inevitable round of birth and death. The Northern myth of creation and world destruction itself reflects the human cycle, but there is a depth of victory which is implicit in the attitude of the Norse gods even to this Fate. The victor who achieves a consciousness of superiority without pride is indeed in possession of an unusual wisdom. In the speech of Hrothgar, who is called "of great heart" (*rūmheort*) (1799), Beowulf is warned against the pride of the ruler and against the consequent neglect and misuse of that destiny with its share of honor which will fall to his lot. It is when all the world meets his desire that the keeper of the soul slumbers, and the ruler's doom approaches unawares.

> Bebeorh þē ðone bealonīð,   Bēowulf lēofa,
> secg betsta,   ond þē þæt   sēlre gecēos,
> ēce rǣdas;   oferhȳda ne gȳm,
> mǣre cempa!   (1758–61)

(Keep yourself from such destructive passions, beloved
Beowulf, best of warriors, and choose for yourself that
better part, lasting profit.   Care not for pride,
famous hero!)

The speech of Hrothgar closes the second episode. Beowulf has completed the wandering in foreign lands, and expresses his intention of returning to Hygelac. This implies the opening of a new phase in his career. The judgment passed on his initial labors has been a satisfactory one, and there remains for him the stage of kingship. A period of transition intervenes. Hygelac is killed and the land of the Geats comes under the rule of Beowulf. He rules well for fifty years as the guardian of his people, but as implied in the speech of Hrothgar, royal greatness—the confident possession of power—was regarded by the Germanic mind as the prelude to a disaster of some kind (1761 ff.).[22] The Northern sense of the irony of existence should not be confused with that of Hellenic literature. To the Greek, tragedy followed an inevitable sequence. The first step was dissatisfaction founded on satiety which resulted in the act of *hybris* and ended in disaster. However unavoidable the sequence might appear and however complete the hero's subjection to Fate was represented to be, the end still took the form of some kind of retribution. This attitude was evidently not that of the Northern mind. Retributive justice was ultimately irrelevant in appraising what was still felt to be the ordained pattern of human existence.

As a background to Beowulf's last battle, there is the atmosphere of a "doom" or judgment for which no excuse is made since, obviously, in the eyes of the poet and his contemporaries no excuse is required. Interspersed with the joys of the gift hall is a spirit of foreboding which seems to grow as the dragon fight approaches. The various successes recorded are reduced to failure but the failure is inevitable and seems to bear no relation to the value or scope of the events which lead up to it. It is, at first, difficult to relate the dragon fight to the other two episodes. In the *Volsungasaga*, Sigurd, the young hero, begins his career by slaying the dragon, so that the incident parallels Beowulf's battles with Grendel and his mother. If it is remembered that other versions of the myth speak of the dragon as a water spirit to whom human victims were sacrificed,[23] the connection is made even more definite. The version which fits the narrative of the *Beowulf* is that of the old hero who, at the end of his career, attacks the dragon and kills it but also perishes himself. In the *Voluspa*, Thor attacks the serpent Miðgarðsormr (Encircler of the World), and slays it, yet not only does he perish in the end, but the universe is destroyed in the general conflagration.[24] This last fight of the Norse gods contains all the elements of Beowulf's battle with the dragon. Especially interesting is Thor's attitude of mind. He is aware that Ragnarök, the doom of the gods, is inevitable and that his last hour has come, but this knowledge does not hold him from attacking the serpent, nor is he, at the last, reduced to a state of fear. He appears to be neither desperate nor resigned but retains complete possession of his characteristic energy and courage.[25]

The last episode is introduced by an account of the manner in which the hoard was violated and its guardian tricked by the cunning of a thief (*þēofes cræfte*) (2219). The poet is careful to point out that the invader who provoked the dragon did so out of necessity and not of his own free will. Once in the retreat, he lessened the treasure and presented it to his prince. The dragon is provoked and begins his depredations throughout the countryside. Like Miðgarðsormr, the Encircler of the World, he encompasses the land with fire and finally burns the gift hall of Beowulf. The aged king who, in his youth, had gained fame by battling monsters such as Grendel is now faced by an enemy who is also a guardian, the protector of an enchanted treasure. Grendel's depredations had been undertaken solely out of a spirit of malice and not for the purpose of protecting his possessions. The dragon is, like Beowulf, a guardian and a protector and so their motives for engaging in battle are related. In the first two episodes, the conflict was between the hero and a kind of *diabolus ex machina* who reflected inversely his attitude and status. The same relationship may be found between Beowulf and his fire-breathing antagonist. This time, he is left in his old age to defend not his possessions which are already in flames, but his integrity as the protector of his people. The use of conventional epithets skilfully recalls the two earlier episodes. His own abode, the best of buildings, reminds the audience of Heorot. The throne of the Geats (*gifstōl Gēata*) melting in the surges of fire (*brynewylmum*) (2326)[26] recalls the earlier reference to the throne and the wave-surges stained with blood. After surviving the flood of waters, Beowulf is faced with destruction by fire. He searches his memory for some unremembered sin, the transgression of an ancient law, and is sorely troubled. It is even possible to detect the feeling that he is this time abandoned by the Eternal Lord to Fate which he calls the master of every man (*metod manna gehwæs* (2527). But he claims integrity of mind and dispenses with the formality of boasting. His unblemished character recalls the demands made upon the scapegoat or sacrificial victim in the age-old rites of atonement. The author of *Beowulf* might have been acquainted with these rites through the Biblical account of Isaac and the priesthood of Aaron, or through the medium of his own Northern myths. The older belief in the sacrificial atonement of the divine king is effectively blended with the Christian conception of the savior and redeemer who lays down his life for his people.

In his speech before the battle, the aged hero, for he has reassumed his original role, shows that he is willing to discard his sword as he did formerly, but the enemy is too strong. The dragon is called the keeper of the barrow or cave—foreshadowing Beowulf's burial mound. By challenging it, the old warrior hopes to win the hoard for his people and thus restore the balance of fortune. He offers himself directly as the sacrificial victim, and is prepared to provide the atonement for the evils visited on his subjects.[27] The battle begins, and Beowulf finds himself in the midst of a ring of fire. The companions take refuge in flight. From this dismal plight Wiglaf seeks to rescue him but in vain. The young fighter cannot do for Beowulf what Beowulf had done originally for Hrothgar, although he does assist in killing the dragon. The man who may be said to receive the mantle of the hero is not his equal. Beowulf has not been granted an heir to succeed him. While he lies mortally wounded, he passes judgment on his doom, and rejoices in it. He seeks one thing more and that is the sight of the gold and the treasures which he has won for his land. Again he is confronted with the work of giants—treasure sufficient to overpower any man (*gumcynnes gehwone / oferhīgian*) (2765–66). It is significant that the curse has not yet taken effect, and the hoard is unspoiled. In his last speech, Beowulf gives thanks to the Eternal Lord that he has been able to win for his people the hoard of treasures, instructs Wiglaf how he shall be buried, and confers on him the golden ring and the armor.

The bard ends the description of Beowulf's passing with the statement that his soul sought the judgment of the true (*sōð fæstra dōm*) (2820). The old warrior has attained the heroic apotheosis.

As far as the central character of the epic is concerned, the "doom" or measure of his actions has been completed. The significance of the aftermath is that it reveals the triumph of the curse on the treasure and the uselessness, from the human point of view, of the hero's last stand and the ostensible reason for it. He has succeeded once more in cleansing the land of a baleful influence but not in lifting the curse from the hoard for which he had exchanged his life. In fact, the curse descends with the warrior's last breath to deprive the coveted riches of all value. The ancient princes to whom the original treasure once belonged had placed a ban upon it till the day of judgment. In violating the malediction connected with it, Beowulf, with an apocalyptic energy, anticipated the Last Judgment. By doing so, he staged for himself a preview of that drama. Even if, in person, he did not originally invade the dragon's lair, the purpose of his challenge was to wrest the accumulated treasure of ancient times possessed by the "titans" from its guardian. But before the challenge was ever issued, the flames of the enemy were already devouring his hall and throne. While he was still speaking of the battle, seated on the headland, he was restless in mind as he felt the approach of death and the Fate which was to seek the actual treasure of his soul (*sēcean sāwle hord*) (2422).[28] The hero was in himself the real treasure which he had come to find, and it is significant that he finds his life through losing it.[29] It is as if the bard would say that the real treasure could only be found in the ashes of this world's possessions. No "reason" whatever is given for the hero's defeat; he is in no way culpable. In the spirit of an *imitatio Christi*, Beowulf's death was a blameless sacrifice, for he was not even represented as the immediate cause of strife. The one who actually provoked the dragon's raid which led to the hero's death was, like a Judas Iscariot, entirely unworthy of Beowulf's sacrifice. He was a cowardly and frightened man caught in a situation which was beyond him, and it was he who became the thirteenth man in the troop, forced in his misery to lead the way to the cave. If, however, Beowulf was not responsible for the fiery devastation, he was caught up into the midst of it. Surely, the hero recognized in this, his last battle, the doom of a Ragnarök and also the vision of a Last Judgment, the latter making him the heir to a new promise.

Seen from the perspective of this last battle, the effect of the epic is transformed. The first two episodes may be considered as stages through which the hero passes and defeats the essential embodied evils which seem to bar his advance. The fight with Grendel is seen to be the struggle with the gloom which has descended on the stronghold of Heorot and threatens to render the achievement which it represents of no avail. The companions of Hrothgar are desolate, and the gift hall is bereft of joy. The coming of Beowulf is the restoration of joy but, during the feast which follows his reception, doubt is cast upon his ability and renown by the speech of Unferth. Beowulf answers the challenge of insufficiency by a speech showing the strength of his purpose which Hrothgar detects and in which he rejoices.

gehȳrde on Bēowulfe
folces hyrde   fæstrǣdne geþōht. (609–10)

(The protector of the people heard in
Beowulf a resolute purpose.)

In the first battle, therefore, he resolutely defeats the malignant offensive and slays the son of the mere-woman.

The source of the evil is not yet removed nor is Heorot utterly cleansed while the mere remains haunted by the mother of Grendel. Thus, the first battle is a preliminary to the second. The second represents a more formidable undertaking, since it is easier to repel an incursion than to strike at its source. In this, as in other respects, the epic displays unity of theme and treatment. The only boon that Beowulf asks before meeting Grendel is that the corslet of Wēland[30] should be sent to Hygelac in the event of his death. Before entering the mere, however, the hero remembers his comrades, and hopes that Hrothgar will act as their lord and protector if he should not return. On his arrival, he had encountered the jealousy of Unferth but now he has been given the sword, Hrunting, by his former antagonist. In the first encounter he awaits the enemy and defeats him, but in the second he goes to meet the mere-woman and is seized and brought to her lair. The challenge to which the hero responds is in each instance individual in its immediate application, social in its significance, and universal in its implications, for his victories involve the world of men. For this reason, the home-coming and the report to Hygelac form a link between the cleansing of Heorot and the fight with the dragon. The period of "withdrawal" has been completed. The initial stage of temptation or challenge has elicited a victorious response. The "adversary" in the form of the race of Grendel who has sought to destroy the hero and draw him into the Abyss has been overcome, and Beowulf returns to Hygelac.

In the Christian tradition and in that of the Northern sagas, the world is represented as suffering two cataclysmic upheavals—one by water and one by fire. With the former is associated purgation and renewal, with the latter, death and transfiguration. Beowulf is, therefore, rescued from the power of the flood in the second battle, and the imagery suitably suggests the Biblical Deluge. The subsequent passages describing the home-coming and the struggles connected with political and dynastic ambitions are a prelude to the last battle. While looking forward to the fulfillment of Beowulf's prophecy regarding the engagement of Freawaru and Ingeld and the ensuing wars, the reader finally discovers that he is looking backward at the illustrious career of Beowulf after a reign of fifty years. This atmosphere of reminiscence is interwoven with the narrative of the depredations of the Dragon. The sudden change is striking.

þā wæs Bīowulfe   brōga gecȳðed
snūde tō sōðe,   þæt his sylfes hām,
bolda sēlest   brynewylmum mealt,
gifstōl Gēata.   (2324–27)

> (Then straightway the terror was made known
> to Beowulf that in truth his own abode, the
> best of buildings, the throne of the Geats,
> was melting in the surges of flame.)

The immediate suddenness of the catastrophe overwhelms Beowulf, for the destruction of his throne is the destruction of the natural field of the hero's experience, and it foreshadows with dramatic irony the end of his earthly career. The pattern of his *dōm* passes before him, and he prepares to engage in his last battle.

This last battle with the fiery antagonist is in the form of an apocalypse which reveals the theme of judgment as the ordained conclusion to that of redemption. In the first encounter, the companions in the festive hall of Heorot arouse the Satanic invader by their feasting and by singing the song of Creation. Like Satan in Milton's *Paradise Lost,* Grendel journeys from his hell-world in the subterranean cave through the chaotic waters of the mere to the human world, and his journey is a vision of the incursion of the evil will into the cosmos, placed in the Christian tradition prior to the fall of Adam. This theme is specifically developed in the next episode, in which Beowulf enters the troubled waters of the mere and is seized by Grendel's dam and dragged down into the cave. From this state he is redeemed when defeat seems inevitable, and returns to enter into the joy of his lord. His redemption is followed in due time by the acquisition of kingship and finally by the apocalyptic battle with the dragon.

> And the great dragon was cast out, that old serpent,
> called the Devil and Satan, which deceiveth the whole
> world: he was cast out into the earth, and his angels
> were cast out with him. (Revelation xii.9)[31]

Either in terms of the Norse myth or the Christian tradition, this is the consummation of a catastrophic vision of judgment. The tragic hero loses himself and is represented as a failure through his self-will, pride, and presumption. But although there are the overtones of sorrow, even the death of this epic hero is a triumph in the midst of apparent catastrophe.

At the close of the epic, the twelve sons of the chieftains ride about the burial mound of Beowulf to lament the king and exalt his heroic life. Their tribute recalls the beginning of the epic and its theme, and the work is thus effectively completed. It must be borne in mind that the structure of the narrative was known to the audience. This accounts for the fact that the outcome of the three mythical battles is stated, in each instance, before the actual struggle is well under way. Suspense was not felt to be important; it was the meaning of the heroic adventure which counted, and it is in the meaning, with its wealth of suggestive imagery, that the unity of the *Beowulf* is to be found. The pattern which this imagery produces is not without coherence, and it is not difficult to see the outline of an heroic achievement expressed in a way which reflects the impact of Christian ideals upon the world of the Northern saga. As in the *Iliad,* it is the story of Beowulf and the figure of Beowulf which focus the bard's complete vision of life. The hero becomes the universal type of humanity and of the life of humanity in all its greatness, in its wonder and sorrow. Achilles is described as the man of swiftest doom (ὠκυμορώτατος) ; for if man himself is of swift doom, the hero is the intensification of the life of the race (*Iliad* I. 505).[32] Although the story of Beowulf does not emphasize the brevity of human existence, it does emphatically concentrate on the mortal fate which conflicts with the glory of heroic achievement and yet is the basis of redemption. Beowulf is never wholly free from despair but he triumphs over it, and in this triumph the author successfully completes his theme of judgment after recounting the trials of his hero.

NOTES

1. Fr. Klaeber, *Beowulf* (3d. ed., New York, 1950), p.*li–iii.*

2. In this connection, informed opinion has been based on the following: J. R. R. Tolkien, "Beowulf: The Monsters and the Critics," *Proc. British Acad.* 22:271–72 (1936) ; R. W. Chambers, "Beowulf and the 'Heroic Age' in England," *Man's Unconquerable Mind* (London, 1939), p. 68–70; Kemp Malone, "Beowulf," *English Stud.,* 29:161–72 (1948) ; J. L. N. O'Loughlin, "*Beowulf*—Its Unity and Purpose," *Medium Ævum* 21:1–13 (1952).

3. As A. G. Brodeur states ("The Structure and the Unity of *Beowulf*," *PMLA* 68:1186 [Dec. 1953]), "a time gap of more than fifty years, confronted its poet with a problem more difficult than Homer had to face," because the poet obviously felt the irrelevance of the events of those fifty years. For the defence of the symbolical interpretation see Adrien Bonjour, "Monsters Crouching and Critics Rampant," *PMLA* 68:304–12 (Mar. 1953).

4. Aristotle, *Poetics,* XXIV, 1459B. Cf. Beowulf, ed. by C. L. Wrenn (London, 1953), p.41: "*Beowulf* may best be described as an heroic poem rather than an epic, since the Classical name at once suggests structural qualities which the poet did not aim at."

5. Among the Hindus, the scriptural writings (*sāstra*) were divided into four categories of which one included the collections of ancient legends (*purāna*) comprising the cosmogonic works from which their epics were immediately derived. With reference to the Hebraic writings, it might be objected that Job should be placed in the third class, that the books dealing specifically with the Law are inappropriate, that Psalms and the wisdom literature fit awkwardly into the scheme, and that the prophets were moving in the direction of an individualistic rather than a racial point of view. But it must also be remembered that the first type is close to the origin of all three, and may conceivably contain examples of the other two within it, along with much of what—to our Aristotelian palates —may appear "irrelevant" matter.

6. Klaeber (*Beowulf,* p.*cvii*) dates the epic not later than the beginning of the eighth century, well before the Danish invasions. He describes the anonymous author (p.*cxix*) as a "man well versed in Germanic and Scandinavian lore, familiar with secular Anglo-Saxon poems of the type exemplified by *Widsið Finnsburg, Deor,* and *Waldere,* and a student of biblical poems of the Cædmonian cycle, a man of notable taste and culture and informed with a spirit of broad-minded Christianity."

7. *Beowulf,* 2. Hereafter line numbers will be given parenthetically in the text.

8. Joseph Campbell in his book on the significance of the hero in myth and legend (*The Hero with a Thousand Faces* [New York, 1949], p.245 ff.) summarizes in outline the heroic adventure.

9. Cited by R. W. Chambers, *Beowulf* (Cambridge, Eng., 1921), p.370.

10. C. J. Engelhardt ("*Beowulf:* A Study in Dilatation," *PMLA* 70:834–35 [Sept. 1955]), describes Unferth as "a man in whom force of mind has been supplanted by cunning. Even his name suggests paronomastically the lack of this spiritual force or *ferhð.*" Klaeber (*Beowulf,* p.148) rejects this interpretation in favor of *Unfrið*—"mar-peace"—as do Wrenn (*Beowulf,* p.317) and others.

11. Cited by O. F. Emerson, "Legends of Cain," *PMLA* 21:867 (1906). See Louis Ginzberg, *Legends of the Bible* (New York, 1956), p.59.

12. Cf. I John iii.12: "Not as Cain, who was of that wicked one, and slew his brother."

And wherefore slew he him? Because his own works were evil, and his brother's righteous."

13. Augustine, *In Epistolam Joannis ad Parthos* (Tract. v, chap. iii), referred to Cain as *filius diaboli;* cf. *Anglo-Saxon Chronicle,* Anno 675 (the writ of Pope Agatho). For Cain's descent from Satan or Samael, the Angel of Death, see Ginzberg, *Legends of the Bible,* p.54: "Cain's descent from Satan, who is the angel Samael, was revealed in his seraphic appearance. At his birth, the exclamation was wrung from Eve, 'I have gotten a man through an angel of the Lord'."

14. *Early English Text Society* 57:1065–660.

15. *Canterbury Tales,* x(1), 1015. This may serve as a possible explanation of lines 168–69 in *Beowulf,* if *gifstōl* means the throne of God from which Cain was forever banished.

16. Compare Beowulf's magnanimity with that of Aristotle's magnanimous man (*Ethics* IV.3) who possesses "greatness of soul" (μεγαλοψυχια), rather than being possessed by unwarranted pride (ὕβρις).

17. *Metod* probably had the original meaning of 'ruler,' and in the pre-Christian period was closely associated with the idea of "Fate." The word was perhaps derived from *metan* 'to measure' and may be compared with Old Norse *mjqtuðr* 'ordainer of fate.'

18. The *Bear's Son Tale* is certainly the literal analogue of *Beowulf*—the "bee-wolf" or "bear." He may also be called the "innocent abroad" who conquers cunning and experience, like a Galahad. There is a possible comparison here with Parsifal, the "guileless fool" of the Grail legend.

19. *Beowulf,* 2327 ff.; Augustine, *De Civ. Dei,* lib. XIV, chap. 8–9.

20. *Beowulf,* 1681; Genesis IV.22.

21. The universal nature of the trials of the epic hero is emphasized. Christ was called the "young hero" (*geong hæleð*) in the *Dream of the Cross* (l. 39)—a term used to describe Beowulf throughout the epic. If Beowulf is to be the typical Christian hero, his struggle should reflect by analogy the archetypal passion of Christ. "And it was about the sixth hour, and there was a darkness over all the earth until the ninth hour. And the sun was darkened, and the veil of the temple was rent in the midst" (Luke XXIII. 44 ff.; cf. Matthew XXVII. 45 and Mark XV. 33 ff.). *"Ðā cōm nōn dæges"* (*Beowulf,* 1600). Allusion is also made to the theme of purgation and renewal in that part of the *Poetic Edda* where the Norse pagan deity Odin is crucified on the mysterious tree for nine nights (tr. by H. A. Bellows, [New York, 1923], *Hovamol,* 139).

22. In sacrificing himself for his people, Beowulf performs an act of public service amounting to the liturgical rite of sacrifice of the earlier conception of the divine king and the dying god. See R. C. Sutherland, "The Meaning of *Eorlscipe* in *Beowulf,*" *PMLA* 70:1139–40 (Dec. 1955).

23. J. G. Frazer, *The Golden Bough* (London, 1951), v. 2, p.155.

24. *Poetic Edda,* tr. by H. A. Bellows (New York, 1926), *Voluspa,* 55 ff.

25. Contrast this with the attitude of the Olympian deities living "without sorrow," and decreeing "for miserable mortals that they should live in pain" (*Iliad* XXIV. 525–26). The classical outlook should not be confused with the Germanic in this respect. C. L. Wrenn (*Beowulf,* p.41–42) applies a classical standard to a Germanic epic when he calls the "Germanic hero" a "tragic hero," and at the same time speaks of his "glorious death" without which "a Germanic hero would be incomplete." Surely, the tragic hero is such because he fails in the heroic adventure and his death is not glorious. The suffering and death of the Germanic hero, however, is far from tragic, for it demonstrates the measure of his heroic virtue.

26. Cf. Kemp Malone, "Coming Back from the Mere," *PMLA* 69:1299 (Dec. 1954), and the statement that "our study of the art of the *Beowulf* poet needs to take into account the parallelism of parts and other structural features to an extent greater than has been usual in the past." The parallelism here suggested serves to unite the dragon fight to the so-called "Grendel part" and is reinforced by two references (2351 ff., 2521) which Klaeber (*Beowulf,* p. li–lii) too readily dismisses as "being quite cursory and irrelevant."

27. That courage which distinguished the "lost cause" was dear to the Germanic heart. In the *Battle of Maldon,* the Saxon chief who is mortally wounded is praised for this quality (146–48), and later, in the speech by Byrhtwold, the same attitude of mind is encouraged (312–13).

28. Fate (*wyrd*) and the Lord of Fate (*metod*) are here aligned as the providential means of the hero's redemption. Cf. A. G. Brodeur, "Structure and Unity of *Beowulf*," p.1187. Fate is surely not merely "a power which God is no longer concerned to forestall," but rather one which has come to serve the larger purpose of the hero's salvation through suffering and loss.

29. Cf. Matthew x. 39; xvi. 25; Mark viii. 35; Luke xvii. 33; John xii. 25.

30. This Anglo-Saxon form of the name of the mythical blacksmith, Wayland Smith, corresponds to Old Norse *Volundr* (German *Wieland*). Like Hephaestus in the *Iliad,* he, a supernatural figure, had forged the armor of the hero. Like Arthur's Excalibur and the Shield of Achilles, Beowulf's Corslet bore witness to his heroic stature.

31. The parallel is drawn in the spirit of Tolkien and against that of O. F. Emerson ("Legends of Cain," p.882) and T. M. Gang. Surely the reader can assume that Christianity's Satanic Dragon, the prince of this world, and the Norse Miðgarðsormr, the encircler of the world, were in the mind of the author who gave us Beowulf's antagonist. See A. E. DuBois, "The Dragon in *Beowulf*," *PMLA* 72:819–22 (Dec. 1957).

32. Cf. E. T. Owen, *The Story of the Iliad* (Toronto, 1946), p. 247–48.

John M. Steadman

THE "SUFFERING SERVANT"

MESSIANIC MINISTRY AS EPIC EXEMPLAR

In the Christ of *Paradise Regain'd* recent scholarship has recognized Milton's answer to the classic problem of the Renaissance epic poet—the choice of an exemplary hero. In both of his epics the perfect "pattern of a Christian hero"[1] he exhibits not in a secular "king or knight," but in the Son of God himself—the "Most perfect *Heroe,* try'd in heaviest plight Of Labours huge and hard, too hard for human wight." In the protagonist of *Paradise Regain'd* [Merritt Y.] Hughes saw "the culmination of the faith of the Reformers in an exemplar Redeemer, the Word of Saint John's Gospel, as it fused with the cravings of the critics and poets of the later Renaissance for a purely exemplary hero in epic poetry."[2] [Frank] Kermode found in this figure an idea of Christian heroism surpassing that of the pagan worthies both in virtue and in rewards: "We learn . . . why Christ is the exemplary hero by watching him in the act of confuting or transcending all the known modes of heroism. We are taught the rewards of Christian heroism by a demonstration based on the superseded rewards of the old heroes."[3] Finally, [A. S. P.] Woodhouse has focused attention on "two ideas . . . embodied in the Christ of *Paradise Regain'd*"—"the idea of obedience to God as the beginning and end of virtue, and the idea of Christian heroism as something new and distinctive, different not simply in degree, but in kind, from every other."[4]

Nevertheless, the attempt to interpret Milton's Christ against the background of Renaissance heroic tradition involves us in a certain paradox. While acknowledging that Christ himself provides the heroic norm *par excellence,* we may find ourselves, notwithstanding, in the position of regarding him as the embodiment of ethical concepts which are extrinsic to the Biblical Messiah—of explaining his character as a reflection of Milton's personal preference for a particular heroic ideal: magnanimity or charity, action or contemplation, doing or suffering, the military fortitude displayed in "Warrs" or "the better fortitude Of Patience and Heroic Martyrdom."

In actuality (Milton would have insisted) the true heroic paradigm is implicit in Christ, and any valid conception of the heroic norm must inevitably be derivative from his example. He is, strictly speaking, the *arche-*

"The 'Suffering Servant.'" From John M. Steadman, *Milton's Epic Characters: Image and Idol* (Chapel Hill: University of North Carolina Press, 1968), p.58–71. Reprinted by permission of the publisher. First published, in somewhat different form, in *The Harvard Theological Review* 54: 29–43 (1961).

type rather than the *embodiment* of Christian heroism. As the perfect "pattern of a Christian hero" is, *ipso facto,* Christ himself, Milton modeled his exemplary hero not on any ideal extrinsic to the Biblical Messiah, but on the character of the historic Christ as revealed in the Scriptures and interpreted by Protestant theologians. He did not "lay" the heroic norm in this figure, as he might have done in the case of some "king or knight, before the conquest."[5] Instead, it was precisely from the Son of God that he derived his heroic paradigm.

The norm of heroic excellence in both epics is Biblical both in origin and in authority. In the lineaments of his poetic Christ, Milton sought to imitate those of the historic Messiah—the "suffering servant" of Isaiah's prophecy, the redeemer in "the form of a servant" of Philippians. In both of these poems the supremely heroic enterprise is Messiah's ministry of redemption, and in the twofold aspects of this ministry—Messiah's humiliation and exaltation—lies the perfect exemplar of Christian heroism and its rewards. This is the true prototype of the heroic pattern in both *Paradise Lost* and *Paradise Regain'd,* and for the characterization of Christ in either poem the concepts of Renaissance ethical theory are of secondary importance.

Milton's search for the ideal exemplar of Christian heroism led him, then, from the inferior imitation to the archetype, from the Christian "king or knight" to Christ himself. In choosing the Messiah as his "pattern of a Christian hero," he pursued to its logical conclusion an axiom of Renaissance poetic theory—that the poet must imitate the idea. Poetry is more philosophic than history, Aristotle had insisted, "since its statements are of the nature rather of universals, whereas those of history are singulars."[6] In such epic heroes as Achilles, Odysseus, Aeneas, and Godfrey, Renaissance critics had recognized the "idea" of a valiant warrior, a prudent commander, a virtuous leader, or a Christian prince. Similarly, in looking for some "king or knight, before the conquest," in whom he might "lay the pattern of a Christian hero," Milton had been seeking an appropriate vehicle for the *idea* of Christian virtue—a particular historical example, in which he might delineate the universal norm. In the case of all of these secular worthies the heroic paradigm is an ideal really extrinsic to the men themselves, a universal which the poet may *embody* in a particular individual. In the instance of Milton's Christ, however, the relationship of the historical particular to the universal norm is radically different. Here the example is himself the Idea; the historical individual is himself the universal norm. In Christ, the suffering servant, Milton found the very archetype of Christian heroism.

I

Not only is Christ himself the heroic exemplar in both of Milton's epics, but his ministry of redemption is likewise the supremely heroic or "godlike" enterprise. At best the secular worthy could bring a superficial and temporary deliverance to a mere fraction of humanity. Christ's satisfaction, on the other hand, enabled him to offer a genuine and eternal deliverance to all mankind—"to save . . . the whole Race lost," "to save A World from utter loss." Moreover, the secular hero achieved fame largely through acts of destruction. Messiah, on the other hand, not only surpassed them in destructive might (witness his victory over the rebel angels), but also was capable of a still loftier mode of valor—both to create and to restore his fallen creation; "to create" the angelic choir reminds us, "is greater than created to destroy." Finally, the earthly conqueror had inevitably been overcome by Sin and Death. Messiah, on the other hand, overcame both of these "grand foes" in his ministry of redemption. The ministry of redemption is thus the supremely heroic act of the "Most perfect *Heroe*," and it is to the dual aspects of this ministry—Christ's humiliation and exaltation[7]—that we must look for the archetypal pattern of Christian heroic virtue and its reward.

Christ's humiliation and exaltation (Milton declared in the *De Doctrina Christiana*) provide a normative pattern for all Christian believers. The conformity[8] of the faithful to his image was a major objective of his ministry of redemption: "The second object of the ministry of the Mediator is, *that we may be conformed to the image of Christ, as well in his state of humiliation as of exaltation.*"[9] Like Christ, the faithful must endure suffering, but, with Christ, they would receive an eternal "reward" or "recompense"[10] of heavenly glory:

> Rom. viii, 29, "to be conformed to the image of his Son . . ."; [Rom.] viii, 17, "if so be that we suffer with him, that we may be also glorified together . . ."; 2 Tim. ii, 11, 12, "if we be dead with him, we shall also live with him . . ."; 1 Pet. iv. 13, "rejoice, inasmuch as ye are partakers of Christ's sufferings, that when his glory shall be revealed, ye may be glad also."

> John xii. 32, "I, if I be lifted up from the earth, will draw all men unto me."; [John] xvi. 22, "the glory that thou gavest me, I have given them."; Ephesians ii. 5, 6, "God hath quickened us together with Christ . . . and hath raised us up together, and made us sit together in heavenly places in Christ Jesus."

Again, in a passage Milton cites frequently in his chapter "Of the Ministry of Redemption," St. Paul exhorts the Philippians (2:5–9) to imitate the example of Christ's humiliation:

> Let this mind be in you, which was also in Christ Jesus: Who, being in the form of God, thought it not robbery to be equal with God: But made himself of no reputation, and took upon him the form of a servant, and was made in the likeness of men: And being found in fashion as a man, he humbled himself, and became obedient unto death, even the death of the cross. Wherefore God also hath highly exalted him, and given him a name which is above every name.[11]

In Christ's humiliation and exaltation—an example normative for all believers—Milton found his ideal "pattern" of Christian heroism and its reward.

II

In Messiah's humiliation Milton found an ethical pattern diametrically opposed to that of the secular hero. Where the worldly hero sought glory, Christ had voluntarily renounced glory for shame. Where the wordly hero strove to win "high repute," Christ had made himself of "no reputation," Where the worldly hero aspired to regal dignity, Christ had assumed the form of a servant. Where the worldly heroes had usurped divine title ("and must be titl'd Gods, Great Benefactors of mankind, Deliverers, Worship't with Temple, Priest and Sacrifice; One is the Son of *Jove,* of *Mars* the other"), Christ had resigned the "form of God" and the privileges of divinity. In this concept of heroic humility—a heroism characterized by obedience, lowliness, and suffering—Milton found the antithesis of the world's opinion of the hero.

Let us briefly examine the use Milton makes of this conception of the "suffering servant" as heroic archetype, first in *Paradise Lost* and afterwards in *Paradise Regain'd.*

Christ's humiliation (Milton declared in the *De Doctrina*) is "that state in which under his character of God-man he voluntarily submitted himself to the divine justice, as well in life as in death, for the purpose of undergoing all things requisite to accomplish our redemption." The first object of his ministry of redemption was "the satisfaction of divine justice on behalf of all men"; and in accomplishing this satisfaction he "fulfilled the law by perfect love to God and his neighbor, until the time when he laid down his life for his brethren, being made obedient unto his Father in all things."[12]

In *Paradise Lost* these concepts emerge with exceptional clarity in the celestial council of Book III. Here the Son of God "voluntarily submits himself to the divine justice" on man's behalf. The particular virtues he manifests on this occasion—"immortal love To mortal men" and "Filial obedience"—are the moral qualities especially demanded for his satisfaction. In accepting the Father's challenge to "satisfie for Man," he displays that "magnanimous resolution to die,"[13] which, in Tasso's opinion, characterized the ideal epic hero. In this scene he voluntarily makes "himself of no reputation" and becomes "obedient unto death."

> Account mee man; I for his sake will leave
> Thy bosom, and this glorie next to thee
> Freely put off, and for him lastly die
> Well pleas'd on me let Death wreck all his rage. . . .

In this passage, crucial for the celestial strategy in the Holy War, the heroic norm is clearly based on the doctrine of Christ's humiliation. After first presenting the Messiah in "the form of God" and as "equal to God," Milton shows him volunteering to "take upon him the form of a servant," for the sake of accomplishing his ministry of redemption. This deliberate renunciation of glory for shame ("no reputation") stands in striking opposition to Satan's motivation in the analogous scene in Hell ("the high repute Which he through hazard huge must earn").

Again, Milton stresses Messiah's humiliation in Book X, when the Son of God assumes "the forme of servant" immediately after passing judgment on Adam and Eve:

> . . . [He] disdain'd not to begin
> Thenceforth the forme of servant to assume,
> As when he wash'd his servants' feet, so now
> As Father of his Familie he clad

> *Thir nakedness with Skins of Beasts, or slain* . . . :
> *Nor hee thir outward onely with the Skins*
> *Of Beasts, but inward nakedness, much more*
> *Opprobrious, with his Robe of righteousness,*
> *Araying cover'd from his Fathers sight.*

Later, in his mediatorial function, he intercedes with the Father (X, 228; XI, 21–44) on behalf of the guilty pair. Finally, in Book XII, Michael recapitulates the essential details of Christ's humiliation and satisfaction (XII, 390–435):

> *The Law of God exact he shall fulfil*
> *Both by obedience and by love, though love*
> *Alone fulfil the Law; thy punishment*
> *He shall endure by coming in the Flesh*
> *To a reproachful life and cursed death.* . . .

In this passage, as in Book III, the poet emphasizes the two allied virtues, obedience and love—both requisite for Christ's mission "to satisfie for Man." It is from Michael's account of Christ's humiliation that Adam learns the better fortitude of "suffering for Truth's sake" and the merit of obedience.

If Messiah's humiliation constitutes the norm of Christian heroism in *Paradise Lost,* his exaltation provides the pattern of the Christian's reward—a *remuneratio aeterna* of celestial glory:

> *The exaltation of Christ* is that by which *having triumphed over death, and laid aside the form of a servant, he was exalted by God the Father to a state of immortality and of the highest glory, partly by his own merits, partly by the gift of the Father, for the benefit of mankind; wherefore he rose again from the dead, ascended into heaven, and sitteth on the right hand of God.* . . . This exaltation consists of three degrees; his resurrection, his ascension into heaven, and his sitting on the right hand of God. . . .[14]

In Book III the Son himself prophesies his triumph over death and his victorious return to Heaven "with the multitude of my redeem'd" (III. 247–65). That his exaltation is the reward for his humiliation is stated, however, even more explicitly by the Father (III. 305–17):

> *Because thou hast, though Thron'd in highest bliss*
> *Equal to God, and equally enjoying*
> *God-like fruition, quitted all to save*
> *A World from utter loss, and hast been found*
> *By Merit more than Birthright Son of God,*
> *Found worthiest to be so by being Good,*
> *Far more than Great or High; because in thee*
> *Love hath abounded more than Glory abounds,*
> *Therefore thy Humiliation shall exalt*
> *With thee thy Manhood also to this Throne;*
> *Here shalt thou sit incarnate, here shalt Reigne*
> *Both God and Man, Son both of God and Man,*
> *Anointed universal King.* . . .

Again, in Book III, Michael foretells Messiah's exaltation and entrance into glory and foresees the heavenly reward of the faithful (XII. 456–65).

III

In *Paradise Regain'd*, as in the earlier epic, the heroic norm is to be found in Christ's ministry of redemption—in the humiliation which precedes his ultimate exaltation. Although the temptation is itself an aspect of this humiliation, the poet's primary emphasis falls on future events. The temptation is basically an "apprentissage"—a schooling in spiritual combat preliminary to a greater battle. In this preparatory "exercise" the protagonist must "first lay down the rudiments Of his great warfare" against Sin and Death. As he is to conquer these "grand foes" not by physical weapons, but by "Humiliation and strong Sufferance," he must learn the particular virtues requisite for his future satisfaction—obedience, humility, reliance on Providence (I, 290–93), and patience. These are the necessary moral equipment for his "reproachful life" and the supreme agony of the crucifixion—a death "ignominious in the highest degree." In this epic, as in its predecessor, the virtues Milton stresses as normative for Christian heroism are those particularly characteristic of the "suffering servant"—obedience and the "better fortitude" of patience. Both of these virtues are actually based on the concept of Messiah's humiliation, and it is significant that Milton's Christ recognizes that suffering and obedience, exercised in "humble state," are necessary prerequisites for his ultimate exaltation (III. 188–97):

> What if he hath decreed that I shall first
> Be try'd in humble state, and things adverse,
> By tribulations, injuries, insults,
> Contempts, and scorns, and snares, and violence,
> Suffering, abstaining, quietly expecting
> Without distrust or doubt, that he may know
> What I can suffer, how obey? who best
> Can suffer, best can do; best reign, who first
> Well hath obey'd; just tryal e're I merit
> My exaltation without change or end.

In the spiritual duel between Christ's wisdom and Satan's "hellish wiles," Milton skillfully exploited the antithesis between the "form of God" which Messiah had laid aside and the "form of a servant" which he had assumed, for some highly effective irony. Throughout the poem Satan has assayed to discover the identity of "this glorious Eremite"—

> In what degree of meaning thou are call'd
> The Son of God, which bears no single sense;

yet it is not until the third and final temptation that he realizes that the "Son of *Joseph* deem'd" is identical with Jehovah's "first-begot," whose "fierce thunder drove us to the deep." And this he learns by a miracle; only when Messiah is able "to stand upright" on the "highest Pinnacle" does his adversary recognize him.

Satan's inability to recognize the Son of God in the state of humiliation is quite consistent with the belief (shared by several Reformation
theologians) that Christ's divinity was "hidden" in the state of his humiliation, but nevertheless manifested itself on occasion in miracles. Polanus
maintained that "Christ humbled himself in respect of his Deity . . . by
hiding it under the forme of a servant which he had assumed. . . ."[15] Wolleb
asserted that when Christ "stript himself of the forme and glory of the
Divinity," he "did not cast off the Divinity, but hid it in the assumed form
of a servant: And . . . the Deity of Christ did manifest it selfe in the state
of his Humiliation, chiefly by miracles. . . ."[16] Milton exploits this conception poetically for the sake of complicating his Fable. It enables him to achieve
"the finest form of Discovery"—"one attended by Peripeties, like that
which goes with the Discovery in *Oedipus*."[17]

It is the essential identity of the Son—the continuity of his divine Sonship
in the state of humiliation as in that of exaltation—that the "Angelic
Quires" emphasize in their final hymn:

> *True Image of the Father, whether thron'd*
> *In the bosom of bliss, and light of light*
> *Conceiving, or remote from Heaven, enshrin'd*
> *In fleshy Tabernacle, and human form,*
> *Wandr'ing the Wilderness, whatever place,*
> *Habit, or state, or motion, still expressing*
> *The Son of God, with Godlike force indu'd*
> *Against th' Attempter of thy Father's Throne. . . .*

Whether in the "form of God" or in the "form of a servant," Messiah remains the "first-begot" of the Father, and it is to "His Father's business"
—the ministry of redemption—that the final lines of the angelic chorus
commit him:

> *. . . on thy glorious work*
> *Now enter, and begin to save mankind.*

Humiliation and suffering—these are, paradoxically, the "matchless Deeds"
whereby he must "express [his] matchless Sire."

Negatively, the pattern of Christ's humiliation determines in part the
character of the "manlier objects . . . such as have more show Of Worth,
of honour, glory, and popular praise," whereby his antagonist attempts to
try his constancy. Wealth, honor, arms, arts, kingdoms, empires, glory, fame
(IV, 368–69, 536)—these are not merely inferior to the *remuneratio aeterna*
which Messiah merits for mankind; they are also fundamentally at variance
with the nature of his mediatorial office, with the theological purpose of his
humiliation. In order to carry out "His Father's business"—the ministry
of redemption—Messiah must reject all ends or means incompatible with
the character of the "suffering servant." The enterprises and rewards which
Satan proposes are, indeed, characteristic of secular opinions of heroic activity, but, inasmuch as they are diametrically opposed to the Messianic
pattern of humiliation, they are obstacles, rather than means, to his destined
enterprise—the redemption of mankind.

If, on the one hand, Satan attempts to divert Messiah from his mission of redemption by tempting him to choose ends and means inconsistent with his humiliation, on the other hand he depicts the Messianic norm of humiliation as an evil to be eschewed. He pretends to find in the stars a prediction of ignominy and death, and he interprets this pattern of adversity as an obstacle to the execution of the Biblical prophecies concerning the Messiah, rather than as a means to their fulfillment (IV. 382-88, 477–80):

> *Now contrary, if I read aught in Heaven, . . .*
> *Sorrows and labours, opposition, hate,*
> *Attends thee, scorns, reproaches, injuries,*
> *Violence and stripes, and lastly cruel death.*
>
> *If thou observe not this, be sure to find,*
> *What I foretold thee, many a hard assay*
> *Of dangers, and adversities and pains,*
> *Ere thou of* Israel's *Scepter get fast hold. . . .*

As Satan elsewhere shows familiarity with the prophecies[18] about the future Messiah (III. 178; IV. 381, 502), it seems apparent that he has in mind the Scriptural predictions concerning the suffering servant and is deliberately wresting them to his own purposes. Certainly, Christ himself recognizes in these prophecies the pattern of humiliation and suffering (I. 259–67), and his mother is likewise aware that the future contains not "Honour," but "trouble" (II. 86–87).

> *This having heard, strait I again revolv'd*
> *The Law and Prophets, searching what was writ*
> *Concerning the Messiah, to our Scribes*
> *Known partly, and soon found of whom they spake*
> *I am; this chiefly, that my way must lie*
> *Through many a hard assay even to the death,*
> *E're I the promis'd Kingdom can attain,*
> *Or work Redemption for mankind, whose sins*
> *Full weight must be transferr'd upon my head.*

The phrase "many a hard assay" appears first on Christ's lips and afterwards on Satan's.[19] By this verbal echo Milton attempts to underscore the contrasting attitudes of the two figures towards the Biblical prophecy of the suffering servant. Whereas Christ, recognizing that his humiliation must precede his exaltation, rejects all alternatives to his destined ministry of redemption, Satan attempts to seduce the hero from the Messianic path of humiliation by proposing contrary ends or means on the one hand and by presenting the idea of the suffering servant as a degradation to be shunned, on the other. Christ, in his "wisdom," interprets the Old Testament prophecy of a suffering Messiah in its correct sense. Satan, by his "hellish wiles," deliberately distorts it.

In this context, the emphasis that Reformation discussions of Messiah's humiliation and exaltation placed on proof texts concerning the Old Testament prophecies of the suffering servant seems especially significant. Polanus[20] cited Luke 24:26, with its specific application of these predictions of Jesus: "O fools, and slow of heart to believe all that the prophets have spoken: Ought not Christ to have suffered these things, and to enter into his glory? And beginning at Moses and all the prophets, he expounded unto them in all the scriptures concerning himself." Similarly, Wolleb, explaining that in the state of humiliation Christ administered his regal office "in gathering together a Church by his word and Spirit, so, that in their [*sic*] appeared no sign of Regal Majesty," adduced the following corollary: "In vain do the Jews dream of *Messiah's* corporal and earthly Kingdome."[21] In support of this "Rule" he cited three Old Testament prophecies concerning the suffering servant—Isaiah 42:2 and 53:2–3 and Zechariah 9:9,

> He shall not cry, nor lift up, nor cause his voice to be heard in the street. . . . he hath no form nor comeliness: . . . He is despised and rejected of men; a man of sorrows, and acquainted with grief: . . . he was despised, and we esteemed him not.

> . . . behold, thy King cometh unto thee: he is just, and having salvation; lowly, and riding upon an ass. . . .

In these prophecies of his humiliation Christ could recognize an ideal absolutely contradictory to the ends and means Satan proposed to him.[22] From the same prophecies[23] his tempter could acquire some knowledge of the nature of the ministry of redemption and evolve a strategy designed to frustrate the Messianic way of humiliation.

IV

In Messiah's ministry of redemption Milton found the norm of Christian heroism for both of his epics, but not (paradoxically) an epic subject. Except for the incomplete lines on "The Passion," he never, apparently, devoted a poem to what would seem to be the logical material for a Christian heroic poet—the crucifixion and resurrection.[24] Though both of his epics represent these "godlike acts" as the supremely heroic enterprise, the actual arguments of both poems concern events preliminary to this "glorious work." In *Paradise Regain'd* the heroic norm is the "great warfare" on the cross, whereby Messiah is to defeat Sin and Death; but instead of taking the victory over Death and Sin as his subject, Milton chooses the theme of the temptation in the wilderness, where Christ is acquiring the "rudiments" of his subsequent warfare. In *Paradise Lost* the poet declares that Messiah is to triumph through his death and resurrection—by paying "the rigid satisfaction, death for death," and afterwards rising "Victorious" to "subdue" the "vanquisher"; the real argument of this poem, however, is not Christ's triumph, but Adam's fall. Milton never assayed a *Christiad,* the logical objective for a Christian poet.

Perhaps the fact that Vida ("Cremona's Trump") had anticipated him served as a deterrent. Nevertheless there was an additional, and possibly more cogent, objection to writing an epic on the Passion and Resurrection. The detailed account in the Gospels left the poet little scope to invent, to alter and rearrange his materials in the interests of verisimilitude and the epic marvellous, or to adapt his sources to the laws and conventions of heroic poetry. In the subjects Milton *did* choose—the fall of man and the temptation of Christ—the brevity of the Biblical narrative was a distinct asset; it afforded him ample opportunity for "feigning." It is significant that both Tasso and Milton's own nephew recognized the advantages of a subject brief or obscure enough to leave scope for invention and fiction. "In [sacred] histories of the first quality," declared Tasso, "the poet scarcely dares to extend his own hand. . . . Feigning is hardly permissible in such cases, and the writer who does not feign and imitate . . . is not really a poet, but a historian." In choosing his subject (Tasso continues) the poet should select his argument from the history of a remote nation or period since it affords greater freedom in imitation. For Edward Phillips, "it is not a meer Historical relation, spic't over with a little slight fiction . . ., which makes a *Heroic Poem;* but it must be rather a brief, obscure, or remote Tradition, but of some remarkable piece of story, in which the Poet hath an ample field to inlarge by feigning of probable circumstances, in which . . . Invention . . . principally consisteth. . . ."[25]

In both of Milton's epics the supreme exemplar of heroic virtue and its reward—the perfect pattern of that "suffering for Truths sake" which is "fortitude to highest victorie" and receives a recompense of celestial glory— is ultimately based on Christ's humiliation and exaltation. Though manifested *par excellence* in Messiah himself, this heroic norm of the "suffering servant"[26] who endures "Universal reproach" or violence in his single-handed obedience to the divine will and his isolated witness to the divine truth also recurs on the angelic and purely human levels in such "heroes of faith" as Abdiel, the faithful "Servant of God," who maintains "against revolted multitudes the Cause of Truth," in the occasional "Just Man" of Old Testament history (Enoch, Noah, Abraham, etc.), and finally in the persecuted minority of Christians who bear witness to the Gospel in its purity and "in the worship persevere of Spirit and Truth."

NOTES

1. . . . See A. S. P. Woodhouse, "Theme and Pattern in *Paradise Regained,*" *University of Toronto Quarterly,* 25:167–82 (1956); see also Arnold Stein, *Heroic Knowledge: An Interpretation of Paradise Regained and Samson Agonistes* (Minneapolis, 1957); Stein's "underlying assumption" (p.17) is "that *Paradise Regained* is a dramatic definition of 'heroic knowledge,' not of heroic rejection; and that the contest is a preparation for *acting transcendence in the world,* by uniting intuitive knowledge with proved intellectual and moral discipline"; cf. *ibid.* p.205, "The key for Milton is knowledge, the self-knowledge of thought tested by deed, heroic knowledge maintained against the pressing claims of immediate knowledge and action."

2. Merritt Y. Hughes, "The Christ of *Paradise Regained* and the Renaissance Heroic Tradition," *Studies in Philology* 35:277 (1938).

3. Frank Kermode, "Milton's Hero," *RES,* n. s. 4:330 (1953).

4. Woodhouse, p.167.

5. See *"The Reason of Church Government,"* in *The Prose Works of John Milton* (Bohn Library; London, 1883), v.2, p.478.

6. Aristotle, *On the Art of Poetry,* tr. by Ingram Bywater (Oxford, 1951), p.43.

7. See Milton's *Christian Doctrine,* tr. by Charles R. Sumner, in *Prose Works,* 5vs. (London, 1848–64), v. 4, p.304, "Having treated of the mediatorial office, and its threefold functions, we are now to consider the manner in which it is discharged. This includes the state of humiliation to which our Redeemer submitted, as well as his state of exaltation." For the relationship of the theology of the *De Doctrina* to that of *Paradise Lost,* see Maurice Kelley, *This Great Argument* (Princeton, 1941).

8. In representing Christ himself as the heroic exemplar in both of his epics, Milton was following not only the theological doctrine of "the conformation of the faithful to the image of Christ" (*Prose Works,* v. 4, p.309), but also the Renaissance critical principle of conformity to the moral example of the epic hero. Thus Tasso maintains, in his *Discorsi del Poema Eroico,* that heroic poems and discourses on their composition should be especially dear to those who seek to conform their minds to the example of their fathers' virtues. The intellect acts like a painter, depicting in the soul the forms of fortitude, temperance, prudence, justice, and other virtues, both acquired and infused. Torquato Tasso, *Prose,* ed. by Francesco Flora (Milan and Rome, 1935), p.319.

9. Milton, v. 4, p.316. Cf. Amandus Polanus, *The Substance of Christian Religion,* tr. by Thomas Wilcocks (London, 1608), p.121. "The state of the humiliation of Christ, was that state of his in which hee did abase himselfe, that so by his obedience, hee might satisfie for our disobedience." According to John Wolleb's *Abridgment of Christian Divinitie,* tr. by Alexander Ross (London, 1660), p.135, "The state of Humiliation is, in which he took the forme of a Servant being in the forme of God, and gave obedience to his Father for us . . . : And in this State he so performed his Prophetical, Sacerdotal, and Regal office, that in a manner he stript himselfe of the forme and glory of the Divinity." In *The Reason of Church Government,* Milton declared (v. 2, p.483) that "the form of a servant was a mean, laborious, and vulgar life, aptest to teach; which form Christ thought fittest, that he might bring about his will according to his own principles, choosing the meaner things of this world, that he might put under the high."

10. Milton, v. 4, p.317. "So far, therefore, as regards the satisfaction of Christ, and our conformity to his humiliation, the restoration of man is of merit; in which sense those texts are to be understood which convey a notion of recompense and reward."

11. *Ibid.,* p.304–8, 316–17; cf. p.118, 145.

12. *Ibid.,* p. 304, 309–10.

13. Tasso, p.368, "ma l'illustre de l'eroico è fondato . . . sopra il magnanimo proponimento di morire. . . ."

14. Milton, v. 4, p.307–8.

15. Polanus, p.150. Cf. *Paradise Regain'd,* III, 21–23, "These God-like Vertues wherefore dost thou hide? Affecting private life, or more obscure In savage Wilderness . . . ?"

16. Wolleb, p.135–36. For Milton's indebtedness to Wolleb, see Maurice Kelley, "Milton's Debt to Wolleb's *Compendium Theologiae Christianae,*" *PMLA* 50:156–65 (1935); T. S. K. Scott-Craig, "Milton's Use of Wolleb and Ames," *MLN* 55:403–7 (1940).

17. Bywater, p.47. Cf. Merritt Y. Hughes, ed., *Paradise Regained* (New York, 1937), p.351 n.; Ida Langdon, *Milton's Theory of Poetry and Fine Art* (New Haven, 1924).

18. Nevertheless, despite his knowledge of these prophecies Satan does not really understand the means whereby Christ will establish his kingdom; cf. *Paradise Regain'd,* IV. 152–53, "Means there shall be to this, but what the means, Is not for thee to know, nor me to tell."

19. Instead of achieving his kingdom "in short time with ease" (*Paradise Regain'd,* IV. 378), as Satan proposes, Christ must attain it only by "many a hard assay" and in the "fulness of time." Satan not only attempts to persuade Jesus to employ means contrary to those set forth in the Messianic prophecies, but also tries to induce him to act prematurely. Christ manifests his obedience through his willingess to await the "due time" which "The Father in his purpose hath decreed" (*Paradise Regain'd,* III. 182–86), whereas Satan argues that the present moment is "full age, fulness of time, thy season" (*Paradise Regain'd,* IV. 380).

20. Polanus, p.120–21.

21. Wolleb, p.156.

22. Satan's offer of "the kingdoms of the world, and the *glory* of them" obviously constitutes a direct challenge to the whole concept of Christ's humiliation. Cf. *Paradise Lost,* III. 238–40 ("I for his sake will leave Thy bosom, and *this glorie next to thee* Freely put off, and for him lastly die") and 311–14 ("because in thee Love hath abounded *more than Glory abounds,* Therefore thy Humiliation shall exalt With thee thy Manhood also to this Throne"). Italics mine.

23. Satan attempts to wrest the prophecies to his own ends, either by representing the values he offers as means of fulfilling the Old Testament predictions concerning the Messiah, or else by maintaining that the prophecies themselves are not absolute but conditional— that their fulfillment is contingent upon Jesus' adopting the means and occasions he offers. Cf. *Paradise Regain'd*, III. 177–80, 351–56; IV. 106–8.

24. The Trinity Manuscript does, however, contain a brief outline of a drama on "Christus Patiens." See James Holly Hanford, *A Milton Handbook* (4th ed., New York, 1947), p.181 n.

25. Torquato Tasso, *Prose Diverse*, ed. by Cesare Guasti, I, 110–11: "L'istoria di secolo o di nazione lontanissima pare per alcuna ragione soggetto assai conveniente al poema eroico; però che, essendo quelle cose in guisa sepolte nell'antichità, ch'a pena ne rimane debole ed oscura memoria, può il poeta mutarle e rimutarle, e narrarle come gli piace." See J. E. Spingarn, ed., *Critical Essays of the Seventeenth Century* (Oxford, 1908), v. 2, p.267.

26. For a bibliography of studies on the "suffering servant" of Isaiah 53, see Christopher R. North, *The Suffering Servant of Isaiah: An Historical and Critical Study* (2d ed.; London, 1956), p.240–53. "Until the close of the eighteenth century," North observes (p.1), "Christian writers—with almost the sole exception of Grotius, who thought of Jeremiah— were unanimous that Isa. liii was Messianic prophecy"; cf. *ibid.*, p.23–27.

Brian Wilkie

THE WAY OF THE HERO

Wordsworth's most significant critical statement on the epic is to be found in a letter to Southey written about 1815: "My opinion in respect to epic poetry is much the same as that of the critic whom Lucien Bonaparte has quoted in his preface. Epic poetry, of the highest class, requires in the first place an action eminently influential, an action with a grand or sublime train of consequences; it next requires the intervention and guidance of beings superior to man, what the critics, I believe, call machinery; and lastly, I think with Dennis that no subject but a religious one can answer the demand of the soul in the highest class of this species of poetry." Wordsworth then goes on to discuss the limitations of a stanzaic movement in epic writing (a subject much debated in neoclassic theory), and in the course of this discussion he gives us the nearest approximation to his own epic canon. He names Tasso, Spenser, Homer, Virgil, and Milton, an almost perfectly orthodox list.[1]

The applicability of this epic formula to *The Prelude* is the general subject we are concerned with, but a few points require immediate notice. The words "what the critics, I believe, call machinery" are astonishing; it seems almost incredible that this term, one of the most hackneyed in neoclassic theory, should have been only vaguely familiar to Wordsworth. The implication is that he knew at first hand almost none of the standard treatises, and it is true that references to the Augustan critics are very few in Wordsworth's writings. On the other hand, Wordsworth's phrase may have an element of pose about it, like the similar "Aristotle, I have been told" of the Preface to *Lyrical Ballads;* that is, Wordsworth may have wanted to strike a superior attitude by affecting ignorance of musty laws. If so, the affectation would be entirely in keeping with the role often assumed by the epic poet.

Also worth scrutiny is Wordsworth's third requirement for epic poetry, that the subject be religious. The word "religious" is almost certainly not to be taken in the common, relatively narrow sense in which Wordsworth understands the term when, late in his life, he points out with regret how many people read *Paradise Lost* "not as a poem, but a religious Book."[2]

"The Way of the Hero." From Brian Wilkie, *Romantic Poets and Epic Tradition* (Madison and Milwaukee: The University of Wisconsin Press; © 1965 by the Regents of the University of Wisconsin), p.60–77 and 238–43. Reprinted by permission of the publisher.

Wordsworth is not likely to have condemned readers for applying to the work which for him most nearly represented the epic law and the prophets the very criterion he had himself declared to be essential. It is much more likely, as Miss [Abbie Findlay] Potts indicates, that in his definition of the epic he is using "religious" in the sense which he assigns to the word in a letter to Landor written in 1824. Here he identifies religious poetry with imaginative sublimity: "even in poetry it is the imaginative only, viz., that which is conversant [with], or turns upon infinity, that powerfully affects me,—perhaps I ought to explain: I mean to say that, unless in those passages where things are lost in each other, and limits vanish, and aspirations are raised, I read with something too much like indifference—but all great poets are in this view powerful Religionists."[3]

Finally, the reference to "the critic whom Lucien Bonaparte has quoted" is of some importance. The brother of Napoleon had published in 1814 an epic poem entitled *Charlemagne, ou L'Eglise Délivrée,* which was translated a year later into English.[4] The only piece of criticism quoted in the Preface is Clement's seventh letter to Voltaire. The entire passage follows:

> Without doubt, the intervention of God, of angels, and saints, ought not to be employed to enliven our poetry, as Homer employed Mars, Juno, Vulcan, Venus and her cestus. The marvellous of our religion, which tends only to grandeur and sublimity, ought not to be prodigally introduced, and indeed cannot be employed with too much caution and judgment; but in our system, as in that of the ancients, the marvellous ought to animate the whole poem: the poet who calls himself inspired, and who ought to be so, should be seized, if I may so express it, with a divine spirit like the ancient prophets; so that he may read in Heaven the decrees of Providence; may see the chain which links the events of this world to the divine will, and the supernatural agents which direct and influence mankind. The entire action of the poem ought to be connected with the marvellous: so that Heaven should decree, and mankind conduct themselves accordingly. From the beginning to the end we should see the supernatural agents give an impulse to the actors, and man every where under the direction of God.[5]

The view of machinery expressed here is a fairly sophisticated one. It should manifest itself not in isolated, magical events, but rather in an air of inspired prophecy and supernatural wonder diffused throughout the entire poem, a spiritual atmosphere which shows the mysterious link between man and an order more powerful than and superior to man. Now, it is in very nearly this manner that Wordsworth, half metaphorically, describes in *The Prelude* the interaction between himself and his own "machinery." But of this more later.

The extent of Wordsworth's epic traditionalism and of his traditionalism in general is both conditioned by and reflected in his reading. His frankness in confessing the gaps in his literary background (rather surprising when we consider how vain Wordsworth often was), his self-criticism for scholarly indolence at Cambridge, the magnitude of his intellectual debt to Coleridge, the anti-intellectualism of certain poems in *Lyrical Ballads,* his vagueness in *The Prelude* about the influence of specific books, and the literary rebelliousness of the 1800 Preface have combined, along with other influences, to create a Wordsworthian equivalent of the "native wood-notes wild" theory. Yet, whatever limitations Wordsworth's general reading may have had, they certainly do not apply to poetry. English poetry he knew thoroughly, especially eighteenth-century poetry and that of the great masters he acknowledged: Chaucer, Shakespeare, Spenser, and Milton.[6] He discusses knowingly the poetry of Ovid, Juvenal, Virgil, Homer, Horace, Lucretius, and Catullus.[7] Italian poetry was one of his passionate loves, and references to Tasso and Ariosto are frequent in his correspondence.[8] The authors he knew best, such as Milton and Virgil, he knew with a particular, microscopic intimacy. His taste gravitated sincerely toward the literary giants of the past, so that he seldom needed to apply that distinction between the personal and objective estimates which Matthew Arnold prescribes as necessary for good criticism. Nor did Wordsworth simply feel a vague awe for the monuments of the past, the kind of feeling he attributes to himself upon his first arrival in London.[9]

> A weight of ages did at once descend
> Upon my heart; no thought embodied, no
> Distinct remembrances, but weight and power,—
> Power growing under weight.   (*Prelude* VIII. 552–55)

His comments on the great writers often have a kind of sincere casualness which rings very true, and he was capable of finding fault with even the greatest of poets. Though he admired Dante's style early in his life, he later confessed a dislike for Dante's "grotesque and fantastic fictions," and he admitted finding The *Divine Comedy* tedious for various reasons. He expressed varying estimates of Homer's poetry, generally rating it high. Yet he was frank in acknowledging his distaste for Homeric "manners."[10]

From three of Wordsworth's letters, two written in early 1804 and one, to Sir George Beaumont, in June, 1805 (most of the original *Prelude* was written between these two dates), we know that at this important period Wordsworth contemplated writing a narrative or epic poem and not simply the philosophic poem which was later partially realized in *The Excursion*.[11] His failure to write the epic, like his failure to complete *The Recluse,* has been explained by his having achieved both aims earlier than he immediately recognized, that is, in *The Prelude*.[12] If this is true, the references to epic in the letters, especially the 1805 letter to Beaumont, do not describe a definite project which Wordsworth had in mind so much as they reflect the pattern which, perhaps half-consciously, was emerging in *The Prelude* itself. Stated as unsubtly as I have put it, this explanation might seem to deny Wordsworth's conscious artistry, but the inference would not be valid; in the psychology of the creative process it is not at all uncommon for one's notion of what he has accomplished to lag far behind what has actually been done, even though quite specific decisions have been made at every stage in accordance with a distinct if incompletely formulated pattern. This is especially likely to be true when the subject, like that of *The Prelude,* is profoundly personal and when the poet's mind, like Wordsworth's, is so seamless. As further evidence we might consider Wordsworth's tendency to write poems over periods of years, in snippets and segments whose final use was unforeseen. Yet the resulting poems are usually coherent. That such unity was achieved indicates that the organizing power of Wordsworth's mind often operated at a deeper psychological level than is usual, a level less schematic than is implied by deliberate planning for *a* philosophic poem and *an* epic poem.

Perhaps the best evidence that in *The Prelude* Wordsworth was building more heroically than he completely recognized is that his later revisions of the poem almost consistently point up the epic pattern, strong as that pattern already is in the 1805 version; I shall try to ilustrate this fact along my way. Because I am interested chiefly in the epics of the high Romantic age, and because I am mainly though not exclusively concerned with the early Wordsworth rather than with the Wordsworth of later years, I have chosen the 1805 text as the basis of my analysis, but to compare the earliest and latest versions of the poems is to be convinced that the relatively latent epic form of the 1805 *Prelude* came to be ever more markedly the dominant one.

There is little need to establish once more the fact, recognized by several critics in recent years, that Wordsworth's epic theme is meant deliberately to compete with those of earlier epics.[13] Wordsworth in *The Prelude* was following the precedent of earlier epic poets by which they claim to herald a higher and more spiritual ideal than had prevailed in the past and in epics before them. The time has come, Wordsworth declares explicitly in the poem, to celebrate the loftiest subject of all, the mind of man. The poet is to explore this theme through tracing the growth of the only mind whose vicissitudes he knows at first hand, his own. But this almost exclusive emphasis by critics on thematic innovation has its dangers, for to call *The Prelude* an epic in some loose sense or to imply that it is an epic because of its lofty subject, as though that alone (or mere ambitiousness of intent or tone) could make a poem an epic, is to reinforce, perhaps unintentionally, the mistaken idea that the "true" epic was dead in the Romantic age.

I should therefore like to concentrate on the epic *pattern* of *The Prelude,* a matter which has been much less adequately treated. Nevertheless, some discussion of the poem's theme is in order, if only to make my discussion of the pattern more coherent. A more important reason for retracing part of this familiar territory is that Wordsworth's definitive statements about his heroic theme are grounded in the details of epic tradition in much more specific ways than has been generally appreciated.

The best key to Wordsworth's epic creed is the passage from Book I of *The Prelude* (157–271) in which he draws up a poetic balance sheet and measures the demands of various heroic subjects against his literary powers. The many Miltonic allusions in this passage and the similarity between the problems it raises and those that Milton felt in his own search for a noble theme indicate beyond much doubt that Wordsworth was placing himself in the heroic tradition exemplified by his great mentor. What Wordsworth tells us here seems to furnish both an index to his own ideas on epic and his version of the history of epic. He begins with a general analysis of the personal endowments required of a poet with such lofty aims as his. They include "that first great gift . . . the vital soul," "general truths," "external things," including forms and images, and other aids of "less regard" but needful for the poet. (The priority of the mind and general truths to techniques, images, and other aids of "less regard" is important in Wordsworth's theory of poetry as a whole.) But all these are essentially prerequisites, even the "external" images stored in the mind and soul; the poet must objectify his inner endowments by finding "Time, place, and manners"—in short, a theme. This aim is to "summon back from lonesome banishment" some "little Band of yet remember'd names" and "make them inmates in the hearts of men / Now living, or to live in times to come." The subject, then, should be taken from the past, but not the utterly obscure past— a compromise perfectly consonant with much neoclassic theory. (Wordsworth seems most conscious of epic theory when, as here, he is still groping toward a theme.) A further implication is that the past must be linked with the present or the future in some meaningful way.

Wordsworth then lists a series of contemplated subjects for heroic treatment. The first is "some British theme, some old / Romantic tale, by Milton left unsung." Next he considers a pastoral-chivalric tale. Or, "more sternly mov'd," he would tell of Mithridates, who "became / That Odin, Father of a Race, by whom / Perish'd the Roman Empire," or of Sertorius' friends and followers, who settled in the Fortunate Isles and left there a tradition of liberty which fifteen hundred years later inspired a gallant struggle against the Europeans. Or he would tell how

> in tyrannic times some unknown Man,
> Unheard of in the Chronicles of Kings,
> Suffer'd in silence for the love of truth,

or narrate the avenging expedition of Dominique de Gourges to Florida in the sixteenth century, or Gustavus I's liberation of Sweden from Danish oppression, or Wallace's fight for Scotland and his bequeathal of his name and deeds as ghostly tokens of "independence and stern liberty" in his country.

Abandoning his list of martial themes, Wordsworth considers as another possibility "Some Tale from my own heart, more near akin / To my own passions and habitual thoughts," lofty but "with interchange of gentler things." The heroic subject, he admits, puts an unnatural strain on his powers. Lastly he mentions his favorite aspiration, a

> philosophic Song
> Of Truth that cherishes our daily life;
> With meditations passionate from deep
> Recesses in man's heart, immortal verse
> Thoughtfully fitted to the Orphean lyre.

But he draws back in fear and self-distrust before the "awful burthen" he envisages, and the passage ends with a thick cluster of Miltonic reminiscences, two of "Lycidas" and one of the sonnet "On His Blindness." Like the mourning shepherd shrinking from premature effort, Wordsworth takes refuge in the timorous hope "That mellower years will bring a riper mind / And clearer insight," and, again like the shepherd, he thinks longingly of the "vacant musing, unreprov'd neglect / Of all things, and deliberate holiday" which are the tempting alternative to stern ambition. The whole passage ends with the allusion to the "Blindness" sonnet when Wordsworth compares himself to "a false Steward who hath much received / And renders nothing back," though doubtless the Biblical influence was also direct.[14]

Several important facts emerge from this passage. First, the epic impulse which Wordsworth feels is in part the same kind of generalized ambition to do something great that Milton expresses in much of his literary autobiography before *Paradise Lost*—in the *Vacation Exercise*, in "Elegy VI," in the *Apology for Smectymnuus*, in *The Reason of Church-Government*.[15] Wordsworth chides himself for having

> no skill to part
> Vague longing that is bred by want of power
> From paramount impulse not to be withstood.
> (I. 240–42)

This generalized ambition is related to Wordsworth's great capacity, often illustrated in *The Prelude,* for expectations whose intensity depends in part on their vagueness; such were his expectations of Mount Blanc before its "soulless image" had "usurp'd upon a living thought / That never more could be" (VI. 454–56). A more important implication of this vague longing for a great theme is the personal nature of the search. Wordsworth's problem is not merely to find an adequate theme, but, more important, to find the theme best for him. Epic, according to this view, exists first in the mind of the poet, as an undirected, potential force which must then be channeled into a particular theme, as electric power is stored in a battery before it is used to run a motor or heat an element. Yet the theme is by no means accidental, and herein Wordsworth's approach differs from Southey's, for the theme must be peculiarly right for the poet as an individual; it must be an appropriate fulfillment of his own aspirations. In any event, the search for a theme becomes an occasion for introspection and solemn self-analysis.

Secondly, Wordsworth's list of possible subjects is a catalogue of the various traditional epic subjects. He mentions the "romantic tale," the vehicle used by Spenser and Tasso and ultimately rejected by Milton. In the Mithridates story he has a tale of empire suggestive of Virgil, though Wordsworth's story would tell of the destruction of an empire rather than its origin. Some of the themes (Gustavus, Wallace) are primarily national, as much neoclassic theory believed epic subjects should be, and possibly Wordsworth is considering Biblical material in his reference to "the Chronicles of Kings," though probably the phrase means something different.[16] The stories of Mithridates and Sertorius are tales of wandering, like the *Odyssey* and the first half of the *Aeneid*. Even the "Tale from my own heart" and the "philosophic Song" are to be treated in a lofty way.

Thirdly, all the subjects have a spiritual significance and often they are "influential" in the light of later history, the apparent exceptions being the personal and philosophic subjects. (They are, in fact, only apparent excep-

tions.) Many of them have for their theme liberty, certainly a spiritual ideal
for Wordsworth. Like his master Milton, Wordsworth rejects the purely martial idea of a hero. It is interesting that the only theme listed which in the
early version is not moral by statement of implication is the chivalric tale,
and this is expanded in later revision from the simple pastoral theme of the
1805 version to a conception of

> a song that winds
> Through ever changing scenes of votive quest
> Wrongs to redress, harmonious tribute paid
> To patient courage and unblemished truth,
> To firm devotion, zeal unquenchable,
> And Christian meekness hallowing faithful loves.
>   (I. 180–85)

Fourthly, there is a fairly definite progression in Wordsworth's list from
subjects which most strictly confine themselves to things, manners, and other
externals (like the romantic tale as briefly described in the 1805 version),
through expressions of political idealism, to the most universal theme, the
"philosophic Song / Of Truth." There is also a movement from those subjects
most remote from modern man's experience through those, remote in time
but morally or politically relevant, to those most directly bearing on contemporary life or of greatest personal significance to the poet himself. Unless the order in which the themes are mentioned is an accident, Wordsworth is implying
a conception of epic as a growing rather than a static form.

Finally, the position of the pastoral theme at the head of Wordsworth's list
is probably important. Renaissance convention held that the interest in
pastoral poetry was an early stage in the development of the epic poet. Virgil
had furnished the precedent; Spenser and Milton conformed to it. And in view
of the echoes of "Lycidas" in the passage we are examining and Wordsworth's
insistence later in the poem on the difference between his version of pastoral
and the older, idyllic one, it is a reasonable inference that Wordsworth was
recalling the pastoral-to-epic tradition.[17] In fact, the place of pastoralism in
The Prelude has great significance, for it symbolizes the general direction
of the poet-hero's developing mind—from love of Nature to love of Man.
Pastoralism is one example of Wordsworth's belief that his literary forms
are not replicas of older models but rather developments of them. *The Prelude*
is in part a modern pastoral, and Wordsworth, though he apparently discards
the themes listed in Book I, actually uses nearly all the types there represented
in his poem. There is a coloring of romance and the supernatural, description
of a war for liberty, a philosophic song. A national theme is prominent—
"national" in the sense which is applicable to *Joan of Arc,* where England is
not glorified but English ideals are closely scrutinized. And, of course, the
autobiographical nature of the poem fulfills the promise of the "Tale from my
own heart." But all these elements are finally subordinated to his main epic
theme, the mind of man.

Like the great epic poets of the Renaissance, Wordsworth felt the need
for a new heroic ideal. Milton, Tasso, and Camoëns had all exalted their
heroes' exploits above those of antiquity. All three had made the heroic ideal

Christian, and Milton in particular had pointed the way for Wordsworth by making the essential heroic attribute not deeds but a state of mind. The deepest hell is within Satan, and to Adam is revealed a "paradise within thee, happier farr." The triumphant Christ in *Paradise Regained* wins victory through the maintenance of inner integrity rather than through action.

Thus Wordsworth had ample precedent for making the heroic ideal an interior one. Yet he believed he was making a new departure, and he was right. For one thing, his method is basically different from Milton's and those of the other writers of literary epic. Wordsworth does not simply depict the heroic ideal in action; he is even more concerned with its genesis and growth in the individual hero, namely—and embarrassingly for Wordsworth—himself. The "action" of *The Prelude,* the story of Wordsworth's mental growth, is justified by the final product—the poet's mature mind.[18] The action is purposeful and "influential," as the wanderings and struggles of Aeneas influence the growth of Rome and as the fall of Adam influences the whole later history of the world. (The analogy is not merely fanciful, nor on the other hand should it convict Wordsworth of being a megalomaniac, since his subject—the human mind—is indeed a grand one, and since Wordsworth's personal history is mainly an *exemplum* of the mind's development.) In Virgil and Milton heroism is a given quality, a means toward an end, the end being action or the adoption of a moral stance or both. But in Wordsworth heroism is the *product* of the influences and actions described in the poem. Aeneas's *pietas* helps to build the Roman Empire, and Adam, exemplifying heroism in a negative way, acts to bring "Death into the World, and all our woe," but in *The Prelude* the heroic ideal—mental equipoise, the harmony between man and his environment—is primarily an end and not a means, at least within the boundaries defined by the story of Wordsworth's early life. This last qualification is important; I shall argue presently that *The Prelude* too points toward action beyond the acquisition itself of Wordsworth's version of heroism, that the poem is not content to state an ideal of *being.* But that action is not part of the pattern of development traced in the *events* of the poem.

The emphasis on origins and development permeates much of *The Prelude,* and not merely in a narrow autobiographical sense. Wordsworth's attempt to define heroism is itself rooted in the epic poems and heroic ideal of the past. This way of thinking is probably best illustrated in Wordsworth's description of his native region as lovelier than all the beautiful paradises of fable (VIII. 119–58). As De Selincourt observes, the passage is based on Milton's description of Eden as surpassing all other delectable gardens.[19] But Wordsworth's passage is not a mere echo. The allusion is to a passage in *Paradise Lost* which, like many other passages in that poem, vaunts the superiority of its subject matter over fables and traditionally heroic tales. The implication of Wordsworth's allusion, in connection with other such comparisons in *The Prelude,* is the still greater loftiness of his own theme; in other words, Wordsworth implies a kind of growth and progress in earlier epics toward his own subject, "the mind of man." Another example of this technique is the thorough discussion of the difference between the ancient pastoral life and the more vital pastoralism of the shepherds Wordsworth knew (see, for example, VIII. 182–428).

But it is not only in the function he assigns to heroism that Wordsworth differs from the traditional epic poets; the heroic ideal itself is new. Its concentration on the inner man has precedents, as we have seen, but the degree of emphasis is far greater than in previous epic writers. And there are still other innovations. Wordsworth's climactic statement of his great theme, the theme toward which Book I shows him as groping, suggests the main new elements in his heroic code.[20]

> Of Genius, Power,
> Creation and Divinity itself
> I have been speaking, for my theme has been
> What pass'd within me. Not of outward things
> Done visibly for other minds, words, signs,
> Symbols or actions; but of my own heart
> Have I been speaking, and my youthful mind.
> O Heavens! how awful is the might of Souls,
> And what they do within themselves, while yet
> The yoke of earth is new to them, the world
> Nothing but a wide field where they were sown.
> This is, in truth, heroic argument,
> And genuine prowess . . .
> Points have we all of us within our souls,
> Where all stand single; this I feel, and make
> Breathings for incommunicable powers.
> Yet each man is a memory to himself,
> And, therefore, now that I must quit this theme,
> I am not heartless; for there's not a man
> That lives who had not had his godlike hours,
> And knows not what majestic sway we have,
> As natural beings in the strength of nature.
>   (III. 171–94)

There are three basic elements in the heroic ideal offered here: an emphasis on spiritual and psychological qualities ("my theme has been / What pass'd within me"), a form of egalitarianism ("there's not a man / That lives who hath not had his godlike hours"), and individualism ("Points have we all of us within our souls, / Where all stand single"). All these are fairly novel in the light of the traditional heroic pattern, especially as it exists in epic "orthodoxy"—the inner emphasis because of the enormous importance which Wordsworth gives it, the egalitarianism because it goes so far out of the way to deny that the hero is unique, the individualism because Wordsworth makes it a universal and markedly philosophical ideal.

The main emphasis in the quoted passage is on the spiritual and psychological nature of the theme. Despite the lengthy treatment of the French Revolution, the poem's values are antimartial (though, as in Southey, not strictly pacifist), and the older concept of a hero as a great warrior is nowhere in evidence, not even in Beaupuy, who is glorified mainly as a thinker. Wordsworth's antimilitarism leads him to confess with some sense of guilt that he once was led by French military victories to confound them with another victory "far higher and more difficult, / Triumphs of unambitious peace at home / And noiseless fortitude" (X. 591–93). Later he rejoices that the "wiser mood" has been re-established which sees "little worthy or sublime / In what we blazon with the pompous names / Of power and action" (XII. 45–49). His description of the pathetic separations and the domestic havoc wrought by war (IX. 273–79) is very much like Southey's in *Joan of Arc*. Southey too might, with slight modifications, have written what Wordsworth wrote in 1794: "I am a determined enemy to every species of violence. I see no connection, but what the obstinacy of pride and ignorance renders necessary, between justice and the sword, between reason and bonds."[21] By 1802 Wordsworth had modified his views somewhat, but he still believed that "excessive admiration was paid in former times to personal prowess and military success; it is so with the latter even at the present day, but surely not nearly so much as heretofore."[22] It is one of the more striking bits of evidence for the "lost leader" theory that in 1816 Wordsworth's views had been so transformed that he believed that "martial qualities are the natural efflorescence of a healthy state of society," and that he cites in support of this thesis the authority of Milton, among others.[23] But it is equally significant that Wordsworth never deleted from *The Prelude* the passages I have just mentioned, for the poem always retained for him an integrity of pattern independent of his self-revelation. Even the brief temptation to join forces with the revolutionists is mainly a reaction to the French need for guidance and moral authority (X. 129–58).[24] And, significantly, one of Dorothy's great restorative services is to "soften down" her brother's "over-sternness" (XIII. 226–27).

When in announcing his theme Wordsworth states that he rejects "outward things," "Symbols or actions," in favor of "What pass'd within me," he is not describing his poem with complete exactness, for *The Prelude* contains many pictures of the great world and of momentous events. But this passage was almost certainly written at a time when the whole poem was still intended to be only five books long and more limited in scope than it turned out to be.[25] In the full poem Wordsworth takes pains to show the reality, indeed the practicality, of his theme. This insistence on the reality and truth of his subject is one of the things that place Wordsworth most directly in the tradition of literary epic. "What pass'd within me" is not the stuff of dreams; the "godlike hours" are part of our empire "As natural beings in the strength of nature." In his early days of revolutionary zeal he had rejoiced that his efforts and the efforts of men like him would be exercised "Not in Utopia," but "in the very world which is the world / Of all of us" (X. 724–27), and on regaining his emotional health after his moral crisis he seeks "good in the familiar face of life," and not in "sanguine schemes" (XII. 65–67).

No statements could illustrate better than these the difference between Wordsworth's heroic standard and the standards expressed by Southey and Landor. All three poets define heroism idealistically, but Wordsworth's brand of idealism is at the more utilitarian end of the idealist's spectrum, whereas Southey and Landor preach a much simpler doctrine, bordering on escapism. The utopian ideal which helps to inform *Madoc* and the political quietism of

Gebir are both foreign to Wordsworth's intentions in *The Prelude,* for in emphasizing psychology at the expense of martial heroism Wordsworth is not retreating from the field of human action except in what he would consider a superficial sense of the word *action,* despite his frequent praises of rural and domestic retirement. On the contrary, in exploring the mind of man he claims to be focusing on the area of human life where the most truly significant action occurs, the area which is most "substantial." It is Wordsworth's concern with the real applicability of his message which explains why *The Prelude,* if it had been published in 1805, might have been doctrinal to an age and nation in a way that was not possible for the contemporary epics of Southey and Landor. When Wordsworth, having reviewed his past life near the end of the poem, confirms his dedication to a newer, more truly heroic program, he ponders "How oft high service is perform'd within" (XII.226). But, although one terminus of the events narrated in *The Prelude* is the poet's decision to write verse which will celebrate the inner nature of men in humble life, he declares that in this enterprise he will "Deal boldly with substantial things, in truth / And sanctity of passion" (XII. 234–35);

> it shall be my pride
> That I have dared to tread this holy ground,
> Speaking no dream but things oracular,
> Matter not lightly to be heard by those
> Who to the letter of the outward promise
> Do read the invisible soul.
>
> (XII. 250–55)

Wordsworth does not preach subjectivism; he simply believes that mental experience is entirely real and, furthermore, that the greatest practical problem of his own age is not material or institutional, but spiritual.[26] One can readily surmise the effect this creed must have had on one of Wordsworth's disciples, the author of *Culture and Anarchy*.

Far from being neglected, external narrative has a special importance in Wordsworth's poem. It is through the action of the poem that ideas and ideals are made concrete—the ideal of true liberty, for example, through the poet's experiences with the French Revolution. Furthermore, as in Virgil, the action traces the origin, growth, and cause of the resultant—which, in *The Prelude,* is a man's mature mind. But Wordsworth's special emphasis on psychology needs external narrative not only as symbolic explanation (as in the Snowdon episode) but also as factual example. In the Wordsworthian hero, as typified by the author himself, the inner and outer worlds are in equipoise and thus interact with each other. Hence external contingencies and action in the world are important as specific proof of the part played by the experience of external things in shaping the imagination and thought of the developing man.

The other chief ingredients in Wordsworth's heroic ideal, democratic egalitarianism and individualism, are closely dependent on each other. It had been at least half-assumed by most earlier epic poets that the hero was a great leader enjoying special gifts of Nature and Fortune. He relied on himself in all that was within human power and is distinctly contrasted with his less gifted fellows. Though Wordsworth sometimes speaks in such terms, it is in a different context. . . ; in general, Wordsworth's individualism has a more philosophic cast than in older versions of heroism. And since it is democratic, it applies to all men ("Points have we all of us within our souls, / Where all stand single"). We "stand single"—the individual is unique. But this is true of "all of us," and therefore individualism is formulated as a universal, democratic ideal.

This democratic note pervades *The Prelude;* Wordsworth denies, for example, that love requires "Retirement, leisure, language purified / By manners thoughtful and elaborate" (XII. 189–90). Yet he cannot deny the differences between men or the rarity of individuals who satisfy his heroic ideal, and the problem troubles him. The dignity of individual man—"no composition of the thought," but "the man whom we behold / With our own eyes"—is a fact of experience, but

> Why is this glorious Creature to be found
> One only in ten thousand? What one is,
> Why may not many be?
>
> (XII. 83–92)

Wordsworth's heroic ideal postulates, not a great individual hero, but a great race of individualists. The message of serious literary epic is usually a collective one in some sense, and Wordsworth's justification in turning his personal memoirs into heroic argument is his belief that, as Shelley was to put it, we have one human heart.

NOTES

1. *LWY* [*The Letters of William and Dorothy Wordsworth: The Middle Years,* ed. by Ernest De Selincourt, 2vs. (Oxford, 1937)], v. 2, p.633. Another reference to Dennis occurs in a letter to Catherine Clarkson written slightly earlier (*LMY,* v. 2, p.617, Dec., 1814); here we find Wordsworth in agreement on the nature of poetic passion. But Wordsworth makes few such references to neoclassic critics.
See Hugh Thomas Swedenberg, *Theory of the Epic in England,* 1650–1800 (Berkeley and Los Angeles, 1944), p.340–42, for an index to and summary of English neoclassic theory on verse form in the epic.
I have no certain evidence that Wordsworth knew Camoëns during early or middle life, but his generally strong admiration for W. J. Mickle, who published his well-known translation of the *Lusiad* in 1776, makes it very likely that he did. See Wordsworth's letters to W. Mathews, *LLY* [*The Letters of William and Dorothy Wordsworth: The Later Years,* ed. by Ernest De Selincourt, 3vs. (Oxford, 1939)], v. 3, p.1334, Oct. 24, 1795, and to Allan Cunningham, *LLY,* Nov. 23, 1823. On Nov. 15, 1844, Wordsworth wrote a letter to John Adamson, the biographer of Camoëns, expressing his interest in Portuguese literature, stating that Southey and Wordsworth's son-in-law, Edward Quillinan, had made Wordsworth familiar with the country and its literature. In this letter, as it happens, Wordsworth criticizes Mickle's translation sharply See E. H. A., "Letters of Wordsworth," *Notes and Queries,* 8th series, 12:86 (Jl. 1, 1897). But just when he first read the translation is uncertain.
2. *LLY,* March 9, 1840, to Edward Quillinan.
3. *LLV,* Jan. 21, 1824; Potts, *Wordsworth's "Prelude,"* p.337.
4. The identification is made by De Selincourt in a note to the letter.
5. *Charlemagne; or The Church Delivered,* tr. by Samuel Butler and Francis Hodgson, 2vs. (London, 1815), v. 1, p.*xiv–xv.*
6. See, for example, *LLY,* Nov. 23, 1823, to Allan Cunningham; *LLY,* Nov. 16, 1824, to Alaric Watts.
7. See, for example, *LMY,* v. 1, p.458d, Jan. 18, 1808, to Walter Scott; *LLY,* April 20, 1822, to Landor.

8. See, for example, *EL* [*The Early Letters of William and Dorothy Wordsworth* (1787–1805), ed. by Ernest De Selincourt (Oxford, 1935)], March 21, 1796, to W. Mathews; *EL*, Oct. 17, 1805, to Sir George Beaumont; *LLY*, Jan. 18, 1840, to Thomas Powell. George McLean Harper mentions that Wordsworth took with him a copy of *Orlando Furioso* during his 1790 tour through the Alps. [See] *William Wordsworth: His Life, Works, and Influence,* 2vs. (2d. ed., New York, 1923), v. 2, p.43.

9. As explained later in this chapter, the text except where otherwise indicated is the 1805 version, in *The Prelude,* ed. by Ernest De Selincourt, rev. by Helen Darbishire (Oxford, 1959).

10. *LLY,* Jan. 21, 1824, to Landor; *LLY,* v. 1, 506–7, to Henry N. Coleridge, 1830. It is true, of course, that Dante's reputation was not quite so high a century and a half ago as it is today, admired though he was by most of the Romantics.

11. For the 1804 letters see *EL,* p.355 (exact date uncertain, to Francis Wrangham) and *EL,* p.370, March 6, 1804, to Thomas De Quincey. For the letter to Beaumont, see *EL,* p.497, June 3, 1805. The letter to Beaumont uses the phrase "narrative Poem of the Epic kind"; the other two letters mention a "narrative" poem without adding the epic label. But the similarity in context implies strongly that all three letters refer to the same projected poem. Nor is it at all likely that the narrative poem is *The Excursion,* which later appeared as part of *The Recluse,* that is, part of the philosophic poem which Wordsworth in the letters distinguished explicitly from the narrative-epic one. Furthermore, *The Excursion* can hardly be called a narrative work. Most students of Wordsworth have missed this sharp distinction between the narrative and philosophic poems.

12. See, for example, Arthur Beatty, *William Wordsworth: His Doctrine and Art in their Historical Relations,* (2d. ed.: Madison, 1927), p.234–36; Elizabeth Sewell, *The Orphic Voice: Poetry and Natural History* (New Haven, 1960), p.302.

13. See, for example, Lascelles Abercrombie, *The Art of Wordsworth* (New York, 1952), esp. p.41–42; Sewell, *The Orphic Voice,* p.302–9; Karl Kroeber, *Romantic Narrative Art* (Madison, 1960), p.78–112; Herbert Lindenberger, *On Wordsworth's "Prelude"* (Princeton, 1963), p. 9–15. (In a more casual way *The Prelude* has been called an epic countless times.) Most of these treatments emphasize the epic theme while admitting or implying that *The Prelude* fails to achieve epic shape or texture. Miss [Abbie Findlay] Potts's study [*Wordsworth's "Prelude": A Study of its Literary Form* (Ithaca, 1953)] is an exception. . . .

14. Herbert Lindenberger (*On Wordsworth's "Prelude,"* p.110) sees in this passage the demoralized sensibility of the modern poet—"procrastinating, self-analytical, recoiling from the burden of his task"—and contrasts it with Milton's sensibility as revealed in the invocations of *Paradise Lost.* But Milton too had been apprehensive that the greatness of his theme, "sufficient of it self" to raise his name, might succumb to the handicaps of "an age too late, or cold/Climat, or Years" (*PL* IX. 44–45), and it is even more important to recognize that Milton's literary "autobiography," which Wordsworth knew thoroughly, represents Milton too as groping hesitantly, not only toward a theme but in many ways toward a form as well. The passage from Book I of *The Prelude* which we have been discussing invokes Milton's precedent through echoes of "Lycidas" and therefore shows a sense of kinship with the epic tradition rather than alienation from it. See the following note.

15. Wordsworth's discipleship to Milton is a famliar topic, but even so readers are likely to underestimate the extent of parallelism between the two poets in their views and especially in their self-images. The principal documents of Milton's literary autobiography molded Wordsworth's conception of his own literary evolution in powerful and very specific ways, of which the gradual channeling of diffused ambition into a particular theme is only the most obvious. The beginning of *The Prelude* shows Wordsworth retiring from the city and his "unnatural self" to espouse what, in heroic and monastic terms, he calls "The holy life of music and of verse" (I. 23, 50–54); here the situation and ascetic emphasis suggest Milton's address to Diodati in "Elegy VI," 9–78. The mention of a romantic tale "by Milton left unsung" recalls the kind of subject which Milton first considered and then rejected, as we learn from *Mansus,* the *Epitaphium*

Damonis, the *Apology for Smectymnuus,* and the Cambridge MS. if the order of subjects listed there is significant. (One wonders whether Wordsworth had seen the Milton MS. at the university.) The passage about the Druids in *Prelude,* XII. 312–54, resembles the lines (41–43) about the Druids in *Mansus;* here both Wordsworth's and Milton's contexts celebrate the national past and the universal bond which unites poets. Wordsworth's distrust of his poetic powers has precedents not only in "Lycidas" but also in Milton's hint that his first difficulty in treating a heroic theme was stylistic (*Epitaphium Damonis,* ll. 155–60). The poet's *apologia* for himself near the end of *The Prelude* and subsequent distinction between earthly love and a higher kind (XIII. 128–65) is, especially as expanded in the 1850 version, much like Milton's defense of himself against charges of licentiousness and his panegyric on Platonic love in the *Apology for Smectymnuus* (Columbia ed., III, 301–6). Wordsworth liked to apply to his own poetry and views the famous passage from Book Two of *The Reasons of Church-Government* (III. 235–41); see *LMY,* April 28, 1814, to Poole; *LLY,* Sept. 3, 1821, to Landor. In the same passage Milton, like Wordsworth (*Prelude,* VI. 64–69), tells of having felt great literary ambition for the first time in an academic setting. Milton's embarrassment about autobiographical intimacy and defense of it are strikingly like Wordsworth's sentiments in *Prelude,* XIII. 386–90, and Milton's statement that the poet should teach, though by indirect means, is close to the view once expressed by Wordsworth (*LMY,* June 5, 1808, to Wrangham) and implied in Wordsworth's poetry in general. And, of course, it is in the *Church-Government* passage that Milton declares his view that the hero should be a model Christian and the poet's life itself a poem.

16. Although Wordsworth may have been thinking of a Biblical subject, another possibility is a tale, like some of those listed in the Cambridge Milton MS., derived from the English chroniclers. But Professor Carl Woodring has suggested to me the likelihood that Wordsworth, under the influence of the English republican writers of the seventeenth century, had in mind an unsung hero modeled on Algernon Sydney or some such figure. For a discussion of Wordsworth's intellectual debt to the English republican writers, see Z. S. Fink, "Wordsworth and the English Republican Tradition," *Journal of English and Germanic Philology* 47:107–26 (1948).

17. Miss Potts (*Wordsworth's "Prelude,"* p.295) cites the precedent of Spenser for this pastoral-to-epic motif in *The Prelude.*

18. See *ibid.,* p.336.

19. *The Prelude,* p.568–69.

20. The words "now that I must quit this theme" would seem to say that the theme Wordsworth announces is not at all the general theme of the poem but rather the theme of the first books. But by "quit this theme" Wordsworth is on the simplest level implying no more than that he is closing out an episode in his life and beginning another. Immediately afterward he writes, "Enough: . . . A Traveller I am, / And all my Tale is of myself." The phrase "quit this theme" is one of almost countless modulating phrases by means of which Wordsworth shifts back and forth between private statement and generalization about man. . . .

21. *EL,* p.120–21, June, 1794, to W. Mathews.

22. *EL,* p.296, June, 1802, to John Wilson.

23. *LMY,* June 11, 1816, to John Scott.

24. Z. S. Fink distinguishes between Wordsworth's temporary conception of himself as divinely appointed leader and lawgiver, and the opposite, Burkean view according to which institutions arise through a long process of historical evolution. In *The Prelude* Wordsworth places himself in the tradition which held that "states were best contrived when they were made all at once by a single great institutor or legislator whose disinterestedness was guaranteed by the fact that he had no place in the government which he set up and retired from the scene once the state was established." [See] "Wordsworth and the English Republican Tradition," p.119–22.

25. See De Selincourt, ed., *The Prelude* (Oxford, 1926 ed.) p.*xxxv–xxxviii.* Book III was probably written partly during the years 1801–3 and partly in 1804 before March 24. But on March 19, 1804, Wordsworth had not worked on the poem for nearly three

weeks, and on March 6 he had completed four books and still believed that one more would conclude his poem. Almost certainly, then, all of Book III had been written by March 6 or a few days later, and very possibly long before that date.

26. Mario Praz, in his stimulating book *The Hero in Eclipse in Victorian Fiction* (New York, 1956), p.41–53, sees in Wordsworth's apparent retirement from the world of action and revolutionary zeal a symptom of typically *bourgeois* values later characteristic of the Victorians: sentimentalism, cozy domesticity, the sense of duty, the stress on the beauties of nature, the belief in humble life as somehow heroic. There is a sense in which these remarks are valid, and in that sense Wordsworth might have shamelessly pleaded guilty to the charges; he knew where his ideas led. We cannot, therefore, beg the very questions that Wordsworth was raising by simply condemning him peremptorily as a proto-Victorian; he might well have answered, *"Et donc?"* But it is even more important to recognize that in *The Prelude* Wordsworth's most important ideal, the Imagination, has little to do with class milieu or special environment, whatever he may say about his own debt to nature. He does not idealize nature and cozy domesticity for their own sakes; they are, rather, favorable conditions for what he considers the noble life of Imagination, which life as he depicts it far transcends *Gemütlichkeit* of the Victorian or any other variety. Wordsworth did, in Praz's phrase, turn from the world of the Revolution to "the little world of his own childhood" (p.43), but the spiritual and psychological dimensions which he gives to that world are anything but little. Finally, we must recognize his championing of domestic life in the country as in part a rhetorical device used to dramatize the distinction between inner heroism and superficial activism.

LANGUAGE

G. S. Kirk

HOMERIC SUBJECTS
AND STYLES

The *Iliad* and *Odyssey* far exceed the normal and natural length of oral compositions, and each presupposes an unusual motive and a deliberate intention on the part of an individual to create a definitely monumental structure. It is already clear that they are substantially constructed from traditional elements: traditional vocabulary, traditional fixed phrases, traditional themes and episodes. These were worked together and expanded so as to form the two great epics, each of which displays as a whole an undeniable unity of technique, purpose and effect. Therefore we shall expect to find in such poems the evidence both of a single monumental plan and of the variability and disparity that characterize all traditional poetry. In other words, if the *Iliad* and *Odyssey* are both monumental and oral, then they must contain signs both of unity and of plurality of authorship. This duality has been the background of an over-protracted war between Analysts and Unitarians. . . .

Some kinds of literary anomaly or incoherence are caused not by the use of disparate materials but by deliberate or unconscious alterations of style and method on the part of the composer. Unitarians have often pointed out that a single author may use different styles in different books or even in different parts of the same book. Admittedly the oral poet has less capacity for variation than the writer, since he works with an inherited stock not merely of word-units but also of phrase-units. His expression and style are to some extent predetermined. Even so he can achieve different stylistic effects by his way of combining phrase-units, as well as by adaptations and new creations of his own. The phrases are usually quite short, two to five words, and this means that their effect on style is not overpowering; yet the sentences that can be built from them may differ in individuality and effect, they may be rhetorical or ironic, pathetic or factual, redundant or colourless. Within the broad limits of the heroic style there is much room for variation. Sometimes this variation will show the virtuosity of a single singer; sometimes it will suggest a difference of singers and perhaps even of periods.

Changes of style are often conditioned by changes of subject. The *Iliad* may be thought of as unusually homogeneous in subject: it is a war poem,

Originally "Subjects and Styles." From G. S. Kirk, *Homer and the Epic* (New York: Cambridge University Press, 1965), p.126–38. Reprinted by permission of the publisher.

its main scene restricted to the Trojan plain. Yet even the descriptions of fighting are strikingly diverse, ranging from mere catalogues of victims to elaborate set-pieces with taunts and counter-taunts. Moreover, the battle is only a part of the poem; the main motif is the wrath of Achilles, and when this too is left in the background there are many other different scenes and subjects to vary the action: scenes among the gods on Olympus and Ida or human scenes in the Achaean camp or in Troy; major digressions like the making of the shield of Achilles in XVIII and the funeral games in XXIII; lists and catalogues of many kinds, of ships and warriors, of legendary parallels, of ancestors, gifts, horses, heroines, or Nereids; elaborate and frequent similes; summaries of other legends outside the Trojan tale—the attacks on Thebes and the prowess of Tydeus, Heracles, Meleagros and Bellerophon; detailed descriptions of sacrifices, tactical devices, the handling of ships or the preparation of heroic meals.

In the *Odyssey*, with its more complex plot and its multiple setting, there is less need for other kinds of diversification. So there are fewer similes than in the *Iliad*, where they had served to relieve the potential monotony of the battle-poetry, and fewer inorganic episodes. Not that the *Odyssey* is free from medium-scale digressions; we have seen that, in a poem describing palace life, the device could be used of reporting the songs of the court singer, Phemius in Ithaca or Demodocus in Phaeacia. Thus the song of the love of Ares and Aphrodite occupies a hundred lines of Book VIII, and part of the story of the Trojan Horse is given in more summary form in the same book. The visit of Telemachus to the palaces of Nestor and Menelaus, itself something of a digression, gave an opportunity for further reminiscences beyond the range of the main plot. But the chief diversion consists of the stories of his adventures which Odysseus recounts to the Phaeacians in Books IX–XII. These, although put in the form of a reminiscence by Odysseus, form an important part of the action of the poem as a whole, and are set against a background remote not only from Ithaca or Troy or Pylos but from the whole world of ordinary experience.

Some of these changes of subject-matter impose consequential changes of style. Sometimes a particular manner of presentation, within the limitations of oral poetry, is demanded by a particular kind of material. Thus a bare list, whether of proper names or of things, allows only insignificant variation. This is hardly a matter of true style—though we may for convenience talk of a "catalogue-style"—but rather of a taste for a certain kind of subject. Such a taste may in itself carry implications of date: for example certain long and purely decorative catalogues in Homer, notably the list of Nereids at XVIII. 39–49, typify the love of codification which inspires the *Theogony* of Hesiod and probably belong to a relatively late stage of oral epic. Normally style only comes into question when there is a choice of presentation, when content can be expressed in at least two different ways. Even here we must be careful to distinguish styles which might be adopted by almost any singer, from those which are so individual that they are likely to belong to one particular singer, region or period.

As an example of the first kind one may take what might be called the *succinct narrative style* as exemplified in the opening book of both the *Iliad* and the *Odyssey*. Each book has to set the scene and foreshadow the action as briefly and forcefully as possible; there are different ways in which this could be done, and we might therefore look for a distinguishable style. The general approach of each book is indeed rather similar. An elegant and informative use is made of dialogue (by Agamemnon and Chryses, Agamemnon and Achilles, Telemachus and Athene); between the speeches come passages of condensed narrative, devoid of imagery though not of all decoration, clear and uncomplicated in effect. This produces a stylistic impression slightly different from that of the bulk of the narrative in each poem, which tends to be more diffuse and is constructed from longer and more complex sentences. Succinct narrative, on the other hand, tends to be divided into sentences or clauses each of which occupies one verse:

> For nine days through the army went the shafts of the god,
> and on the tenth to assembly Achilles called the host;
> for this in his mind did white-armed goddess Hera put,
> for she was troubled for the Danaans, because she saw them dying.
> When they, then, were assembled and gathered all together,
> to them, standing up, did swift-footed Achilles speak
>
> (I. 53 ff.)

(In this and some others of the translations I have deliberately reproduced the Greek word-order fairly closely, regardless of elegance.) Yet we should hesitate to associate this power of succinct narrative with a particular singer or period, even though it was a power which the main composer of each poem clearly possessed. The style implies complete mastery of the traditional language, and exemplifies the oral technique in one of its most impressive aspects. However unusual the subject, the sense is advanced rapidly, smoothly and without straining the predominantly formular language. This is seen in a technical passage like the building of Odysseus's raft, for example [*Od.*] V. 254–57:

> Within he made a mast and a yard-arm fitted to it;
> then he attached a rudder in order to steer the craft.
> He fenced it all along with willow-branches
> to be a bulwark against the wave, and heaped much brushwood over.

> ἐν δ' ἱστὸν ποίει καὶ ἐπίκριον ἄρμενον αὐτῷ·
> πρὸς δ' ἄρα πηδάλιον ποιήσατο, ὄφρ' ἰθύνοι.
> φράξε δέ μιν ῥίπεσσι διαμπερὲς οἰσυΐνῃσι,
> κύματος εἶλαρ ἔμεν· πολλὴν δ' ἐπεχεύατο ὕλην.

From the brevity of this succinct narrative must be distinguished the more extreme compression of what may be called an *abbreviated-reference style*, which reveals itself in summaries of epic incidents lying outside the main plot of the *Iliad* or *Odyssey*. Often these condensations and summary references seem to be based on other poems. They tend to contain stylized phrases which do not occur elsewhere, most of which are probably to be explained not so much as survivals from earlier poetry but as devices used by later singers to glide over familiar developments in a well-known story or to gloss over legendary incidents the details of which were unfamiliar or forgotten. This accounts for their characteristic vagueness. So in the abbreviated story of Bellerophon:

> Killing him [*sc.* Bellerophon] he [Proitos] avoided, for he had shame for this in his heart, but sent him to Lycia, and bestowed baneful signs, scratching on folded tablet many life-destroying things, and bade him show them to his [Proitos's] father-in-law, that he [Bellerophon] might be destroyed. But he went to Lycia under the blameless escort of the gods. . . .

> κτεῖναι μέν ῥ' ἀλέεινε, σεβάσσατο γὰρ τό γε θυμῷ,
> πέμπε δέ μιν Λυκίηνδε, πόρεν δ' ὅ γε σήματα λυγρά,
> γράψας ἐν πίνακι πτυκτῷ θυμοφθόρα πολλά,
> δεῖξαι δ' ἠνώγειν ᾧ πενθερῷ, ὄφρ' ἀπόλοιτο.
> αὐτὰρ ὁ βῆ Λυκίηνδε θεῶν ὑπ' ἀμύμονι πομπῇ.

> (VI. 167 ff.)

The phrase "he had shame for this in his heart" is used but once more in Homer, in another abbreviated reference in the same book. "Baneful signs" and "many life-destroying things" have a similar formular appearance but do not recur in Homer, where such a reference to writing is unique. *Their* unspecific quality, then, is due mainly to the arcane nature of what they describe. On the other hand the vagueness of another formular phrase in the same passage, "under the blameless escort of the gods," θεῶν ὑπ' ἀμύμονι πομπῇ, must be caused by the attempt either to summarize too much in too short a phrase or to cover a deficiency of precise information. What was this escort? We do not know, any more than we know what were the "portents of the gods" which Bellerophon obeyed, θεῶν τεράεσσι πιθήσας, when he killed the Chimaera a few lines later.

Many of these phrases concern the activity of gods, and many of the compressed episodes and reminiscences in which they occur are suggested by their language (which is often Odyssean, even in the *Iliad*), and sometimes by their content, to belong to a relatively late stage of composition. Even apart from these vague compendious phrases a frequent characteristic of the style is its complication and general lack of clarity—another result of compression not ideally carried out. This is to be seen in some of the Nestor reminiscences and is well exemplified in the Bellerophon passage just quoted, where the reference of the personal pronouns is not immediately clear (which accounts for the clumsy parentheses in the translation) and where the rapid changes of subject are confusing.

The use of vague or loose expressions is not restricted to an abbreviated-reference style. Odd and imprecise language, often formular or tending to become so, occurs at intervals throughout both poems in contexts of many different kinds. Frequently such language belongs to what may be termed a *tired or second-hand formular style:* one from which the freshness of the best Homeric poetry is absent, in which there is an unusually high proportion of repeated lines and half-lines, and in which abundant traditional elements are combined in a turgid, imprecise and banal manner. At its best, and particularly when its subject-matter is not too familiar, this style can be restful. So it is in the interlude of the highly concentrated opening book of the *Iliad*, where at lines 430–87 Odysseus sails off and returns Chryseis to her father. Here is a plethora of traditional phrases and of lines and half-lines which appear elsewhere and to greater effect; in addition there are genre passages with descriptions of ship-handling, sacrifice and feasting which must have been extremely familiar to the Homeric audience. In this case one notices no conspicuous imprecision or looseness of phraseology. At its worst, though, the tired style rejoices in phrases like ἢ θέμις ἐστί, "which is lawful," used as little more than automatic and insignificant additions to fill out the line. Another cause of a stale or flaccid oral style is the too frequent use of pleonastic and pointlessly repetitious phrases like "to make war and to fight," "in his mind and in his heart," "knows and has learned" (πολεμίζειν ἠδὲ μάχεσθαι, κατὰ φρένα καὶ κατὰ θυμόν, οἶδέ τε καὶ δεδάηκε). I have already observed that such prosaic expressions are commoner in the *Odyssey* than the *Iliad*.

At other times the mishandling or misunderstanding of traditional formulas, or the loose formation of new ones on the analogy of old, leads to expressions which are, by any reasonable standards, almost meaningless. . . . Such misuses of the traditional phraseology were probably due to rhapsodic types of elaboration rather than to the singers of the full oral period. This pretentious style is commonest in sections which seem to belong to the post-Homeric stages of composition; but so thorough has been the mixture of tradition and innovation in the poems as a whole, and so liable to later rhapsodic elaboration were their most popular episodes, that these perverted expressions can occur even in passages which are otherwise well established in the tradition and relatively old. They are no rarer in the *Iliad* than in the *Odyssey*.

It would be a mistake to conclude that what is stylistically devious or complex is necessarily incompetent or meaningless. In contrast with the succinct narrative style, or the rounder and more periodic language of much of the *Iliad*, or the somewhat toneless effect of much of the *Odyssey*, one occasionally, and especially in the *Iliad*, finds a manner of expression so compact, so involuted in its component words and phrases, that it gives a superficial appearance of confusion. To further inspection—or, better, on further hearing—it reveals itself as sensitive, subtle, and sometimes pathetic. An example is XI. 242 f., where Trojan Iphidamas falls at the hands of Agamemnon and sleeps a brazen sleep,

> pitiable, away from his wedded wife, helping his fellow-townsmen, his young wife, from whom he saw no recompense, but gave much for her . . . ,

> οἰκτρός, ἀπὸ μνηστῆς ἀλόχου, ἀστοῖσιν ἀρήγων,
> κουριδίης, ἧς οὔ τι χάριν ἴδε, πολλὰ δ' ἔδωκεν. . . .

This interweaving of themes and clauses is ultimately a result of the *paratactic* nature of Homeric poetry, that is, of the unsophisticated tendency to state logically subordinate ideas as separate, grammatically co-ordinate propositions.[1] When it is not carefully controlled this tendency can lead to incoherence, as in the story of Meleagros, who at IX. 556 ff. "lay by his wedded wife, fair Cleopatra, daughter of fair-ankled Marpessa daughter of Euenos, and of Ides, who was the strongest of men on earth at that time—and he against lord Phoebus Apollo took up his bow for the sake of the fair-ankled maid: her then in their halls did her father and lady mother call by the name Alkyone, because . . ."—and so on for another ten lines and two or three new themes before a major stop. Now the compression in this instance is probably produced by the condensation of a longer poem. The result is a special form of the abbreviated-reference style, which on this occasion has resorted not to vague generalization but to an excessive concentration of detail. Yet the rapid sequence of new ideas expressed in short clauses can be used more artistically, to give a deliberate effect of confused emotion. The best illustration is Achilles's reply to the envoys in IX; his turmoil of mind, caused by the attempt to delve deeper into motives than was usual for heroes or could easily be expressed in the heroic language designed to describe their actions and passions,[2] is admirably reproduced in a complex and impulsive speech full of rapid transitions and passionate short sentences: "Nor shall I at all compound counsel with him [*sc.* Agamemnon], nor indeed action; for thoroughly has he deceived me and transgressed against me; nor could he once again beguile me with words; let it be enough for him—but let him go to destruction his own way, for his senses has counsellor Zeus taken away. Hateful to me are the gifts of that man, and I esteem him in the portion of a splinter" (IX. 374–78).

Let us turn to a more tangible stylistic phenomenon. At certain dramatic and solemn moments in the *Iliad* the language becomes lofty and sonorous to match the event. One may tentatively distinguish a *majestic style* from the less emphatic manner of the ordinary flow of narrative. A familiar example is Zeus's confirmation of his oath to Thetis at I. 528–30:

> He spoke and with his dark-blue brows the son of Kronos nodded; then did the lord's ambrosial locks stream forward from his immortal head; and he shook great Olympus.

Athene is described in a similar style as she prepares for battle:

> Into the flaming chariot with her feet she went, and grasped her spear, heavy, great, massive, with which she subdues the ranks of men, of heroes with whom she of the mighty father is wroth.

> ἐς δ' ὄχεα φλόγεα ποσὶ βήσετο, λάζετο δ' ἔγχος
> βριθὺ μέγα στιβαρόν, τῷ δάμνησι στίχας ἀνδρῶν
> ἡρώων, οἷσίν τε κοτέσσεται ὀβριμοπάτρη.
>
> (V. 745–47.)

Here the first line contains a redundant expression, "went with her feet," reminiscent of the mannerisms of the tired style, and a rather ineffective hyperbole in the description of the goddess's chariot as "flaming." There is an element, too, of fantastic exaggeration in this style: Hector is inspired by Zeus in his attack on the Achaean ships, and

> Foam around his mouth was formed, his eyes shone out from under dreadful brows, and about his temples terribly shook his helmet as he fought. . . .

> ἀφλοισμὸς δὲ περὶ στόμα γίγνετο, τὼ δέ οἱ ὄσσε
> λαμπέσθην βλοσυρῇσιν ὑπ' ὀφρύσιν, ἀμφὶ δὲ πήληξ
> σμερδαλέον κροτάφοισι τινάσσετο μαρναμένοιο. . . .
>   (XV. 607–9.)

The magnificent effect, which is achieved in part by the use of long, sonorous words, is on the brink of becoming absurd.

There is no reason for thinking that the majestic style, if it is to be associated with one singer or a single stage of the tradition—and that is not certain, even if it may seem possible—is older than the monumental composer of the poem. Yet it is curiously rare, and sometimes conspicuously absent from passages where it could have heightened the drama. Thus when Achilles approaches Hector in Book XXII his appearance is so terrible that Hector is panic-stricken and simply takes to his heels. To motivate this panic one might have expected an unusual and majestic description of Achilles at this crucial moment. Admittedly, we are told that he was like Enyalios the war-god, that he waved his great spear over his right shoulder, that bronze gleamed around him like fire or the sun. Yet these descriptive elements are too familiar to be truly forceful; in sum they produce a certain effect, yet not a particularly unusual one, and they lack the special sonority of the majestic style. It is significant that at this crucial point, as at others which are essential to the basic monumental plot, the majestic style is absent even when it might have had something to contribute; and where it appears is often in episodes which could be elaborations. In the *Odyssey,* indeed, the majestic style is almost entirely lacking, though fantasy and exaggeration are to be found in the visit to the underworld or the vision of Theoclymenus.

Closely akin to the majestic style, and similarly absent in its extreme form from the *Odyssey,* even though it uses a vocabulary more Odyssean than Iliadic, is a *decorated lyical style* which makes its appearance especially in descriptions of gods. Indeed this style is almost restricted to the single long episode of the Beguilement of Zeus by Hera, which, with its prelude and immediate consequences, occupies a substantial part of books XIII–XV. Thus when Poseidon descended from the peaks of Samothrace "trembled the tall hills and forest under the immortal feet of Poseidon as he went" (XIII. 18 f.); then at the fourth step he reached Aigai, where in his divine home in the depths of the sea he made ready his chariot and horses with golden mane, and then drove over the waves:

> sea-beasts gambolled beneath him, coming from their lairs from all directions, nor did they fail to recognize their lord, and with rejoicing the sea stood asunder . . . (27–29).

The lyrical fantasy is paralleled by the account of the love-making of Zeus and Hera at XIV. 347–51:

For them, beneath, the divine earth brought forth new-burgeoning grass, and dewy clover and crocus and hyacinth thick and tender which kept them from the ground. In this did they lay themselves down, and clad themselves over with cloud fair and golden, and sparkling dew-drops descended.

> τοῖσι δ' ὑπὸ χθὼν δῖα φύεν νεοθηλέα ποίην,
> λωτόν θ' ἐρσήεντα ἰδὲ κρόκον ἠδ' ὑάκινθον
> πυκνὸν καὶ μαλακόν, ὃς ἀπὸ χθονὸς ὑψόσ' ἔεργε.
> τῷ ἔνι λεξάσθην, ἐπὶ δὲ νεφέλην ἔσσαντο
> καλὴν χρυσείην· στιλπναὶ δ' ἀπέπιπτον ἔερσαι.

This is fine poetry, more reminiscent of Sappho or *Midsummer Night's Dream* than of the heroic epic, and probably reflecting the sophisticated taste of Ionian audiences towards the end of the oral period. Its persistent romantic undertone is a rarity in Homer, though there are hundreds of brief lyrical touches scattered throughout the poems—no less effective because they only extend to an epithet or a phrase but not amounting to a unified style.

It is for this last reason of brief and sporadic occurrence that one is cautious about a *rhetorical style* in Homer. Yet many devices of emphasis and variation, depending on the careful arrangement of words and phrases, occur regularly through the poems. Important among these are rhetorical questions by the poet, like "Who of mortal men could relate all those sufferings?"; appeals by the poet for divine aid or inspiration, or dramatic addresses to a particular character, for example, "Then for you, Patroclus, appeared the end of life"; the emphatic repetition either of single words, like "strongest were they that were reared of men on earth, strongest they were and with the strongest they fought," or of phrases, like "Against him shall I go, even if his hands are like fire, his hands like fire and his might like gleaming iron"; comments by anonymous bystanders, for example, "Thus did one say, looking towards another nearby . . ."; antithesis, as in αἴδεσθεν μὲν ἀνήνασθαι, δεῖσαν δ' ὑποδέχθαι (VII. 93); assonance and alliteration, which though sometimes fortuitous in Homer are often not—for example I. 49, δυσμόρῳ, ὃς δὴ δηθὰ φίλων ἄπο πήματα πάσχει (dusmoröi, hos dē dētha philōn apo pēmata paschei).

Word-plays, as when Achilles has the ash-spear of *Peleus,* from the crest of Mount *Pelion,* which he alone could wield, *pēlai,* or tropes like Patroclus's rebuke to Achilles, "Cruel man, your father was not horse-man Peleus nor Thetis your mother, but the grey sea bore you, and precipitous rocks, since your mind is unyielding," are equally rhetorical in flavour. Yet only rarely can one detect a continuous rhetorical urge, as in the seventh book of the *Iliad*. There one finds a heavy concentration of assonance and alliteration, and, more important, a persistent attempt to design balanced antithetical phrases to correspond with and reproduce a balance in events. Yet a continuous style in any true sense remains doubtful. The Embassy to Achilles, Book IX of the *Iliad*, might be expected to exemplify such a style, if one existed; and indeed the flavour of this episode is undeniably rhetorical with its speeches of appeal, argument and rejection, employing such artifices as allegory (the Prayers) and paradigm (the story of Meleagros). But in the main this rhetorical flavour is produced by the deployment of arguments rather than by the verbal quality which is an essential part of style, and the same is true of the speeches and laments in the last book of the *Iliad*.

It is tempting to consider any kind of rhetoricism as relatively late in the oral tradition, and some extreme examples occur in contexts which there are other grounds for identifying as accretions. Conversely, rhetorical devices are absent from many stretches of the poems which possess an apparently (though perhaps deceptively) archaic simplicity. It is also true that subsequent Greek literature shows a progressive interest in rhetoric. Yet before we try to use these devices as evidence for comparative dating or different authorship we should remember that even primitive literature tends to delight in simple tropes and metaphorical artifices, on the level of the Homeric description of oars as the wings of ships or the fame of a song as reaching to the broad sky; and that the *Iliad* and *Odyssey* are by no means primitive. The most that can be said, then, is that rhetoricisms seem to have been used more commonly in the later stages of the oral tradition, and that the most violent of them exemplify that love of novelty and variety which is characteristic of elaborations at the end of the oral period.

The stylistic analysis of Homer is, I know, an occupation to be indulged at one's peril. It was common in the later half of the last century, but was done in so insensitive and careless a manner, and led to results so blatantly contradictory, that since then there has been a common tendency to consider questions of style as beyond the scope of true scholarship. This approach seems feeble and unjustified. It is obvious enough that the estimation of literary style is an abstract and subjective activity. Yet certain stylistic differences are easily recognizable in the *Iliad* and *Odyssey*, and there could be little disagreement about, say, the decorated lyrical style of the *Iliad*. I have deliberately concentrated on some easily recognizable differences of stylistic *effect*—have done no more than that; and I have emphasized that many differences of style are likely to be due to changes of subject rather than of composer. At the same time certain stylistic effects seem particularly frequent in contexts which there are other grounds for considering as being relatively late in construction—as belonging either to the stage of monumental composition itself or to a subsequent stage of elaboration. Here the study of the means by which the effects are achieved is fruitful, and in particular the relation of these means to the traditional formular equipment of the Homeric singer.

This has been illustrated by a useful examination of the different ways in which wounds and death are described in the *Iliad*. Wolf-Harmut Friedrich decided that the only hope of detecting different personal styles was to take a subject that recurs throughout the poem and see how the description of this subject varies from context to context.[3] Clearly the battle-poetry is the best such subject, and in particular the nature of wounds, fatal or not. These are usually described in a careful and formal way which nevertheless admits considerable variety of detail. Often the same kind of death, as when a charioteer is hit by a spear and topples from his chariot, is described in two or three different parts of the poem with slight variations. Sometimes it seems possible to say of such closely similar but not identical passages that one must be prior in composition and has been subjected to more or less appropriate variation in its other uses. Unfortunately, though, there is no justification for concluding, in a traditional poem, that the context of an apparently original description was composed earlier than that of an apparent derivative. The derivative might itself be quite old, both it and the original may have been floating around in the tradition for a generation or more, and the passage containing the derivative version, in a poem like the *Iliad,* may actually have been put together before the passage containing the original.

For this reason the analytical results achieved by the application of Friedrich's method are limited and sometimes, no doubt, misleading. More important is his perception of a more purely stylistic tendency for the secondary variants and elaborations of recurrent martial incidents to become fantastic and improbable, despite a frequent veneer of specious realism. Thus XVI. 612 f. (= XVII. 528 f.) describes quite credibly how a spear, having missed its object, quivers in the ground:

> it was buried in the earth, and the butt of the weapon quivered; then mighty Ares took away its force.

But at XIII. 442–44 this vignette is elaborated into something which, immediately one thinks about it, is physiologically impossible and artistically rather absurd:

> The spear was fixed in his heart, which in its palpitation made the butt of the weapon, also, quiver; then mighty Ares took away its force.

Similarly with two episodes involving Antilochus: at XIII. 396 ff. he hit a charioteer, and "he gasping fell from the well-wrought chariot," and Antilochus drove off the horses; but at V. 580 ff. another charioteer was hit by Antilochus, and he too "gasping fell from the well-wrought chariot." This time, though, something fantastic happens: the victim falls head-first in soft sand and sticks there upside-down until his horses knock him over. Again this shows a desire to elaborate the direct description, to go one better than what seems to be the traditional version. This desire is likely to be more characteristic of later singers and rhapsodes than of the main monumental composer or his predecessors. Again we must beware of abusing this conclusion and applying it mechanically to many less extreme cases, where the description of impossible events may be due not to second-hand elaboration and the desire for novelty for its own sake but to a keen poetical and dramatic imagination—as for example when a victim's eyes fall out when he is struck in the face by a spear.

In short there is something to be learned from the search for different styles in Homer. Obviously, different styles do not necessarily entail different authors; it would be fantastic to imagine that the main poet of the *Iliad* (or indeed any competent singer) was incapable of composing in something like the majestic style, if he wished, as well as in the succinct narrative style or the much commoner "normal" style to which we can attach no special description. The question is whether and when he did so wish. In general, as one would expect on *a priori* grounds, poetry which may have been taken over more or less intact from the shorter epics of the pre-Homeric period tends to be simpler, more direct, less elaborate. The main composer of the *Iliad* probably brought an increase in subtlety and variation, but where the elaboration becomes excessive there are often grounds for seeing the operation of declining singers or rhapsodes. The *Odyssey* has a markedly narrower stylistic range than the *Iliad,* and its excesses are more strictly confined to large-scale expansions like the last book. At least the diversity and unity that must be expected in any oral poem of monumental scope are certainly present, in stylistic terms, in both poems. The diversity carries certain strong implications for the complex oral ancestry of the poems, though often—as the critic must be constantly aware—it arises simply from the diversity of parts possessed by any work of art whatever.

NOTES

1. For a good brief account of the paratactic style see Pierre Chantraine, *Grammaire Homérique,* 2 vs. (Paris, 1958–63), v. 2, p.351 ff.
2. Adam Parry, "The Language of Achilles," *TAPhA* 87:1–7 (1956), repr. in G. S. Kirk, ed., *The Language and Background of Homer* (Cambridge, Eng., 1964–65).
3. Wolf-Harmut Friedrich, *Verwandung und Tod in der Ilias* (Göttingen, 1956).

William Whallon

BIBLICAL POETRY AND HOMERIC EPIC

In the first chapter of *Mimesis*—hereafter cited from the English translation by Willard R. Trask (Princeton, 1953), but with the page numbers from the German edition (Bern, 1946) in brackets—Erich Auerbach contrasted the narrative about Odysseus' scar (from the nineteenth book of the *Odyssey*) with the narrative about Abraham's offering of Isaac (from the twenty-second chapter of Genesis). The analysis is brilliant; and yet the two texts do not seem wholly comparable. For Homeric epic is no more analogous to Old Testament prose than to the poetry; it is episodic like the one, but formulaic like the other—the argument from style that Homeric epic derived ultimately from an oral culture cannot be extended to Old Testament prose but can in large measure be extended to the poetry. So the passage about Odysseus' scar answers, in one way, to the passage about the offering of Isaac, but in another way, equally good, to a chapter from Habakkuk. In considering how Old Testament prose may be unlike the poetry, we shall keep Homeric epic as a touchstone, and bring Auerbach, quoting him as extensively as need be, under judgment.

A. OLD TESTAMENT POETRY LACKS DISTINCTIVE CHARACTERIZATION

Herein lies the reason why the great figures of the Old Testament are so much more fully developed, so much more fraught with their own biographical past, so much more distinct as individuals, than are the Homeric heroes. Achilles and Odysseus are splendidly described in many well-ordered words, epithets cling to them, their emotions are constantly displayed in their words and deeds—but they have no development, and their life-histories are clearly set forth once and for all. So little are the Homeric heroes presented as developing or having developed, that most of them—Nestor, Agamemnon, Achilles—appear to be of an age fixed from the very first. Even Odysseus, in whose case the long lapse of time and the many events which occurred offer so much opportunity for biographical development, shows almost nothing of it. Odysseus on his return is exactly the same as he was when he left Ithaca two decades earlier. But what a road, what a fate, lie between the

Jacob who cheated his father out of his blessing and the old man whose favorite son has been torn to pieces by a wild beast!—between David the harp player, persecuted by his lord's jealousy, and the old king, surrounded by violent intrigues, whom Abishag the Shunnamite warmed in his bed, and he knew her not. The old man, of whom we know how he has become what he is, is more of an individual than the young man; for it is only during the course of an eventful life than men are differentiated into full individuality; and it is this history of a personality which the Old Testament presents to us as the formation undergone by those whom God has chosen to be examples. Fraught with their development, sometimes even aged to the verge of dissolution, they show a distinct stamp of individuality entirely foreign to the Homeric heroes.

(Mimesis 17–18[22–23])

It will be convenient to borrow from Auerbach, for the sake of showing how far we agree with him, two spatial metaphors. The one concerns depth: it contrasts a background (of matters in obscurity) with a foreground (where all is made clear). The other contrasts verticality (or succession in time) with horizontality (or contemporaneity). Let us apply both metaphors to Old Testament prose and Homeric epic (after the manner of Mimesis), and then to Old Testament poetry as well.

Content. Old Testament prose implies a background and develops with suspense. The prosateur sets down only whatever matters are crucial; no ancillary material is allowed to claim attention for itself. Many things that might be expressed are left to be inferred. Nor can we accurately predict much of what is about to happen.

And Rebekah took goodly raiment of her eldest son Esau, which were with her in the house, and put them upon Jacob her younger son: And she put the skins of the kids of the goats upon his hands, and upon the smooth of his neck: And she gave the savoury meat and the bread, which she had prepared, into the hand of her son Jacob. And he came unto his father, and said, My father: and he said, Here am I; who art thou, my son? And Jacob said unto his father, I am Esau thy firstborn; I have done according as thou badest me: arise, I pray thee, sit and eat of my venison, that thy soul may bless me. And Isaac said unto his son, How is it that thou hast found it so quickly, my son? And he said, Because the Lord thy God brought it to me. And Isaac said unto Jacob, Come near, I pray thee, that I may feel thee, my son, whether thou be my very son Esau or not. And Jacob went near unto Isaac his father; and he felt him, and said, The voice is Jacob's voice, but the hands are the hands of Esau.

(Gen. 27:15–22)

Homeric epic occurs in the foreground and has less suspense. The poet works into the narrative by one device or another whatever seems likely to hold the interest of his audience. He understands everything fully and leaves nothing obscure. We can predict some events because they are explicitly foretold.

And warm tears were flowing from their brows to the ground as they grieved in longing for their charioteer, and their rich manes were stained as they streamed from the yoke-pads by the yoke on both sides. Seeing the two of them in grief, the son of Cronus pitied them, and shaking his head he said to himself: Ah, wretched ones, why did we give you to lord Peleus, a mortal, when you yourselves are ageless and immortal? Was it that among unhappy men you should have your own sorrows? For I suppose that of all the things that breathe and creep on the earth there is nothing more miserable than man. But Hector Priamides is certainly not going to mount on you and the resplendent chariot; I will not allow it. Isn't it enough that as things are he has the arms and prides himself on them? But I shall send courage into your knees and your heart, so that you may save Automedon from the war and bring him to the hollow ships. For I shall still stretch out glory to the Trojans to slay, until they come to the well-benched ships, and the sun sets and the sacred darkness comes on. (*Il.* XVII. 437–55)

Old Testament poetry occurs in the foreground and has no suspense. Not details about political intrigues but truths known to every generation, not new facts but new insights, engage the poet's special eloquence. We lack any incentive to predict; nothing will take place that is memorable as history.

(Having long been barren, Hannah conceived a son; when he was weaned she prayed as follows:)

> My hearth rejoiceth in the Lord,
> mine horn is exalted in the Lord:
> my mouth is enlarged over mine enemies;
> because I rejoice in thy salvation.
> There is none holy as the Lord:
> for there is none beside thee:
> neither is there any rock like our God.
> Talk no more so exceeding proudly;
> let not arrogancy come out of your mouth:
> for the Lord is a God of knowledge,
> and by him actions are weighed.
> The bows of the mighty men are broken,
> and they that stumbled are girded with strength.
> They that were full have hired out themselves for bread;
> and they that were hungry ceased:
> so that the barren hath born seven;
> and she that hath many children is waxed feeble.
> The Lord killeth, and maketh alive:
> he bringeth down to the grave, and bringeth up.
> The Lord maketh poor, and maketh rich:
> he bringeth low, and lifteth up.
> He raiseth up the poor of the dust,
> and lifteth up the beggar from the dunghill,
> to set them among princes,
> and to make them inherit the throne of glory:
> for the pillars of the earth are the Lord's,
> and he hath set the world upon them.
> He will keep the feet of his saints,
> and the wicked shall be silent in darkness;
> for by strength shall no man prevail.
> The adversaries of the Lord shall be broken to pieces;
> out of heaven shall he thunder upon them:
> the Lord shall judge the ends of the earth;
> and he shall give strength unto his king,
> and exalt the horn of his anointed. (I Sam. 2:1–10)

Old Testament prose is vertical in showing a procession of figures after the usual fashion of a chronicle, and in showing that a long passage of time has affected certain figures in the usual way. But Homeric epic is horizontal since the casts of the *Iliad* and *Odyssey* are somewhat identical, and since the passage of time—each poem taking place in a few days, and only ten years lying between them—is too brief for much aging. And Old Testament poetry is horizontal in rather like manner: no great while is needed for the dialogue in Job, and everyone is the same at the end as at the beginning.

Style. Old Testament prose suggests a background by using only such descriptive elements as cannot be spared, and stands vertical because these elements always give point to the moment at hand; character is drawn without the use of clichés. But Homeric epic evenly illuminates its foreground with descriptive elements that are interesting for their own sake, and lies horizontal because these elements are timeless. Being loaded now with treasure to ransom the body of Hector (*Il.* XXIV. 189), and now with clothing that Nausicaa and her handmaids will wash at the shore (*Od.* VI. 72), a wagon is a "wagon well-wheeled, mule-drawn" ἄμαξαν ἐύτροχον ἡμιονείην. Character is sketched by assigning to everyone certain traits and titles that may be repeatedly mentioned without regard for their appropriateness in any particular passage. Not that all are alike: Achilles and Odysseus, since their names are identical in meter, could have shared their epithets between them, and the same is true for Hector and Ajax, or Athene and Apollo. But there is no change: there is never a time when we are sure that Achilles will not be called "swift-footed," and those who are prominent in both poems—Odysseus, Nestor, Menelaus, and Helen—are described in the same way early and late. Old Testament poetry creates a foreground of Homeric leisure and serenity by restating every concept, and lies horizontal because its idiom has a Homeric timelessness and inevitability. A mountain of any kind brings mention of a hill: "I will get me to the mountain of myrrh, and to the hill of frankincense" (S. of Sol. 4:6); "contend thou before the mountains, and let the hills hear thy voice" (Mic. 6:1). Character is not here an important subject, yet "Jacob" and "Israel," synonymous names, are balanced in forty verses; there is no development, no contrast.

It may be helpful to extend what Tolstoi, *What is Art? and Essays on Art,* tr. by Aylmer Maude (London, n.d.), p.208, remarked about Wagnerian opera: "There is one fixed combination of sounds, or *leit-motiv,* for each character, and this *leit-motiv* is repeated every time the person whom it represents appears; and when anyone is mentioned the *motiv* is heard which relates to that person. Moreover each article also has its own *leit-motiv* or chord. There is a *motiv* of the ring, a *motiv* of the helmet, a *motiv* of the apple, a *motiv* of fire, spear, sword, water, etc., and as soon as the ring, helmet, or apple is mentioned, the *motiv* or chord of the ring, helmet, or apple, is heard." None of this pertains to Old Testament prose, but if we change *leitmotiv* to *epithet* there are resemblances to Homeric epic, and if we change it to the *synonym,* or antonym, completing a word pair—there are resemblances to Old Testament poetry. With regard to background versus foreground, and verticality versus horizontality, both metaphors being applied in particular to characterization, Old Testament prose belongs on the left,

Homeric epic and Old Testament poetry belong together on the right. Without debating whether, if all the factors were weighed, the figures of the Old Testament really would seem to have, as Auerbach claimed for them, an individuality foreign to the Homeric heroes, we observe that even the analysis behind this conclusion is valid only for the prose and not in the least for the poetry.

In contrasting Old Testament prose, on the one hand, with Homeric epic and Old Testament poetry, on the other, we say nothing about which is the nobler or has the more forcible effect on the mind. We say only that certain differences can be noted: the reportorial against the creative, the naturalistic against the nonnaturalistic, the suggestiveness of what is withheld as internal against the handsomeness of what is revealed as external, the nonformulaic against the formulaic, low against high style. To give these qualities in a slightly different order we may notice that, in contrasting Old Testament prose with Homeric epic, Auerbach defined the latter by its "fully externalized description, uniform illumination, uninterrupted connection, free expression, all events in the foreground, displaying unmistakable meanings, few elements of historical development and of psychological perspective" (*Mimesis* 23 [18]). Every term in the list applies also to Old Testament poetry.

B. OLD TESTAMENT POETRY CONSISTS OF NONNATURALISTIC SPEECH

> With the utmost fullness, with an orderliness which even passion does not disturb, Homer's personages vent their inmost hearts in speech; what they do not say to others, they speak in their own minds, so that the reader is informed of it. Much that is terrible takes place in the Homeric poems, but it seldom takes place wordlessly: Polyphemus talks to Odysseus; Odysseus talks to the suitors when he begins to kill them; Hector and Achilles talk at length, before battle and after; and no speech is so filled with anger or scorn that the particles which express logical and grammatical connections are lacking or out of place.
>
> (*Mimesis* 6 [10])

One fact Auerbach failed to discuss is that, unlike Old Testament prose, Homeric epic and Old Testament poetry had special requirements, and became circumlocutory, and formulaic, as a consequence. A concept had to be expressed under exacting conditions (of meter in the one, parallelism in the other), and these conditions were fulfilled in perhaps the easiest way possible (by such means as the use of epithets to create phrases of the desired meter in the one, by the use of synonyms and antonyms to create word pairs of the desired parallelism in the other). And whenever the same problem recurred the poet ordinarily supplied the same answer because it came most quickly to mind. For this reason, Thetis, Diomedes, Andromache, and Eumaeus all speak with like epithets to accompany like nouns; Hannah, Job, Lemuel, and Isaiah all speak with the same word pairs. It was not from any wish for decorum, but primarily for the sake of convenience, that the poet never allowed his figures, no matter how strong the passions that might govern them, to mar their eloquence with solecisms, stammerings, and anacolutha.

No one in Homeric epic used "swift-footed" because he was intended to emphasize that term in particular, but solely because the poet needed to stretch out the name "Achilles"; no one in Old Testament poetry used "hills" because he was intended to be interested in them, but solely because the poet needed to complement the noun "mountains." Whether "swift-footed" or "hills" occurs in a line is accordingly somewhat fortuitous, the deciding factors being "Achilles" and meter, or "mountains" and parallelism. Here is a further aspect, not in Old Testament prose but in Homeric epic and Old Testament poetry, of an analogy with the *leitmotiv:* W. H. Auden, "Mimesis and Allegory," in *English Institute Annual, 1940* (New York, 1941), p.5–6, remarks that it "was Wagner who showed the surrealists that the primitive, the illogical, the chance-determined was the true revolutionary art and who preceded Sibelius and Gertrude Stein in the discovery that if you repeat the same thing four times it has little effect, but that a remarkable effect can be gained by repeating it four hundred times."

Some speech in the Old Testament is prose, some poetry; but all the poetry —a fact noticed by few besides Paul Dhorme, O.P., *Le Livre de Job* (2d. ed., Paris, 1926), p.*li*—is speech. In the historical books the main narrative, in prose, is broken only for the quotation of a blessing (Gen. 49:1–27), a song of victory (Jud. 5), a prayer of thanksgiving (1 Sam. 2:1–10), or one of the other subjects of poetry. In Job the prologue and epilogue are in prose (except that Satan speaks in poetry: "From going to and fro in the earth, and from walking up and down in it"), and the assignment of the speeches and the introduction of Elihu are in prose; but Job and his friends converse in poetry, Elihu gives his monologue in poetry, and the Lord speaks in poetry from the whirlwind. In the books of psalms and proverbs prose is used for attributing, now and then, a passage of poetry to an author, or for naming the circumstances behind its creation; and in the books of prophecy prose introduces, comments upon, and otherwise gives continuity to the words of the prophets, which are characteristically in poetry. The distinction between the forms, low against high style, is exact and uniform. In Homeric epic there is nothing comparable: the narrator speaks in the idiom of his heroes: the words of Priam resemble those of Telemachus, and both are like what the poet says as spectator; the high style is never interrupted. In this respect there is a distinction between the Old Testament and Homer, and it is precisely the opposite of what was asserted by Auerbach—who so far has been censurable only for having possibly misled us by giving all his attention to Old Testament prose and none to the poetry, but here for once is certainly mistaken:

> From the rule of the separation of styles which was later almost universally accepted and which specified that the realistic depiction of daily life was incompatible with the sublime and had a place only in comedy or, carefully stylized, in idyl—from any such rule Homer is still far removed. And yet he is closer to it than is the Old Testament. (*Mimesis* 22 [28])

This assertion, which stands near the close of the first chapter, is not peripheral or incidental to the arguments Auerbach developed throughout his book, for it reappears near the middle of the third chapter: "In the Judaeo-Christian tradition, as we have previously pointed out, there was no separating the elevated style from realism" (*Mimesis* 63 [68]). The assertion is not peripheral but central, and it is wrong. For the separation of styles is not further to seek in the Old Testament than in Homeric epic; it is immeasurably closer at hand; indeed it is obvious. Prose is used for the naturalistic description of events, poetry for all speech that is elevated or sustained.

Paul J. Alpers

SPENSER'S POETIC LANGUAGE

The question we are asking of the verse of *The Faerie Queene* is: what is the relation between stanza and sentence, or between lines and parts of a sentence? The stanza from the *Prothalamion* suggested that in Spenser's verse the formal requirements of line and stanza carry the sentence, whose structure has little or no independent force. We shall find that this phenomenon is characteristic of the verse of *The Faerie Queene,* and it well explains the "dream-like" or "musical" qualities that readers through the centuries have found in the poem. But it is not so easy as one thinks to say specifically what we mean when we say that sentence structure has little independent force in Spenser's verse. We at first think of the contrast between what Coleridge called the "fluent projection" of Spenser's verse, as opposed to "the deeper and more inwoven harmonies of Shakespeare and Milton."[1]

> There, as in glistring glory she did sit,
> She held a great gold chaine ylincked well,
> Whose vpper end to highest heauen was knit,
> And lower part did reach to lowest Hell;
> And all that preace did round about her swell,
> To catchen hold of that long chaine, thereby
> To clime aloft, and others to excell:
> That was *Ambition,* rash desire to sty,
> And euery lincke thereof a step of dignity.
> (2.7.46)

> High on a Throne of Royal State, which far
> Outshone the wealth of *Ormus* and of *Ind,*
> Or where the gorgeous East with richest hand
> Show'rs on her Kings *Barbaric* Pearl and Gold,
> Satan exalted sat, by merit rais'd
> To that bad eminence; and from despair
> Thus high uplifted beyond hope, aspires
> Beyond thus high, insatiate to pursue
> Vain War with Heav'n, and by success untaught
> His proud imaginations thus display'd.[2]

Selections from ["Spenser's Poetic Language, in] Paul J. Alpers, *The Poetry of* The Faerie Queene (copyright © 1967 by Princeton University Press), p.77–98. Reprinted by permission of Princeton University Press.

In Spenser's stanza, each line is a self-contained component of the sentence. It is significant that the one enjambment (after "thereby") produces a line in which the two halves are syntactically parallel, and which thus maintains the correspondence between line and sentence component. The contrast with Milton's postponed verbs and continual enjambments is obvious and is immediately felt when one reads the passages aloud. Yet when we try to use these points of comparison as criteria for analyzing Spenser's verse, we find that they are not so decisive as we had hoped. If simply the use of enjambment is to be a criterion, there are many more enjambments in *The Faerie Queene* than we expect. Similarly the correspondence between verse line and sentence component is too frequent in other Elizabethan narrative poems to be considered a distinguishing characteristic of Spenser's verse.

There is an obvious difficulty in using *Paradise Lost* as a gauge for *The Faerie Queene*. Milton so conspicuously complicates sentence structure that he does not help us determine whether Spenser's verse corresponds to or deviates in its own way from a norm for narrative verse. Similarly lyric poetry cannot provide the basis for a systematic examination of the verse of a heroic poem, even though considering Donne and Sidney is a useful starting point for dealing with Spenser. The relevant comparisons will be between *The Faerie Queene* and other Elizabethan narrative poems, and of these I have chosen Marlowe's *Hero and Leander* and Drayton's *The Barons Warres*. The first seems to me the one Elizabethan narrative as masterful in its mode as Spenser's, and the second is a heroic poem by a disciple of Spenser. If Spenser's verse is really as specialized as it seems, we ought to be able to discriminate it from these poems.

The most useful way to examine sentence structure in these poems is not to distinguish lines and sentences on the basis of inherent structural features, but to pay attention to what happens in the act of reading them.[3] Take the following lines from the *Barons Warres:*

> Whilst EDWARD takes but what they [his advisers]
>   onely give,
> Whose Nonage crav'd their carefullest Protection,
> Who knew to rule, and he but learn'd to live,
> From their Experience taking his Direction.
>
>   (6.11)[4]

This passage is very similar to Spenser's verse in the way individual lines are managed and the way in which sentence components are distributed among lines of verse. What distinguishes it from Spenser is the mental activity required of us when we recognize that "Whose" in line 2 refers to the young king, while "Who" in line 3 refers to his advisers. Simply to understand the lines requires a distinct consciousness of the sentence structure; this demand is particularly striking because we must resist the suggestion that "Whose" and "Who" refer to the same person became they appear in the same position in successive lines of verse.

"Consciousness of sentence structure" may seem an elusive criterion, but we can show with some exactness that Drayton and Marlowe require it, while Spenser does not. Here is another stanza from *The Barons Warres:*

> But never doth it surfet with Excesse,
> Each Dish so savorie, season'd with Delight,
> Nor nothing can the Gluttonie suppresse,
> But still it longs, so liquorish is the sight,
> Nor having all, is in desire the lesse,
> Till it so much be tempted, past the Might,
> That the full stomacke more than well suffic'd,
> Vomits, what late it vilely gourmandiz'd.
>
> (6.23)

We have to recognize that line 2 is an absolute construction, not the subject or object of an ensuing verb, and in line 4 we must recognize that neither "longs" nor "so liquorish" has an ensuing complementary construction. The rejected alternatives are not remote possibilities, but arise perfectly naturally. We again find ourselves resisting some of the suggestions of the verse, and the conflict between verse form and sentence structure accounts for our feeling that our progress through the stanza is rather bumpy. (Drayton increases this effect when, having persuaded us that no line carries over into what follows, he goes against our expectation that the sentence will end at line 5 and pushes it through to the end of the stanza.) The going is bumpy even when we are dealing with parallel constructions, because Drayton makes us work out the grammatical construction of almost every line:

> By which, the King with a selected Crue,
> Of such as he with his Intent acquainted,
> Which he affected to the Action knew,
> And in revenge of EDWARD had not fainted,
> That to their utmost would the Cause pursue,
> And with those Treasons that had not been tainted;
> Adventured, the Labyrinth t'assay,
> To rowse the Beast, which kept them all at bay.
>
> (6.49)

The effort with which we make our way through the first six lines is capped in the seventh, where we are forced to go back to line 1 to find the subject of "Adventured." A comparison of *The Barons Warres* (1603) with its first version, *Mortimeriados* (1596), shows that Drayton intended us to work consciously at sentence structure.[5] No doubt he meant the effect of difficulty to be a heightening or dignifying of his verse. But it becomes a real vice in *The Barons Warres,* because it so often involves a struggle against verse form: the stanzas more often strike us as fragmented than coherent. Indeed these stanzas from Drayton may suggest to us that the lucidity and ease with which a sentence unfolds in Spenser's stanza is a sign of mastery of language, not of an inability to exploit its resources.

Our consciousness of sentence structure can be most clearly observed when there are structural ambiguities or at least genuine possibilities of misconstruing sentence structure. The following lines render Hero's confusion after she has unwittingly allowed herself to invite Leander to her tower:

> And like a planet, mooving severall waies,
> At one selfe instant, she poore soule assaies,

> Loving, not to love at all, and everie part
> Strove to resist the motions of her hart.[6]

"At one selfe instant" can modify either "mooving" or "assaies"; each syntactic choice produces a distinct intonation of the phrase and movement of the line in which it occurs. For two reasons, the phrase is best taken with "mooving." This construction more precisely renders the phenomenon which makes planetary motion an apt simile for Hero's confusion. Second, this choice involves an enjambment and divides the second line; it thus requires a more active use of the speaking voice to keep alive both sentence structure and verse form, and Marlowe continues to exploit this active speaking voice in the interjected "poore soule" and in controlling the rhythm of the hypermetrical third line. Even if this argument is disputed and the other sentence structure preferred, it is clear that the way we speak and mentally grasp these lines depends on which of the two sentence structures we choose.

The next example is not genuinely ambiguous, but it is thoroughly confusing until the right sentence structure is discerned:

> Home when he came, he seem'd not to be there,
> But like exiled aire thrust from his sphere,
> Set in a forren place, and straight from thence,
> Alcides like, by mightie violence,
> He would have chac'd away the swelling maine,
> That him from her unjustly did detaine.
> *(Hero and Leander, 2.117–22)*

The first couplet does not make a complete sentence, and having recognized this, we must avoid treating "Set in a forren place" as parallel to "thrust from his sphere." The voice must register the fact that the second line depends on "Set in a forren place" and that that phase, in its turn, modifies "he." The lines are rather hard to get into focus and might be thought faulty in the way Drayton's stanzas were. But the very active sentence structuring here demanded of us is turned to poetic use: the concentrated effort we give to these lines supports the sense of heroic expenditure of strength in those that follow. Our attention to sentence structure is exploited in a very different way in the opening description of Hero:

> She ware no gloves, for neither sunne nor wind
> Would burne or parch her hands, but to her mind,
> Or warme or coole them, for they tooke delite
> To play upon those hands, they were so white.
> *(Hero and Leander, 1:27–30)*

I think it natural to mistake the first couplet for a complete sentence, but even without making this error, we see how forcible is the enjambment from "to her mind" to "Or warme or coole them." The attention secured by this enjambment makes us particularly heed the meaning of "warme or coole" (as opposed to "burne or parch"), and our sense of discriminating attention to language encourages us to participate in the elements' delighting solicitude for Hero.

The consciousness of sentence structure that Marlowe expects is simply the normal attention to language that makes us, in actual speaking and listening, choose one of the possible interpretations of such ambiguous sentences as "The man was killed by the machine" or "They were entertaining women." But in *The Faerie Queene* we are not intended to make a choice when sentence structure is ambiguous. The following lines describe Amoret's appearance in the masque of Cupid:

> After all these there marcht a most faire Dame,
> Led of two grysie villeins, th'one *Despight*,
> The other cleped *Cruelty* by name:
> She dolefull Lady, like a dreary Spright,
> Cald by strong charmes out of eternall night,
> Had deathes owne image figur'd in her face,
> Full of sad signes, fearefull to liuing sight.
> (3.12.19)

"Cald by strong charmes" can modify either "Lady" or "Spright," and the important point is that there is no need to make a decision either way. Indeed it is essential to the poetry that we somehow have it both ways. Amoret, the prisoner of a diabolical sorcerer, has literally been "Cald by strong charmes out of eternall night," and it is because we feel the line applies to her that the next two lines are so immediate and awesome. Yet the force of the line would be diminished if it modified "Lady" alone. The double syntax makes us feel not simply that Amoret has been "Cald by strong charmes," but that she is "a dreary Spright," and we now see that this phrase has two meanings, both of which are allowed to come into play by the ambiguous structure of the sentence.[7]

Our next example presents a more complicated use of a structural ambiguity:

> And that new creature borne without her dew,
> Full of the makers guile, with vsage sly
> He taught to imitate that Lady trew,
> Whose semblance she did carrie vnder feigned hew.
> (1.1.46)

We cannot, and again we need not, decide whether "with vsage sly" modifies "taught" or "imitate." The double grammar makes the allegorical point that the false Una is the creature of Archimago: what characterizes the one characterizes the other. There is a further point of interest here. In line 2, we entertain for a moment the possibility that "with vsage sly" is syntactically parallel to the preceding two phrases (it seems a close echo of "without her dew") and thus modifies "creature." In Marlowe's verse this possibility would be rejected, and our perception of the sentence structure would produce a vigorous enjambment from line 2 to line 3. But the enjambment does not occur here. We continue to entertain the apparent syntax of "with vsage sly," because it makes little difference to the meaning of the passage: it simply makes line 2, rather than line 3, bring out the identity of the false Una and her creator. Note that we do not *choose* the wrong syntax. Rather this is a case of extreme permissiveness; we seem not to have to make the decisions about sentence structure that we ordinarily make.

Before going on to other instances of ambiguous sentence structure in *The Faerie Queene,* I would like to discuss the phenomenon that makes examples like the last one possible. Consider the following stanza:

> Her scattred brood, soone as their Parent deare
> They saw so rudely falling to the ground,
> Groning full deadly, all with troublous feare,
> Gathred themselues about her body round,
> Weening their wonted entrance to haue found
> At her wide mouth: but being there withstood
> They flocked all about her bleeding wound,
> And sucked vp their dying mothers blood,
> Making her death their life, and eke her hurt
>   their good.   (1.125)

"Groning full deadly" can modify either "Parent deare" (and thus parallel "falling to the ground") or "all" (and thus parallel "Weening . . . "). In this case we cannot have it both ways. The first of these choices creates an enjambment from line 2 to line 3, a strong caesura in line 3, and another enjambment from line 3 to line 4. The second choice makes line 3 an independent unit, because sentence structure now corresponds to the lines of verse: the subordinate clause ends at the end of line 2, and line 3 gives the subject of the main clause.[8] But on what basis do we make our choice here? There is really no difference in meaning. As the final lines make explicit, with their play on "death" and "dying," we can equally well think of the parent dragon emitting a death groan or of the children giving a deathlike groan at her death. But we must make a choice, and I think we choose the second alternative simply because it is easier: it more readily makes sentence structure compatible with the allocation of words to different lines of verse. The basis of our choice here is a rule that Spenser's verse almost never makes us violate: follow the path of least resistance. This rule, we may note, succinctly states the reason that modern critics dislike Spenser and romantic critics loved him.

We are brought back to the phenomenon that we saw was so important . . . —the independence of the line as unit in Spenser's verse. We now see that we do not treat the line as a unit at the expense of sentence structure; rather Spenser's ways with sentence structure encourage us to treat the line as a unit. Let us consider a more complex example than the last:

> By them the Sprite doth passe in quietly,
> And vnto *Morpheus* comes, whom drowned deepe
> In drowsie fit he findes: of nothing he takes keepe.
>   (1.1.40)

On first reading, the enjambment between the last two lines seems strong. We assume that "drowned deepe in drowsie fit" is a single, inseparable constituent and thus that a structural necessity forces us to continue from one line to the next. But the two halves of the phrase are quite independent of each other. Spenser could just as well have written "whom in drowsie fit

he findes" or "whom drowned deepe he findes" (the preceding stanza tells us
that Morpheus' dwelling is where "*Tethys* his wet bed / Doth euer wash, and
Cynthia still doth steepe / In siluer deaw his euer-drouping hed"). Hence
it would be perfectly possible to rewrite these lines, "whom drowned deepe
/ He findes in drowsie fit." As the lines stand, the immediate echo of
"drowned" in "drowsie" makes us feel that this is a single phrase, and the resulting effect of a strong enjambment is poetically important. When we go
from the tentative possibility that "drowned deepe" is literal to find "in
drowsie fit," we are made to see both the point of a fable—telling us about
the steeping of Morpheus' head is a way of telling us about sleep—and the
force of a metaphoric locution, "to be drowned in sleep." But the point to observe here is that our sense of a strong enjambment comes not from a genuine
structural necessity in the phrase, but from the order of words in the last line.
It is, as it were, an enjambment after the fact. Even in this instance our principle of taking the path of least resistance is confirmed. We read these lines
correctly by assuming that sentence structure has the easiest relation to the
disposition of words into lines, and by thus expecting only a subject and
a main verb after "whom drowned deepe."

Structural ambiguity is a genuine poetic resource for Spenser, not
just a freakish by-product of his loose sentence structures. The following lines
render the invigoration of the Red Cross Knight by Una's call, "Add faith
vnto your force":

> That when he heard, in great perplexitie,
> His gall did grate for griefe and high disdaine,
> And knitting all his force got one hand free,
> Wherewith he grypt her gorge with so great paine,
> That soone to loose her wicked bands did her constraine.
>
> (1.1.19)

We cannot tell whether "so great paine" refers to the knight's painful efforts
or to the pain he causes the dragon. This ambiguity is immediately succeeded
by another. "That" in the last line is either a relative pronoun or correlative
to "so"—in which case the last line is a result clause and we silently supply
"he." If we interpret the pain as the dragon's, we are likely to make "That"
a relative pronoun; if the pain is the knight's, then "That" will be treated as
a conjunction introducing a result clause. But these alternatives are not
mutually exclusive. It is possible to make either meaning of "paine" go
with either use of "That," and this overlap, or blur, helps us hold in our minds
both ways of construing the sentence. Thus, it might be argued that the
effect works by our recognizing the ambiguity in "paine" and simply treating
"That" as a relative pronoun, which of course retains the ambiguous reference.
(This cannot be the only correct reading, because "so . . . that" imposes itself
too strongly to be ruled out.) The sentence is exceptionally permissive, and it
is able to be so because we are used to treating each line as a unit—
an expectation which none of the preceding lines in the stanza violates. We
fully take in the next to last line before going on to the last, which in its turn
satisfies any or all of our grammatical expectations. We can put this another

way by saying that the independence of lines means their separation from each other, and that Spenser's verse keeps us from inspecting the connection between the lines in a way that would make us treat structural possibilities as alternative choices.

An ambiguity like this is a poetic resource for Spenser, because it brings to life a basic assumption of allegory—in this case, that the struggle depicted occurs within a single mind. A related instance occurs in Arthur's battle with Orgoglio, where syntactic ambiguity brings out a connection between Duessa and her beast that is similar to that between Archimago and the false Una:

> The proud *Duessa* full of wrathfull spight,
> And fierce disdaine, to be affronted so,
> Enforst her purple beast with all her might
> That stop out of the way to ouerthroe,
> Scorning the let of so vnequall foe.
>
> (1.8.13)

"Enforst . . . to ouerthroe" can be construed either as "compelled" (*OED* 10) plus a complementary infinitive or as "strengthened" (*OED* 3) plus a purpose clause. The two meanings overlap (the purpose of her strengthening him is the same action that she is compelling him to do), but it is nevertheless important for us to take in the double syntax. It focuses our attention on line 3 (which is made a complete clause by the meaning "strengthened") before we move on to line 4, and in this way the simple narrative action—the rider compelling her steed—is made an allegorical reality. Duessa, we see, is literally filling the beast with her might: her characteristics are his. We may already have noticed that the description of Duessa in the first two lines closely matches the lines describing the beast in the preceding stanza:

> Her dreadfull beast, who swolne with bloud of late
> Came ramping forth with proud presumpteous gate,
> And threatned all his heads like flaming brands.
>
> (1.8.12)

The identity of Duessa and her beast is brought out in a delightful way in the second half of stanza 13. We are told that Timias would not "To *her* yeeld passage, . . . / But with outrageous strokes did *him* restraine" (my italics).

The passages we have examined, though immensely instructive, are of course exceptional. We would like to know what is the normal usage of which such moments are intensifications. The following passage in which the satyrs kneel before Una, contains both a normal and an abnormal bit of sentence structure:

> Their frowning forheads with rough hornes yclad,
> And rusticke horror all a side doe lay,
> And gently grenning, shew a semblance glad
> To comfort her, and feare to put away,
> Their backward bent knees teach her humbly to obay.
>
> (1.6.11)

We at first treat "feare to put away" as parallel to "to comfort her," but as we continue reading we see that it must go with the last line. The initial mistake seems inevitable, because it is so naturally produced by the ordinary way of reading the verse, and I think we must regard it as a fault. Spenser's verse, unlike Marlowe's, does not encourage or allow us to make the kind of syntactic decision that is required here. In rereading these lines we must either undergo the jolt of the mistake again, or adopt the unusual tactic of remembering the sentence structure that lies ahead. In the lines just before these, on the other hand, we have a normal example of Spenserian sentence structure. If we read the first two lines with particular attention to sentence structure, we find that Spenser apparently wants us to imagine the satyrs laying aside their foreheads, and the visual absurdity is strengthened by the phrase, "with rough hornes yclad." But this difficulty goes unnoticed in our normal reading of the lines. "Rusticke horror" makes perfect sense as the object of "lay aside" (here in a very common metaphoric sense) and we are not at all prompted to seek out the earlier direct object. The separation of lines partly causes this effect, but even more important is the fact that "rusticke horror" recapitulates the preceding line, so that we are willing to understand it as the complete direct object of the verb. The formula includes both the satyrs' physical appearance and their frowns, which are what they can actually be thought to be laying aside.

We read these lines correctly by taking the path of least resistance, but there is a sense in which this rule applies to any grammatical discourse that is not ambiguous. We assume that a poet's sentences will be grammatical, and we often read without paying particular attention to their structure. At the same time, however, we assume that paying attention to sentence structure will be helpful and interesting, and in *Hero and Leander* it is. But particular attention to sentence structure is almost never helpful in reading *The Faerie Queene*. This is the general rule, whose intensified version is that we do not have to make a choice between alternatives when sentence structure is ambiguous. It seems a disagreeable prospect to have to avoid paying attention to sentence structure. But as we shall see, the requisite minimum of attention is secured not by prohibition, but by a firm and involving use of other aspects of language.

The mental processes by which we recognize that a sentence is grammatical are very complex, but no one, I think, would claim that they are conscious. We assume that any utterance is a grammatical sentence, and our awareness of sentence structure needs to become conscious attention only when this expectation is threatened. A deviant usage makes us ask, "Is this sentence really grammatical?" An ambiguity makes us ask, "How is this sentence grammatical?" Except for explicit problems like these, the reader or listener takes his sentence structure as it comes. We can see the difference between conscious attention and unconscious awareness in the following passage from *Hero and Leander*:

> Yet as she went, full often look'd behind,
> And many poore excuses did she find,
> To linger by the way, and once she stayd,
> And would have turn'd againe, but was afrayd,
> In offring parlie, to be counted light.
> So on she goes, and in her idle flight,

> Her painted fanne of curled plumes let fall,
> Thinking to traine Leander therewithall.
>
> (2.5–12)

If we make the natural mistake of treating "was afrayd" (line 4) as the completion of a clause, we must consciously restructure the sentence when we discover the complementary infinitive in the next line. But in the last three lines, sentence structure takes care of itself; the participial phrase in the last line in no way makes us question the fact that or the way in which the sentence is grammatical. However, recognizing that a sentence is grammatical is the minimum condition, not the full act, of understanding. A good reading of these lines possibly requires and is certainly facilitated by a conscious attention to sentence structure. There is a great difference between the last line as it stands and the ostensible equivalent, "She thought to traine Leander therewithall." The latter would be simply a knowing remark, set apart from the action. "Thinking" immediately enters the sentence to modify "she," and thus makes us reinterpret "let fall" as an act of volition the moment after we have seen it as an accident. The wit of the line lies in the precision with which the grammatical turn renders our seeing through Hero's helpless little attempt to fool Leander and herself. At every point in the passage conscious attention to sentence structure makes for better reading. To see that lines 3 and 4 are grammatical, we need only read line by line, as we read *The Faerie Queene*. But the lines come to life dramatically when we heed the force of "and," and connect, as a single action, Hero's stopping and her desire to turn.

In *Hero and Leander* the speaking voice structuring a sentence is played off against the formalities of meter, not as a special effect, but as a normal mode of verse that delights. In Spenser's verse, on the other hand, sentence structure is consistently subordinated to the steady progression of lines and the verbal formulas they carry:

> And all that preace did round about her swell,
> To catchen hold of that long chaine, thereby
> To clime aloft, and others to excell:
> That was *Ambition*, rash desire to sty,
> And euery lincke thereof a step of dignity.
>
> (2.7.46)

"Thereby" arouses certain grammatical expectations which are satisfied in the next line, but we should treat this syntactic link in the loosest way. If we pay conscious attention to it, "clime aloft" can have only its physical meaning in the allegorical narrative, whereas taken by itself, it has the force of both narrative action and moral phrase. But not attending to sentence structure cannot be a simply negative action. If it is natural and a sign of poetic strength, then there must be something to which we *are* paying attention. Here and everywhere in Spenser's verse, we pay attention to individual lines and verbal formulas. Instead of looking between the lines at the syntax of "thereby to clime aloft," we look within them at the progression from a formula that renders physical action ("to catchen hold . . .") to one that combines physical and moral phenomena ("to clime aloft") to the purely moral

"others to excell." The verse renders not an action, but an allegorical reality—
a permanent condition of the human spirit. The sequence of formulas reaches
its peak in the naming of Ambition and its definition as "rash desire to sty
[ascend]," which exploits elements of all three preceding formulas. For example, the impetuousness suggested by "rash" is indebted to the purely physical
"to catchen hold," rather than to the moral formulas.

It is to some extent misleading to speak of Spenser's specialized sense of
language. Loose sentence structure, double syntax, and the like are found in
much Elizabethan poetry—most notoriously, perhaps, in Shakespeare's sonnets. As a linguistic phenomenon, Spenser's ways with sentence structure
should be regarded as a specialized development of characteristics and potentialities that belong to Elizabethan English and Elizabethan verse. But this
does not mean that Spenser's underplaying of sentence structure is any the
less radical or decisive. The following stanza strikingly justifies our rule that it
is not helpful to pay attention to sentence structure in the verse of *The
Faerie Queene:*

> All cleane dismayd to see so vncouth sight,
> And halfe enraged at her shamelesse guise,
> He thought haue slaine her in his fierce despight:
> But hasty heat tempring with sufferance wise,
> He stayde his hand, and gan himselfe aduise
> To proue his sense, and tempt her faigned truth.
> Wringing her hands in wemens pitteous wise,
> Tho can she weepe, to stirre vp gentle ruth,
> Both for her noble bloud, and for her tender youth.
>
> (1.1.50)

In lines 5 and 6, it seems unquestionably desirable to heed sentence structure.
If we register the syntactic link between "aduise" and its complementary infinitives, the voice will stress the infinite verbs more than the nouns, and our
reading will bring out the Red Cross Knight's dramatic intent—"To *proue* his
sense, and *tempt* her faigned truth." But several factors, all characteristic of
Spenser's verse, encourage us to read line 6 as an independent unit, with the
stress falling about equally on verbs and nouns. First, the inversion in line 4
thwarts dramatic clarity and thrust. We would be more likely to heed the
structural force of the verbs in the next two lines if line 4 read: "But tempring
hasty heat with sufferance wise." Second, "gan himselfe aduise" need not
have a complement (cf. *OED* 5). Finally line 6, with its doubling of the infinitive phrase, fulfills only one syntactic function, so that it is perfectly easy
to take in the structure of the sentence by following the path of least resistance. We read the stanza, then, as a normal piece of Spenserian verse, and the
question is whether we pay a real price in losing the dramatic intonation of
line 6. I think we do not and that Spenser gives us all that the rejected reading does and more. The stanza is devoted not to dramatizing, but to making us
see the forces that arise and clash in a spiritual conflict like this. Our suggested rewriting of line 4 would render a single, definitive act of dealing with
the passions. Spenser's word order underplays the act of control and more
strongly suggests that "hasty heat" and "sufferance wise" are separate forces

in the mind, fixed in opposition to each other. The poetic force of the phrase "tempt her faigned truth" comes not from its registering a dramatic intent, but from the fact that it has one meaning for the Red Cross Knight and another for us. While it is a direct reminder to us that this is the false Una, it also expresses the knight's moral indignation—"I will test the faith which (I now see) she pretended to me." The double meaning makes us vividly aware how self-thwarting and helpless the soul can be in such a conflict. Note that we have no difficulty at all in grasping the Red Cross Knight's meaning of "faigned truth." We are conscious of his mind and feelings throughout the stanza, and the first two lines are predominantly from his point of view. But his meaning of "faigned truth" arises as a meaning of the phrase, quite independently of the sentence in which it occurs.

There are dozens of stanzas in *The Faerie Queene* that might legitimately be thought to challenge what we have said, and we cannot examine even a fraction of them here. The next two examples, two consecutive stanzas from the Cave of Mammon canto, seem to require some attention to sentence structure; what we say about them can serve to represent the kind of argument that would be brought against other apparent exceptions to our rules. The first stanza follows the arrival of Guyon and Mammon at Mammon's abode:

> So soone as *Mammon* there arriu'd, the dore
> To him did open, and affoorded way;
> Him followed eke Sir *Guyon* euermore,
> Ne darkenesse him, ne daunger might dismay.
> Soone as he entred was, the dore streight way
> Did shut, and from behind it forth there lept
> An vgly feend, more fowle then dismall day,
> The which with monstrous stalke behind him stept,
> And euer as he went, dew watch vpon him kept.
>
> (2.7.26)

There are three forcible enjambments in this stanza, and the question is whether a right reading of them involves attention to sentence structure. There is no doubt that Spenser is *using* sentence structure here. Lines 1, 5, and 6 each impels us into the next line by introducing a new sentence constituent in the middle of the line and by leaving it syntactically incomplete. But it requires no attention to sentence structure to apprehend that "dore" and "dore streight way" require verbs, and that "forth there lept" requires a subject. Here as elsewhere, Spenser underplays the connections between lines and draws our attention to the lines of verse themselves. We feel the link between the two verbs in line 2 much more strongly than the link between "the dore" and "did open." Our interest here is not so much in what the door does (it can only open or remain shut) as in the nature of a heroic entrance into an evil realm. Spenser is concerned to contrast the formula of line 2, which suggests a willing yielding, with the sense of hostility and terror in the lines that follow. The disparity we feel between lines 2 and 4 leads us into lines 5 and 6, where the enjambments generate real narrative excitement: "forth there lept" forces us on to discover *what* leaped forth. But line 7 then detaches itself from the sentence, and we pay attention to it alone. The verse does not attempt to show us the action rendered by the whole sentence, but rather moves us, by means of consciously melodramatic excitement, from the general formula, "Ne darkenesse him, ne daunger might dismay" to a more concrete and terrifying version of it, "An vgly feend [cf. "daunger"], more fowle then dismall day [cf. "darknesse"]." The enjambments in this stanza simply intensify our linear progression from line to line. Compare the following lines from *Hero and Leander:*

> Therefore unto him hastily she goes,
> And like light Salmacis, her body throes
> Upon his bosome, where with yeelding eyes,
> She offers up her selfe a sacrifice,
> To slake his anger, if he were displeas'd.
>
>   (2.45–49)

There are no enjambments as forceful as those in Spenser's stanza, but as we proceed from line to line, we must retain our grasp of the whole sentence and the relation of its parts. We would seriously misunderstand the last two lines if we did not remember where Hero has thrown and how she is offering herself. Indeed, the wit of the next line—"O what god would not therewith be appeas'd?"—exploits the disparity between the action depicted by the whole sentence and the more solemn suggestions of the last two lines when taken by themselves.

A different problem of sentence structure confronts us in the next stanza:

> Well hoped he, ere long that hardy guest,
> If euer couetous hand, or lustfull eye,
> Or lips he layd on thing, that likt him best,
> Or euer sleepe his eye-strings did vntye,
> Should be his pray. And therefore still on hye
> He ouer him did hold his cruell clawes,
> Threatning with greedy gripe to do him dye
> And rend in peeces with his rauenous pawes,
> If euer he transgrest the fatall *Stygian* lawes.
>
>   (2.7.27)

The first five lines are a periodic sentence, but even with a postponed main verb, Spenser makes it easy for us to avoid paying attention to sentence structure. By making lines 2, 3, and 4 a sequence of parallel clauses, he encourages us to entrust the grammatical working out of the sentence to the unfolding of the stanza. Moreover, far from being an essential conclusion to the sentence, "Should be his pray" at first strikes us as the flattest phrase in it. We can see why this is so by considering that if the words followed line 3, they would do no more than fulfill two expectations. As readers of romance we expect such a fate if the hero fails his test, and as readers of allegory we expect that moral failures will be punished in kind: thus "pray" simply confirms what is suggested by "couetous hand, or lustfull eye." But when we read "Should be his pray" not within the structure of a sentence, but in a sequence of lines, we see the poetic life the words have. Coming after "Or euer sleepe his eye-strings did vntye," "pray" surprises us by reintroducing the force of "couetous" and "lustfull," we realize that in this trial a natural human need is a weakness as potentially disastrous as a moral fault. Merely to be human is a danger here, and the sense of being threatened is developed in the final lines with formulas that expand "pray." The increasing terror in lines 6–8 comes not simply from the increasing energy of the verbs, but also from the moral progression from "cruell" to "greedy" to "rauenous," which increasingly brings out the potential identity of the fiend with the hero who fails. Hence when the alexandrine returns to the "If euer" with which the stanza began, the conditions of the trial impress us as genuinely awesome. The fiend is no longer dependent on the moral error (presumably avoidable) of a "hardy guest"; he has become identified with "the fatall *Stygian* lawes."

Finally we should note that there are some real exceptions to our rules for reading Spenser's verse. The question we must ask of these passages is whether the attention to sentence structure they require arises naturally in the specific poetic context. When it does not, as in the example (1.6.11) discussed above, the verse is faulty.[9] But in other instances, Spenser secures the right kind of attention:

> Thereat the feend his gnashing teeth did grate,
> And grieu'd, so long to lacke his greedy pray;
> For well he weened, that so glorious bayte
> Would tempt his guest, to take thereof assay:
> Had he so doen, he had him snatcht away,
> More light then Culuer in the Faulcons fist.
> Eternall God thee saue from such decay.
> But whenas *Mammon* saw his purpose mist,
> Him to entrap vnwares another way he wist.
>   (2.7.34)

Following the path of least resistance does not produce the right tone of voice in lines 5 and 6. The awe with which those lines should be said depends on our heeding the syntactic connection between them: the voice must connect "snatcht away" with the adverbial of manner in the next line. But in this case the verse enables us to produce the right intonation by making us feel the incursion of the narrator's speaking voice in line 5. That Spenser wants this effect is shown by the frank emergence of the narrator's voice in "Eternall God thee saue from such decay." That he secures the effect naturally is shown by the fact that it exploits a basic feature of the stanza—the special opportunity it provides for a poetic choice at the beginning of line 5.

The lines and stanzas of *The Faerie Queene* are not conceived as the utterances of a speaker who has a dramatic identity and presence. This fact is apparent not only in Spenser's ways with syntax, but also in his use of individual words and formulas. Consider the following stanza:

> Thus being entred, they behold around
> A large and spacious plaine, on euery side
> Strowed with pleasauns, whose faire grassy ground
> Mantled with greene, and goodly beautifide
> With all the ornaments of *Floraes* pride,
> Wherewith her mother Art, as halfe in scorne

> Of niggard Nature, like a pompous bride
> Did decke her, and too lauishly adorne,
> When forth from virgin bowre she comes in th'early
>   morne.   (2.12.50)

In Marvell's "The Mower against Gardens," a poem similar to this stanza in both subject and point, the speaker has a precise dramatic relation to the world of man and the world of nature:

> Luxurious Man, to bring his Vice in use,
> Did after him the World seduce:
> And from the fields the Flow'rs and Plants allure,
> Where Nature was most plain and pure.[10]

But in Spenser's stanza, we cannot imagine that "goodly beautifide" and "too lauishly adorne" are uttered by the same speaker about the same "ornaments." The purpose of the stanza is not to define a dramatic attitude, but to unfold the meanings of the formula at the center of the stanza, "all the ornaments of *Floraes* pride." As we come to it, this line expresses the natural attractiveness of a pastoral landscape. But the next line turns the apparently casual personification of Flora into decisive one; at the same time, the conventional metaphor in "ornaments" is taken seriously and is made to render a sense of artificial excess. We might argue that these lines make the true meaning of line 5 apparent, were it not for the alexandrine, which again represents "*Floraes* pride" as natural and wholesome. In "The Mower against Gardens," the speaker's tone is often elusive, but we have a fairly definite sense of his mixture of wonder and scorn, and we rightly assume that precise definition of his tone improves our grasp of the poem. But in reading this stanza, it is positively wrong to try to define the tone with which one says, "With all the ornaments of *Floraes* pride." The line includes meanings that would dictate very different tones of voice in a speaker dramatically conceived.

For Spenser the meanings of locutions and formulas are inherent in them, and are as independent of a putative speaker as they are independent of specific dramatic situations within the poem. This sense of language is most directly manifested when Spenser brings to life and puts us in possession of the full meaning of conventional formulas and phrases:

> And oft inclining downe with kisses light,
> For feare of waking him, his lips bedewd,
> And through his humid eyes did sucke his spright,
> Quite molten into lust and pleasure lewd.
>   (2.12.73)

"Molten into lust" is brought alive by the literal liquidity of "bedewd" and "humid." (It in turn brings out the dissipation of self that both Acrasia and her lover experience—for the last line, in true Spenserian fashion, can refer to either or both of them.) The sense of a moral metaphor can be drawn out by other means than reference to the physical phenomena that underlie it:

> The one [spirit] vpon his hardy head him plast,
> And made him dreame of loues and lustfull play,

> That nigh his manly hart did melt away,
> Bathed in wanton blis and wicked ioy.
>
> (1.1.47)

Here two stock locutions vivify each other. A fuller and more complex instance shows that this is not a casual device, but a basic poetic resource that truly reflects a habit of mind:

> There *Atin* found *Cymochles* soiourning,
> To serue his Lemans loue: for he by kind,
> Was giuen all to lust and loose liuing,
> When euer his fiers hands he free mote find:
> And now he has pourd out his idle mind
> In daintie delices, and lauish ioyes,
> Hauing his warlike weapons cast behind,
> And flowes in pleasures, and vaine pleasing toyes,
> Mingled emongst loose Ladies and lasciuious boyes.
>
> (2.5.28)

The stanza is a beautiful illustration of the way Spenser, as W. B. C. Watkins says, "sets up a kind of vibration of interrelated meanings among various seemingly simple, direct statements."[11] The meaning of "loose liuing" is unfolded in a series of formulas and conventional phrases, so that even in a sequence of which Spenser was obviously conscious—"pourd out his idle mind," "flowes in pleasures," and "Mingled emongst loose Ladies"—we feel that the connected meanings lie in the phrases themselves, and are not produced or joined together by the will or wit of the poet.

Our relation to the language of *The Faerie Queene* is illustrated by so many of the passages analyzed elsewhere that we need not now examine any more stanzas like those that have been quoted. What we should recognize here is that the treatment of poetic language as if meanings were inherent in it pervades the verse of *The Faerie Queene*. It underlies the most intimate verbal details, as well as those passages in which we consciously attend to the full meaning of words. Watkins has a fine discussion of such a detail:

> Sensitivity to sound values is so instinctive in Spenser that some of his effects which we have been taught to explain by such devices as alliteration, assonance, internal rhyme rather seem to develop meaning through sound relationships, just as in the process of creation selection of imagery at the start seems to beget subsequent images and in part control the development of the poem. For example:
>
> > Sleepe after toyle, port after stormie *seas,*
> > *Ease* after warre, death after life does greatly
> > *please.*
> >
> > (*Faerie Queene*, 1.9.40)

And in *Richard II.*, the Shakespearean play nearest to Spenser as well as to Marlowe, we find not only similar structural balance, but also this special sound relationship, which cannot be satisfactorily explained either by "internal rhyme" or "pun":

> But whate'er I be,
> Nor I nor any man that but man is

> With nothing shall be pleased, till he be *eased*
> With being nothing.
>
> (*Richard II*, 5.5.38–41)

Here the rhyme really represents a common element of meaning in the two words. Even here Shakespeare makes Spenser's simple statement (ease does please) sharper and more causal (nothing doth please *till* ease); the intellectual, soon to precipitate metaphysical wit, enters.[12]

The comparison with Shakespeare shows that in *The Faerie Queene* the common element of meaning seems really to be in the words, independent of a dramatically conceived speaker.

NOTES

1. Samuel Taylor Coleridge, *Miscellaneous Criticism,* ed. by T. M. Raysor (Cambridge, 1936), p.33.

2. John Milton, *Paradise Lost,* ed. by Merritt Y. Hughes (New York, 1962), II. 1–10.

3. It is surprising to find that no mechanical test is adequate or genuinely revealing when we compare the relation between verse form and sentence structure in these poems. By mechanical test I mean one based on some characteristic of language or verse form that exists independently of these particular poems—for example, the use of a particular grammatical construction or of inversions or of enjambments. For example, I could find no significant difference between Spenser's and Marlowe's use of infinitives, or between the syntax of the enjambments in Book I, canto 1 of *The Faerie Queene* and sestiad 2 *Hero and Leander.* Some mechanical tests produce revealing symptoms, but not explanations. A canto of *The Barons Warres* has more postponed main verbs than a canto of *The Faerie Queene,* but if this difference is important it must reflect a more basic difference between characteristics that are equally present in stanzas that do not contain periodic sentences. Similarly, there are rarely two or more consecutive enjambments in *The Faerie Queene,* whereas there are several stretches of consecutively enjambed verse in *Hero and Leander.* But *Hero and Leander* also contain long stretches of verse with few or no enjambments. Obviously we must describe a characteristic of all the verse in *Hero and Leander* that makes Marlowe able or liable, as Spenser is not, to produce a series of enjambments.

4. All quotations from Drayton are from Michael Drayton, *Works,* ed. by J. William Hebel, 5 vs. (Oxford, 1931–41).

5. Compare *Mortimeriados,* 2347–443, with the stanza just quoted; all Drayton's changes increase the effort required of the reader.

6. Christopher Marlowe, *Hero and Leander,* 1.361–64, in *Elizabethan Minor Epics,* ed. by Elizabeth Story Donno (London, 1963).

7. For a slighter example of the same structural ambiguity, see 1.1.38.2–3.

8. Actually "with troublous feare" is a sentence modifier—it can be construed with either subject or predicate. There is thus still an enjambment from line 3 to line 4, but it is not so strongly felt as it is when we choose the first of the alternative structures.

9. Other stanzas that have faults of this sort are 1.6.10 and 2.5.14.

10. Andrew Marvell, *Poems and Letters,* ed. by H. M. Margoliouth, 2 vs. (Oxford, 1952).

11. W. B. C. Watkins, *Shakespeare and Spenser* (Princeton, 1950), p.284.

12. *Ibid.,* p.286.

·VI·

MAGNITUDE AND THE EPIC VISION

Simone Weil

THE "ILIAD," POEM
OF MIGHT

The true hero, the real subject, the core of the *Iliad,* is might. That might which is wielded by men rules over them, and before it man's flesh cringes. The human soul never ceases to be modified by its encounter with might, swept on, blinded by that which it believes itself able to handle, bowed beneath the power of that which it suffers. Those who dreamt that might, thanks to progress, belonged henceforth to the past, have been able to see its living witness in this poem: those who know how to discern might throughout the ages, there at the heart of every human testament, find here its most beautiful, most pure of mirrors.

Might is that which makes a thing of anybody who comes under its sway. When exercised to the full, it makes a thing of man in the most literal sense, for it makes him a corpse. There where someone stood a moment ago, stands no one. This is the spectacle which the *Iliad* never tires of presenting.

> . . . the horses
> Thundered the empty chariots over the battle-lanes
> Mourning their noble masters. But those upon earth
> Now stretched, are dearer to the vultures than to
> their wives.

The hero is become a thing dragged in the dust behind a chariot.

> All about the dark hair
> Was strewn; and the whole head lay in dust,
> That head but lately so beloved, Now Zeus had
> permitted
> His enemies to defile it upon its native soil.

The bitterness of this scene, we savour it whole, alleviated by no comforting fiction, no consoling immortality, no faint halo of patriotic glory.

> His soul from his body took flight and sped towards
> Hades

"The 'Iliad,' Poem of Might." From Simone Weil, *Intimations of Christianity Among the Ancient Greeks,* translated and collected by Elizabeth C. Geissbuhler (Boston: Beacon Press, 1958), p.24–55. Originally titled "L'Iliade, ou le poème de la force," in Simone Weil, *La Source Grecque* (Paris: Editions Gallimard, Copyright 1953), p.9–43. Reprinted by permission of Editions Gallimard.

> Weeping over its destiny, leaving its vigor and
>   its youth.

More poignant still for its pain of contrast is the sudden evocation, as quickly effaced, of another world, the far-off world, precarious and touching of peace, of the family, that world wherein each man is, for those who surround him, all that counts most.

> Her voice rang through the house calling her
>   bright-haired maids
> To draw a great tripod to the fire that there might be
> A hot bath for Hector upon his return from combat.
> Foolish one! She knew not that far away from hot baths
> The arm of Achilles had felled him because of green-
>   eyed Athena.

Indeed he was far from hot baths, this sufferer. He was not the only one. Nearly all the *Iliad* takes place far from hot baths. Nearly all of human life has always passed far from hot baths.

The might which kills outright is an elementary and coarse form of might. How much more varied in its devices; how much more astonishing in its effects is that other which does not kill; or which delays killing. It must surely kill, or it will perhaps kill, or else it is only suspended above him whom it may at any moment destroy. This of all procedures turns a man to stone. From the power to transform him into a thing by killing him there proceeds another power, and much more prodigious, that which makes a thing of him while he still lives. He is living, he has a soul, yet he is a thing. A strange being is that thing which has a soul, and strange the state of that soul. Who knows how often during each instant it must torture and destroy itself in order to comform? The soul was not made to dwell in a thing; and when forced to it, there is no part of that soul but suffers violence.

A man naked and disarmed upon whom a weapon is directed becomes a corpse before he is touched. Only for one moment still he deliberates, he strives, he hopes.

> Motionless Achilles considered. The other drew near,
>   seized
> By desire to touch his knees. He wished in his heart
> To escape evil death, and black destiny. . . .
> With one arm he encircled those knees to implore him,
> With the other he kept hold of his bright lance.

But soon he has understood that the weapon will not turn from him, and though he still breathes, he is only matter, still thinking, he can think of nothing.

> Thus spake the brilliant son of Priam
> With suppliant words. He hears an inflexible reply . . .
> He spoke; and the other's knees and heart failed him,
> He dropped his lance and sank to the ground with
>   open hands,
> With both hands outstretched. Achilles unsheathes
>   his sharp sword,

Struck to the breastbone, along the throat, and then
    the two-edged sword
Plunges home its full length. The other, face down upon
    the ground,
Lay inert, his dark blood flowed drenching the earth.

When, a stranger, completely disabled, weak and disarmed, appeals to a warrior, he is not by this act condemned to death; but only an instant of impatience on the part of the warrior suffices to deprive him of life. This is enough to make his flesh lose that principal property of all living tissue. A morsel of living flesh gives evidence of life first of all by reflex, as a frog's leg under electric shock jumps, as the approaching menace or the contact with a horrible thing, or terrifying event, provokes a shudder in no matter what bundle of flesh, nerves and muscles. Alone, the hopeless suppliant does not shudder, does not cringe; he no longer has such licence; his lips are about to touch that one of all objects which is for him the most charged with horror.

None saw the entrance of great Priam. He paused,
Encircled Achilles' knees, kissed those hands,
Terrible slayers of men, that had cost him so many sons.

The spectacle of a man reduced to such a degree of misery freezes almost as does the sight of a corpse.

As when dire misfortune strikes a man, if in his own
    country
He has killed, and he arrives at another's door,
That of some wealthy man; a chill seizes those who
    see him;
So Achilles shivered at the sight of divine Priam,
So those with him trembled, looking from one to the other.

But this only for a moment, soon the very presence of the sufferer is forgotten:

He speaks. Achilles, reminded of his own father, longed to
    weep for him.
Taking the old man by the arm, he thrusts him
    gently away.
Both were lost in remembrance; the one of Hector,
    slayer of men,
And in tears he faints to the ground at Achilles feet.
But Achilles wept for his father and then also
For Patroclus. And the sound of their sobbing rocked
    the halls.

It is not for want of sensibility that Achilles had, by a sudden gesture, pushed the old man glued against his knees to the ground. Priam's words, evoking his old father, had moved him to tears. Quite simply he had found himself to be as free in his attitudes, in his movements, as if in place of a suppliant an inert object were there touching his knees. The human beings around us exert just by their presence a power which belongs uniquely to themselves to stop, to diminish, or modify, each movement which our bodies design. A person who crosses our path does not turn aside our steps in the same manner as a street sign, no one stands up, or moves about, or sits down again in quite the same fashion when he is alone in a room as when he has a visitor. But this undefinable influence of the human presence is not exercised by those men whom a movement of impatience could deprive of their lives even before a thought had had the time to condemn them. Before these men others behave as if they were not there; and they, in turn, finding themselves in danger of being in an instant reduced to nothing, imitate nothingness. Pushed, they fall; fallen, they remain on the ground, so long as no one happens to think of lifting them up. But even if at last lifted up, honoured by cordial words, they still cannot bring themselves to take this resurrection seriously enough to dare to express a desire; an irritated tone of voice would immediately reduce them again to silence.

> He spoke and the old man trembled and obeyed.

At least some suppliants, once exonerated, become again as other men. But there are others, more miserable beings, who without dying have become things for the rest of their lives. In their days is no give and take, no open field, no free road over which anything can pass to or from them. These are not men living harder lives than others, not placed lower socially than others, these are another species, a compromise between a man and a corpse. That a human being should be a thing is, from the point of view of logic, a contradiction; but when the impossible has become a reality, that contradiction is as a rent in the soul. That thing aspires every moment to become a man, a woman, and never at any moment succeeds. This is a death drawn out the length of a life, a life that death has frozen long before extinguishing it.

A virgin, the daughter of a priest, suffers this fate:

> I will not release her. Before that old age shall
>   have taken her,
> In our dwelling, in Argos, far from her native land
> Tending the loom, and sharing my bed.

The young wife, the young mother, the wife of a prince suffers it:

> And perhaps one day in Argos you will weave cloth
>   for another
> And you shall fetch Messeian or Hyperian
>   water
> In spite of yourself, under stress of dire necessity.

The child heir to a royal sceptre suffers it:

> These doubtless shall depart in the depths of
>   hollow ships
> I among them; you, my child, will either go with me
> To a land where humiliating tasks await you
> And you will labour beneath the eyes of a pitiless master. . . .

Such a fate for her child is more frightful to the mother than death itself, the husband wishes to perish before seeing his wife reduced to it. A father calls down all the scourges of heaven upon the army that would subject his daughter to it. But for those upon whom it has fallen, so brutal a destiny wipes out damnations, revolts, comparisons, meditations upon the future and the past, almost memory itself. It does not belong to the slave to be faithful to his city or to his dead.

It is when one of those who made him lose all, who sacked his city, massacred his own under his very eyes, when one of those suffers, then the slave weeps. And why not? Only then are tears permitted him. They are even imposed. But during his servitude are not those tears always ready to flow as soon as, with impunity, they may?

> She speaks in weeping, and the women moan
> Taking Patroclus as pretext for each one's private
> anguish.

On no occasion has the slave a right to express anything if not that which may please the master. This is why, if in so barren a life, a capacity to love should be born, this love could only be for the master. Every other way is barred to the gift of loving, just as for a horse hitched to a wagon, the reins and the bridle bar all directions but one. And if by miracle there should appear the hope of becoming again someone, to what pitch would not that gratitude and that love soar for those very men who must still, because of the recent past, inspire horror?

> My husband, to whom my father and my revered mother gave me,
> I saw before the city, transfixed by the sharp bronze.
> My three brothers, born of our one mother,
> So beloved! have met their final day.
> But you, when swift Achilles killed my husband
> And laid waste the city of divine Mynes,
> Did you not allow me to weep. You promised me that the divine
> Achilles
> Would take me for his legitimate wife and carry
> me off in his vessels
> To Phthia to celebrate our marriage among the
> Myrmidons.
> Therefore without ceasing I weep for you who have
> always been so gentle.

One cannot lose more than the slave loses, he loses all inner life. He only retrieves a little if there should arise an opportunity to change his destiny. Such is the empire of might; it extends as far as the empire of nature. Nature also, where vital needs are in play, wipes out all interior life, even to a mother's sorrow.

> For even Niobe of the beautiful hair, had thought
> of eating,
> She who saw twelve children of her house perish,
> Six daughters and six sons in the flower of youth.
> The sons Apollo killed with his silver bow
> In his anger against Niobe, the daughters, Artemis,
> lover of arrows, slew.
> It was because Niobe made herself equal to Leto saying:
> "She has two children, I have given birth to many."

> And those two, although only two, brought death to all.
> Nine days they lay dead; and none came to bury them.
> The neighbours had become stones by the will of Zeus.
> On the tenth day they were interred by the Gods of
> the sky,
> But Niobe had thought of eating, when she was weary
> of tears.

None ever expressed with so much bitterness the misery of man, which renders him incapable of feeling his misery.

Might suffered at the hands of another is as much a tyranny over the soul as extreme hunger at the moment when food means life or death. And its empire is as cold, and as hard as though exercised by lifeless matter. The man who finds himself everywhere the most feeble of his fellows is as lonely in the heart of a city, or more lonely, than anyone can be who is lost in the midst of a desert.

> Two cauldrons stand at the doorsill of Zeus
> Wherein are the gifts he bestows, the evil in one,
> the good in the other. . . .
> The man to whom he makes evil gifts he exposes to outrage;
> A dreadful need pursues him across divine earth;
> He wanders respected neither by men nor by Gods.

And as pitilessly as might crushes, so pitilessly it maddens whoever possesses it. None can ever truly possess it. The human race is not divided, in the *Iliad,* between the vanquished, the slaves, the suppliants on the one hand, and conquerors and masters on the other. No single man is to be found in it who is not, at some time, forced to bow beneath might. The soldiers, although free and well-armed, suffer no less outrage.

> Every man of the people whom he saw he shouted at
> And struck with his sceptre and reprimanded thus:
> "Miserable one, be still, listen while others speak,
> Your superiors. You have neither courage nor strength,
> You count for nothing in battle, for nothing in the
> assembly."

Thersites pays dear for these words, though perfectly reasonable and not unlike those pronounced by Achilles:

> He strikes him so that he collapses with tears fast flowing,
> A bloody welt rises upon his back
> Beneath the golden sceptre; he sits down, frightened.
> In a stupor of pain he wipes his tears.
> The others, though troubled, found pleasure and
> laughed.

But even Achilles, that proud unvanquished hero, is shown to us at the beginning of the poem weeping for humiliation and frustrating pain after the woman he had wanted for his wife was carried away under his very eyes and without his having dared to offer any opposition.

> . . . But Achilles,
> Weeping, sat down at a distance far from his companions,
> Beside the whitening waves, his eyes fixed upon
>   the boundless sea.

Agamemnon humiliates Achilles deliberately to show that he is the master.

> . . . Thus you will realize
> That I have more power than you, and all others shall tremble
> To treat me as an equal and to contradict me.

But a few days later even the supreme leader weeps in his turn, is forced to humble himself, to plead and to know the sorrow of doing so in vain.

Neither is the shame of fear spared to a single one of the combatants. The heroes tremble with the others. A challenge from Hector suffices to throw into consternation all the Greeks without the least exception, except Achilles and his men, who are absent.

> He speaks and all were silent and held their peace;
> They were ashamed to refuse, frightened to accept.

But from the moment that Ajax advances, fear changes sides:

> The Trojans felt a shiver of terror through their limbs,
> Even Hector's heart bounded in his breast,
> But he no longer had licence to tremble or
>   seek refuge.

Two days later, it is Ajax's turn to feel terror:

> Zeus, the father, from above causes fear to mount
>   in Ajax;
> He stands, distraught, putting his seven-skinned
>   shield behind him,
> Trembling before the crowd like a beast at bay.

It happens once, even to Achilles: he trembles and groans with fright, not, it is true, before a man but before a great river. Himself excepted, absolutely all are at some moment shown vanquished. Valour contributes less in determining victory than blind destiny, which is represented by the golden scales of Zeus:

> At this moment Zeus the father makes use of his
>   golden scales.
> Placing therein the two fates of death that reaps all,
> One for the Trojans, breakers of horses, one for the
>   bronze-clad Greeks.
> He seized the scales in the middle; it was the fatal day of the
>   Greeks that sank.

Because it is blind, destiny establishes a sort of justice, blind also, which punishes men of arms with death by the sword; the *Iliad* formulated the justice of retaliation long before the Gospels, and almost in the same terms:

> Ares is equitable, he kills those who kill.

If all men, by the act of being born, are destined to suffer violence, that is a truth to which the empire of circumstances closes their minds. The strong man is never absolutely strong, nor the weak man absolutely weak, but each one is ignorant of this. They do not believe that they are of the same species. The weak man no more regards himself as like the strong man than he is regarded as such. He who possesses strength moves in an atmosphere which offers him no resistance. Nothing in the human element surrounding him is of a nature to induce, between the intention and the act, that brief interval where thought may lodge. Where there is no room for thought, there is no room either for justice or prudence. This is the reason why men of arms behave with such harshness and folly. Their weapon sinks into an enemy disarmed at their knees; they triumph over a dying man, describing to him the outrages that his body will suffer; Achilles beheads twelve Trojan adolescents on Patroclus' funeral pyre as naturally as we cut flowers for a tomb. They never guess as they exercise their power, that the consequences of their acts will turn back upon themselves. When with a word one can make an old man be silent, obey, tremble, does one reflect upon the importance in the eyes of the gods of the curses of the old man, who is also a priest? Does one abstain from carrying off the woman Achilles loves when one knows she and he cannot do otherwise than obey? While Achilles enjoys the sight of the unhappy Greeks in flight, can he think that this flight, which will last as long and finish when he wills, may cost the life of his friend and even his own life? Thus it is that those to whom destiny lends might, perish for having relied too much upon it.

It is impossible that they should not perish. For they never think of their own strength as a limited quantity, nor of their relations with others as an equilibrium of unequal powers. Other men do not impose upon their acts that moment for pausing from which alone our consideration for our fellows proceeds: they conclude from this that destiny has given all licence to them and none to their inferiors. Henceforth they go beyond the measure of their strength, inevitably so, because they do not know its limit. Thus they are delivered up helpless before chance, and things no longer obey them. Sometimes chance serves them, at other times it hinders, and here they are, exposed, naked before misfortune without that armour of might which protected their souls, without anything any more to separate them from tears.

This retribution, of a geometric strictness, which punishes automatically the abuse of strength, became the principal subject of meditation for the Greeks. It constitutes the soul of the Greek epic; under the name of Nemesis it is the mainspring of Aeschylus' tragedies. The Pythagoreans, Socrates, Plato, take this as the point of departure for their thoughts about man and the universe. The notion has become familiar wherever Hellenism has penetrated. It is perhaps this Greek idea which subsists, under the name of Kharma, in Oriental countries impregnated by Buddhism; but the Occident has lost it and has not even in any one of its languages a word to express it; the ideas of limit, of measure, of equilibrium, which should determine the conduct of life, have no more than a servile usage in its technique. We are only geometricians in regard to matter; the Greeks were first of all geometricians in the apprenticeship of virtue.

The progress of the war in the *Iliad* is no more than this play of the scales. The victor of the moment feels himself invincible, even when only a few hours earlier he had experienced defeat; he forgets to partake of victory as of a thing which must pass. At the end of the first day of combat recounted in the *Iliad,* the victorious Greeks could doubtless have obtained the object of their efforts, that is, Helen and her wealth; at least if one supposes, as Homer does, that the Greek army was right to believe that Helen was in Troy. The Egyptian priests, however, who ought to have known, affirmed later to Herodotus that she was in Egypt. In any case, on that particular evening, the Greeks did not want her.

> "Let us at present accept neither the wealth of Paris
> Nor of Helen; each one sees, even the most ignorant,
> That Troy now stands at the edge of doom."
> He spoke and all among the Achaeans acclaimed.

What they want is no less than all. All the riches of Troy as booty, all the palaces, the temples and the houses as ashes, all the women and all the children as slaves, all the men as corpses. They forget one detail; this is that all is not in their power; for they are not in Troy. Perhaps they may be there tomorrow, perhaps never.

Hector, that very day, succumbs to the same fault of memory:

> For this I know well in my entrails and in my heart;
> That day will come when holy Ilion shall perish
> And Priam of the mighty sword and Priam's nation.
> But I think less of the sorrow prepared for the Trojans,
> Less of Hecuba herself, and of King Priam,
> And my brothers, so many and so brave,
> Who will fall to the dust beneath the enemy's lash,
> Than of you, when one of the Greeks in bronze
> armour
> Shall drag you away weeping, and rob you of your liberty.
> For myself: may I be dead and may the earth cover me
> Before I hear your cries or see you dragged away.

What would he not give at this moment to avoid such horrors which he believes inevitable? All that he can offer must be in vain. Yet only two days later the Greeks fled miserably, and Agamemnon himself wanted to take to the sea again. Hector, who by giving way a little might easily have obtained the enemy's departure, was no longer willing to allow them to leave with empty hands:

> Let us build fires everywhere that their brilliance
> may enflame the sky
> For fear lest into the darkness the long-haired Greeks
> May flee away and throw themselves upon the broad
> back of the seas. . . .
> Let more than one carry a wound to digest even at
> home,

> And thus may all the world be afraid
> To bring to the Trojans, tamers of horses, the
> misery of war.

His desire is carried out, the Greeks remain, and the next day, at noon, they make a pitiable object of Hector and his forces.

> They, fleeing across the plain, were like cattle
> Which a lion coming in the night drives before him. . . .
> Thus the mighty Agamemnon, son of Athens, pursued them,
> Killing without pause the hindmost; thus they fled.

In the course of the afternoon, Hector regains advantage, withdraws again, then puts the Greeks to rout, is set back in his turn by Patroclus' fresh forces. Patroclus, pushing his advantage beyond its strength, ends by finding himself exposed, unarmed, and wounded by Hector's javelin, and that evening the victorious Hector receives with severe reprimand Polydamas' prudent advice:

> "Now that I have received from the crafty son
>   of Kronos
> A glorious victory near the ships, forcing the Greeks into
>   the sea,
> Fool! Never voice such counsel before the
>   people.
> No Trojan will listen to you; as for me, I
>   forbid it."
> Thus spoke Hector, and the Trojans acclaimed him.

The next day Hector is lost. Achilles has pushed him back across the whole plain and will kill him. Of the two, he has always been the stronger in combat; how much more so now after several weeks of rest and spurred on by vengeance to victory against a spent enemy! Here is Hector alone before the walls of Troy, completely alone awaiting death and trying to gather his soul to face it.

> Alas! if I should retreat behind the gate and the
>   rampart
> Polydamas would be first to shame me. . . .
> Now that by my folly I have destroyed my people,
> I fear the Trojans, and the long-robed
>   Trojan women.
> And I fear to hear it said by those less brave
>   than I:
> "Hector, too confident of his strength, has lost
>   our land."
> But what if I put away my arched shield,
> My stout helmet, and leaning my lance against
>   the rampart
> I went forth to meet the illustrious Achilles?
> But why now should my heart give me such counsel?
> I will not approach him; he would have no pity,
> No regard; he would kill me if I were thus naked,
> Like a woman.

Hector escapes none of the grief and ignominy that belong to the ruined. Alone, stripped of all the prestige of might, the courage that upheld him outside the walls cannot preserve him from flight:

> Hector, at the sight of him was seized with
> trembling. He could not resolve
> To remain. . . .
> It is not for a ewe nor for an ox-hide,
> Nor for the ordinary compensations of the hunt that
> they strive.
> It is for a life that they run, that of Hector,
> tamer of horses.

Fatally wounded, he augments the triumph of the victor by his vain entreaties.

> I implore thee by thy life, by thy knees, by thy
> parents.

But those who are familiar with the *Iliad* know the death of Hector was to give but short-lived joy to Achilles and the death of Achilles brief joy to the Trojans, and the annihilation of Troy but brief joy to the Achaians.

For violence so crushes whomever it touches that it appears at last external no less to him who dispenses it than to him who endures it. So the idea was born of a destiny beneath which the aggressors and their victims are equally innocent, the victors and the vanquished brothers in the same misfortune. The vanquished is a cause of misfortune for the victor as much as the victor is for the vanquished.

> An only son is born to him, for a short life; moreover
> He grows old abandoned by me, since far from home
> I linger before Troy, doing harm to you and to your sons.

A moderate use of might, by which alone man may escape being caught in the machinery of its vicious circle, would demand a more than human virtue, one no less rare than a constant dignity in weakness. Further, moderation itself is not always without peril; for the prestige which constitutes three-fourths of might is first of all made up of that superb indifference which the powerful have for the weak, an indifference so contagious that it is communicated even to those who are its object. But ordinarily it is not a political idea which counsels excess. Rather is the temptation to it nearly irresistible, despite all counsels. Reasonable words are now and then pronounced in the *Iliad;* those of Thersites are reasonable in the highest degree. So are Achilles' words when he is angry:

> Nothing is worth life to me, not all the rumoured
> wealth of Ilium, that so prosperous city. . . .
> For one may capture oxen and fat sheep
> But a human life, once lost, is not to be recaptured.

Reasonable words fall into the void. If an inferior pronounced them he is punished and turns silent. If a leader, he does not put them into action. If need be he is always able to find a god to counsel him the opposite of reason.

At last the very idea that one might wish to escape from the occupation bestowed by fate, that to kill and to be killed, disappears from the consciousness.

> . . . we, to whom Zeus
> From our youth to old age, has assigned the struggle
> In painful wars, until we perish even to the last one. . . .

Already these combatants, as so much later Craonne's, felt themselves "wholly condemned."

They are caught in this situation by the simplest of traps. At the outset their hearts are light, as hearts always are when one feels power within one and against one only the void. Their weapons are in their hands; the enemy is absent. Unless one's soul is stricken by the enemy's reputation, one is always stronger than he during his absence. An absent enemy does not impose the yoke of necessity. As yet no necessity appears in the consciousness of those who thus set forth, and this is why they go off as if to a game, as if for a holiday freed from the daily grind.

> Where have our braggings gone, our vaunted bravery,
> Which we shouted so proudly at Lemnos
> While gorging upon the flesh of horned bullocks,
> And drinking from cups overflowing with wine?
> Saying: against an hundred or two hundred Trojans
> Each one would hold combat; and here only one is
> too much for us!

Even when war is experienced, it does not immediately cease to appear as a game. The necessity that belongs to war is terrible, wholly different from that belonging to peaceful works; the soul only submits to the necessity of war when escape from it is impossible; and so long as the soul does escape, it lives irresponsible days, empty of necessity, days of frivolity, of dream, arbitrary and unreal. Danger is then an abstraction, the lives which one takes seem like toys broken by a child, and no more important; heroism is a theatrical pose soiled by artificial braggings. If, added to this, an influx of vitality comes to multiply and inflate the power of action, the man believes that, thanks to divine intervention, he is irresistible, providentially preserved from defeat and from death. War is easy then, and ignobly loved.

But for the majority of soldiers this state of soul does not last. The day comes when fear, defeat or the death of beloved companions crushes the warrior's soul beneath the necessity of war. Then war ceases to be a play or a dream; the warrior understands at last that it really exists. This is a hard reality, infinitely too hard to be borne, for it comprises death. The thought of death cannot be sustained, or only in flashes from the moment when one understands death as a possible eventuality. It is true that every man is destined to die and that a soldier may grow old among his comrades, yet for those whose souls are subservient to the yoke of war, the relationship between death and the future is different than for other men. For those others death is the acknowledged limit pre-imposed upon their future; for these warriors, death itself is their future, the future assigned to them by their profession. That men should have death for their future is a denial of nature. As soon as the practice of war has revealed the fact that each moment holds the possibility of death, the mind becomes incapable of moving from one day to the next without passing through the spectre of death. Then the consciousness is under tension such as it can only endure for short intervals. But each new dawn ushers in the same necessity. Such days added to each other make up years. That soul daily suffers violence which every morning must mutilate its aspirations because the mind cannot move about in a time without passing through death. In this way war wipes out every conception of a goal, even all thoughts concerning the goals of war. The possibility of so violent a situation is inconceivable when one is outside it, its ends are inconceivable when one is involved in it. Therefore no one does anything to bring about its end. The man who is faced by an armed enemy cannot lay down his arms. The mind should be able to contrive an issue; but it has lost all capacity for contriving anything in that direction. It is completely occupied with doing itself violence. Always among men, the intolerable afflictions either of servitude or war endure by force of their own weight, and therefore, from the outside, they seem easy to bear; they last because they rob the resources required to throw them off.

Nevertheless, the soul that is dominated by war cries out for deliverance; but deliverance itself apears in tragic guise, in the form of extreme destruction. A moderate and reasonable end to all its suffering would leave naked, and exposed to consciousness, memories of such violent affliction as it could not endure. The terror, the pain, the exhaustion, the massacres, the deaths of comrades, we cannot believe that these would only cease to ravage the soul if they were drowned in the intoxication of force. The thought that such vast efforts should have brought only a negative or limited profit, hurts too much.

> What? Shall we allow Priam and the Trojans, to glory
> In Argive Helen, she for whom so many Greeks
> Have perished before Troy, far from their native
>   land?
> What? Would you abandon Troy, the city of wide streets,
> For which we have suffered so many afflictions?

What does Helen matter to Ulysses? Or even Troy with all its wealth, since it can never compensate for the ruin of Ithaca? Troy and Helen matter to the Greeks only as the causes of their shedding so much blood and tears; it is in making oneself master that one finds one is the master of horrible memories. The Soul, which is forced by the existence of an enemy, to destroy the part of itself implanted by nature, believes it can only cure itself by the destruction of the enemy, and at the same time the death of beloved companions stimulates the desire to emulate them, to follow their dark example:

> Ah, to die at once, since without my help
> My friends had to die. How far from home
> He perished, and I was not there to defend him.
> Now I depart to find the murderer of one so beloved:
> Hector. I will receive death at whatever moment
> Zeus and all the other gods shall accomplish it.

So it is that the despair which thrusts toward death is the same one that impels toward killing.

> I know well that my fate is to perish here,
> Far from my loved father and mother; but still
> I will not stop till the Trojans have had their
> glut of war.

The man torn by this double need for death belongs, so long as he has not become something different, to another race than the living race. When the vanquished pleads that he may be allowed to see the light of day, what echo may his timid aspiration to life find in a heart driven by such desperation? The mere fact that the victor is armed, the other disarmed, already deprives the life that is threatened of the least vestige of importance. And how should he who has destroyed in himself the very thought that there may be joy in the light, how should he respect such humble and vain pleadings from the vanquished?

> I am at thy knees, Achilles; have pity, have regard
> for me;
> Here as a suppliant, O Son of Zeus, I am worthy of
> respect:
> It was first at your house that I ate the bread of
> Demeter,
> When from my well-tended vineyard you captured me.
> And selling me, you sent me far from my father and
> my own,
> To holy Lemnos; a sacrifice of one hundred oxen were
> paid for me.
> I was redeemed for three hundred more; Dawn breaks
> for me
> Today the twelfth time since I returned to Ilium
> After so many sorrows. Again at the mercy of your
> hands
> A cruel fate has placed me. How Zeus the father
> must hate me
> To have delivered me to you again; for how small
> a part in life
> Did my mother, Laothoe, daughter of the ancient
> Altos, bear me.

See what response this feeble hope gets!

> Come friend, you must die too! Who are you to
> complain?
> Patroclus was worth much more than you, yet he
> is dead.
> And I, handsome and strong as you see me,
> I who am of noble race, my mother was a goddess;
> Even over me hangs death and a dark destiny.
> Whether at dawn, in the evening, or at noon
> My life too shall be taken by force of arms. . . .

Whoever has had to mortify, to mutilate in himself all aspiration to live, of him an effort of heart-breaking generosity is required before he can respect the life of another. We have no reason to suppose any of Homer's warriors capable of such an effort, unless perhaps Patroclus. In a certain way Patroclus occupies the central position in the *Iliad,* where it is said that: "he knew how to be tender toward all," and wherein nothing of a cruel or brutal nature is ever mentioned concerning him. But how many men do we know in several thousand years of history who have given proof of such divine generosity? It is doubtful whether we could name two or three. In default of such generosity the vanquished soldier is the scourge of nature; possessed by war, he, as much as the slave, although in quite a different way, is become a thing, and words have no more power over him than over inert matter. In contact with might, both the soldier and the slave suffer the inevitable effect, which is to become either deaf or mute.

Such is the nature of might. Its power to transform man into a thing is double and it cuts both ways; it petrifies differently but equally the souls of those who suffer it, and of those who wield it. This property of might reaches its highest degree in the midst of combat, at that moment when the tide of battle feels its way toward a decision. The winning of battles is not determined between men who plan and deliberate, who make a resolution and carry it out, but between men drained of these faculties, transformed, fallen to the level either of inert matter, which is all passivity, or to the level of blind forces, which are all momentum. This is the final secret of war. This secret the *Iliad* expresses by its similes, by making warriors apparitions of great natural phenomenon: a conflagration, a flood, the wind, ferocious beasts, any and every blind cause of disaster. Or else by likening them to frightened animals, trees, water, sand, to all that is moved by the violence of external forces. Greeks and Trojans alike, from one day to the next, sometimes from one hour to the next, are made to suffer in turn these contrary transmutations.

> Like cattle which a murderous lion assaults
> While they stand grazing in a vast and marshy meadow
> By thousands . . .; all tremble. So then the Achaians
> In panic were put to rout by Hector and by Zeus the
>   father.
> All of them. . . .
> As when destructive fire runs through the depths
>   of a wood;
> Everywhere whirling, swept by the wind, when the trees
> Uprooted are felled by pressure of the violent fire;
> Even so did Agamemnon son of Athens bring down the heads
> Of the fleeing Trojans.

The art of war is nothing but the art of provoking such transformations. The material, the procedures, even the inflicting of death upon the enemy, are only the means to this end; the veritable object of the art of war is no less than the souls of the combatants. But these transformations are always a mystery, and the gods are the authors of them because it is they who excite men's imaginations. However this comes about, this double ability of turning men to stone is essential to might, and a soul placed in contact with it only escapes by a sort of miracle. Miracles of this sort are rare and brief.

The frivolity, the capriciousness of those who disrespectfully manipulate the men or the things which they have, or believe they have at their mercy, the despair which drives the soldier to destroy, the crushing of the slave and of the vanquished, the massacres, all these contribute to make a picture of utter, uniform horror. Might is the only hero in this picture. The resulting whole would be a dismal monotony were there not, sprinkled here and there, luminous moments, brief and divine moments in the souls of men. In such moments the soul which awakes, only to lose itself again to the empire of might, awakes pure and intact; realizes itself whole. In that soul there is no room for ambiguous, troubled or conflicting emotions; courage and love fill it all. Sometimes a man is able to find his soul in deliberating with himself when he tries, as Hector did before Troy, without the help of gods or of men, all alone to face his destiny. Other moments wherein men find their souls are the moments when they love; almost no type of pure love between men is lacking from the *Iliad*.

The tradition of hospitality, carried through several generations, has ascendancy over the blindness of combat:

> Thus I am for you a beloved guest in the heart of
> Argos. . . .
> Let us avoid one another's lances, even in
> the fray.

The love of a son for his parents, of a father, or of a mother, for the son, is constantly expressed in a manner as moving as it is brief:

> Thetis replied, shedding tears:
> You were born to me for a short life my child,
> as you say. . . .

Likewise fraternal love:

> My three brothers born of our same mother
> So cherished. . . .

Married love, condemned to misfortune, is of a surprising purity. The husband, in evoking the humiliations of slavery which await his beloved wife, omits to mention that one of which only to think would be to forecast memories that would soil their tenderness. Nothing could be more simple than the words spoken by his wife to the husband who goes to his death:

> . . . It were better for me
> If I lose you, to be under the ground, I shall have
> No other refuge, when you have met your fate,
> Nothing but griefs.

No less moving are the words addressed to the dead husband:

> You are dead before your time, my husband; so
> young, and I your widow
> Am left alone in the house; with our child still
> very little,

Whom we bore, you and I, the ill-fated. And I
    doubt
He will ever grow up. . . .
For you did not die in bed stretching
    your hands to me,
Nor spoke one wise word that for always
I might think on, while shedding tears day
    and night.

The most beautiful friendship, that between companions in combat, is the
final theme of the epic.

. . . But Achilles
Wept, dreaming of his much-loved companion;
    and sleep
That overcomes all, would not take him; as he
    turned himself from side to side.

But the triumph, the purest love of all, the supreme grace of all wars, is that
friendship which mounts up to brim the hearts of mortal enemies. This quells
the hunger to avenge the death of a son, of a friend. It spans, by an even greater miracle, the breach that lies between the benefactor and the suppliant, between the victor and the vanquished.

But when the desire to drink and to eat was appeased,
Then Dardanian Priam began to admire Achilles;
How mighty and handsome he was; he had the look
    of a god.
And Dardanian Priam, in turn, was admired by
    Achilles,
Who gazed at his beautiful visage and drank in
    his words.
And when both were assuaged by their contemplation
    of each other. . . .

Such moments of grace are rare in the *Iliad,* but they suffice to make what
violence kills, and shall kill, felt with extremest regret.

And yet such an accumulation of violences would be cold without that accent of incurable bitterness which continually makes itself felt, although often
indicated only by a single word, sometimes only by a play of verse, by a run-
over line. It is this which makes the *Iliad* a unique poem, this bitterness, is-
suing from its tenderness, and which extends, as the light of the sun, equally
over all men. Never does the tone of the poem cease to be impregnated by this
bitterness, nor does it ever descend to the level of a complaint. Justice and love,
for which there can hardly be a place in this picture of extremes and unjust
violence, yet shed their light over the whole without ever being discerned otherwise than by the accent. Nothing precious is despised, whether or not destined to perish. The destitution and misery of all men is shown without dis-
simulation or disdain, no man is held either above or below the common level
of all men, and whatever is destroyed is regretted. The victors and the vanquished are shown equally near to us, in an equal perspective, and seem, by

that token, to be the fellows as well of the poet as of the auditors. If there is a difference it is the affliction of the enemy which is perhaps the more keenly felt.

> Thus he fell there, overcome by a sleep of bronze,
> The ill-fated, far from his wife, while defending
> his people. . . .

What a tone to use in evoking the fate of the adolescent whom Achilles sold at Lemnos!

> Eleven days his heart rejoiced among those he loved
> Returning from Lemnos; on the twelfth once again
> God delivered him into the hands of Achilles,
> who would
> Send him to Hades, although against his will.

And the fate of Euphorbus, he who saw but a single day of war:

> Blood drenches his hair, hair like that of the Graces.

When Hector is mourned:

> . . . the guardian of chaste wives and of little
> children.

These words are enough to conjure up a picture of chastity ruined by violence and of little children taken by force of arms. The fountain at the gates of Troy becomes an object of piercing nostalgia when the condemned Hector passes it running to save his life.

> There were the wide wash basins, quite near,
> Beautiful, all of stone, where splendid vestments,
> Were washed by the wives of Troy and by its most
> beautiful daughters,
> Formerly, during the peace, before the advent of
> the Achaeans.
> It was this way that they ran, fleeing, and the
> other following behind.

The whole *Iliad* is overshadowed by the greatest of griefs that can come among men; the destruction of a city. This affliction could not appear more rending if the poet had been born in Troy. Nor is there a difference in tone in those passages which tell of the Achaeans dying far from home.

The brief evocations of the world of peace are painful just because that life, the life of the living, appears so full and calm:

> As soon as it was dawn and the sun rose,
> From both sides blows were exchanged and men fell.
> But at the very hour when the woodsman goes home to
> prepare his meal
> From the valleys and hills, when his arms are wearied
> From cutting down great trees,
> and a great longing floods his heart,
> And a hunger for sweet food gnaws at his entrails,

> At that hour, by their valour, the Danaans broke
>   the front.

All that has no part in war, all that war destroys or threatens, the *Iliad* envelops in poetry; this it never does for the facts of war. The passage from life to death is veiled by not the least reticence.

> Then his teeth were knocked out; from both sides
> Blood came to his eyes; blood that from his lips
>   and nostrils
> He vomited, open-mouthed; death wrapped him in
>   its black cloud.

The cold brutality of the facts of war is in no way disguised just because neither victors nor vanquished are either admired, despised or hated. Destiny and the gods almost always decide the changing fate of the combatants. Within the limits assigned by fate, the gods have sovereign power to mete out victory and defeat; it is always they who provoke the madness, the treachery, by which, each time, peace is inhibited. War is their particular province and their only motives are caprice and malice. As for the warriors themselves, the similes which make them appear, victors or vanquished, as beasts or things, they cannot make us feel either admiration or disdain, but only sorrow that men could be thus transformed.

The extraordinary equity which inspires the *Iliad* may have had other examples unknown to us; it has had no imitators. One is hardly made to feel that the poet is a Greek and not a Trojan. The tone of the poem seems to carry direct proof of the origin of the most ancient passages; although history may never give us light thereon. If one believes with Thucydides that eighty years after the destruction of Troy the Achaeans in turn were conquered, one may wonder whether these songs, in which iron is so rarely mentioned, may not be the chants of a conquered people of whom perhaps some were exiled. Obliged to live and to die "very far from the homeland" like the Greeks before Troy, having, like the Trojans, lost their cities, they saw their likeness in the victors, who were their fathers, and also in the vanquished, whose sufferings resembled their own. Thus the truth of this war, though still recent, could appear to them as in the perspective of years, unveiled either by the intoxication of pride or of humiliation. They could picture it to themselves at once as the fallen and as the conquerors, and thus understand what never the defeated nor the victorious have ever understood, being blinded by one or the other state. This is only a dream; one can hardly do more than dream about a time so far distant.

By whatever means, this poem is a miraculous object. The bitterness of it is spent upon the only true cause of bitterness: the subordination of the human soul to might, which is, be it finally said, to matter. That subordination is the same for all mortals, although there is a difference according to the soul's degree of virtue, according to the way in which each soul endures it. No one in the *Iliad* is spared, just as no one on earth escapes it. None of those who succumb to it is for that reason despised. Whatever, in the secret soul and in human relations, can escape the empire of might, is loved, but painfully loved because of the danger of destruction that continually hangs over it.

Such is the spirit of the only veritable epic of the western world. The *Odyssey* seems to be no more than an excellent imitation, now of the *Iliad*, then of some oriental poem. The *Aeneid* is an imitation which, for all its brilliance is marred by coldness, pomposity and bad taste. The *chansons de geste* were not able to attain grandeur for want of a sense of equity. In the *Chanson de Roland* the death of an enemy is not felt by the author and the reader in the same way as the death of Roland.

Attic tragedy, at least that of Aeschylus and of Sophocles, is the true continuation of the epic. Over this the idea of justice sheds its light without ever intervening; might appears here in all its rigidity and coldness, always accompanied by its fatal results from which neither he who uses it, nor he who suffers it, can escape. Here the humiliation of a soul that is subject to constraint is neither disguised, nor veiled by a facile piety; neither is it an object of disdain. More than one being, wounded by the degradation of affliction, is here held up to be admired. The Gospels are the last and most marvellous expression of Greek genius, as the *Iliad* is its first expression. The spirit of Greece makes itself felt here not only by the fact of commanding us to seek to the exclusion of every other good "the kingdom of God and his righteousness" but also by its revelation of human misery, and by revealing that misery in the person of a divine being who is at the same time human. The accounts of the Passion show that a divine spirit united to the flesh is altered by affliction, trembles before suffering and death, feels himself, at the moment of deepest agony, separated from men and from God. The sense of human misery gives these accounts of the Passion that accent of simplicity which is the stamp of Greek genius. And it is this same sense which constitutes the great worth of Attic tragedy and of the *Iliad*. Certain expressions in the Gospels have a strangely familiar ring, reminiscent of the epic. The adolescent Trojan, sent against his will to Hades, reminds one of Christ when he told St. Peter: "Another shall gird thee and carry thee where thou wouldst not." This accent is inseparable from the idea which inspired the Gospels; for the understanding of human suffering is dependent upon justice, and love is its condition. Whoever does not know just how far necessity and a fickle fortune hold the human soul under their domination cannot treat as his equals, nor love as himself, those whom chance has separated from him by an abyss. The diversity of the limitations to which men are subject creates the illusion that there are different species among them which cannot communicate with one another. Only he who knows the empire of might and knows how not to respect it is capable of love and justice.

The relations between the human soul and destiny; to what extent each soul may mould its own fate; what part in any and every soul is transformed by a pitiless necessity, by the caprice of variable fortune; what part of the soul, by means of virtue and grace, may remain whole—all these are a subject in which deception is easy and tempting. Pride, humiliation, hate, disdain, indifference, the wish to forget or to ignore—all these contribute toward that temptation. Particularly rare is a true expression of misfortune: in painting it one almost always affects to believe, first, that degradation is the innate vocation of the unfortunate; second, that a soul may suffer affliction without being marked by it, without changing all consciousness in a particular manner which belongs to itself alone. For the most part the Greeks had such strength of soul as preserved them from self-deception. For this they were recompensed by knowing in all things how to attain the highest degree of lucidity, of purity and of simplicity. But the spirit which is transmitted from the *Iliad* to the Gospels, passed on by the philosophers and tragic poets, has hardly gone beyond the limits of Greek civilization. Of that civilization, since the destruction of Greece, only reflections are left.

The Romans and the Hebrews both believed themselves exempt from the common misery of man, the Romans by being chosen by destiny to be the rulers of the world, the Hebrews by the favour of their God, and to the exact extent in which they obeyed Him. The Romans despised foreigners, enemies, the vanquished, their subjects, their slaves; neither have they any epics or tragedies. The Hebrews saw a trace of sin in all affliction and therefore a legitimate motive for despising it. They saw their vanquished as an abomination in God's sight and therefore condemned to expiate their crimes. Thus cruelty was sanctioned and even inevitable. Nor does any text of the Old Testament sound a note comparable to that of the Greek epic, unless perhaps certain parts of the poem of Job. The Romans and Hebrews have been admired, read, imitated in actions and in words, cited every time there was need to justify a crime, throughout twenty centuries of Christianity.

Furthermore, the spirit of the Gospels was not transmitted in all its purity to successive generations of Christians. From the earliest times it was believed to be a sign of grace when the martyrs joyfully endured suffering and death; as if the effects of grace could be realized more fully among men than in the Christ. Those who remember that even the incarnate God Himself could not look on the rigours of destiny without anguish, should understand that men can only appear to elevate themselves above human misery by disguising the rigours of destiny in their own eyes, by the help of illusion, of intoxication, or of fanaticism. Unless protected by an armour of lies, man cannot endure might without suffering a blow in the depth of his soul. Grace can prevent this blow from corrupting the soul, but cannot prevent its wound. For having too long forgotten this the Christian tradition has been able only very rarely to find that simplicity which makes each phrase of the accounts of the Passion so poignant.

Despite the brief intoxication caused, during the Renaissance, by the discovery of Greek letters, the Greek genius has not been revived in the course of twenty centuries. Something of it appears in Villon, Shakespeare, Cervantes, Molière, and once in Racine. In the *École des Femmes,* in *Phèdre,* human misery is revealed in its nakedness in connection with love. That was a strange century in which, contrary to what happened in the epic age, man's misery could only be revealed in love. The effects of might in war and in politics had always to be enveloped in glory. Doubtless one could add still other names. But nothing of all that the peoples of Europe have produced is worth the first known poem to have appeared among them. Perhaps they will rediscover that epic genius when they learn how to accept the fact that nothing is sheltered from fate, how never to admire might, or hate the enemy, or to despise sufferers. It is doubtful if this will happen soon.

C. M. Bowra

VIRGIL AND THE IDEAL
OF ROME

When Virgil lay on his death-bed at Brundisium in 19 B.C. he called for his manuscript of the *Aeneid* with the intention of destroying it, and his will directed that his executors should publish nothing but what he himself had already edited. But on Augustus' instructions these last wishes were overridden, and the *Aeneid* was given to the world to win an immediate success and a continuous renown without parallel in history. More than any other book it dominated Roman education and literature. It became a "set book" for centuries of schoolboys and was admired by almost every writer from Petronius to St. Augustine. Servius composed his massive commentary on its interpretation, text, grammar and mythology; Donatus expatiated on the moral lessons to be drawn from it; Macrobius devoted his *Saturnalia* to a discussion of its problems. It survived both the rise of Christianity and the fall of Rome. In the Dark Ages it kept a special prestige and was studied successively by Bede, by Alcuin and by Anselm. In the Middle Ages Dante exalted Virgil to the highest place among all poets and saw in him the embodiment of earthly knowledge:

> tu duca, tu segnore e tu maestro, (*Inf. II.* 140)
> [Thou art my guide, my master and my lord.]*

while Chaucer regarded him as the perfect master whom others should honour and follow:

> Glory and honour, Virgil Mantuan,
> Be to thy name! and I shal as I can
> Folow thy lantern as thou gost biforn.

In the Renaissance the *Aeneid* became the great poem which many poets tried forlornly to rival. It kept its pre-eminence and became in turn a school of good manners for the seventeenth century and of noble style for the eighteenth, while doubting spirits of the nineteenth found in it anticipations of their own hesitant misgivings before the problems of life and death. In two thousand

---

"Virgil and the Ideal of Rome." From C. M. Bowra, *From Virgil to Milton* (New York: St. Martin's Press, 1963), p.33–70. Reprinted by permission of St. Martin's Press and Macmillan and Company of London and Canada.

* Bracketed passages consist of translations made or supplied by C. M. Bowra. These and other footnotes have been moved to the body of the essay for this edition.

years of history the *Aeneid* has kept a central place in European literature and survived vast changes both secular and religious. It has shown an unparalleled variety of appeal and has been admired at different times for very different reasons. Whatever faults the dying Virgil found in it, it has succeeded in doing something that no epic has done before or since, and helped many generations of men to formulate their views on the chief problems of existence.

Virgil was not the first to write the epic of Rome. In the third century B.C. Naevius had used the old Saturnian measure for his *Punic War* and in the next century Ennius' *Annals* traced the Roman story from Romulus to his own day. The first of these poems must have had many similarities to oral epic or even to ballad; the second, despite its use of the hexameter and many effective adaptations of the Homeric manner, was built on the annalistic plan which is always liable to appear when poetry annexes history. Virgil knew both works, and his own poem must have been meant to supersede them and to give in a more satisfactory form the truth about Rome as it had been revealed to his own generation. To do this he adopted a remarkable method. He abandoned the annalistic scheme and instead of versifying history presented the Roman character and destiny through a poem about a legendary and largely imaginary past. His concern was less with historical events than with their meaning, less with Rome at this or at that time than as it was from the beginning and for ever, less with individual Romans than with a single, symbolical hero who stands for the qualities and the experience which are typically Roman. By skilful literary devices, such as prophecies spoken by gods or visions seen in Elysium or scenes depicted on works of art, Virgil links up the mythical past with recorded history and his own time. But such excursions are exceptional and take up less than 300 lines in a total of nearly 10,000. The main action of the *Aeneid* takes place some three hundred years before the foundation of Rome; the leading hero and his followers are not Romans nor even Italians but Trojans whose ancestral connection with Italy is dim and remote; much of the action takes place outside Italy, and when it moves there, is confined to a small area around the Tiber; Aeneas himself is a homeless wanderer who asks for no more than a few acres for himself and his company. This remote past is connected with the present by many ingenious ties. The Trojan heroes are the ancestors of famous Roman families and bear names honoured in Roman history; their ceremonies, their habits, their games, forecast what are later to be characteristic of Rome; they touch at places familiar to every Roman; into their story local legends and traditions are woven; the gods who support and sustain them are those whose cults formed the official religion of the Roman people. And more significant than these external connections are the Roman spirit, virtues and outlook which the Trojans display. The difficulties encountered by these first ancestors, their relations to the gods, their emotions and their ideals, their family loyalties, their behaviour in peace and war, their attitude to the divine task laid upon them, are somehow typical and representative of the Romans as they were believed to have always been. Virgil is less concerned with origins than with a permanent reality as it was displayed from the first and is still being displayed in his own time.

Such a plan and such a purpose demanded a new kind of poetry, and when we turn from the *Iliad* to the *Aeneid*, it is clear that the whole outlook is different and that Virgil has a new vision of human nature and of heroic virtue. Homer concentrates on individuals and their destinies. The dooms of Achilles and Hector dominate his design; their characters determine the action. But from the start Virgil shows that his special concern is the destiny not of a man but of a nation, not of Aeneas but of Rome. Though he opens with "Arms and the man" and suggests that his hero is another Achilles or Odysseus, he has, before his first paragraph is finished, shown that he reaches beyond Aeneas to the long history that followed from him:

> genus unde Latinum
> Albanique patres atque altae moenia Romae.
>
> (I. 6–7)
>
> [whence came the Latin race,
> The Alban sires and lofty walls of Rome.]

Soon afterwards, when he has noted the obstacles which the Trojans meet in their wanderings, he again ends a period on a similar note:

> tantae molis erat Romanam condere gentem. (I. 33)
>
> [So vast a task to found the Roman race.]

Then, when Venus complains that her son, Aeneas, is unjustly treated, Jupiter replies not only by promising that all will be well with Aeneas but by giving a prophetic sketch of Roman history to Julius Caesar. The reward which the ancestor of the Roman race is to receive is much more than his own success or glory, more even than his settlement in Italy; it is the assurance of Rome's destiny, of universal and unending dominion:

> his ego nec metas rerum nec tempora pono:
> imperium sine fine dedi. (I. 278–79)
>
> [To them I give no bounds in space or time
> But empire without end.]

At the outset Virgil shows what kind of destiny is the subject of his poem. The wanderings and sufferings and ultimate success of Aeneas and his followers are but a preliminary and a preparation for a much vaster theme. It was with reason that Petronius, like Tennyson, called the poet "Roman Virgil."

The fundamental theme of the *Aeneid* is the destiny of Rome as it was revealed in this mythical dawn of history before Rome itself existed. This destiny is presented in the person of Aeneas who not only struggles and suffers for the Rome that is to be but is already a typical Roman. If his individual fortune is subordinate to the fortune of Rome, his character shows what Romans are. He is Virgil's hero in a new kind of heroic poem, and in him we see how different Virgil's epic vision is from Homer's. Aeneas is Virgil's own creation, conceived with the special purpose of showing what a Roman hero is. Unlike Homer, Virgil owes little in his hero's character to tradition. Whereas Homer had to conform to established notions and make his Achilles "swift of foot," his Agamemnon "king of men" and his Odysseus "of many wiles," Virgil was bound by no such obligations. He could find his characters where he chose and shape them to suit his own purpose. His Aeneas owes something to Homeric precedent in being a great warrior and a devout servant of the gods, but he has taken on a new personality and is the true child of Virgil's brooding meditation and imaginative vision. The persons of the *Aeneid* are created and fashioned for a special purpose. They contribute to the main design, and everything that they say or do may be considered in the light of Rome's destiny. For this reason it is wrong to treat them as if they were dramatic characters like Homer's. They are more, and they are less. They are more, because they stand for something outside themselves, for something typically and essentially Roman; they are types, examples, symbols. And they are less, because any typical character will lack the lineaments and idiosyncrasies, the personal appeal and the intimate claims, of a character who is created for his own sake and for the poet's pleasure in him. Moreover, because Aeneas is typical of Rome, the events through which he passes are equally so. The difficulties which he has to surmount, the burden which the gods have laid on him, the human beings who ensnare or hinder him, the obstacles which he finds in his circumstances or in his followers or in himself, represent what may happen to any Roman. Aeneas behaves as a Roman would in conditions familiar to Roman experience. Therefore though the action takes place in a kind of historical past, it transcends history in a way that the Trojan War does not for Homer. Each action in the *Aeneid* may be interesting for its own sake, but its special claim is that it typifies a class of actions and situations in which great questions are raised and great issues are at stake. That is partly why Virgil tells a story less well than Homer. His task prevents him from really enjoying a tale for its own sake, from concentrating entirely on the excitement of what happens. Beyond the actual events there is always something else, a problem or a principle or a hint that what occurs has some other claim than its immediate interest.

Virgil worked at the *Aeneid* for twelve years, and was at the end profoundly discontented with it. It seems unlikely that what moved him to demand its destruction was its incomplete state. For even the unfinished lines have often a beauty of their own, and the artistry of his language and versification has won him centuries of devoted admiration. It seems more likely that he felt something wrong in his whole conception, as if he had undertaken a task for which after much work he still did not feel properly qualified. Before his death he wrote to Augustus that he had begun the poem, *paene vitio mentis,* almost in a perversion of mind, and this suggests that what discouraged and depressed him was some failure in his main plan. Whether this is so or not, most readers of the *Aeneid* would agree that in deciding to write a heroic epic on his Roman theme Virgil embarked on a task of extraordinary difficulty. On the one hand his epic was to be in some ways a rival to the *Iliad* and the *Odyssey;* it was to present a hero comparable to Achilles and Odysseus; it was to have all the Homeric accoutrements. So much his time demanded of him. The Augustan age felt that anything less than Homeric epic was unworthy of its great achievements. Just as Alexander had lamented that he had no Homer to sing of his conquests, so Augustus seems to have determined that Virgil should be a second Homer. But this new epic was also to be something else. It was to present an ideal of Roman *virtus* quite unlike the Homeric ideal of manhood, and it must somehow make this conform to the old-fashioned epic plan. Such a task was not entirely suited to Virgil's gifts. In his self-depreciatory way he seems to have felt this. Fortunately others saw that his successes quite outweighed his failures, and saved his poem for posterity.

Virgil's first obstacle in writing a heroic poem was his own temperament. He was enormously impressed by Homer and felt that many of his effects should be Homeric. At the same time he recognised the portentous nature of such a task and said that it was as easy to take his club from Hercules as a line from Homer. None the less he persevered and often competed with Homer on his own ground. It is in such passages that Virgil is most open to criticism. He had little of Homer's understanding of the fury and frenzy of war. So far from feeling that war was exciting, he felt that it was odious and horrible. He had to make Aeneas a great warrior and to depict scenes of carnage, but he seems to have postponed them as long as possible, and his first attempt at heroic battle comes in Book X. Then laboriously and conscientiously he tries to recreate in his own sensitive and melodious language what Homer had done so naturally and so brilliantly. Virgil tries his utmost to make his battles interesting. He varies them with contemporary devices of warfare such as cavalry, siege-engines and battering rams. But these are not enough, and over his battles there hangs a sense of effort, as if the poet's heart were not in them. The slayings of men in Homer are not to modern taste, but they have their own vitality and certainly much more poetry than a passage like this from Virgil:

> Caedicus Alcathoum obtruncat, Sacrator Hydaspen
> Partheniumque Rapo et praedurum viribus Orsen,
> Messapus Cloniumque Lycaoniumque Erichaeten.
> (X. 747–49)

> [Caedicus kills Alcathous, Sacrator
> Hydaspes, Rapo kills Parthenius
> And mighty Orses, and Messapus kills
> Clonius and Erichaetes, Lycaon's son.]

The faint ghostly figures behind the resounding names have no part in the story; their fates are without pathos or interest. Such a passage bears no relation to experience and is purely literary. Virgil wrote it because he felt that his poem demanded it, but he did not give life to it or make it really his own.

Even when Virgil is more successful than here, his meditative, literary, highly educated self seems to impose barriers between his Homeric original and his attempt to reproduce it in new circumstances. For instance, when Homer tells of the fatal pursuit of Hector by Achilles and says that the two did not run for a sacrificial ox or a tripod such as are given for prizes in foot-races,

> ἀλλὰ περὶ ψυχῆς θέον Ἕκτορος ἱ ποδάμοιο,
> (*Il.* XXII. 161)

> [But they ran for the life-blood of Hector, the tamer of horses.]

the point is true and magnificently made. It comes straight from the heroic world where the qualities needed for athletic prowess are needed also for war, and all that differs between the two kinds of race is the stake for which each is run. Virgil tries to copy this effect when Aeneas pursues Turnus:

> neque enim levia aut ludicra petuntur
> praemia, sed Turni de vita et sanguine certant.
> (XII. 764–65)

> [No light or worthless prize
> They seek, but fight for Turnus' life and blood.]

The Latin eloquence makes its point clearly enough, but it hardly arouses our pity and horror as Homer's direct approach does. The imagery of the race, so real and so true for Homer, is somehow not so real for Virgil. He did not look on physical and athletic prowess with an expert soldierly eye and he can hardly have enjoyed the excitement of racing as Homer did. Something of freshness and truth has gone from the comparison.

Virgil's inability to rival Homer on his own ground and his distrust of himself in trying to do so were partly due to his circumstances and reflected the temper of his time. The generation to which Augustus appealed so deeply with his promises of peace and order had known too much of war to believe that it was really exciting or enjoyable. No one was more conscious of this than Augustus himself, and he took care that one of his chief claims to power was the restoration of peace. In his own account of his actions he laid great emphasis on it; peace was indissolubly connected with his name in the prayers offered for his protection; the Temple of Janus was closed, as a sign that peace reigned by land and sea. The Augustan world was weary of war and was ready to sacrifice its liberty that it might enjoy peace. Virgil shared this feeling. In his youth he had known the confiscation of his lands by soldiers of the Civil War, and he joined in the chorus of praise for the man who had brought peace to Rome and to the world. His Jupiter prophesies the coming of Augustus who shall make an end of war:

> aspera tum positis mitescent saecula bellis. (I. 291)

> [Then wars shall cease, and the rude age grow mild. (C. J. Billson)]

In this Virgil was at one with most Romans. The sight of embattled legions which Lucretius was able to bear with a philosophic equanimity was too much for Virgil's war-worn generation. Yet into this world, with its longing and admiration for peace, he had to introduce his epic with its inevitable accounts of battle and of the heroic spirit. He could not, even if he had the right gifts, present war as Homer had presented it. He could not even re-echo the tramp of armies and the confident spirit of victory which still sound in the fragments of Ennius. If he was to write an epic which was really significant for his time, he must treat of war in a way that appealed to contemporary experience of it and show what part it played in the Roman conception of life.

In this Virgil was not entirely successful, but he was more successful than is often allowed, and at certain places he created a new poetry, which his contemporaries understood and appreciated, about the tragedy and confusion of war. It is significant that Book II, his most sustained and most finished scene of battle, did not meet with the approval of Napoleon, who said that Virgil was "nothing but the regent of a college, who had never gone outside his doors and did not know what an army was." By the austere standards of a Staff College this is true. Virgil does not write as a general nor even as an old soldier. He sees war from the standpoint of a suffering civilian as a chaos of horror and muddle. This standpoint is perfectly human, and there is much tragic beauty as well as eternal truth in Virgil's Sack of Troy. In war horror and muddle inevitably play a large part, and Virgil added a new realm to poetry when he wrote about them. No ordinary soldier will deny the reality and the realism of this famous narrative, from the simple but cunning device of the Wooden Horse, which brings the invaders inside the beleaguered city, to the final scene where the conquerors collect the booty and place a guard over it, while the prisoners wait in a long row by them. There are aspects of war which mean little to the hero or to the general but are well known to the common man. Of these Virgil is the poet.

Virgil's Sack of Troy gives the poetry of defeat from the point of view of the defeated. Such a theme is familiar to heroic epic, but Virgil works differently. The defeat which he describes is not heroic and glorious as in the *Battle of Maldon* or the *Song of Roland*. In them the defeated almost choose to die when they might escape, and their choice is a sign of their heroic natures, of their belief that death is better than dishonour. Virgil's Troy has no such choice; it is doomed from the beginning, when Laocoön is devoured by Neptune's serpents for doubting the honest intentions of the Wooden Horse, and at the end the predestined character of its fall is marked by the menacing vision of revengeful gods:

> apparent dirae facies inimicaque Troiae
> numina magna deum.   (II. 622–23)

> [The dreadful faces throng, and, hating Troy,
> Great presences of gods.]

All through the events of the capture this inevitable doom is clear. When the ghost of Hector appears to Aeneas in a dream, it makes no appeal for a fight; —all is lost, the fate of Troy is sealed, and the only wise course is to flee. The Greeks fall on Troy like some irresistible natural force, like fire upon corn-fields or a mountain stream upon tilth and woodland. The Trojans are entirely unprepared and peacefully asleep when the attack comes. They are caught unawares, have no leadership and no plan, and are trapped by the enemies in their midst. They fight with the courage of despair, as Aeneas shows when he calls upon his comrades:

> moriamur et in media arma ruamus.
> una salus victis nullam sperare salutem.
>   (II. 353–54)

> [Forward to death in battle's midst!
> One chance the conquered have, to hope for none.]

This is not the authentic spirit of heroism. When the Old Companion in the *Battle of Maldon* calls on his men to fight to the last, he knows what he is doing, and his decisions rise from his belief that in such a desperate resistance manhood really reaches its heights. The Trojans have no such belief. Their disaster is tragic but not heroic. The old conception of a fight to the finish has been replaced by something nearer to life and in its way more painful and more appalling.

Poetry like Virgil's Sack of Troy almost inevitably raises great questions about the nature of heroism and the worth of the old heroic ideal. If war is really like this, Homer can hardly have been right in treating warriors as if they were supermen, Virgil does not shirk any of the questions raised by his story and implicitly criticises the heroic ideal by showing to what baseness it can degenerate. His Trojans are noble enough, but they lack the qualities necessary to victory and cannot be called heroes. His Greeks, whose names and actions come from the Homeric and post-Homeric epics, are not redeemed by nobility or mercy or chivalry. The agent, Sinon, who secures the introduction of the Wooden Horse into Troy, is a master of perjured falsehood who does not shrink from invoking the most holy powers to confirm his lies, or from winning his way by playing on the Trojans' noble compassion and sense of justice for a man whom they think grievously misused. The guilefulness which Homer portrayed so humanly and attractively in Odysseus has become sinister and bestial and alien to decency and truth. Sinon is the corruption of one heroic type, the clever soldier as a later, disillusioned age saw him. Equally unattractive is the type of relentless fighter, as Virgil presents it in Neoptolemus. The son of Achilles inherits his father's proud temper and martial fury, but he is brutal and bloodthirsty. He is compared to a poisonous snake, and with remorseless cruelty he kills the boy Polites in front of his old father, Priam, and then kills Priam himself. The hideous horror of such a death is conveyed in Virgil's words:

> iacet ingens litore truncus,
> avulsumque umeris caput et sine nomine corpus.
> (II. 557–58)

> [The great corpse lies upon the shore,
> A severed head, a trunk without a name.]

The hateful brutality of the Greeks increases the helpless appeal of the Trojans, of Cassandra dragged by the hair from the sanctuary of Pallas, of Hecuba and her daughters clustering like frightened doves about the sacred hearth, of Priam girding on his useless sword and throwing his pathetic, ineffectual spear at Neoptolemus. In such a fight it is the best who perish, like Rhipeus

> iustissimus unus
> qui fuit in Teucris et servantissimus aequi
> (dis aliter visum). (II. 426–28)

> [Of the Trojans he
> Most just and most observant of the right,—
> The gods thought otherwise.]

Such a victory has no glamour and no glory. It is won by treachery and cruelty. To this Homer's Achaeans have degenerated.

The criticism of the heroic type which Virgil gives in his Sack of Troy is not his only approach to it. It shows one side of the question as he saw it, but only one side. It was as clear to him, as to others, that an ideal which had in its time exerted so great an influence on the world, could not be entirely like this, though at times it might degenerate to this. Indeed his task almost forced him to take another, more favourable view of it; for if the Augustan Romans sought to be compared with heroes, the heroic ideal must have some dignity and appeal. Virgil's more friendly feelings about it may be seen in his characterisation of Turnus. The Rutulian prince who defends Latium against Aeneas and his Trojans is one of Virgil's most convincing creations. He has the vitality and nobility of a Homeric hero, and we are forced to admire him and even to sympathise with him. Virgil delineates him with care and love, and in him, much more than in the degenerate Neoptolemus, we learn the poet's feelings about a hero. Turnus is a second Achilles, as the Cumaean Sibyl tells Aeneas:

> alius Latio iam partus Achilles,
> natus et ipse dea, (VI. 89–90)

> [In Latium is a new Achilles born,
> Himself a goddess' son.]

and such his actions prove him to be. Like Achilles, he lives for honour and for renown, especially in war. When he hears that the stranger has landed in Latium and is destined to take his affianced bride from him, his immediate impulse is to fight for his rights and his honour. Feeling that his pride has been insulted, he turns furiously to his weapons. Virgil's similes show the strength and energy of Turnus. When he attacks the Trojan camp, he is like a hungry wolf circling round a sheepfold (IX. 59–64); when he is driven slowly and reluctantly from the battlefield, he is like a lion that refuses to turn and fly (IX. 790–96); he falls on Pallas as a lion falls on a bull (X. 454–56); he is again like a wounded lion when he sees the failing spirit of his companions and refuses to admit defeat (XII. 4–8). These comparisons are based on the *Iliad* and show Turnus in his heroic magnificence as a peer of Achilles and Ajax. Virgil takes pains to make Turnus live up to the old heroic standards and shows how in the best traditions of his type he rallies his troops, attacks the Trojan camp, deals deadly blows to all who come in his way, and fights with heroic courage in his last encounter against hopeless odds. He is a true hero by Homeric standards and finds in battle proper scope for his great gifts.

Turnus is more than a great warrior. He believes, not entirely without reason, that he is fighting for his country. He calls on his countrymen to see the issues at stake, and there is something of Hector in him when he appeals to the Latin Council:

> nunc coniugis esto
> quisque suae tectique memor, nunc magna referte
> facta, patrum laudes. (X. 280–82)

> [Let each remember now
> His wife, his home. Recall your fathers' acts,
> Great deeds that brought them praise.]

Unlike Achilles, he does not exult over his fallen enemies, and though the slaying of Pallas is to cost him his own life in the end, he does not maltreat the body nor gloat in triumph over it, but with a generous gesture gives it back for burial. Nor is his confidence of the kind that collapses with the first signs of failure. He takes heavy blows, the defeat of his troops, the failure of his diplomatic overtures to Diomedes, the half-hearted support of his colleagues and the ill-concealed envy of his rivals, and he still retains a proud trust in his Latin allies (XI, 428 ff.). He is eager to devote his own life in single combat for his country, no matter against how powerful an enemy, and even when his hopes grow dim and death is all but certain, he is still ready to shoulder his burden, though the gods are against him, and he keeps his honour untainted to the last. Since he may not live, he will die like a man and worthily of his race:

> usque adeone mori miserum est ? vos o mihi, Manes,
> este boni quoniam superis aversa voluntas.
> sancta ad vos anima atque istius inscia culpae
> descendam magnorum haud unquam indignus avorum.
> (XII. 646–49)

> [Is death a sorrow? Spirits of the dead,
> Be kind to me, since Heav'n has turned away.
> A soul unstained, unblamed, I shall go down,
> In naught unworthy of my mighty sires.]

In the final fight he is not afraid of his antagonist, but only of the gods; he refuses to abase himself before the triumphant Aeneas and says proudly:

> non me tua fervida terrent
> dicta, ferox; di me terrent et Iuppiter hostis.
> (XII. 894–95)

> [Thy hot words daunt me not,
> Proud man,—Heav'n daunts me and Jove's enmity.]

Though he begs Aeneas to spare his life, it is because he thinks of his old father, and because he cannot believe that Aeneas will pursue hatred and revenge when he has won all that he desires. In Turnus there is much of Achilles, much too of Hector; there is nothing of Sinon or of Neoptolemus. He is the hero who fights for honour and for home. In him the heroic qualities have lost none of their grandeur or their fascination, and we may be sure that Virgil admired him as much as we do.

Virgil does more than admire Turnus; he feels deeply for him, especially in the final fight with Aeneas. Turnus has no hope of victory; for the gods have abandoned him. But he does not give up the struggle. There is a tragic pathos in his frustration when he lifts his last weapon, a huge stone, and throws it, in vain, against his enemy. Nowhere in the *Aeneid* are lines so intimate and so tender as the simile which shows the futility of Turnus' efforts:

> ac velut insomnis, oculos ubi languida pressit
> nocte quies, nequiquam avidos extendere cursus
> velle videmur et in mediis conatibus aegri

succidimus—non lingua valet, non corpore notae
sufficiunt vires nec vox aut verba sequuntur:
sic Turno, quacunque viam virtute petivit,
successum dea dira negat.   (XII. 908–14)

[And as in sleep, when night has sealed the eyes
In drooping rest, in some long race we seem
To strive in vain, and in our striving fail
And fall; our tongue fails, our familiar strength
Is useless, and our words and voice fail too;
So wheresoever Turnus sought a way,
That goddess dread denied success.]

This is something quite outside Homer. Though the bare outlines of the simile come from the *Iliad* where the pursuit of Hector by Achilles is compared to the pursuit of one man by another in a dream:

ὡς δ' ἐν ὀνείρῳ οὐ δύναται φεύγοντα διώκειν,
οὔτ' ἄρ' ὁ τὸν δύναται ὑποφεύγειν οὔθ' ὁ διώκειν·
ὡς ὁ τὸν οὐ δύνατο μάρψαι ποσίν, οὐδ' ὃς ἀλύξαι,
                              (*Il*. XXII. 199–201)

[As in a dream a man cannot catch whom he pursueth,
Neither the one can escape in flight, nor the other pursue him,
So the one could not surpass in the race, nor the other elude him.]

the Homeric simile is much less pathetic, much less concerned with the feelings of the defeated than Virgil's is. Homer sees the struggle from outside while Virgil sees it in all the horror and despair and frustration that it means to Turnus. The climax comes, and Turnus is killed, and with his death the poem ends, not on a note of success or triumph or even of duty done, but almost with a lamentation for the great spirit sent to an untimely doom. In the *Aeneid* it is not of Aeneas but of Turnus that we are made to think at the finish:

ast illi solvuntur frigore membra
vitaque cum gemitu fugit indignata sub umbras.
                          (XII. 951–52)

[His limbs grow faint and cold,
And, wailing, his indignant life takes flight.]

The poem of imperial Rome closes not with a patriotic paean or a hope of high national achievements but with the pathos of a young man's death. We cannot doubt that Virgil meant us to feel that Turnus was a noble and heroic figure and that his death was not a mere incident in the foundation of Rome nor a punishment for resisting the divine plan. He stresses the nobility and the pathos of Turnus, and both must have had some relevance to his general plan.

Turnus is a tragic figure and his death is a tragic event. He dies because he opposes the inevitable and predestined rise of Rome, but that does not mean that we should rejoice in his death or condemn him in all that he does. The

rise of such a power as Rome demands sacrifices of this kind. They are inescapable, but they are not necessarily matter for rejoicing. Virgil treats Turnus
as a tragic hero, as a great man who is highly gifted and in many ways admira-
ble but falls through a single fault. The scheme is more Sophoclean than Homeric. For the fault which ruins Turnus is also the source of his greatness; it is
his heroic pride and sense of his own worth. Such a scheme fits naturally into
the epic pattern and gives depth and significance to the story. Turnus opposes the divine mission of Aeneas because the gods decide that he shall and
Juno, who herself opposes it, uses him as her instrument. But this does not
mean that Turnus is an unwilling victim or puppet in the hands of the gods.
He acts like this because he is the kind of man to set his own pride before
any other consideration. He fails to see how great are the powers that fight
for Aeneas and believes that his own destiny can match them. He is therefore
blind to the portents and deaf to the prophecies which reveal the meaning
of Aeneas' arrival in Italy and affects to believe that the mere arrival of Aeneas
is all that matters and that with it the oracles are fulfilled. For this reason he
is not afraid of them:

> nil me fatalia terrent,
> si qua Phryges prae se iactant, responsa deorum:
> sat fatis Venerique datum, tetigere quod arva
> fertilis Ausoniae Troes.   (IX. 133–36)

> [They daunt me not, these dooms
> And oracles of which the Phrygians boast.
> Enough for Fate and Venus that they touched
> Ausonia's rich fields.]

So confident is he of his own destiny and in his own judgment that he makes
fatal mistakes, first when he gladly and confidently takes up arms against the
Trojans and secondly when there is a good chance of peace but, instead of
taking it, he follows his own wild ambition and decides to renew the battle and
display his own prowess. His love of battle and of glory blinds him to the
wrong that has been committed. The result is that he is forced to fight Aeneas
alone and is killed. His high temper impairs his judgment, and he does
not know where to stop. He is an example of that tragic ὕβρις or pride
which leads a man too far and works his destruction. In the end he dies
because he attempts what is beyond his powers. Virgil conveys this in a significant way. When Turnus kills Pallas, he takes an embossed belt off the body,
and Virgil comments:

> nescia mens hominum fati sortisque futurae
> et servare modum rebus sublata secundis!
>   (X. 501–2)

> [Blind heart of man, blind to its coming doom,
> That keeps no bounds in arrogant success.]

Turnus shows his exultant spirit by taking the belt; at the end, when he
himself lies helpless before Aeneas and begs for his life, there is a chance

that he will be spared until Aeneas, on the point of yielding, sees the belt and is inflamed by the sight to kill him. Turnus is not, strictly speaking, punished for killing Pallas; for that is a legitimate act of war. He is killed because he lives a life of war and inevitably resorts to war when his will is crossed. He represents that heroic world which contains in its ideals the seeds of its own destruction, and in him Virgil shows that he understood the heroic type and even admired it but knew that it was no longer what the world needed.

Turnus is not Virgil's only presentation of a heroic type. With him we may in many ways compare Dido, Virgil's most complete and most successful woman in the *Aeneid*. Just as Turnus obstructs Aeneas in the course of his destiny, so in her own way does Dido. She too is an instrument of Juno; she too evokes our admiration and our sympathy. Dido does not come from Homer and has no roots in heroic story. Virgil has given her a heroic status in his own manner and for his own reasons. She is an example of what a woman can be if her character is like that of a heroic man. In her case too Virgil conceives the story in a tragic spirit and shapes it almost like an Attic tragedy. It opens with a conversation between Dido and her confidante, like that between Phaedra and the Nurse in Euripides' *Hippolytus;* it marches inevitably to a crisis and a catastrophe, but the poetry is put more into speeches than into accounts of action; the injured woman decides to kill herself, but first lays a hideous curse on the man who has, as she believes, wronged her; then the end comes peacefully with a *deus ex machina,* when Iris releases Dido from her dying agony. There are even passages, like the account of Atlas or of Rumour, which are like choral odes and provide lyrical interludes in the grim story. The tone and construction of Book IV come from Greek tragedy, and we are right to respond to Dido's catastrophe as to a tragic disaster. The tears which St. Augustine deplored that he had wasted on her in his misguided youth show that at least his literary judgment was not at fault. Behind this external resemblance to tragedy we can see also a tragic vision and intention, a scheme which relates Dido to other great women whose character is their doom.

Dido, like Turnus, has a tragic fault. She has taken a vow to be faithful to the spirit of her dead husband, Sychaeus, but she breaks it when she unites herself to Aeneas. This is the *culpa* which eventually proves her undoing. But for it she would never have fallen so much in love with him or have felt his desertion so deeply. While Dido still hesitates to yield to her passion, she says:

> si non pertaesum thalami taedaeque fuisset,
> huic uni forsan potui succumbere culpae
> (IV. 18–19)

> [Were I not tired of bridal torch and bower,
> I might perhaps give in to this one fault.]

and later when she has yielded, Virgil repeats the word *culpa* to set his meaning beyond doubt:

> nec iam furtivum Dido meditatur amorem:
> coniugim vocat, hoc praetexit nomine culpam.
> (IV. 171–72)

[Nor longer dreams of secret love, but calls
It wedlock, and with this name decks her fault.]

The fault would seem more grave to a Roman than to us. Not only would he feel a special sanctity in an oath taken to a dead husband, but in theory at least he would hold that a woman ought not to have more than one husband in her lifetime. So when Dido yields to her passion, she is not entirely blameless. On the other hand her punishment is far beyond her deserts. Virgil is explicit about the source of her sorrows, but he does not say that she deserves them all, and the judgment of posterity has been that she suffers unjustly. It is she and not Aeneas who wins our sympathy, she whose sufferings call out Virgil's most splendid poetry. Like Turnus she is built on a heroic scale. She has conducted a great and hazardous enterprise in founding Carthage, and until Aeneas arrives she is a great ruler. For this reason the catastrophe is all the greater when it comes. In her dying hours we forget her initial fault, and we appreciate the justice with which in the Underworld, where she is united again to her dead husband, she turns scornfully away from Aeneas' apologetic attempts to make his peace with her.

The modern world sympathises with Dido against Aeneas, and on the whole the Romans seem to have done the same. Perhaps Ovid is partly responsible for this; for in his *Letter of Dido to Aeneas* he wholeheartedly took her side and set an example which others followed. But even without Ovid's example, it seems likely that the Romans would have supported Dido. St. Augustine shed tears over her in his youth, and in later life noticed Aeneas' hardness of heart in his treatment of her. Once Virgil had presented her as he did there was almost no alternative to accepting her as a much-injured woman. Yet to Virgil's first readers Dido might not have been expected to make so immediate and so powerful an appeal. In reading about her they might well have felt suspicion and distrust. Virgil must have been conscious of this, and his presentation of Dido shows how he was able to make his Roman public rise above national passions to a more impartial outlook. For his Dido must inevitably have called to mind the influence of another foreign queen on Roman history and her fatal hold on a great Roman. The episode of Antony and Cleopatra proved how dangerous the East was to the West, and the general relief over Cleopatra's death may be seen in Horace's almost hysterical outburst of joy over it. That Virgil shared the common view of her is clear from her place on the Shield of Aeneas:

sequiturque, nefas, Aegyptia coniunx.   (VIII. 688).

[And follows, shame on it! th' Egyptian bride.]

The damning word *nefas* leaves no doubt about the wickedness of Antony's relations with Cleopatra. It is against this background of hatred, fear and horror that we must set Virgil's Dido. She is not Cleopatra. Yet the two women have enough in common for Dido to suggest the lures and perils which the Romans knew to have lurked in Egypt. The two queens have certain superficial and accidental resemblances. Each reigns in Africa, and has in youth been driven from her heritage by a brother; each falls in love with a famous Roman, if so Aeneas may be called, and each ends by killing herself. More important are resemblances of character. Each is imperious and self-willed, capable of desperate action and able to promote great enterprises and to rule a people surrounded by enemies; each has the passionate temperament of a woman who is bound by no Roman proprieties and has all the forceful independence of one born to rule. There was in Cleopatra, as in Dido, much to compel respect and admiration. In a Roman world these great figures stand remarkably apart. Virgil must have seen that, when he created Dido, his readers would remember Cleopatra and would, consciously or unconsciously, revive for Dido much of their old feeling for the Egyptian queen and see yet another example of the dangers which the East held for the West. Such doubts would need all Virgil's art to allay them, and yet he seems to have succeeded in doing so.

Dido might be equally suspect for another reason. She was a Carthaginian, a ruler of the people which had been the greatest menace known to Rome and of which little good was said long after the destruction of Carthage. The official and no doubt popular view of Carthage is clear from Livy's judgment on the great Hannibal. In this soldier, whose achievements still stir the imagination, he sees the exemplar of cruelty, unscrupulousness and "more than Punic treachery" (XI. 4, 17). The same spirit breathes in some of Horace's odes, when he dwells on the treachery of Carthage and regards its ruin as a proper punishment for its impiety. Similar feelings had been held by Cicero who made an exception to the honourable enemies of Rome in the "treaty-breaking Carthaginians and cruel Hannibal" (*De Officiis*, I, 38). Virgil knew these suspicions and to some degree shared them; he saw that Dido, as the foundress of Carthage, would invite distrust. He adopts a bold solution. When Dido finds that she has been abandoned by Aeneas, she curses him and his descendants, and her curse forecasts the hideous struggles of the Punic Wars, and the rise of Hannibal:

> exoriare aliquis nostris ex ossibus ultor
> qui face Dardanios ferroque sequare colonos,
> nunc, olim, quocumque dabunt se tempore vires.
>> (IV. 625–27)

> [Let some avenger rise up from my bones
> To chase Troy's wanderers with fire and sword,
> Now, afterwards, whenever strength is ours.]

In her death-hour Dido invokes vengeance on Rome, and for the moment seems to be responsible for the Punic Wars. Yet she does this because Aeneas has deserted her, and so Aeneas is hardly less responsible than she. It is true that this might well cause Roman readers to dislike or condemn Dido as the enemy of their race, yet such is the power of Virgil's poetry that he makes us sympathise even with Dido's curse. He seems to take her side so wholeheartedly that the Romans must almost have been forced to forget their national grievances in their sympathy with her tragic destiny.

Virgil in fact makes Dido's misfortunes awake a compassion and a sympathy which outweigh and even obliterate legitimate considerations of what such a woman might mean to Rome. He uses every means to make her majestic, human and tragic. He dwells on her greatness of character and of heart. When she first appears, she is a great queen and a great woman. She has founded and built Carthage; she has led a large company from Tyre to the waste shores of Africa where she is building a city so splendid that it must have recalled the temples and palaces which Augustus was building in Rome; the welcome which she gives to Aeneas and his Trojans is as warm as it is sincere. She makes no reservations in her offers of hospitality, invites the Trojans to stay in Carthage and promises to make no discrimination against them:

> Tros Tyriusque mihi nullo discrimine agetur. (I. 574)
>
> [Trojans and Tyrians—I shall deem them one. (C. J. Billson)]

She recalls the ancient ties between her own house and that of Aeneas, and shows what the ancient world would have thought a becoming modesty when she says that her own sufferings have taught her to succour the distressed:

> me quoque per multos similis fortuna labores
> iactatam hac demum voluit consistere terra.
> non ignara mali miseris succurrere disco.
>
> (I. 628–30)
>
> [Me, too, like fortune through a world of woe
> Hath tossed, and in this land late rest hath given
> My own wounds teach me to salve others' pain (C. J. Billson)]

Her regal style displays itself in her feasts and her gifts, in her ceremonies for the gods, in her court with its attendants and minstrels and its talks prolonged into the night, in the kindness which she lavishes on the boy Ascanius. More even than Turnus she is a ruler of men who carries out her duties with a fine conscience and a high style. It was not like this that the Romans saw Cleopatra. Dido appeals to deep-seated Roman feelings such as their respect for power and hospitality and generosity. She is a true heroine in her great gifts and her noble instincts.

Even in her relations with Aeneas Dido is presented in an unexpectedly favourable light. She is wrong to break her oath to her first husband, but after this it is not easy to condemn her conduct. She is in love with Aeneas, and Virgil never says that he is in love with her. In her love she believes that their union is a real marriage. Nor is she entirely wrong. The two first consummate their love in a cave into which a storm has driven them, and Virgil describes the circumstances:

> prima et Tellus et pronuba Iuno
> dant signum; fulsere ignes et conscius aether
> conubiis, summoque ulularunt vertice Nymphae.
>
> (IV. 166–68)
>
> [Old Earth and spousal Juno give
> A sign; bickering fires and conscious sky
> Witness the rite, and mountain Nymphs cry hail.]

The events are less simple than they look. What happens is that powers of earth and sky carry out in their own way the ceremony of an ancient marriage. Mother Earth and Juno, goddess of wedlock, give the signal for the rites to begin; the lightning-flashes correspond to the marriage torches; the air is a witness, and the Nymphs raise the nuptial cry. All is in order and correct for a marriage, but it is carried out not by human beings but by natural powers. The conclusion is inevitable that the marriage is in some sense valid. Dido does not wed Aeneas as a Roman woman weds a Roman man, but she weds him with the approval of nature and believes that the marriage is real. In this belief she never falters, and to it she appeals when she begs Aeneas not to leave her:

> per conubia nostra, per inceptos hymenaeos.　(IV. 316)

> [By wedlock that is ours, by rites begun.]

But it is precisely in this that the tragic discord lies. Aeneas, already a typical Roman, does not share her belief. In his answer to her he denies that they were ever married:

> nec coniugis unquam
> praetendi taedas aut haec in foedera veni.
> (IV. 338–39)

> [I never lit
> A bridal torch or entered on this pact.]

He knows that, since his destiny calls him to Italy, no ties with Dido can be binding. Between the two points of view there is an irreconcilable conflict. Dido has committed her whole life to her love for Aeneas, and when he rejects it, there is nothing else for her but death; for life has no meaning for her without it. This conflict rises from a deeper discord. Different in origin and in destiny, she and Aeneas cannot be united in any real or abiding way. Each believes that she or he is right, and each has good reason for it. By giving in to her original fault and indulging her passion for Aeneas, Dido opens the way to her own doom. The consummation in the cave is the beginning of the end:

> ille dies primus leti primusque malorum
> causa fuit.　　　　　　(IV. 169–70)

> [That day the first of woe and first of death
> Was cause.]

Once she believes that Aeneas is hers, she is determined to keep him at all costs and forgets everything else in her love for him. The result is that, when he leaves her, she kills herself.

The parallel between Dido and Turnus is close. Each comes to a tragic end through a relatively small fault, and each wins compassion and sympathy. Just as Turnus' last hours set him beyond all condemning or critical judgments, so we forget that Dido is partly responsible for her own catastrophe and take her side when she invokes the powers of heaven and hell to carry out her curse:

> Sol, qui terrarum flammis opera omnia lustras,
> tuque harum interpres curarum et conscia Iuno,
> nocturnisque Hecate triviis ululata per urbes

et Dirae ultrices et di morientis Elissae. . . .
(IV. 607-10)

[Thou Sun, whose beams survey all works of earth,
And Juno, witness of my agony,
Hecate, at the cross-roads wailed at night,
Avenging Curses, and my gods of death. . . .]

Virgil is more than fair to her. He allows his poetic imagination full rein in his treatment of her and presents her case with great pity and understanding. Yet she too, like Turnus, illustrates the limitations and the dangers of the heroic outlook. Her high spirit makes her act in defiance of her better nature and brings her to her doom. She lives in the last resort for herself, for her own emotions and passions and pride. Once her love for Aeneas dominates her nature and engages her vanity, nothing else matters to her. When she first falls in love, she forgets about Carthage and neglects the great task which she has begun:

pendent opera interrupta minaeque
murorum ingentes aequataque machina caelo.
(IV. 88-89)

[Half-built the works hang, and the great
Menacing walls and cranes that touch the sky.]

So when she knows that Aeneas is leaving her, she thinks only of herself and her injured pride, and turns on him; if he will not stay with her, let him perish in a hideous death and let the world of their descendants be convulsed in war. Her heroic nature, despite all its great qualities, lives for itself. When it is frustrated and injured, it can only turn to destroy others and itself. Virgil seems to have felt that the heroic type, which he understood and in many ways admired, had this fatal fault, that, because it lives for its own glory and satisfaction, it is bound to cause destruction. It is a just comment, and Virgil was entitled to make it. It shows why the old heroic and Homeric outlook was inadequate either to him or to Augustan Rome. His world had enough experience of this reckless self-assertion to know what harm it can cause.

Against these imperfect types Virgil had to set his own reformed and Roman ideal of manhood. His task was indeed difficult. He had to create a man who should on the one hand be comparable to the noblest Homeric heroes in such universally honoured qualities as courage and endurance and on the other hand should present in himself the qualities which the Augustan age admired beyond all others but which had meant nothing to Homer. Virgil's treatment of Dido and Turnus shows that his new hero could not be ruled by the self-assertive spirit and cult of honour which inspired the heroic outlook; he must be based on some other principle more suited to an age of peace and order. But if he was to rival Achilles and Odysseus, he must be a great man and a ruler of men. Virgil had to present a hero who appealed both by his greatness and by his goodness, by his superior gifts and by his Roman *virtus*. On the one hand he must be a fitting member of the heroic age to which legend assigned him, and on the other he must represent in its fullness and variety the new idea of manhood which Augustus advocated and proclaimed as characteristically Roman. The result was Aeneas, a character so compounded of different elements that he has often been derided even by those who love Virgil. Yet to him Virgil gave his deepest meditations and some of his finest poetry. To understand him we must try to recapture some of the ideas and sentiments of the Augustan age.

Aeneas comes from Homer, and in the *Aeneid* he is presented as a great warrior who is almost the equal of Hector. To him Hector appears after death, as to his legitimate successor in the defence of Troy. Andromache associates him with Hector when she asks if the boy Ascanius has the courage and spirit of his father Aeneas and his uncle Hector. Aeneas' fame has spread through the whole world, and Dido knows all about him before she sees him, while in Italy Pallas is amazed that so renowned a man should appear before him on the Tiber. He has the heroic qualities of divine blood, prowess in war, personal beauty and power to command men. But he has something more than this. His essential quality, as his distinguishing epithet of *pius* shows, is his *pietas*, his devotion to the gods and to all their demands. When Ilioneus speaks of him to Dido, he shows the combination of qualities in Aeneas:

> rex erat Aeneas nobis, quo iustior alter
> nec pietate fuit, nec bello major et armis.
> (I. 544–55)
>
> [A king we had, Aeneas: none more just,
> More righteous, more renowned in war and arms.]

Aeneas is not only a great soldier; he is a good man. So, to some degree, Homer had made him when he told of his many sacrifices to Poseidon, but Virgil enlarges the concept of this goodness until it covers much more than the performance of religious rites. Aeneas' *pietas* is shown in his devotion to his country, to his father, to his wife, to his child, to his followers and above all to the many duties and the special task which the gods lay on him. He is *pius* because he does what a good man should. The epithet which Virgil gives him is unlike the epithets which Homer gives to his heroes. For while these denote physical characteristics or qualities useful in war, *pius* indicates a spiritual quality which has nothing to do with war and is specially concerned with the relations between Aeneas and the gods. Thus at the start Virgil's hero is set in a different order of things and claims a different kind of attention. In this unprecedented epithet for an epic hero and in all that it implies is the clue to Virgil's conception of Aeneas.

Aeneas is *pius*, but he is not a perfect and ideal man throughout the poem. The indignation which he has excited in more than one critic for his obvious faults shows not that Virgil's idea of goodness was singularly unlike our own but that he chose to show a good man in the making and the means by which he is made. To understand Aeneas we must understand the scheme by which Virgil presents him, a scheme based on the moral views of the Augustan age but modified by Virgil's own beliefs and admirations. The clue to Aeneas is that he is built on a Stoic plan. St. Augustine hints at this when he touches on Aeneas' treament of Dido and treats it as being typically Stoic because while he sheds tears for her, his purpose is not shaken by her sufferings:

mens immota manet, lacrimae volvuntur inanes.   (IV. 449)

[His mind unmoved, his tears fall down in vain.]

It is not certain that St. Augustine interprets the line correctly, but his main conclusion is right. Aeneas has undeniably something Stoic about him which accounts for the alleged paradoxes and contradictions of his character. There is nothing strange in this. In the moral reforms which Augustus preached and planned a revived Stoicism took a prominent place. It breathes through the patriotic odes of Horace, and it survived through the first two centuries A.D. Originally Stoicism was a creed to meet the horrors of an age in which there was no political or personal security. Against this disorder it set the citadel of a man's soul in which he could live at peace with himself and with the universe and by subduing his emotions be undismayed at whatever might happen. The Augustan Romans took over this creed and gave it a new reference. It suited them because it disapproved of self-assertion and ambition and laid great emphasis on social duties. It was well suited to an age which hoped to recover from the excesses of unfettered individualism. The quiet, self-denying, self-sacrificing citizen who was prepared to do what he was told was a type dear to Augustus. Virgil knew the theory and the doctrine, and though in his youth he had leaned towards Epicurus, he was deeply affected by them.

The Stoics believed that a man is not born good, or as they called it "wise," but becomes so through testing, *exercitatio,* by which his natural qualities are brought into practice and his character is strengthened and developed. If he responds rightly to this process, he will in the end find that wisdom which is the same as goodness. What matters is the result, the final state of a man. It does not matter if he makes mistakes provided that he learns from them and becomes wise. The great exemplars of Stoic virtue were Hercules and the Dioscuri, men who spent their lives in performing hard tasks and were in the end exalted to deity by their success in them. Into such a scheme the career and character of Aeneas may be fitted. In the first five books of the *Aeneid* he is tested; in the later books he has become wise and good and is a complete man. Since the result is good, it does not matter that in the past he should sometimes have failed; what counts is his ultimate character, and this Virgil sets before us after showing his failings. That this was Virgil's intention is shown by his use of Stoic language at certain important points. The process of testing is revealed twice. The first occasion is when Aeneas is in despair over his failure to settle in Crete, the second when he has seen four of his ships burned in Sicily and thinks of giving up his quest altogether. Both occasions find him at his least confident, and on both he is saved by his father, Anchises, first in the flesh and later as a ghost in a dream who addresses him with the words

nate Iliacis exercite fatis   (III. 182; V. 725)

[Son, tested by the fates of Troy.]

The word *exercite* is technical and means "tested" and almost "tested by ordeal." Seneca says that God tests those whom he loves (*Dialogi*, 1, 4). So the gods love Aeneas and test him. Nearly half the *Aeneid* is concerned with this process, and it explains why Aeneas acts as he does. The naturally good man, who is faithful to his gods and to his family, has been chosen for a special task, and to fit himself for it he must pass through ordeals. He makes mistakes in them, but he learns from his mistakes, and in the end he finds his true self.

The faults of Aeneas are an ancient topic of derision. They may perhaps have been stressed in a lost work by Carvilius Pictor called *Aeneomastix* (*The Scourge of Aeneas*), and they received full attention from the Fathers of the Church who felt that one of their chief opponents was this mythical hero held up to the admiration of Roman youth. Many of the charges against Aeneas are frivolous, but there remain three cases when by the highest standards he fails, in the Sack of Troy, in his relations with Dido, and at the burning of his ships in Sicily. On each of these occasions he allows his emotions to get the better of him and make him act unwisely or wrongly. The Stoics held that the emotions must be entirely subordinated to the reason, and Virgil made use of this belief. Aeneas, for all his natural nobility, begins by being emotional in the wrong way and fails to understand what his duty is or what actions he ought to take. The tests to which he is subjected reveal this weakness in him and in due course teach him how to counter it.

In the Sack of Troy Aeneas behaves courageously enough, but his courage is useless. The Stoics would explain this by saying that real courage is not of a physical or animal kind but a moral quality directed by the reason and that it lies largely in knowing what to do in any given circumstances. This Aeneas lacks. He believes the lying tale of Sinon, though experience should have taught him to distrust the Greeks, and helps to bring the Wooden Horse into Troy, an action in which, as he himself says, he and his friends are

> immemores caecique furore. (II. 244)
>
> [Unmindful, blind with rage.]

They are excited and forgetful, not reasonable and foreseeing; they lack that courage which Cicero calls "memory of the past and foresight for the future" (*De Senectute*, 78) and they allow their emotions to subdue their reason. Even in the actual fighting they do not act as rational beings, but fight in a mad, blind fury, without clear purpose or plan. Again Aeneas condemns himself: when he prepares to fight,

> arma amens capio, nec sat rationis in armis, (II. 314)
>
> [Mad, I take arms, but have not plan enough.]

and when he rushes with his companions into the fray,

> furor iraque mentem
> praecipitant.   (II. 316–17)
>
> [Frenzy and anger drive
> My mind headlong.]

Any foresight that he may possess is subdued by passion and fury. The mood in which the Trojans fight shows that they are a doomed people. Their aimless courage is useless against the far-sighted plans of the Greeks, and it is symptomatic that at one point they kill their own comrades in error. In his excitement and anxiety Aeneas still manages to take his father and son from Troy, but on the way he loses his wife, Creusa, and never sees her again in the flesh. On this failure the Christian Fathers dwelt with some satisfaction, but Virgil showed them the way. He makes Aeneas admit that at the time his mind was confused and that is why he lost Creusa:

> hic mihi nescio quod trepido male numen amicum
> confusam eripuit mentem.   (II. 735–36)

> [Then in my fear some unkind spirit stole
> My frenzied wits.]

Aeneas is at this stage still at the mercy of his instincts and emotions; he has not learned to be master of himself or of his circumstances.

In his relations with Dido Aeneas fails again, though not quite in the way that modern critics find so deplorable. What is wrong is not his desertion of her, which is ordered by the gods and necessary for the fulfilment of his task in Italy, but his surrender in the first place to her love and his subsequent neglect of his real duty which lies away from Carthage. Virgil does not show clearly what Aeneas' motives are; they seem at least not to be love for Dido, for whom he shows little more than grateful affection. But of his fault there is no question; it is neglect and forgetfulness of duty. Mercury, sent by Jupiter, makes it quite clear:

> heu, regni rerumque oblite tuarum!   (IV. 267)

> [Forgetful of thy realm and fate!]

This forgetfulness, due perhaps to sloth and love of ease, is a kind of intemperance, a failure in moderation, a state of false pleasure in which a temporary advantage is mistaken for a real good. Aeneas' duty, as Mercury tells him, is owed to his son, and he must do it. This is precisely what he tells Dido, and though her furious reception of his defence makes it look feeble, it is all that he can say, and it is right. Nor would it perhaps have seemed so weak to a Roman. For his duty is concerned with the foundation of Rome, and it cannot be right to set a woman's feelings before that destiny. Aeneas is fond of Dido and feels pity for her, but his conscience is stronger than his emotions and wins in the end. When he leaves her, he acts as a Stoic should, and undoes, so far as he can, the evil which he has committed by allowing himself to forget his task in her company.

In Book V Aeneas is faced with another crisis. During the Funeral Games of his father, the women of his company, stirred up by Juno's agent, begin to burn his ships with the purpose of keeping him in Sicily. Aeneas sees the havoc that they have started and prays to Jupiter to stop it. Jupiter sends rain and the fire is quenched. But even after this display of divine help, Aeneas is full of misgivings:

At pater Aeneas casu concussus acerbo
nunc huc ingentis, nunc illuc pectore curas
mutabat versans, Siculisque resideret arvis
oblitus fatorum, Italasne capesseret oras.
(V. 700–3)

[But prince Aeneas, by that sad mischance
Sore stricken, rolls the burden of his thoughts
This way and that. There should he make his home,
Heedless of fate, or grasp Italian shores? (C. J. Billson)]

It seems almost incredible that Aeneas should at this juncture think of abandoning his quest. Yet he does, and it shows how deeply his emotions still rule
him. The catastrophe of the burned ships has filled him with such despair that
for the moment he ceases to believe in his destiny. Fortunately he is saved
by the old sailor Nautes, who not only gives him sensible advice about leaving
the women in Sicily and sailing with the rest of his company, but sums up the
situation in a way that must have appealed to every Roman conscience:

nate dea, quo fata trahunt retrahuntque sequamur;
quidquid erit, superanda omnis fortuna ferendo est.
(V. 709–10)

[Go, goddess' son, where fate drives—back or on.
Endurance conquers fortune, come what may.]

The fate which Aeneas should follow is the destiny which the gods have given
him, and he should be master enough of himself to know this. Nautes brings
him to his senses, and when this advice is fortified by words from the spirit of
Anchises, Aeneas recovers his confidence and sets sail for Italy. He never again
allows his feelings to obscure his knowledge of his duty.

Once he lands in Italy Aeneas is a new man. He makes no more mistakes,
and always does what is right in the circumstances. He is never again assailed
by doubt or despair; his only hesitations are about the right means to the
known end, and these after due consideration he finds. The change in him is
clear when he visits the Cumaean Sibyl and says to her:

omnia praecepi atque animo mecum ante peregi. (VI. 105)

[I have foreseen and thought all in my soul.]

The word *praecepi* comes from the technical language of Stoicism. The duty of
the wise and brave man is to foresee, *praecipere*, all possible emergencies and
to be ready for them. Cicero uses the word when he says that the duty of
a great nature is to foresee what can happen, whether good or bad (*De Officiis*,
I, 80), and Seneca quotes Virgil's actual words to illustrate his view of a good
man,—"Whatever happens, he says 'I foresaw it' " (*Epistulae Morales*, 76,
33). When Aeneas touches the fated soil of Italy, he has learned his lessons
and found that self-control and wisdom which the Stoics regarded as the mark
of a good man. His earlier adventures and mistakes have not been in vain. For
they have made him surer of himself and more confident of the divine destiny
which leads him.

The Stoic ideas which inform Virgil's conception of Aeneas' ordeal and development persist to some degree in the later books of the *Aeneid,* but with a different purpose. Aeneas is the just and wise prince, and he must not act unjustly, particularly in such important matters as peace and war, about which the Augustan age had been taught by bitter experience to hold strong views. Aeneas is very like an invader, and he lives in a heroic past, but he must not be allowed to make war as Homer's heroes make it, simply to indulge his own desire for glory. For this reason Virgil makes Aeneas face war with a consciousness of grave responsibilities and of nice distinctions between moral issues. Just as Cicero says that the only right reason for declaring war is that "life may be lived in peace without wrong" (*De Officiis,* I, 34), so Virgil is careful to put Aeneas in the right when war is forced upon him by the Latins. Earlier versions of the story said that the Trojans began the attack and were resisted by the Latins; Virgil reverses the situation and makes Aeneas do everything to secure his aims by peaceful negotiations. His envoy makes the most modest demands of King Latinus, and the king is perfectly willing to accede to them. When war is begun by the Latins, Aeneas conducts it in the spirit which Cicero advocates, "that nothing should be sought but peace" (*De Officiis,* I, 83). Even after the aggression of the Latins, Aeneas tells their envoys, who ask for leave to bury the dead, that he is willing to grant much more than that:

> pacem me exanimis et Martis sorte peremptis
> oratis? equidem et vivis concedere vellem.
> (XI. 110–11)

> [Peace for the dead and slain in war you ask.
> I'd grant it gladly to the living too.]

When the truce is broken, his chief thought is to have it restored. He tries to avert a general slaughter and offers to settle the issue by a single combat between himself and Turnus. He cries out to the excited armies:

> o cohibete iras! ictum iam foedus et omnes
> compositae leges, mihi ius concurrerre soli.
> (XII. 314–15)

> [Oh stay your wrath! The pact is made, and all
> The rules are fixt. My right to fight alone!]

In this we hear the spirit of the Augustan age as its master proclaimed it when he said that he himself had never made war "without just and necessary reasons" and that he always pardoned his enemies when the general safety allowed. Such an attitude towards war bears no resemblance to anything heroic or Homeric. War has become an evil which may be undertaken only when there is no alternative, and it must be conducted in a spirit of chivalry and clemency.

Though Aeneas is built largely on a Stoic plan and conforms in some important respects to the Stoic ideal of the wise man, he is not only this. He has other qualities which lie outside the Stoic purview and are even hostile to it. This is not hard to understand. The Stoic ideal, interesting though it is as an attempt to set a man above his troubles and his failings and to provide him with a feeling of security in a disordered society, failed to conquer mankind because it denied the worth of much that the human heart thinks holy and will not willingly forgo. St. Augustine was not alone in feeling that the Stoics were inhuman in their attempt to suppress all emotions, no matter how reputable. Many other men felt that such an exaltation of reason is wrong in so far as it dries up the natural springs of many excellent actions. Though Virgil used Stoic conceptions for the development of Aeneas' character, his warm-hearted, compassionate temperament was not satisfied with an ideal so cold and so remote. If Stoicism provides a scheme by which Aeneas is tested and matured, it does not explain much else in him. Aeneas, with all his faults and contradictions, is essentially a creature of emotions. It is true that at first these are the cause of his failures and may be condemned, but Virgil did not believe that his ideal Roman should lack emotions altogether. His confident Aeneas of the later books is still highly emotional, but his emotions are now in harmony with his appointed purpose and help him in his pursuit of it.

The most important of these divagations from the Stoic norm is the part played by pity in the character of Aeneas. For many readers this is the most Virgilian of all qualities, the most typical and most essential feature of the *Aeneid*. When Aeneas sees the episodes of the Trojan War depicted in stone at Carthage, he utters the famous words which have so often been quoted as the centre of Virgil's outlook and message:

> sunt hic etiam sua praemia laudi;
> sunt lacrimae rerum et mentem mortalia tangunt.
> (I. 461–62)

> [Here praise has its rewards,
> Fortune its tears, and man's fate stirs the heart.]

The words do not mean all that is sometimes claimed for them; they are certainly not a declaration that human life is nothing but tears. But they show that Aeneas on arriving in a strange land feels that here too is not only the glory but the pathos of life. In his mind the two are equally important, and such a view is far removed from Stoic detachment. The same quality comes out when Aeneas sees the ghosts of the unburied dead wandering in the underworld and halts his steps:

> multa putans sortemque animo miseratus iniquam.
> (VI. 332)

> [With thought and pity for their unjust lot.]

He allows his compassion here to assert itself at the expense of a divine ordinance and to criticise the government of the universe. No correct Stoic would dream of doing such a thing, and it shows how strong pity is in Aeneas and what importance Virgil attaches to it. It makes a remarkable appearance when Aeneas is fighting in Italy. When he kills the young Lausus, he is deeply affected:

> at vero ut vultum vidit morientis et ora,
> ora modis Anchisiades pallentia miris,

ingemuit miserans graviter dextramque tetendit,
et mentem patriae subiit pietatis imago. (X. 821–24)

[But when Anchises' son looked on the face
And dying eyes, so marvellously pale,
He groaned aloud with pity, stretched his hand,
And saw the semblance of his filial love.]

Aeneas is not merely sorry for the dying boy; his pity is deeply rooted in his own domestic affections and sanctities. He feels pity for Lausus' father, and he thinks of his own father, Anchises, who might so easily have lost his son in this way. The great patronymic *Anchisiades* helps to convey this sense of a tie between father and son and gives reality and depth to what might otherwise be a stray, unfounded emotion.

Behaviour of this kind is alien to Stoic principles. For the Stoics pity was as wrong as any other emotion and was condemned, in the words of their founder, Zeno, as a sickness of the soul. They believed that it was caused by the mistaken notion that a man's sufferings are really evils and claimed that more could be done by a reasonable act of clemency than by the emotion of pity. With this theory few Romans agreed completely. It is true that Seneca calls pity "the vice of a feeble mind which succumbs at the sight of the sufferings of others" (*De Clementia*, II, 5, I), but more often the Romans tended to accept the Aristotelian view that pity was useful for helping others to endure calamity and that liberality was impossible without it. Yet Aeneas' pity is not even of this utilitarian kind. He cannot help the ghosts of the unburied dead; he does not spare Lausus. His pity is part of his nature and must be valued, as it has been, for its own sake. Virgil follows no doctrine and no theory in giving this quality to his hero and seems rather to obey the dictates of his own sensitive and compassionate soul.

More surprising than Aeneas' outbursts of pity are his outbursts of anger and fury, which continue after he has arrived in Italy and are evidently essential to his mature personality. The Stoics would have disapproved of them without qualification. They defined anger as the desire for revenge and thought it odious because it makes deliberate and considered action impossible. Seneca says that it is the result not of goodness but of weakness, often frivolous or flippant, and that any good it may do in the way of punishment or correction can be better done from a sense of duty. Even Marcus Aurelius, who in many ways resembles Aeneas and seems to embody the ideal Roman in his historical self, condemns anger with majestic austerity. In anger, he says, the soul wrongs itself; it is senseless against wrongdoers because they act unwillingly through ignorance, and it is not a proper function of man. Yet Virgil made anger part of Aeneas' character and a potent force in his warlike doings. It rises at the death of Pallas and takes the form of a violent desire to punish Turnus, though for a time it is exercised at the expense of others like Magus, Tarquitus and Lucagus, who do not share Turnus' responsibility for killing Pallas. In the second part of Book X Aeneas is driven by a wild fury against all his opponents. He takes the four sons of Sulmo to be a human sacrifice at Pallas' pyre, and not all the admiration of Donatus,—"how great Aeneas' virtue is shown to be, how great his devotion in honouring the memory of the dead,"—can make us feel that he is acting humanly or even rationally. When Magus makes a pitiful appeal for mercy, Aeneas refuses with heartless irony and tells him that his death is demanded by the dead Anchises and the boy Iulus. He throws Tarquitus to the fishes and denies him the decencies of burial with the derisive taunt that his mother will not bury him nor lay his limbs in the ancestral tomb. When Lucagus appeals for mercy in the name of a father's love for his son, Aeneas kills him without a qualm. When Turnus lies helpless before him and asks for his life, Aeneas remembers the death of Pallas and kills him

> furiis accensus et ira
> terribilis.   (XII. 946–47)
>
> [With fury flamed, and wrath
> Most fearful.]

When Aeneas acts like this, he is indeed formidable and strangely unlike the man who pities the dying Lausus.

The combination of such qualities in a single hero demands some explanation. It is sometimes said that in it Virgil modelled Aeneas on Achilles and did not reconcile the obvious discords. It is true that these episodes have their parallels in the furious revenge which Achilles exacts for the death of Patroclus. But if so, Virgil has failed to make his hero convincing or consistent. These outbursts of heroic fury ill suit the exponent of Roman virtues with his strong distaste for war. But another explanation is possible. Virgil liked and admired Augustus, and at the same time knew that Augustus' dominion was based on force. In his youth he had risen to power by a series of violent acts, which he justified as the vengeance for the death of Julius. Legends had gathered round this vengeance and portrayed Augustus as moved by violent and angry feelings. They may not be true, but they were circulated and known and had become part of Augustus' myth. After Philippi Augustus was said to have behaved much as Aeneas behaves after the death of Pallas. Aeneas refuses burial to Tarquitus and tells him that the birds and fishes will lick his wounds; when a dying man asked Augustus for burial, he said that the birds would soon settle that question. Aeneas is so angry that no appeal to the names of his father and his son moves him to spare Lucagus; Augustus is said to have made a father play a game with his sons to decide which should live and then looked on while both were killed. Aeneas sacrifices the sons of Sulmo at Pallas' pyre; Augustus was said to have sacrificed three hundred prisoners of war after Perusia on the Ides of March at the altar of Julius. Whether these tales are true or not, Augustus undoubtedly took a fierce revenge for the murder of his adopted father, and it is possible that Virgil modelled Aeneas' revenge for Pallas on it. He seems to have felt that there are times when it is right even for a compassionate man like Aeneas to lose control of himself and to be carried away by anger. This anger is thought to be good not only in its cause but in its results. It helps Aeneas to secure his destiny and to overcome those who resist it. Normally considerate and compassionate, he is slow to anger, but some things so shock him that they awake it, and, when it comes, it is terrible. At the back of his mind Virgil seems to have had a conception of a great man whose natural instincts are all for reason and agreement, but who, when he finds that these are useless, shows how powerful his passions can be. Aeneas, who has to subdue so much of himself, has also at times to subdue his gentler feelings and to allow full liberty to more primitive elements which are normally alien to him.

Virgil has put so much into Aeneas that he has hardly made him a living man. But though he lacks human solidity, he is important as an ideal and a symbol. So far from acting for his own pleasure or glory, he does what the gods demand of him. In the performance of this duty he finds little happiness. He would rather at times give up his task, and he envies the Trojans who have settled in Sicily and have no such labours as his. His stay in Carthage shows how easily his natural instincts can conquer his sense of duty, and there is a pathetic sincerity in his words to Dido:

> Italiam non sponte sequor. (IV. 361)

> [I seek not Italy by choice. (C. J. Billson)]

He takes no pride in his adventures, no satisfaction in their successful conclusion. His whole life is dictated by the gods. They tell him what to do and make him do it, and he obeys in an uncomplaining but certainly not a joyful spirit of acceptance. He is aptly symbolised by Virgil's picture of him shouldering the great shield on which Vulcan has depicted the deeds of his descendants:

> attollens umero famamque et fata nepotum. (VIII. 731)

> [His shoulder bears his grandsons' fame and fate.]

On Aeneas the whole burden of Rome seems to lie, and it is not surprising that he lacks the instinctive vigour and vitality of Homer's heroes. The new world which Virgil sought to interpret needed men like this, not heroes like Turnus whose individual ambitions lead to destruction.

William Calin

THE QUEST FOR THE ABSOLUTE: *AMI ET AMILE*

A dominant trait in the *chanson de geste* is a theme which, for want of a better term, we shall call the point of feudal law. *Girard de Roussillon* is concerned with whether, in spite of having been technically released from a feudal relationship to the emperor, Girard still owes him fealty. *Raoul de Cambrai* revolves around the hero's right (or lack of it) to hold King Louis to his word and seize the Vermandois, against the rights of the late Count Herbert's heirs, and whether Raoul's vassal Bernier has the right to break his bond to Raoul in retaliation for having been mistreated. Even the *Song of Roland* takes up a judicial problem: Ganelon's claim that he had the right to defy and destroy Roland in perfect legality, Roland being in Ganelon's eyes merely another particular in the feudal world. *La Chanson d'Ami et Amile* deals with such problems too, but treats them in a quite different way.

The first, perhaps most important point of law concerns whether or not Amile is guilty of the charges brought against him. Hardré, we remember, claimed that the young man had dishonored Charlemagne's daughter by having carnal relations with her. From a strictly legal point of view Hardré is in the right. The facts, as he describes them, are narrated to us directly by the poet. Hardré himself overheard their lovemaking. Amile admits he has acted as felon and enemy of God (vs. 915), though admittedly he is more concerned with having broken his pledge to Ami (not to love Belissant) than with the act itself. Later he formally pleads guilty to Ami, regretting that because of his sin their hostages will perish (vss. 983–95). And Belissant echoes this confession in the most categorical fashion:

> "Si m'ait dex, que tout ainsiz fu il,
> Com Hardrez l'a et jure et plevi,
> Que il n'i a d'un tout seul mot menti."[1] (vs. 1436)

The case would appear, in current parlance, to be "open and shut." But it is not. The very same Belissant urges her lover to challenge Hardré if he ac-

"The Quest for the Absolute: *Ami et Amile*." From William Calin, *The Epic Quest: Studies in Four Old French Chansons de Geste* (Baltimore: The Johns Hopkins Press, 1966), p.83–99. Reprinted by permission of the publisher.

cuses them. For, she says, Amile must surely win, given the fact that Hardré is a felon and traitor (vss. 719–22). Nor is this the only such designation of Hardré. Elsewhere in the same passage and later at the trial scene, as throughout the poem, he is referred to as *fel, losengiers, traitres, renoiez, lerre, gloz,* and *cuivers.* Once, at the time of his accusation, the *trouvère* even calls him *parjure* (vs. 734). Thus, we are led to believe, a man telling the truth is a liar and vice versa!

That the poet does not condemn Amile is confirmed when his side wins the judicial combat. Although the accused finds a substitute (Ami) who is exonerated in his place, this subterfuge in no way affects the problem of Amile's personal guilt or innocence. The fact is, Amile is in no way punished anywhere in the course of the poem. He emerges unscathed from the ordeal, marries Belissant, does not suffer from leprosy, whereas Hardré, his accuser, is mutilated on the first day and perishes on the second. In the early Middle Ages, trial by battle was considered a judgment from God; by its very nature, the *judicium Dei* was a Christian Act infallible in determining truth and justice. Furthermore, any sin (including Amile's) will be punished by God at once. Medieval man had great difficulty in conceiving wickedness triumphant or virtues defeated over a long period of time. Crime contains within itself, and brings about almost immediately, its own retribution. This is the principle of immanent justice.[2] God is personally responsible for the trial's proper functioning. He, who alone knows its outcome, cannot be tricked. If, in certain fabliaux, celestial beings are treated with levity, such is most definitely not the case in *Ami et Amile.* When the author says that God helped Ami (vs. 1512), he is telling us that in God's eyes, his own, and the public's, Amile and Ami are in the right and Hardré in the wrong.

How can this be when, as we have shown, Amile is so obviously guilty? First of all, a good lawyer could cite "mitigating circumstances." Technically the youth has committed an act of lust, compounded by treason to his lord and king. We know, however, that Amile did not pay court to the maiden or seek her favors in any way. She seduced him, preying upon a young man still heavy with sleep. His participation in *luxuria* must be considered passive rather than active. Moreover, having been totally unaware of her identity, he can be absolved of responsibility (*in voluntate*) for dishonoring the king. Of this, by far the more important crime, Amile is for all intents and purposes innocent.

Secondly, Hardré by no means acts from altruistic motives. Twice he threatens to confound Amile as an individual (vss. 738–40, 758–64). He is using a point of law, a question of the king's honor, to further a personal vendetta. His own violence and anger, lack of charity in all senses of the word, draw attention away from the strictly legal issues involved. If Hardré himself goes beyond the law, then we too must judge the case from other than a legal point of view.

Amile is technically guilty of *luxuria.* However, in medieval as well as in modern society, committing the physical act of love, especially with a girl he is quite willing to marry, does not bring down upon a young man the wrath of public opinion. Moralists will denounce, but the literary public forgive, most actions taken in the name of love. Hardré, on the other hand, is a spy and informer. He has committed no crime as such, but is condemned as a scoundrel by the public for acts which, though in a sense useful for the preservation of society, society nevertheless considers loathsome. Contemporary slang terms for Hardré's "type"—*squealer* and *stool pigeon* in English, *mouchard* and *donneuse* in French—indicate that society's attitude has not changed appreciably in this regard. Furthermore, Hardré is a peculiarly despicable stool pigeon. He has informed against Belissant, a lady; thus he has acted unchivalrously toward ladies in general. Ami, on the contrary, claims specifically to be defending *his lady* against felonious accusations (vss. 1378–80). Whereas Ami behaves like Erec, Gawain, and Lancelot, Hardré resembles the lowest of beings in the courtly world, the *losengiers*. A courtly influence is manifest here. *Luxuria* becomes transformed and purified, may reach the level of, or lead to, *caritas*, whereas Hardré's *superbia* and *invidia* are socially and morally despicable, to be condemned at every turn.

Amile is the hero. In certain kinds of literature the hero can do no wrong. He is always right; those who oppose him are in error. The Tristan romances tell of a protagonist and his beloved who commit adultery, perjury, murder, and any number of lesser crimes. Their situation is analogous to that of Ami-Amile and Belissant in the epic. Yet Béroul cannot praise Tristan and Iseut too highly, while their enemies, even though they tell the truth and defend King Mark's honor, are excoriated in no uncertain terms. Although in both stories the heroes commit acts repugnant to society's commonly accepted standards, the very notion of ethics is transformed. Rather than that the hero be considered good because he conforms to given standards, his actions are proved good simply because it is he who commits them. In other words, right and wrong are determined not with reference to a moral code but by the hero himself, who embodies the secret desires and aspirations of society.

The poem's second moral problem resembles the first. It may be stated as follows: given the principle of immanent justice discussed above, why is Ami stricken with leprosy? Several answers have been proposed, by the various medieval poets themselves and by modern scholars. Unfortunately, Radulfus Tortarius, recounting the oldest and, in the opinion of some scholars, most primitive version of the tale, suggests no reason at all for Ami's malady: "Pluribus exactis post haec feliciter annis, / Leprae fis fedis eger, Amice, notis" (vss. 291–92).

Thus we must turn to more recent versions for an answer. One solution especially appealing to the modern reader is that God punishes the young man for having tampered with justice. Although he has perhaps conformed to the letter of the law, by taking his friend's place Ami has flaunted its spirit. Hardré was wicked and therefore had to be destroyed; Ami also sinned and was punished by leprosy. This interpretation is defended in the Middle English *Amis and Amiloun* (unfortunately a relatively late version) and may be supported by a passage in the Latin *Vita* where Amicus says to himself before the combat: "Heu michi, qui mortem huius comitis tam fraudulenter cupio! Scio enim, quod si illum interfecero, reus ero ante supernum judicem, si veru meam vitam tulerit, de me semper oprobrium narrabitur perpetuum."

But has the young man actually committed a misdeed? In medieval France, as in any society which gives rise to epic, the oath is held sacred; false witness is considered a great crime. Hardré too is a false witness, however, if in a different sense; and, to preserve one's honor and that of one's lord, to avoid shame in society, are equally pressing duties for the hero, equally respected by society. The moral problem is once again more complex than it first appears. To condemn Ami, the poet must exonerate, in some measure at least, his archvillain Hardré. Together with Ami he must condemn Belissant and Amile; he must repudiate many of the virtues society holds most dear. Once again poetry triumphs over law, cuts the legal Gordian knot, as it were. The whole case rests on Amile's guilt or innocence. If Amile is guilty he must be punished, and Ami with him for trying to save a guilty man. But since he is innocent, i.e., beyond the law, Ami must not be criticized for going beyond the law to save him. Once again we invoke the Tristan analogy. Although in Béroul the protagonists are clearly guilty of adultery, the author approves of Tristan's ruse (not so different from Ami's) to deceive the court and free Iseut. Jonin has shown that such legal casuistry did exist in the Middle Ages. Significantly, it was condemned by law and canon jurists but approved of under certain circumstances, such as when employed by martyrs of the Church.[3] No medieval public would dream of condemning their hero Ami for having tricked the court into exonerating their other hero Amile.

The twelfth-century *Vita* provides a second explanation for Ami's leprosy. According to the Latin text, neither punishment nor crime is involved; God is merely testing his servant (as he had done in the case of Job): "Amicum vero cum uxore sua manentem percussit Deus morbo lepre, ita ut de lecto surgere non posset, juxta illud quod scriptum est: Omnium filium, quem Deus recipit, corripit, flagellat, et castigat." This solution is perfectly valid. It rests on the belief that both young men are innocent and that God is just. The Lord, in his infinite wisdom, chooses to injure Ami for the greater glory of both Ami and himself. An objection can be raised against the "clerical hypothesis," however. From a literary point of view the *Vita*'s structure suffers from a lack of continuity between the trial and leprosy episodes. God could just as easily test Ami or Amile anytime and the entire trial scene could be left out. And, of course, the author of the one surviving *chanson de geste* himself seems to have rejected this interpretation, and the first one, in favor of still a third.

La Chanson d'Ami et Amile declares that Ami is indeed punished by God, but for the crime of having accepted Belissant's hand in his own name (everyone thinking him to be Amile) even though he is already married to Lubias. An angel of the Lord admonishes him: Formerly you took a wife, and a very beautiful one too; today you swear to take another. God is angry. Martyrdom of the flesh awaits you for it (vss. 1813–16). This explanation for Ami's leprosy has not been accepted by the majority of scholars. Many feel that if the youth is not to be punished for a really serious crime, false witness, he can hardly be condemned for a verbal, unintentional, and non-existent bigamy.[4] Perhaps the *chanson*, in this one episode, is but a weak *rifacimento* of earlier versions. Perhaps, having rejected the two previous explanations, the poet invented his own, which is still less acceptable to a discriminating public. Perhaps indeed all three versions are more or less feeble efforts to rationalize in contemporary terms a folkloric theme whose original meaning had become lost over the years. We believe, however, that every effort should be made to discover whether the version given by the epic text itself cannot yet be justified. In our opinion it is significant that, according to the text, Ami is fully aware of the nature of his actions and the consequences which come from them. Before agreeing to marry Belissant he condemns the forthcoming bigamy in his own heart and asks for counsel from on high, at the same time deciding to plunge ahead come what may (vss. 1768–74). When the angel reveals to Ami his judgment and the penalty of leprosy, the young man still can withdraw. He does not. Instead, persevering in what he believes to be the right, he accepts condemnation in advance:

> "Je n'en puis mais, bonne chose, va t'en.
> La moie char, quant tu weuls, si la prent
> Et si en fai del tout a ton conmant."[5] (vs. 1821)

Thus Ami is warned by his conscience and by a superior being but twice chooses to sacrifice himself for his friend. During the trial Ami had saved Amile's life and reputation. Though he risked his own life (and his wife's chastity), he did not renounce anything, nor was he harmed in any way. But the duel fulfills only half of Ami's mission. If he leaves court directly after the victory, once again Amile will be dishonored—for having left without the king's permission, for having rejected his advice, for having refused his daughter. By remaining, Ami will not only have saved his friend's life but also have united him with the girl he loves. He commits a sin, yes, but in a good cause; he is punished for it, but the punishment serves to consecrate his mission— as friend and martyr. In the public's eyes, of course, he has not sinned at all. The second act of heroism is greater than the first because it implies greater sacrifice, hence greater devotion. Ami's actions are depicted in terms of a progression leading to a climax. If the *trouvère* gave a new interpretation to an old theme, he did so with skill and with a definite artistic and doctrinal purpose.

The same purpose justifies his resolution of the third point of law. This problem, less developed than the other two, concerns whether or not Amile should be condemned for having murdered his sons in order to cure his friend's illness. Amile avows that if he commits the act no one would blame the people for executing him (vss. 2922–23). Later he places himself in the people's hands, expecting, even asking for the death penalty (vss. 3166–67). A double murder and infanticide were considered, then as now, the foulest of crimes. Nonetheless, one of the two victims and Belissant sanction the act; Amile's eldest son speaks so before the murder, the mother afterwards. And the children's resurrection, a miracle from heaven, clearly indicates that God approves of what Amile has done. He too commits an act of sacrifice for his friend. He too is fully conscious of the nature and consequence of his act. Amile's sacrifice is greater than Ami's, because the Lord of Rivière is willing to give up his life whereas the other had only to undergo sickness, poverty, and banishment. The progression in sacrifice is crowned by a climax worthy of the author's subtle preparations: God's double miracle, saving Ami and Amile's children, justifying both acts of sacrifice and restoring both heroes to health, happiness, and public acclaim.

In all three judicial problems the hero is judged, in the eyes of poet and public alike, to be innocent. Ami and Amile are ever in the right, given their *personae* and the literary genre in which they appear. Yet their actions, according to the law, must be condemned. In other words, the poem sets up a tension between heroic idealism and everyday life. Or we may think of the tension as between the letter and spirit of the law, between petrified custom and the living moral code of the people, both contained within the feudal world. In any case we must not consider the ethical situations propounded, or solutions given, to be somehow peculiar to medieval man. A stark contrast between medieval and modern attitudes, in this respect, cannot be maintained. In both societies tensions such as we have been describing exist. In both worlds literature differs from ethics and jurisprudence. A writer will impose "poetic justice" or "poetic injustice" as he chooses. Even though the poet proposes a solution diametrically opposed to the moralist's, his attitude is no less *true*, no less in touch with the deepest springs of human nature. The discussion of juridical problems, crucial to so many *chansons de geste*, in *Ami et Amile* is seen to be hollow. The poet cuts through them to propose a totally different attitude toward life.

From a literary point of view, the point of feudal law exists as a structural and psychological increment. It serves to create dramatic confrontations which will crystallize the narrative and reveal the heroes' fundamental character traits. We must not think of *La Chanson d'Ami*, however, as a "psychological epic." Although the villains, Hardré and Lubias, are endowed with a relatively complex psychology, the heroes are not. Ami and Amile appear no less lifelike or dramatic than their enemies, but they do not present the same complexity of motivation or natural, human reaction to empirical reality. Like Aymeri de Narbonne, they are presented in stylized fashion, as exemplary figures typifying virtues that medieval society considered important. They appear as models to be imitated by all men.

We do not refer specifically to beauty of person, seemingly eternal youth, largess, bravery, or skill in arms. These traits, by no means insignificant, are to be found in heroic poetry generally. More distinctive is a manifestation of goodness, the protagonists' ingrained sense of gentility, kindness, and princely abnegation. We shall not repeat the list of generous thoughts and actions each displays on the other's behalf. Although more than sufficient to prove our point, such actions could be ascribed to friendship, the sentiment uniting Roland and Oliver, Girard and Fouques, and Ogier and Benoît in other works.

No, the companions' goodness is most clearly apparent in their dealings with other people. Ami requests Girard not to accompany him into exile but to remain and inherit the city of Blaye. Two serfs do join their fortunes to his; when the funds necessary to support them have run out, he urges them to return home. He objects strongly to Aymon's being sold into slavery. He sheds tears on seeing Amile come to heal him with his sons' blood. The heroes even respond to evil with kindness. Twice they accept Hardré's lies in good faith (vss. 279–82, 329), although grounds for suspicion are available. Having returned from the Burgundian ambush, Amile defends Hardré against the king's censure (vss. 461–63), on his own initiative, before the villain offers him Lubias. Later the woman's husband makes every effort to reason with her, begging her to prevent him from being starved to death (vss. 2335–45). Harmed by her and by his brothers, Ami forgives them all (vss. 3457–58, 2569–71). In the latter instance his words echo those of the Savior: "Laissiez les fols, certez ne sevent mieuz. / Dammeldex lor pardoingne."[6] With the exception of Hardré, a devil figure and sacrificial victim, neither Ami nor Amile is said to kill any man in the course of the poem. They fight in wars, they take prisoners, but we do not find them shedding blood. This, in a *chanson de geste*, is a rare, almost unique occurrence. It is a clear sign that the comrades are marked for an unusual destiny.

The protagonists embody devotion to each other and all people, temperance, integrity in worldly acts, courage in face of adversity, and humility before God. At one time or another in the poem they demonstrate the four cardinal and three theological virtues. They represent a quality of Christian perfection toward which all men should strive. Of course, the hero as a magnanimous man, an object for emulation, is not rare in the *chanson de geste*. A case can be made for the exemplariness of Roland's behavior throughout the poem bearing his name.[7] The thesis can be applied with great cogency to Vivien (in the *Chanson de Guillaume*) and the elder Girard de Roussillon, both of whom conduct themselves as true knights in the world but die martyrs of the faith. Veritable Christ figures, they are immolated for the betterment of society. Ami and Amile both stand as *vasa electionis*, chosen for great deeds, to exemplify forces and commandments. Now we understand why the author has avoided the issue of intracultural tensions, why his characters exist not to project individual behavior but as *personae*, fulfilling a specific dramatic and didactic role. In this epic, doctrine is more important than story.

La Chanson d'Ami is a poem with a message. It contains a doctrinal core of great importance, one which is not, as some scholars would maintain, limited to the exaltation of friendship. Friendship is not the legend's only possible theme, nor should the poem's clerical aspects be thought of as less important or authentic than the romantic ones. The *trouvère* establishes a clerical atmosphere in the first ten lines:

> Or entendez, seignor gentil baron,
> Que deus de gloire voz face vrai pardon. . . . (vs. 1)

> Ce n'est pas fable que dire voz volons,
> Ansoiz est voirs autressi com sermon;
> Car plusors gens a tesmoing en traionz,
> Clers et prevoires, gens de religion.
> Li pelerin qui a Saint Jaque vont
> Le sevent bien, se ce est voirs ou non.[8] (vs. 5)

Ecclesiastics play an important role in the story. The protagonists' godfather is the pope of Rome; he gives them rich presents and later befriends Ami when he is suffering from leprosy. The Bishop of Blaye, as long as he can, opposes

Lubias' will and refuses to annul her marriage. Amile and Ami are willing to swear on relics before participating in a *judicium Dei*. Both of them, plus Belissant and the queen, pray to God on innumerable occasions, for each other's safety, victory over Hardré, quick reunion. On other occasions they invoke the Lord or thank him for benefits received. The pilgrimage theme is also of prime importance; we will discuss this aspect of the poem later.

Such manifestations of a Christian *Weltanschauung* are not uncommon in *chansons de geste*, though they appear with greater frequency in this epic than is usually the case. The sacramental nature of *Ami et Amile* is made manifest with greatest clarity by the role of miracles in the plot. A total of seven crucial events can be directly ascribed to the hand of God. The heroes' coming into the world is heralded by *sainte annuncion* (vs. 13). They grow up identical in appearance, as if they were twins. In conformity with God's will Ami defeats Hardré instantaneously on the second day of battle. Ami is afflicted with leprosy, either as punishment, a test, or part of his sacrifice. His leprosy is then cured by the blood of Amile's sons, who in turn are brought back to life. And to celebrate the miracle, church bells ring of their own volition. Three times an angel appears to the eyes of men: to announce the protagonists' births, to condemn Ami, to save Ami. These three celestial manifestations outline the poem's structure. They distinguish the heroes' promise of happiness, their sorrow through renunciation, their triumph and attainment of a new, supreme happiness.

Any work of literature so permeated with *merveilleux chrétien* and other aspects of the religious was probably written as a Christian poem and should be so interpreted. We do not wish to minimize in any way the theme of friendship in this *chanson*. Ami and Amile love each other deeply. But they love other people too: their wives, their children, their servants, their lord the king. They love and honor certain abstract concepts and devote their lives to them: public service, law and order, the defense of ladies in distress, secular justice, God's will. Although none of these loves is wrong in itself, love cannot exist in a vacuum. In confrontation with reality it must act; in confrontation with the evil of a Hardré or Lubias it must struggle to survive. It is the dialectic of goodness in relation to evil and to reality that the *Ami* poet seeks to exploit.

For Ami and Amile the answer to their problem is one of abnegation. We have shown how two of the poem's three points of feudal law are decided by means of an extrafeudal, extralegal justification of sacrifice. In fact, the theme of renunciation is interwoven with the heroes' destiny from the beginning. They waste seven years before finding each other. After Amile gives Lubias to his friend, Ami devotes seven more years, away from hearth and home, to stay with Amile at court. Ami again leaves wife and child to risk his life fighting for Amile. He accepts sickness, poverty, and banishment. Amile then sacrifices his children and risks his life to cure Ami. They both renounce family and heritage in favor of a pilgrimage to Jerusalem and die on the return voyage. Each sacrifice parallels the one that has gone before and anticipates the one to come. Seemingly easy at first, the sacrifices become more and more difficult, building up to a magnificent climax.

Great love by necessity implies, even demands, great sacrifice. How else can love be proved genuine except by demonstrating that it goes before all other considerations? Renunciation was central to the love ethos of the troubadours and *trouvères*. Some went to the extreme of rejoicing that their love would never be consummated; only thus could the poet prove himself worthy of his lady. Only thus can the two heroes in our poem exemplify to the utmost the manly love of friendship. Furthermore, reality prevents the companions from satisfying all their loves. Because of the traitors' machinations, they cannot possibly maintain home, family, friendship, and feudal service at the same time. Even if the traitors did not exist, the human condition would forbid such a utopia. The hero cannot succeed in multiple aspirations at the same time. For every idealistic gain he must undergo a corresponding loss: such is man's fate.

Ami and Amile sacrifice all worldly concerns: wife, children, material comfort, service to king, place in the hierarchy. In the end, they sacrifice the entire feudal and material world. This human, feudal world and the loves connected with it must not be considered bad in themselves. They all have a place in the universe. But other, higher values exist—humaneness, forgiveness, charity. These are at least as valid as the calls of feudal society and must enter into conflict with them. The hero is offered a choice, roughly between flesh and the spirit, prowess and charity. He is expected to make a decision, to decide what he shall love most of all. As long as he refuses to make the decision or, rather, ignores that a choice exists and must be made, he is not living up to full potentiality as a man and certainly is not living in a state of grace.

All of Adam's children are subject to original sin. The life the two friends lead in the world is by no means beyond reproach, from a medieval Christian point of view. In the Old French epics Charlemagne's court serves as a focal point for the action. It represents a standard, a norm, for the heroic life. Ami and Amile are formed at court like any other hero of *geste*. The court then perfectly embodies secular life as the poet conceives it. It provides opportunity for glory, responsibility, and happiness, yet can so easily give way to injustice if not outright betrayal. Hardré is in his element. Through flattery and deceit he readily attains most of his ends, while the heroes face blandishments, temptations, an ambush, at every turn. Although Ami and Amile are not said to kill personally, they do participate in war against other Christians. In fact, they fight side by side with Hardré, who brutally hangs the heads of fallen enemies from his saddle. To make matters worse, the companions serve Charles as mercenaries, *soudeiers*. His quarrels are not theirs; theirs are not his. And Amile is mocked for the excessive *soudees* he has purportedly taken from the emperor by having slept with his daughter. Although we know that the young man should not be severely reproached for the Belissant affair, he is to some extent guilty of *luxuria*, as he himself recognizes. His love for her differs little from Ami's attachment to Lubias, who is a far more dangerous creature, *fax Satani*, capable of bringing about unbelievable harm. The riches, the fine meals, the soft bedclothes—these represent aspects of secular life which the Christian must learn to do without. *Vanitas vanitatum*—Ami and Amile at court are not really lacking in *caritas*, but it remains for the most part latent.

They possess great virtues but are, if we may say so, too happy. Neither has suffered; neither is ready for election.

Man must learn to suffer, to merit grace. Without knowledge of what is expected by God, even the best intentioned will stray from the right path. Hence the importance of the "theme of knowing" in this epic. Certain characters learn, grow, become wiser; others do not. Hardré thinks he knows how to confound the two friends. He is able to deceive an unknowing court into believing that he, Hardré, is a hero (the severed heads), that Ami and Amile have perished in battle, that Amile is a traitor deserving to be executed. Neither Hardré nor the court is aware of the real, spiritual nature of the men they are judging nor of the physical substitution in identity. Lubias, in turn, remains oblivious to her husband's inner soul, her ignorance symbolized by a parallel substitution of husbands. Later she thinks he is physically ill whereas in reality it is she, morally a leper, who will eventually be isolated from society. Even the heroes suffer from ignorance. Amile does not recognize the leper begging at his door; an angel must inform Ami of the measures necessary for his cure. But the young men finally do comprehend the realities of existence. Amile will sacrifice everything for his friend; Ami realizes that he can be cured only by God (vss. 2792–94). Having discovered the necessity of sacrifice, the goodness of suffering, they know more at the poem's end than in the beginning. They have achieved lucidity, vision, a kind of anagnorisis.

Since the heroes do not benefit from any single moment of revelation, their growth process is a long, slow one. With them, heroic and Christian virtues exist in a state of tension, not violent opposition, or rather coexist, one leading into, transformed into, the other. Ami and Amile, though human, though guilty of normal, human *cupiditas*, do not flaunt God's will. They voluntarily choose or willingly agree to abandon the old way of life. Knights at Charlemagne's court, they do not participate in any military action after the Burgundian ambush. Ami executes Hardré in almost sacrificial fashion, then leaves the court; Amile had already gone long before the trial. Neither will return. The heroes then devote themselves to their wives and children. Although they love them dearly, leprosy compels Ami to give up his family, and Amile chooses to sacrifice his that Ami might be cured. Immediately thereafter they abandon hearth and home in order to make a pilgrimage. For both protagonists war gives way to love, which in turn gives way to God. Or, in different terms, love of feudal life is transformed into love of family only to become *caritas*, love of God. As in Chrétien's *Perceval*, charity wins out over prowess. Before the end the companions have developed a sense of Christian virtue, have actualized the potential *humilitas, sapientia*, and *caritas* inherent in all men. Their final stage is one of pilgrimage and martyrdom. By renouncing the pleasures of this world (*contemptus mundi*), they demonstrate the highest manifestation of Christian perfection, to the extent of following Christ (*imitatio Dei*) in his Crucifixion. The two friends have sought for the Absolute throughout their lives. God's miracles prove their triumph. By renouncing sovereignty over wives and land, they achieve greater control of self (*ascesio*). By renouncing glory at court, they attain a place among the elect. Instead of the ephemeral renown of secular heroics, they will ever be famous among men for unique deeds of renunciation: ". . . tel renommee, / Que touz jors mais noz sera ramembree / Jusqu'en la fin dou monde" (vss. 3502–4).

Although the epic contains divergent spheres of value, the heroes traverse them to arrive at an absolute—the will of God. This grounding in eternal forces is exemplified in the narrative by a quality of poetic justice. Aymon and Garin, the good serfs, are rewarded with knighthood; the wicked sailors kill each other in a brawl. Girard's loyalty is rewarded (he inherits his father's land), whereas Lubias must undergo the same treatment she gave Ami. Hardré and the friends all die, but the former is tortured, executed, and his corpse vilified as befits that of a traitor,[9] whereas the latter merit a seat in heaven. For all its variety the world exists as one, *sub specie aeternitatis*. History is enacted according to God's will; all tends toward him.

If God deigns to elect Ami and Amile for salvation, he does so presumably not only for his own pleasure and for their sakes, but as an example. Other people—their sons, Belissant, her mother and brother, the two serfs—react favorably in the friends' presence, are made better because of them. The acts of the heroes as individuals affect the love borne to them by friends, relations, and neighbors; this is perhaps the greatest sign of their election. The companions help to regenerate society, to bring forth a collective response from others. Hence one reason why their names will be remembered by people "Jusqu'en la fin dou monde." This is the message of salvation embodied for men to understand.

NOTES

1. "So help me God, it happened entirely just as Hardré has sworn and pledged; not one word he has said is a lie."

2. Paul Rousset, "La croyance en la justice immanente à l'époque féodale," *Moyen Age* 54:225–48 (1948).

3. Pierre Jonin, *Les personnage féminins dans les romans français de Tristan au XIIe siècle* (Aix-en-Provence, 1958), p.99–105, 369.

4. See Philipp August Becker, *Grundriss der altfranzösischen Literatur* (Heidelberg, 1907), p.99–101, and Angelo Monteverdi's refutation, "Rodolfo Tortario e la sua epistola *Ad Bernardum*," *Studi Romanzi* 19:24–25 (1928).

5. "I can do no more, good creature; go. Take my flesh when you wish and do with it whatever you will."

6. See Luke 23:34, "Pater, dimitte illis; non enim sciunt quid faciunt."

7. Alfred Foulet, "Is Roland Guilty of *desmesure?*" *Romance Philology* 10:145–48 (1956–57). Alberto del Monte, "Apologia di Orlando," *Filologia Romanza* 4:225–34 (1957).

8. Now listen, my noble lords, that the God of Glory grant you his pardon. . . . This is not fiction we wish to tell you; rather it is as true as a sermon, for which we call several people to witness: ecclesiastics, priests, and monks. The pilgrims who go to Santiago de Compostela know well whether it is true or not.

9. On the first day, guilty of treason but having told the truth, Hardré is only mutilated. When, on the second day, he turns to the devil for aid, he is executed at once.

·VII·

CONTINUITY AND TRANSFORMATION

George M. Ridenour

MY POEM'S EPIC

While Byron's reading of the myth of the Fall is one of the most important means of organizing the materials of *Don Juan,* it is not the only one. In the first chapter of this study [*The Style of Don Juan*] I attempted an analysis of the Dedication in terms of the poet's evident awareness of the traditional concepts of genre and stylistic level. The second and third chapters emphasized certain points at which stylistic metaphor fused with the metaphor of the Fall, particularly in the imagery of flight or soaring. It was further suggested that while the poet is conscious of moral danger in flight (it leads to a fall like that of Lucifer), some sort of flight is essential to the poetic vocation (Wordsworth sticks to the ground and is savagely attacked for it). It is with this paradox (and the paradoxical world view of which it is a manifestation) that the poet's version of the myth of the Fall is designed to deal.

Now by "soaring" Byron refers to that heroic tradition of which the epic was the supreme expression. "A heroic poem, truly such, is undoubtedly the greatest work which the soul of man is capable to perform." Dryden had said that at the beginning of the Dedication of his translation of Vergil,[1] and Byron had been brought up in that tradition. So it might be well to consider a bit more seriously than is usual Byron's observations on the epic form and the claims he makes for *Don Juan* as an epic. The question, be it understood, is not whether *Don Juan* is or is not an epic, and in what sense. That is not a very interesting question. Just as it is the metaphoric possibilities of the myth of the Fall that interest us, it is the metaphoric implications of the concept of epic with which we are primarily concerned. As was the case with the myth, Byron's interpretation of this traditional material is highly individual; but for our generation, at least, it is the awareness of tradition which must be emphasized.

Byron is very emphatic, both in prose and verse, as to the epic pretensions of *Don Juan.* To confine ourselves to the poem itself, he contrasts himself with "Most epic poets," who "plunge *'in medias res'* " (I. 6). Or, more simply, he announces "My poem's epic," and submits a highly orthodox prospectus:

> My poem's epic, and is meant to be
> Divided in twelve books; each book containing,
> With Love and War, a heavy gale at sea,
> A list of ships, and captains, and king's reigning,

"My Poem's Epic." From George M. Ridenour, *The Style of* Don Juan (New Haven: Yale University Press, 1960), p.89–123. Reprinted by permission of the publisher.

> New characters; the episodes are three:
> A panoramic view of Hell's in training,
> After the style of Virgil and of Homer,
> So that my name of Epic's no misnomer.
>
> (I. 200)

And then from time to time we have passing references to "this Epic" (XVI. 3), or, with more precision, to "this Epic Satire" (XIV. 99). The question here, I suppose, is whether the epic tradition and the fun Byron has with it have any special bearing on the meaning of *Don Juan,* or whether the humor is incidental.

The passage quoted above is surely largely playful. But there are one or two things that deserve comment. There is, for example, the bland pairing of "Love and War" as things which naturally go together and which appear together in epic (primarily, of course, the *Iliad*). I have made some suggestions in the preceding chapter [*The Style of Don Juan*] as to the implications of Byron's initial turning from the warrior to the lover for the hero of his poem. For when we read "I want a hero" we are clearly intended to hear in the background "I sing of arms and the man." Furthermore, Byron's uncertainty as to his hero is not merely a comment on the nineteenth century's presumed inability to supply an acceptable equivalent to Achilles or Aeneas. The whole concept of the warrior-hero is, as we have seen, vigorously called in question. Again and again Byron associates war with the epic and suggests that the traditional heroic poem compromises itself morally by its apparent glorification of bloodshed. In addition to the parody of Spenser cited above, one thinks particularly of the bitter reference to "conquest and its consequences, which/Make Epic poesy so rare and rich" (VIII. 90), or his comment on the savagery of the Cossacks, that "Achilles' self was not more grim and gory" (VII. 14). Or there is the brilliant stanza of Canto VIII where his invocation of the Muse (particularly common in the course of epic battles) takes the form of a curse:

> Oh, blood and thunder! and oh, blood and wounds!
> These are but vulgar oaths, as you may deem,
> Too gentle reader! and most shocking sounds:—
> And so they are; yet thus is Glory's dream
> Unriddled, and as my true Muse expounds
> At present such things, since they are her theme,
> So be they her inspirers! Call them Mars,
> Bellona, what you will—they mean but wars.
>
> (VIII. 1)

It does not, then, seem reckless to suggest that, in his lesser way and from his essentially secular and predominantly rationalist point of view, Byron is attempting as radical a redefinition of the nature of epic and the epic hero as was Milton in *Paradise Lost*.

There is at least one other striking similarity between the epic poems of Milton and Byron: both deal with a loss of innocence. And in both cases the attitude toward this loss is distinctly equivocal. Byron's tone in *Don Juan* had been set many years before in a poem called "To Romance," which appeared in *Hours of Idleness* in 1807. "To Romance" is not a great lyric by any means, but it is interesting in that it suggests attitudes characteristic of the later Byron. It begins:

> Parent of golden dreams, Romance!
> Auspicious Queen of childish joys,
> Who lead'st along, in airy dance,
> Thy votive train of girls and boys;
> At length, in spells no longer bound,
> I break the fetters of my youth;
> No more I tread thy mystic round,
> But leave thy realms for those of Truth.

The poet's attitude toward Romance seems at first wholly sympathetic. She is "Parent of golden dreams' and "Auspicious Queen of childish joys." The first note of qualification is suggested by the adjective "childish"—which may, to be sure, mean no more than "youthful"—and by the insubstantiality of "airy." The second adjective is especially well chosen, suggesting as it does the charm and the weakness of Romance. Then we learn that the "votive train of girls and boys" takes part in the "airy dance" only because it is under a "spell." The "airy dance" and "mystic round" send the unwitting young people pointlessly around and around in a circle getting nowhere, which action is seen imaginatively as forming a fetter. But the poet claims to have broken out of the charmed circle (or chain) and left the realms of Romance for those of Truth. The whole is quite evidently a variant on the lines of Pope . . . :

> That not in Fancy's Maze he wander'd long,
> But stoop'd to Truth, and moraliz'd his song.
> ("Epistle to Dr. Arbuthnot," ll. 340–41)

There is the same opposition between Fancy (l. 13 in Byron's poem) and Truth. The "Maze" corresponds to the "mystic round" and the "stooping to Truth" (the motion of a falcon toward its lure) with the renunciation of "soaring" on "fancied pinions" ("To Romance," l. 28). One sees here an early form of some of the notions and images we have been tracing both in the Dedication and in *Don Juan* itself.

Now one of the most striking characteristics of the *persona* is that he is no longer the man he once was. This is a source of mingled satisfaction and regret:

> "*Non ego hoc ferrem calidus juventâ*
> *Consule Planco*," Horace said, and so
> Say I; by which quotation there is meant a
> Hint that some six or seven good years ago
> (Long ere I dreamt of dating from the Brenta)
> I was most ready to return a blow,
> And would not brook at all this sort of thing
> In my hot youth—when George the Third was King.
>
> But now at thirty years my hair is grey—
> (I wonder what it will be like at forty?
> I thought of a peruke the other day—)
> My heart is not much greener; and, in short, I

> Have squandered my whole summer while 'twas May,
>   And feel no more the spirit to retort; I
> Have spent my life, both interest and principal,
> And deem not, what I deemed—my soul invincible.
>
> No more—no more—Oh! never more on me
>   The freshness of the heart can fall like dew,
> Which out of all the lovely things we see
>   Extracts emotions beautiful and new,
> Hived in our bosoms like the bag o' the bee.
>   Think'st thou the honey with those objects grew?
> Alas! 'twas not in them, but in thy power
> To double even the sweetness of a flower.
>
> No more—no more—Oh! never more, my heart,
>   Canst thou be my sole world, my universe!
> Once all in all, but now a thing apart,
>   Thou canst not be my blessing or my curse:
> The illusion's gone for ever, and thou art
>   Insensible, I trust, but none the worse,
> And in thy stead I've got a deal of judgment,
> Though Heaven knows how it ever found a lodgment.
>
>   (I. 212–15)

The first two stanzas express a mellow, half-amused consciousness of change and loss. In the last two the tone is that of the romantic *cri*—one of Byron's finest efforts in a mode by no means easy to bring off. The trick rhymes of the first two are dropped in the second, to be picked up again in the final "judgment/lodgment" rhyme, as the tone once more begins to lighten.

The theme of the concluding stanzas is the essential subjectivity of human value. It is Coleridge saying (in "Dejection"):

> O Lady! we receive but what we give,
> And in our life alone does Nature live.

Or Madame de Merteuil: "This charm we think we find in others exists in us, and love alone embellishes so much the beloved person."[2] The theist Coleridge is lamenting a fall from grace (he, unlike the Lady, whose imaginative vision is unimpaired, is no longer "guided from above"), so that the fallen world of "Reality's dark dream" exists for him simply as fallen. It is no longer molded and illuminated by the sacramental power of imagination. While this is not too far from what Byron is suggesting in the "Aurora Borealis" passage . . . , here he is in some ways closer to the eighteenth-century courtesan. The young and inexperienced can idealize the object of their love (as does Danceny with Cécile), but with time one learns that the charm was simply projected from oneself. We discover that the glamour we thought we perceived was an "illusion" (I. 215), "The credulous hope of mutual minds" (216). We pass, in other words, from "Fancy's Maze" to the realm of "Truth."

> And yet 'tis hard to quit the dreams
>   Which haunt the unsuspicious soul,
> Where every nymph a goddess seems,

> Whose eyes through rays immortal roll;
> While Fancy holds her boundless reign,
> And all assumes a varied hue;
> When Virgins seem no longer vain,
> And even Woman's smiles are true.
>   ("To Romance," stanza 2)

The motif is persistent in *Don Juan*. As Johnson puts it:

> All, when Life is new,
> Commence with feelings warm, and prospects high;
> But Time strips our illusions of their hue,
> And one by one in turn, some grand mistake
> Casts off its bright skin yearly like the snake.
>   (V. 21)

And he goes on to explain that "Love's the first net which spreads its deadly mesh," only to be followed by "Ambition, Avarice, Vengeance, Glory" (V. 22). What is lost is blamed and regretted; what is gained is welcomed and blamed.

What is gained is called variously "apathy" (IV. 4), "Indifference" (XIII. 4), or "judgment" (I.215), which seems to be roughly synonymous with "insensibility." In a famous passage following hard upon the stanzas on the perils of soaring ("Nothing so difficult as a beginning," IV. 1) the speaker remarks:

> As boy, I thought myself a clever fellow,
>   And wished that others held the same opinion;
> They took it up when my days grew more mellow,
>   And other minds acknowledged my dominion:
> Now my sere Fancy "falls into the yellow
>   Leaf," and Imagination droops her pinion,
> And the sad truth which hovers o'er my desk
> Turns what was once romantic to burlesque.
>   (IV. 3)

The poet's "fall" from the romantic (associated with Fancy and Imagination) to the burlesque is, then, quite a different thing from the fall spoken of two stanzas before, where he is writing of that which comes of soaring higher than one's capacities allow. The thing to be noticed is that it is youth that is primarily the time of imagination and the imaginative flight ("While Youth's hot wishes in our red veins revel, / We know not this"; IV. 2), and that loss of this capacity is part of the process of maturity. One is reminded of the Intimations Ode and the analogous complexity of Wordsworth's attitude toward the "visionary gleam" of youth and the "philosophic mind" of maturity. The poet feels the gain of seeing things as they really are; but he feels the loss, too.

The situation receives perhaps its most succinct expression in a curious little lyric that is usually dismissed with the observation that it shows how little Byron really cared for Mrs. Spencer Smith:

> The spell is broke, the charm is flown!
>   Thus is it with Life's fitful fever:
> We madly smile when we should groan;
>   Delirium is our best deceiver.

> Each lucid interval of thought
>> Recalls the woes of Nature's charter;
> And *He* that acts as *wise men ought,*
>> But *lives*—as Saints have died—a martyr.

Except for the distracting allusion to *Macbeth* in the second line, this is not bad. The second quatrain is, in fact, rather fine in its way. As we find in *Don Juan,* also, the disillusionment that follows on youth is never quite complete. The apathy is broken by upwellings of passion, sensual or otherwise. "Delirium" can momentarily blind us to the realities of the situation; but delirium subsides (in "each lucid interval of thought") and the fact of a fallen world ("the woes of Nature's charter") is not to be escaped. Furthermore, the man who does not permit himself to be deluded, who does not acquiesce in spells and charms and deliriums, suffers like a martyr for his integrity from the pain of encountering a fallen world face on.

With regard to *Don Juan* itself, . . . it is perhaps most useful to cite the very interesting series of stanzas at the beginning of Canto XIII:

> I now mean to be serious;—it is time,
>> Since Laughter now-a-days is deemed too serious;
> A jest at Vice by Virtue's called a crime,
>> And critically held as deleterious:
> Besides, the sad's a source of the sublime,
>> Although, when long, a little apt to weary us;
> And therefore shall my lay soar high and solemn,
> As an old temple dwindled to a column.
>
>   (XIII. 1)

In the first half of the octave the poet is expressing his uneasiness as to the way his satire had been received. A public which so misunderstands what the poet is about (though, to be sure, they did not have the Dedication to help them)[3] deserves punishment in its own terms—the "sad sublime." What Byron was accusing the public of failing to understand was the nature of satire as Pope had understood it and as Byron continued to understand it. To them, says Byron, there is satire, frivolous and socially irresponsible, and there is the "high and solemn" soaring of the heroic muse, socially and morally irreproachable. With the decay of the older tradition and the exaltation of a rather limited conception of the sublime in the latter part of the eighteenth century, it had been forgotten that there had been a sense in which satire could itself be legitimately heroic.

But Byron reminds us. After a rather disorderly rehearsal of the group of themes we have been examining (the loss of "Romance," etc., in XIII. 4–8), Byron turns his attention to a particular artist and a particular work of art— Cervantes' *Don Quixote.* Here again Byron has been greatly underrated. The passage is normally taken as a routine expression of Romantic Cervantes criticism. It is a great deal more than that. Says the poet: I am no longer subject to the powerful feelings either of love or of hate that used to overwhelm me. I should, however,

>   . . . be very willing to redress
> Men's wrongs, and rather check than punish crimes,

> Had not Cervantes, in that too true tale
> Of Quixote, shown how all such efforts fail.
>
> Of all tales 'tis the saddest—and more sad,
>   Because it makes us smile: his hero's right,
> And still pursues the right;—to curb the bad
>   His only object, and 'gainst odds to fight
> His guerdon: 'tis his virtue makes him mad!
>   But his adventures form a sorry sight;—
> A sorrier still is the great moral taught
> By that real Epic unto all who have thought.
>   (XIII. 8–9)

It is important first of all to see what the poet has done with the concept of Romance. Previously associated with the brief period of youthful idealism and with the soaring of imaginative literature, it is here invested with a more specifically moral content—with

> Redressing injury, revenging wrong,
>   To aid the damsel and destroy the caitiff, etc.
>   (XIII. 10)

—in other words, with the traditional idealistic content of the romance epic. The possibility of such belief as the romance epic presupposes is destroyed by experience, especially the kind of experience dramatized in *Don Quixote,* where the author sets out deliberately to attack the world of romance. And in the course of satirizing romance Cervantes has written an epic. It is a *"real* Epic," real in that it, in contrast to the "mere Fancy" of romance, deals with reality, or the way things really are. Like *Don Juan,* it is a creation not of the soaring muse of high imagination, but of the "true Muse" (VIII. 1) of epic satire. But real also in the sense of authentic, or valid. The "true Muse," as we have seen in the Dedication, is capable of her own kind of flight. As Byron observed in his first reply to Bowles, quoting the lines from Pope that echo through much of *Don Juan:* " 'That not in fancy's maze he wandered long, / But *stooped* to Truth, and moralised his song.' He should have written 'rose to truth.' "[4]

I have suggested that *Don Juan* is like *Paradise Lost* in that, in a sense, both poems are attempts to reinterpret and recreate the epic form, and in that they are both concerned with the loss of innocence. Byron deals with the state of innocence in terms of what he calls "Romance." But he makes a rather clear distinction between two kinds of Romance. There is first the natural freshness of the unspoiled child, the Romance of, especially, Haidée. We have already seen something of its charm and its fragility. And then there is the factitious Romance. "An opium dream of too much youth and *reading*" (IV. 19; my italics).[5] This is the artificial innocence of a sophisticated society, a sensibility which is simply a form of self-indulgence (this is the basis of much of his attack on the "Blues"):

> Romance! disgusted with deceit,
>   Far from thy motly court I fly,
> Where Affectation holds her seat,
>   And sickly Sensibility;

Whose silly tears can never flow
    For any pangs excepting thine;
Who turns aside from real woe,
    To steep in dew thy gaudy shrine.
            ("To Romance," stanza 5)

But this too has its charms, not the least of which is that it blends almost imperceptibly into the natural Romance of first love. Juan's boyish agonies over his love for Julia are a delightful mixture of the "natural" and the "literary." The action of nature is obvious enough, but the literary aspect has not been adequately dealt with. Steffan, for example, has lately written of "Juan's bewildered drifting and adolescent mooning around in nature (a burlesque of Wordsworth's theories about man and nature, sts. 86–96)."[6] Now, that there are Wordsworthian echoes in the passage is certain; that they are in any useful sense a "burlesque" is at least questionable; and that the whole of I. 86–96 can be labeled Wordsworthian is simply inaccurate.

In the first place, there are only three clearly Wordsworthian lines in the whole section, the first three lines of stanza 91:

He, Juan (and not Wordsworth), so pursued
    His self-communion with his own high soul,
Until his mighty heart, in its great mood,
    Had mitigated part, though not the whole
Of its disease.

The second and third lines are a fine piece of Wordsworth parody.[7] But that is really all there is.[8] Byron moves on to Coleridge and metaphysics, though the examples he gives have almost as little to do with Coleridge as with Wordsworth. The two stanzas on the lines from Campbell (88–89) are "romantic," to be sure, but not especially Wordsworthian. Stanza 90 seems rather a parody of the lover of courtly romance. It is closer to the *Arcadia* than to *The Prelude*. Stanza 95 informs us that Juan was reading the works of Spanish Petrarchists, while the first part of stanza 87 is a clear Petrarchan parody:

Silent and pensive, idle, restless, slow,
    His home deserted for the lonely wood,
Tormented with a wound he could not know,
    His, like all deep grief, plunged in solitude.

Which may be compared with the opening lines of one of Petrarch's most famous sonnets:

Solo e pensoso i più deserti campi
    vo mesurando a passi tardi e lenti.
            (*Rime*, 39)

And, of course, the Petrarchan tradition is not silent concerning wounds from Amor's arrows and the association between love and solitude.

The literary allusions do tend to fall into two main categories which, for simplicity, we may call the "Wordsworthian" (including Campbell, Coleridge, etc.) and the "Petrarchan" (or Renaissance). It is possible the poet is alluding to these two modes when he observes that

> Nor glowing reverie, nor poet's lay,
> Could yield his spirit that for which it panted.
>
> (I. 96)

"Glowing reverie" will do well enough for the flights of the Wordsworthian sublime, while "poet's lay" covers the ground of Renaissance romance. But in neither case, I would suggest, is there anything so crude as burlesque. The fact that Byron rarely mentions Wordsworth or Petrarch with much admiration does not mean that his attitude is one of simple-minded aversion. Here they participate in both the charm and the foolishness of a very young man in love. Their aptness to his mood is at once a suggestion of their justification and of their peculiar kind of limitation. They are both, in a way, immature —based on a vision which, the poet would insist, is not borne out by a dispassionate view of the way things are.

Briefly to recapitulate, we have seen the period of youth associated with "Romance," which in turn is associated with the imaginative flight and with pride. All of these motifs are found in IV. 3 ("As boy, I thought myself a clever fellow"), commented on above, and they occur repeatedly in various forms throughout the poem. The pattern of association may be compared to the opening lines of Part II of the *Essay on Criticism* (Pope's point is, of course, a different one):

> Of all the Causes which conspire to blind
> Man's erring judgment, and misguide the mind,
> What the weak head with strongest bias rules,
> Is *Pride,* the never-failing vice of fools.
>
> . . . .
>
> Fired at first sight with what the Muse imparts,
> In fearless youth we tempt the heights of Arts.
>
> (ll. 201–4, 219–20)

In any case, we have here a kind of reversal of the traditional order of composition. Byron is turning his back on the "high" and "heroic" in favor of the "low" and "true." In doing so he is following Pope, who wrote his epics (the translation of Homer) first and then turned to the plain style. The Byron of *Don Juan* was criticized by *his* friends:

> You grow correct, that once with Rapture writ.

And, like his master, he replied:

> Truth guards the Poet, sanctifies the line,
> And makes immortal, Verse as mean as mine.

But Byron goes beyond Pope in his suggestion, reinforced by his juggling of traditional rhetorical concepts, of the possibility of a "real Epic," an epic that tells the truth as satire tells the truth.[9] The point need not be labored, for these traditional concepts themselves are merely metaphoric counters the poet uses (as he does the myth of the Fall) to organize his material and to suggest the kind of attitude or world view which is the meaning of *Don Juan*.

I have hinted in passing at a comparison between *Don Juan* and the Immortality Ode. The comparison may be extended. For while Wordsworth is confessing that he has lost something personally valuable ("the visionary gleam"), he is simultaneously asserting that he has moved not only to a profounder view of human experience ("the philosophic mind") but to a higher mode of art. This is made very clear by the highly relevant epigraph—*Paulo majora canamus*. "I am now prepared to write, if not epic, something at least in a rather exalted vein." Looking at Wordsworth's works as a whole, one can think of it as a step toward the unfinished "epic" of the *Recluse*. There is a clear association of the moral (in its broadest sense) with the literary, much in the tradition of the eighteenth century.

Byron's epigraph to *Don Juan* is at least equally significant. So far as I know, no one has thought to ask (in print, at any rate) the reason for his choosing the Horatian *Difficile*—perhaps because it is too obvious, or more likely, because of the general assumption that Byron could not mean very much of anything. However that may be, Willis Pratt has recently taken a step in the right direction by calling attention to Byron's "imitation" of the Latin, the *Hints from Horace:*[10]

> 'Tis hard to venture where our betters fail,
> Or lend fresh interest to a twice-told tale.
>
> (ll. 183–84)

It is clear that *both* verses of the couplet (Pratt carelessly gives only the first) are intended to translate the Latin: *Difficile est proprie communia dicere* (the "*tuque,* etc." is rendered by "And yet, etc."). Interpreted in this manner, the epigraph would be an appeal to the classic and neoclassic doctrine of imitation, and would refer to the choice of subject. "I am, in taking up the story of Don Juan, dealing with material that is already well-known ('a twice-told tale'). It may be hard, but we'll see what I can do with it." The point would be the poet's original use of traditional material.

The reading of the Lovelace manuscript, cited by Pratt, is less clear and may possibly refer to quite a different reading of the line:

> Whate'er the critic says or poet sings
> 'Tis no slight task to write on common things.

Here he might conceivably be interpreting *communia* as "common topics" or "commonplaces," a reading which may be strengthened by the association of "common things" and "common places" in a passage of *Don Juan:*

> This narrative is not meant for narration,
> But a mere airy and fantastic basis,
> To build up common things with common places.
>
> (XIV. 7)

And one fancies that it is not accidental when, only a few stanzas later, the poet observes with regard to the social group under consideration in the last cantos of the poem:

> With much to excite, there's little to exalt;
>   Nothing that speaks to all men and all times;
> A sort of varnish over every fault;
>   A kind of common-place, even in their crimes.
>   (XIV. 16)

Further, in light of what we have seen about the traditional relation between the high (or "sublime") style, satire, and truth, one is struck to observe that the English upper classes had "A want of that *true* nature which *sublimes* / Whate'er it shows with *Truth*" (*ibid.;* my italics).[11]

The point of all this comes out most clearly a little later. In one of the invocations with which Byron decorates his epic he announces, echoing Ariosto:[12]

> Knights and Dames I sing,
> Such as the times may furnish. 'Tis a flight
> Which seems at first to need no lofty wing,
>   Plumed by Longinus or the Stagyrite.
>   (XV. 25)

"Such as the times may furnish." For it is important to recall that at this point Byron is dealing with actual "Knights and Dames," the lords and ladies of the Regency aristocracy, and the social equivalents, at least, of the heroes and heroines of epic and romance. This, he says, is the best we have. If we are to write an epic, and if, in obedience to the laws of decorum, we choose our matter from the life of the higher orders, it is these men and women we must deal with. Further, if we undertake an epic we must be prepared to "soar." But how, asks the poet, can one justify the use of epic flight on such subjects as these?

> The difficulty lies in colouring
>   (Keeping the due proportions still in sight)
> With Nature manners which are artificial,
> And rend'ring general that which is especial.
>   (XV. 25)

Here he is making two further complaints as to the suitability for epic purposes of the material furnished by the age. As epic poet he is obliged to meet the two demands of nature and of generality. In both cases what he is referring to is his obligation to deal with the general, universally valid principles of human nature, as opposed to the merely local and accidental. But one must not ignore the unfavorable associations of the word "artificial." The arts of civilization (with which the poet has no argument in themselves) seem to have got out of hand:

> In the days of old
> Men made the Manners; Manners now make men.
>   (XV. 26)

With the result that:

> With much to excite, there's little to exalt;
>   Nothing that speaks to all men and all times.
>   (XIV. 16)

I have spoken before of Byron's acute awareness of the value and the peril of the arts of civilization. Here a new danger is suggested; civilization has a way of reducing everybody to a dull dead level—so that the epic poet has a serious problem. He must find a hero in an unheroic age and he must attain human generality in an age occupied with factitious trifles. As Byron puts it, he

> . . . must either draw again
> Days better drawn before, or else assume
> The present, with their common-place costume.
>
> (XV. 26)

Whatever the Horatian *Difficile* meant at the beginning of *Don Juan,* it has now come to refer to the commonplace humanity set before the prospective epic poet of the early nineteenth century.

Much earlier in the poem, at the height of the Haidée idyll, Byron's island laureate had sung:

> The heroic lay is tuneless now—
> The heroic bosom beats no more!
> And must thy Lyre, so long divine,
> Degenerate into hands like mine?
>
> ("The Isles of Greece," stanza 5)

And in so speaking he is only echoing what Byron himself had said many years before in the first of the "Turkish Tales." Byron begins *The Giaour* with a meditation on the heroic days of Greece, commenting on its present degradation. Greece is as beautiful as ever, but the moral and spiritual quality of her people has decayed:

> What can he tell who treads thy shore?
> No lengend of thine olden time,
> No theme on which the Muse might soar
> High as thine own in days of yore,
> When man was worthy of thy clime.
>
> (*The Giaour,* ll. 142–46)

Here again the motif of the connection between moral elevation and poetic sublimity. Greece now presents no material for those poetic flights for which her literature is uniquely distinguished. So what shall I write of modern Greece? Not an epic, surely; but a "Turkish Tale." And not even a whole tale; merely "disjointed fragments." The land is Greece, but the principal characters are Turk and Frank. Only the conspicuously frequent and extended "Homeric" similes may remind the reader of the heroic tradition.[13]

He arrives at a somewhat different solution of the problem posed by a colorless aristocracy:

> We'll do our best to make the best on't:—March!
>   March, my Muse! If you cannot fly, yet flutter;
> And when you may not be sublime, be arch,
>   Or starch, as are the edicts statesmen utter.
> We surely may find something worth research:
>   Columbus found a new world in a cutter,

> Or brigantine, or pink, of no great tonnage,
> While yet America was in her non-age.
> (XV. 27)

Here he is simply granting the impossibility of treating his polished patricians as traditional epic heroes. The soaring heroic muse will be forced to "flutter" along. The image is a conventional one for the failure of imaginative *essor*. The word is so used, for example, in the introductory essay to Gifford's *Juvenal*. Of the "heroic" satirist he observes: "His element was that of the eagle, 'descent and fall to him were adverse,' and, indeed, he never appears more awkward than when he flutters, or rather waddles, along the ground."[14] It will be, as it were, a "low" epic. And then again he presents us with one of his most valuable metaphors of the nature of the "real" epic, that of the voyage of exploration. He is harking back to the passage "In the wind's eye I have sailed, etc." (X. 4) . . . and to the fine stanzas only a few pages earlier:

> 'Tis strange—but true; for Truth is always strange—
>   Stranger than fiction: if it could be told,
> How much would novels gain by the exchange!
>   How differently the World would men behold!
> How oft would Vice and Virtue places change!
>   The new world would be nothing to the old,
> If some Columbus of the moral seas
> Would show mankind their Souls' antipodes.
>
> What "antres vast and deserts idle," then,
>   Would be discovered in the human soul!
> What icebergs in the hearts of mighty men,
>   With self-love in the centre as their Pole!
> (XIV. 101–2)

Here he is appealing to the "romantic" associations (or even epic, if one thinks of the *Odyssey*, the *Télémaque*, or, especially, the *Lusiads*) of the voyage of adventure. It is glamorous, and it is in search of truth, a truth, which Byron presents as not only more valuable but more "romantic" than fiction. In words that remind us of the way he has created a subjective version of the romance-epic in *Childe Harold's Pilgrimage: A Romaunt* (where the subtitle indicates the genre against which Byron's poem is constantly to be compared), we learn that the voyage is to be into the heart of social man.[15]

As far, at least, as the incomplete poem we possess is concerned, the voyage comes to its climax in the English cantos. And while it is always well in discussing this section to bear in mind that it is not finished and that we do not know how Byron was going to develop the situation, a few generalizations may perhaps be hazarded. In the first place, it is the only section of the poem which actually deals with a social group, and thus is the only episode that would really fit in any proposed plan of treating the characteristic absurdities of the various peoples of Europe.[16] And it is this section in which he seems to be making his most earnest attempt at dramatizing the possibility of "real Epic."[17] The section is, then, conspicuous not only for its treatment of society and for the number and importance of its evocations of the world of classical epic, but also for the persistence with which it reminds us of the difficulties involved in the notion of reality.

The English cantos, in fact, begin with a consideration of "what is":

> When Bishop Berkeley said "there was no matter,"
>   And proved it—'twas no matter what he said:
> They say his system 'tis in vain to batter,
>   Too subtle for the airiest human head;
> And yet who can believe it? I would shatter
>   Gladly all matters, down to stone or lead,
> Or adamant, to find the world a spirit,
> And wear my head, denying that I wear it.
>
> What a sublime discovery 'twas to make the
>   Universe universal egotism,
> That all's ideal—*all ourselves!*—I'll stake the
>   World (be it what you will) that *that's* no schism.
> Oh Doubt!—if thou be'st Doubt, for which some
>   take thee,
>   But which I doubt extremely—thou sole prism
> Of the Truth's rays, spoil not my draught of spirit!
> Heaven's brandy, though our brain can hardly bear it.
>
>   (XI. 1–2)

The grasp of metaphysics may not be impressive, but the edginess of the passage is of more than biographical interest. The poet wants to base his epic solidly on reality, and he wants to make a point of the fact. And while he is hardly obliged to outline an ontology, it is well at least to forestall objections of excessive naïveté by indicating an awareness of the complexity of the problem. Furthermore, it is to his interest (as well as to his taste) to undermine any systematic formulation of reality, to set system against system (XIV. 1–2), and to exalt the primacy of that immediate experience (what he sometimes calls "fact," or "existence") of which the poet is a peculiarly authoritative spokesman. And finally, the question of reality is important to the poem's social comment.

To restrict ourselves for the moment to this one canto (XI), the introductory stanzas on metaphysics are followed by the episode on Shooter's Hill. Here there is not only an exposure of the seamy side of an ostentatiously free and moral nation, but there is accomplished playing with the notion of heroism (20) and the "great man" (19) much in the manner of Fielding in *Jonathan Wild*. "He from the world had cut off a great man, etc." The difference between a footpad and statesman, it is implied, is largely a matter of social convention (cf. the "sea-sollicitor" Lambro). This is followed immediately by an octave on "Groves, so called as being void of trees"—commenting on a characteristic manifestation of lower middle-class gentility, where the charm and elegance is largely a matter of names. Stanzas 35–37 are concerned with lying. Here the attitude is more complex. Politicians "live by lies, yet dare not boldly lie," in contrast to women, who "won't / Or can't do otherwise than lie—but do it / So well, the very Truth seems falsehood to it" (36). Furthermore, a lie is simply "The truth in masquerade," and lying is indispensable to society as at present constituted (37). Then he undertakes to show the reality of social life, the vicissitudes of the great in their "earthly Paradise of *Or Molu*" (67–75). The brilliant *ubi sunt* and *carpe diem* stanzas with which the canto ends are concluded with some cynical lines on the "play" of life:

> "Life's a poor player,"—then "play out the play,
>   Ye villains!" and above all keep a sharp eye
>   Much less on what you do than what you say:
> Be hypocritical, be cautious, be
> Not what you *seem*, but always what you *see*.
>   (XI. 86)

Byron exploits the possibilities of the play or masquerade theme with some skill. In the passage just quoted he is recommending the deliberate adoption of a role if one wants to advance in society. It is important not to "be oneself" ("what you *seem*"), but the self society expects you to be ("what you *see*"). It is the mingled glamour, pathos, and absurdity of this situation that Byron is trying to suggest when he observes:

> Sometimes, indeed, like soldiers off parade,
>   They break their ranks and gladly leave the drill;
> But then the roll-call draws them back afraid,
>   And they must be or seem what they *were:* still
> Doubtless it is a brilliant masquerade.   (XIV. 17)

These Regency aristocrats caught in their social roles call to mind Sartre's waiter "playing at being a waiter." The very typicality or lack of individuality in the list of guests at Norman Abbey is to the point. He interrupts his catalogue deliberately to remark:

> Good company's a chess-board—there are kings,
>   Queens, bishops, knights, rooks, pawns; the
>   World's a game;
> Save that the puppets pull at their own strings,
>   Methinks gay Punch hath something of the same.
>   (XIII. 89)

It is the inhuman, mechanical rigidity and limitation of personality that seems most profoundly to disturb the poet. In terms of the "Ode to a Lady," this is clearly a world in which love is "a bondage or a trade":

> But coming young from lands and scenes romantic,
>   Where lives, not lawsuits, must be risked for Passion,
> And Passion's self must have a spice of frantic,
>   Into a country where 'tis half a fashion,
> Seemed to him half commercial, half pedantic.
>   (XII. 68)

And Byron delights in references to lawsuits and damages.[18]

But this is too simple to do justice to Byron. The *ubi sunt* and *carpe diem* stanzas toward the end of Canto XI (76–86) remind us that *Don Juan* is a poem that is concerned with time and with the changes that take place in

time, with the emphasis falling heavily on the feeling of loss. With this is
conjoined one stanza on the "business" of love and marriage in England (89)
and three associating the poet's truthfulness and poetic sublimity (87, 89–
90):

> Thus far, go forth, thou Lay, which I will back
> Against the same given quantity of rhyme,
> For being as much the subject of attack
> As ever yet was any work sublime,
> By those who love to say that white is black.
> So much the better!—I may stand alone,
> But would not change my free thoughts for a throne.
>
> (XI. 90)

Now one of the points I am most concerned to make about Byron's method
in *Don Juan* is that it is always extremely important to notice what he is
associating with what. For Byron achieves some of his finest effects by simple
thematic association (such as that of love with war . . .). It may be instructive, therefore, to examine this particular thematic group—time, love, business,
and the sublimity of poetic truth.

One reason why it is especially useful to an enjoyment of *Don Juan* at least
unconsciously to have made this particular association is that the poet appears to pick it up and elaborate it at the beginning of the next canto. And the
beginning of Canto XII marks a turning point of some importance in the
development of the poem.

We hear first of all about the speaker's age. He is "middle-aged," and he
doesn't like it much:

> Too old for Youth,—too young, at thirty-five,
> To herd with boys, or hoard with good threescore,—
> I wonder people should be left alive;
> But since they are, that epoch is a bore:
> Love lingers still, although 'twere late to wive:
> And as for other love, the illusion's o'er;
> And Money, that most pure imagination,
> Gleams only through the dawn of its creation
>
> (XII. 2)

Now that the "illusion" of romantic love is no longer possible (cf. I. 215–16),
the only charm that seems to lie ahead is money and the making of money—
money being as specifically associated with age and experience as romantic
love has been with youth and innocence. And while the poet has been generous
in his appreciation of the charms of love, there is clearly something to be said
for money, too.

> "Love rules the Camp, the Court, the Grove,—for Love
> Is Heaven, and Heaven is Love:"—so sings the bard;
> Which it were rather difficult to prove
> (A thing with poetry in general hard).
> Perhaps there may be something in "the Grove,"
> At least it rhymes to "Love:" but I'm prepared
> To doubt (no less than landlords of their rental)
> If "Courts" and "Camps" be quite so sentimental.

> But if Love don't, *Cash* does, and Cash alone:
>   Cash rules the Grove, and fells it too besides;
> Without cash, camps were thin, and courts were none;
>   Without cash, Malthus tells you—"take no brides."
> So Cash rules Love the ruler, on his own
>   High ground, as virgin Cynthia sways the tides.
> (XII. 13–14)

Money is not only in itself an object of excitement and romance . . . ; it "rules Love the ruler." And the tone is no longer, in this respect, quite that of the Ode. This may not be the way the poet would have it if he had a choice. But he is not merely bitter about the situation. And if the tone is not one of simple amusement, neither is it one of savage satire. "Thus it is," says the speaker. Money is not romantic, perhaps—but in a sense it is. Furthermore, if love is an illusion, money in any case is very real. And the converting of its hard unglamorous reality into a thing of curious beauty is of clear relevance to an "epic" poet who is concerned with writing truth. The notion of the rule of love over human affairs is, says the speaker, "poetic," and poetry tells lies. But the poet of the "truthful Muse," engaged in writing a "real Epic," must be rigorously honest without ceasing to be a poet. Hence the point of the tour de force at the beginning of Canto XII, creating for us a vision of that inevitable change in the life of every man from youth to age—and a vision which presents mutability as more than merely loss. The poet faces the hard facts of experience and finds them not lacking in their own kind of charm.

The point is of clear importance in the working out of the plot. Its elaboration, in fact, seems to be the principal action of the English cantos. For if the world of the English cantos is in some ways analogous to that of the Ode, it is equally clear that a "Lady" is being prepared with whom Juan is to become involved in an affair in every sense more perilous than any of his previous adventures. Adeline is explicitly said to be "The fair most fatal Juan ever met" (XIII. 12). And that is clearly the point of Byron's insistence on the strength of passion of which apparently cold English ladies are capable (XII. 76–77), most notably in the elaborate conceits of the bottle of frozen champagne and the "North-West Passage/Unto the glowing India of the Soul" (XIII. 36–38), referring specifically to Adeline. She is, says the poet like

> . . . a bottle of champagne
> Frozen into a very vinous ice,
>   Which leaves few drops of that immortal rain,
> Yet in the very centre, past all price,
>   About a liquid glassful will remain;
> And this is stronger than the strongest grape
> Could e'er express in its expanded shape.
> (XIII. 37)

The point to be noticed is this: the apparent coldness and the unfavorable social circumstances are seen as contributing factors to the intensity of their love, even as the passion of the Lady of the Ode was refined and made more intense by her own "coldness" and the circumstances which rendered her love a "guilty" one.[19]

The point is worth laboring. Neither the image of ice nor the ideal of restraint has been invested with much grandeur in the course of the poem. We have seen ice in VII. 1–2 as a "wasteland" image over which flashes the aurora borealis of poetry. And the image has been used in the English cantos to express some of the less pleasant aspects of English society (XII. 25, 41, 72). But the attitude toward restraint has been ambiguous throughout. In the discussion of Juan's education, for example, we are led to suppose that the boy was being excessively held down:

> For half his days were passed at church, the other
> Between his tutors, confessor, and mother.
>
> (I. 49)

> They tamed him down amongst them: to destroy
> His natural spirit not in vain they toiled,
>   At least it seemed so.   (I. 50)

The qualifying clause reminds us, however, of the futility of all repression. "Nature," evidently, will out. See the canceled final couplet to II. 10.[20]

But even as he criticizes Donna Inez for being overly repressive in bringing up her son, he is also taking her to task for being too lax:

> Oh ye! who teach the ingenuous youth of nations,
>   Holland, France, England, Germany, or Spain,
> I pray ye flog them upon all occasions—
>   It mends their morals, never mind the pain:
> The best of mothers and of educations
>   In Juan's case were but employed in vain,
> Since, in a way that's rather of the oddest, he
> Became divested of his native modesty.

> Had he but been placed at a public school,
>   In the third form, or even in the fourth,
> His daily task had kept his fancy cool,
>   At least, had he been nurtured in the North;
> Spain may prove an exception to the rule,
>   But then exceptions always prove its worth—
> A lad of sixteen causing a divorce
> Puzzled his tutors very much, of course.[21]
>
> (II. 1–2)

This apparent contradiction serves more than one function. In the first place it brings out the instability of Donna Inez. More important is the suggestion that the alternate severity and laxity tended to cancel each other out (like Fielding's Thwackum and Square), so that when Don Juan goes out into the world he has to deal with it (like Tom Jones) with his own natural resources. The analogy with the sinking ship with "all distinction gone" (II. 44) is clear enough. Both the shipwreck and the mode of Juan's education permit the boy to exercise his own natural capacities unhelped (or hindered) by education or by institutional supports. And finally, there is the suggestion of the value in discipline itself.

. . . I have commented on the speaker's attitude toward the repression of emotion, observing that he often seems to think of it as a purely physical phenomenon, like steam confined and causing an explosion. This is an essential part of that post of detached objectivity which is one of the most obvious qualities of the *persona* in *Don Juan*. He needs it, of course, to make good his claims of speaking truth. He watches, he describes, he sympathizes; but he is reluctant to judge. It is one of the things about *Don Juan* that makes it seem so curiously French. If he is quite merciless in following out the consequences of passion it is not because he acknowledges religious or philosophical sanctions for morality, but because in his own experience as man of the world he has learned that, like it or not, passion *does* end in disaster. It may be worth it, but the consequences are clear and, apparently, inexorable. It is for this reason that he so emphasizes his own worldliness and sophistication. He needs it to validate a particular kind of statement. What might seem the almost Calvinist morality of *Don Juan* is not really morality at all in the usual sense. At least it claims not to be. It presents itself as the observation of a man who is able to offer impressive evidence of his objectivity and first-hand knowledge. The speaker's insistence on his own sophistication may be compared to that of the Ode, or of Donne's "The Relique."

For, as I have already suggested, there is a notable change of emphasis in the course of *Don Juan*. I have ventured to compare the poem with *Paradise Lost* in that both "epics" are concerned with the loss of innocence. And in the early cantos this loss is lamented with some passion: "No more— no more—Oh! never more on me!" But even as the loss is lamented, the fact of gain is at least asserted:

> The illusion's gone for ever, and thou art
> Insensible, I trust, but none the worse,
> And in thy stead I've got a deal of judgment,
> Though Heaven knows how it ever found a lodgment.
>   (I. 215)

And as the poem develops, the emphasis is much less on what has been lost than on what has been gained—on the dangers and opportunities.

> Adversity is the first path to Truth:
> He who hath proved War—Storm—or Woman's rage,
> Whether his winters be eighteen or eighty,
> Hath won the experience which is deemed so weighty.
>   (XII. 50)

Experience is now not so much a thing to be lamented as a thing to test oneself against and a means of arriving at something that may be called truth. The fall is "fortunate."

Early in the first canto there is a stanza (part of which I have already quoted in another context) in which the speaker comments on Juan's boy-love for Julia:

> Silent and pensive, idle, restless, slow,
>   His home deserted for the lonely wood,
> Tormented with a wound he could not know,
>   His, like all deep grief, plunged in solitude:
> I'm fond myself of solitude or so,
>   But then, I beg it may be understood,

> By solitude I mean a Sultan's (not
> A Hermit's), with a haram for a grot.
> (I. 87)

I dare say this is usually taken as simply another example of Byronic digression (or of showing off). It is, in fact, highly relevant. The point of the stanza, and a point that it makes very well, is the enormous gap between the speaker and the protagonist; for both taken together form the third great unifying device of the poem (along with the myth of the Fall and the theory of the styles), and the relations between them are central to an understanding of *Don Juan*. At the beginning of the poem, as the quoted stanza dramatizes, there is a great gulf between them. On the one hand we have the gauche adolescent suffering awkwardly through his first affair. Looking down on him affectionately from Olympian heights is the worldly speaker—who calls attention to his worldliness at this point for very important reasons. One way of defining the action of *Don Juan* would be to say that it consists of a process of gradually narrowing the gap between speaker and protagonist. For if Juan falls from innocence, in the course of the poem he rises to the level of the speaker. The gain is not unequivocal and the process is far from complete when the poem ends. But it is impossible not to feel that the English cantos mark a clear turning point in the development of the poem. By the end the categories of innocence and experience have become largely irrelevant. The very iciness of the world has become a source of potential charm.

All of which, I hope, may suggest that it is very easy to limit too narrowly the scope of *Don Juan*. I am unable to persuade myself that in it Byron is merely "giggling and making giggle," exposing cant, or, especially, writing a treatise on appearance and reality (three popular and representative schools of thought). From this point of view the problem with regard to *Don Juan* is in many ways strongly suggestive of problems raised by *Don Quixote*—and it may have been an implicit awareness of some of this that led Byron to compose his stanzas on the "real Epic." In the course of its long history *Don Quixote* has suffered from two radical interpretations—one seeing it as a farce-satire and the other as a kind of exercise in metaphysics. I think that of the two serious distortions the first is far truer to Cervantes. It is important to perceive, as Erich Auerbach has pointed out, that the whole tone and temper of *Don Quixote* forbids incursions into the ontologically problematic.[22] It is simply untrue that one is aware of metaphysical depths opening before one, or that in the shuffling of "levels of reality" in Part II either Cervantes or the reader is ever for a moment uncertain as to "where" reality actually "is." The point of view may be, in a way, naïve, but in other and more interesting ways it is very refined indeed. And if Cervantes is not Calderon, *Don Juan* is not *The Tempest*. And the point of view of Byron's poem is susceptible of the same charge of naïveté (a charge which one can endure in the company of Cervantes). This is not to say that either *Don Quixote* or *Don Juan* is, as a vision, simple. It is rather that in both Byron and Cervantes the complexity is in the quality of the acquiescence in a world which is, for the most part, simply given. It is because *Don Juan* is, in the sense this study has been an attempt to define, an act of acquiescence in that real world that it can claim to be, like *Don Quixote*, a "real Epic."[23]

NOTES

1. *Essays of John Dryden*, ed. by W. P. Ker, 2vs. (Oxford, Clarendon Press, 1900), v.2, p.154. Cf. the note to *English Bards*, l. 225:

> We beg Mr. Southey's pardon: "Madoc disdains the degraded title of Epic." See his Preface. Why is Epic degraded? and by whom? Certainly the late Romaunts of Masters Cottle, Laureat Pye, Ogilvy, Hole, and gentle Mistress Cowley, have not exalted the Epic Muse; but, as Mr. SOUTHEY's poem "disdains the appellation," allow us to ask—has he substituted anything better in its stead? or must he be content to rival Sir RICHARD BLACKMORE in the quantity as well as quality of his verse?

2. Chaderlos de Laclos, *Les Liaisons dangereuses*, tr. by Richard Aldington (Norfolk, Conn., n. d.), pt. 4, letter 134, p.298.

3. It was not published until 1833.

4. *The Works of Lord Byron, Letters and Journals*, ed. by Rowland E. Prothero, 6 vs. (London, 1898–1901), v. 5, p. 554. Cervantes' emphasis on the "truth" of his "chronicle" has certainly influenced Byron in his development of the motif.

5. Coleridge suggests (*The Works of Lord Byron, Poetry*, ed. by Ernest Hartley Coleridge, 7 vs. [London, 1898–1905], v. 6, p.188, n. 1) that this may refer to De Quincey or Shelley. Neither seems at all likely. I could, however, bring myself to find an allusion to Shelley in IX. 73, ll. 3–5.

6. *Don Juan*, ed. by Truman Guy Steffan and Willis W. Pratt, 4 vs. (Austin, Texas, 1957), v. 1, *The Making of a Masterpiece*, ed. by T. G. Steffan, p. 188, n. 4.

7. Cf., for example: "And all that mighty heart is lying still" ("Westminster Bridge").

8. It is possible that stanza 94 may be a reminiscence of the famous passage on Greek myth in *The Excursion*, Bk. IV, ll. 718–44, 851–87. An argument could also be made for stanza 93, l. 2: "Longings sublime and aspirations high." But eleven lines out of eighty is not very impressive.

9. The point that the epic poet is not strictly confined to truth is made, for example, by Dryden in his essay "Of Heroic Plays" (quoted by Ian Jack, *Augustan Satire* [Oxford, 1952], p.83): "An heroic poet is not tied to a bare representation of what is true, or exceedingly probable; . . . he may let himself loose to visionary objects, and to the representation of such things as depending not on sense, and therefore not to be comprehended by knowledge, may give him a freer scope for imagination" (Ker, v.1, p.153). Uneasiness on this score was not, of course, new in Byron's day. In his "Essai sur la poésie épique," Voltaire, for example, has written of his own *Henriade*: "C'est pour me conformer à ce génie sage et exact qui règne dans le siècle où je vis, que j'ai choisi un héros véritable au lieu d'un héros fabuleux; que j'ai décrit des guerres réelles, et non des batailles chimériques; que je n'ai employé aucune fiction qui ne soit un image sensible de la vérité:" *Œuvres complètes*, 52 vs. (Paris, Garnier Frères, 1877), v. 8, p.363. See also the invocation to the Muse, "auguste Vérité:"

> Viens, parle; et s'il est vrai que la Fable autrefois
> Sut à tes fiers accents mêler sa douce voix;
> Si sa main délicate orna ta tête altière,
> Si son ombre embellit les traits de ta lumière,
> Avec moi sur tes pas permets-lui de marcher,
> Pour orner tes attraits, et non pour les cacher.
>
> (Bk. i. ll. 15–20)

10. *Don Juan*, v. 4, *Notes on the Variorum Edition*, ed. by W. W. Pratt, p.4. Pratt curiously "explains" the sufficiently perspicuous reading of the printed text by the distinctly ambiguous version of the Lovelace manuscript.

11. The "sermon" of XIV. 15 may be a rendering of the Horatio *sermo*, "talk," or "satire," with its strong associations of the plain style. Pope so renders it in *Sat.*, II.ii.9, and in the title of II i.

12. Pratt (*Notes on the Variorum Edition*, p.27) cites the *Aeneid*. But Byron is much closer to the opening lines of the *Orlando Furioso:*

> Le Donne, i Cavalier'! l'arme, gli amori,
> Le Cortesie, l'audaci imprese io canto.

13. Notice especially ll. 68–103, 388–421, 422–38, 505–16, 620–42, 661–64, 945–50, 951– 56, 1159–66. Notice also ll. 640–42, where the pastoral locale is given over to violence.

14. *The Satires of Decimus Junius Juvenalis*, tr. by William Gifford (London, 1806), p.*lxvi*.

15. With reference to this metaphor of the voyage, compare the following lines from the suppressed stanzas on Brougham (*Poetry*, v. 6, p.69, n.):

> I'm sorry thus to probe a wound so raw—
> But, then, as Bard my duty to Mankind,
> For warning to the rest, compels these raps—
> As Geographers lay down a Shoal in Maps.

16. See the letter to Murray, Feb. 16, 1821 (*Letters and Journals*, v. 5, p.242).

17. There is some reason to suspect that the poet is setting up the situation in epic terms. After commenting on the something undefined that Lord Henry lacked (Byron displays an almost Jamesean fondness for the indefinable in these English cantos), the poet makes a striking allusion to the action of the *Iliad:*

> Still there was something wanting, as I've said—
> That undefinable *"Je ne sçais quoi,"*
> Which, for what I know, may of yore have led
> To Homer's Iliad, since it drew to Troy
> The Greek Eve, Helen, from the Spartan's bed;
> Though on the whole, no doubt, the Dardan boy
> Was much inferior to King Menelaus:—
> But thus it is some women will betray us.
>
> (XIV. 72)

I am strongly of the opinion that Byron had the progress of the episode worked out in his own mind, and it seems at least possible that he was preparing to draw on the epic tradition rather more specifically than in the earlier cantos. He may have been amusing himself with the idea of an *Iliad* of which Paris is the hero. And evidently he would have continued to make use of the metaphor of the Fall ("The Greek Eve, Helen").

18. For example, XI. 89; XII. 65, 68.

19. This point has been skillfully developed by Ernest J. Lovell, Jr., in his essay "Irony and Image in Byron's *Don Juan*," in Clarence D. Thorpe, Carlos Baker, and Bennett Weaver, eds., *The Major English Romantic Poets*, (Carbondale, Ill., 1957), p.139.

20.
> Their manners mending, and their morals curing,
> She taught them to suppress their vice—and urine.

21. Cf. I. 25:

> A little curly-headed, good-for-nothing,
> And mischief-making monkey from his birth;
> His parents ne'er agreed except in doting
> Upon the most unquiet imp on earth;
> Instead of quarrelling, had they been both in
> Their senses, they'd have sent young master forth
> To school, or had him soundly whipped at home,
> To teach him manners for the time to come.

22. Erich Auerbach, "The Enchanted Dulcinea," *Mimesis: The Representation of Reality in Western Literature* (Princeton, 1953), p.334–58, esp. 351 ff.

23. Notice that, just at the moment when the issue becomes thematically crucial (after the disastrous end of the affair with Haidée), Byron gives us extended depictions of reaction to adversity in the narrative of the buffo (IV. 81–89), and the description of the captives (V. 7–9), and in the speeches of Johnson (V. 13–25).

George Steiner

HOMER AND TOLSTOY

Hugo von Hofmannsthal once remarked that he could not read a page of Tolstoy's *Cossacks* without being reminded of Homer. His experience has been shared by readers not only of *The Cossacks* but of Tolstoy's works as a whole. According to Gorky, Tolstoy himself said of *War and Peace:* "Without false modesty, it is like the *Iliad,*" and he made precisely the same observation with regard to *Childhood, Boyhood and Youth.* Moreover, Homer and the Homeric atmosphere appear to have played a fascinating role in Tolstoy's image of his own personality and creative stature. His brother-in-law, S. A. Bers, tells in his *Reminiscences* of a feast which took place on Tolstoy's estate in Samara:

> a steeplechase of fifty versts. Prizes were got ready, a bull, a horse, a rifle, a watch, a dressing-gown and the like. A level stretch was chosen, a huge course four miles long was made and marked out, and posts were put up on it. Roast sheep, and even a horse, were prepared for the entertainment. On the appointed day, some thousands of people assembled, Ural Cossacks, Russian peasants, Bashkirs and Khirgizes, with their dwellings, koumiss-kettles, and even their flocks. . . . On a cone-shaped rise, called in the local dialect "Shishka" (the Wen), carpets and felt were spread, and on these the Bashkirs seated themselves in a ring, with their legs tucked under them. . . . The feast lasted for two days and was merry, but at the same time dignified and decorous. . . .[1]

It is a fantastic scene; the millennia dividing the plains of Troy from nineteenth-century Russia are bridged and Book XXIII of the *Iliad* springs to life. In Richmond Lattimore's version:

> But Achilleus
> held the people there, and made them sit down in a wide
> assembly
> and brought prizes for games out of his ships, cauldrons
> and tripods,
> and horses and mules and the powerful high heads of
> cattle
> and fair-girdled women and grey iron.

Like Agamemnon, Tolstoy thrones upon the hillock; the steppe is dotted with tents and fires; Bashkirs and Khirgizes, like Achaeans, race the four-mile course and take their prizes from the hands of the bearded king. But there is nothing here of archaeology, of contrived reconstruction. The Homeric element was native to Tolstoy; it was rooted in his own genius. Read his polemics against Shakespeare and you will find that his sense of kinship with the poet, or poets, of the *Iliad* and *Odyssey* was palpable and immediate. Tolstoy spoke of Homer as equal of equal; between them the ages had counted for little.

What was it that struck Tolstoy as peculiarly Homeric in his collection of early memories? Both the setting, I think, and the kind of life he recalled to mind. Take the account of "The Hunt" in the volume on *Childhood:*

> Harvesting was in full swing. The limitless, brilliantly yellow field was bounded only on one side by the tall, bluish forest, which then seemed to me a most distant, mysterious place beyond which either the world came to an end or uninhabited countries began. The whole field was full of sheaves and peasants. . . . The little roan papa rode went with a light, playful step, sometimes bending his head to his chest, pulling at the reins, and brushing off with his thick tail the gadflies and gnats that settled greedily on him. Two borzois with tense tails raised sickle-wise, and lifting their feet high, leapt gracefully over the tall stubble, behind the horse's feet. Milka ran in front, and with head lifted awaited the quarry. The peasants' voices, the tramp of horses and creaking of carts, the merry whistle of quail, the hum of insects hovering in the air in steady swarms, the odour of wormwood, straw, and horses' sweat, the thousands of different colours and shadows with which the burning sun flooded the light yellow stubble, the dark blue of the forest, the light lilac clouds, and the white cobwebs that floated in the air or stretched across the stubble—all this I saw, heard, and felt.

There is nothing here that would have been incongruous on the plains of Argos. It is from our own modern setting that the scene is oddly remote. It is a patriarchal world of huntsmen and peasants; the bond between master and hounds and the earth runs native and true. The description itself combines a sense of forward motion with an impression of repose; the total effect, as in the friezes of the Parthenon, is one of dynamic equilibrium. And beyond the familiar horizon, as beyond the Pillars of Hercules, lie the mysterious seas and the untrodden forests.

The world of Tolstoy's recollections, no less than that of Homer, is charged with sensuous energies. Touch and sight and smell fill it at every moment with rich intensity:

> In the passage a samovár, into which Mítka, the postilion, flushed red as a lobster, is blowing, is already on the boil. It is damp and misty outside, as if steam were rising from the odorous manure heap; the sun lights with its bright gay beams the eastern part of the sky and the thatched roofs, shiny with dew, of the roomy pent-houses that surround the yard. Under these one can see our horses tethered to the mangers and hear their steady chewing. A shaggy mongrel that had had a nap before dawn on a dry heap of manure, stretches itself lazily, and wagging its tail, starts at a jog-trot for the opposite side of the yard. An active peasant-woman opens some creaking gates and drives the dreamy cows into the street, where the tramping, the lowing and the bleating of the herd is already audible. . . .

So it was when "rosy-fingered Dawn" came to Ithaca twenty-seven hundred years ago. So it should be, proclaims Tolstoy, if man is to endure in communion with the earth. Even the storm, with its animate fury, belongs to the rhythm of things:

> The lightning flashes become wider and paler, and the rolling of the thunder is now less startling amid the regular patter of the rain. . . .

> . . . an aspen grove with hazel and wild cherry undergrowth stands motionless as if in an excess of joy, and slowly sheds bright raindrops from its clean-washed branches on to last year's leaves. On all sides crested skylarks circle with glad songs and swoop swiftly down. . . . The delicious scent of the wood after the spring storm, the odour of the birches, of the violets, the rotting leaves, the mushrooms, and the wild cherry, is so enthralling that I cannot stay in the brichka. . . .

Schiller wrote in his essay *Ueber naive und sentimentalische Dichtung* that certain poets "are Nature" while others only "seek her." In that sense, Tolstoy is Nature; between him and the natural world language stood not as a mirror or a magnifying glass, but as a window through which all light passes and yet is gathered and given permanence.

It is impossible to concentrate within a single formula or demonstration the affinities between the Homeric and the Tolstoyan points of view. So much is pertinent: the archaic and pastoral setting; the poetry of war and agriculture; the primacy of the senses and of physical gesture; the luminous, all-reconciling background of the cycle of the year; the recognition that energy and aliveness are, of themselves, holy; the acceptance of a chain of being extending from brute matter to the stars and along which men have their apportioned places; deepest of all, an essential sanity, a determination to follow what Coleridge called "the high road of life," rather than those dark obliquities in which the genius of a Dostoevsky was most thoroughly at home.

In both the Homeric epics and the novels of Tolstoy the relationship between author and characters is paradoxical. [Jacques] Maritain gives a Thomistic analogue for it in his study of *Creative Intuition in Art and Poetry* [London, 1954]. He speaks "of the relationship between the transcendent creative eternity of God and the free creatures who are both acting in liberty and firmly embraced by his purpose." The creator is at once omniscient and everywhere present, but at the same time he is detached, impassive, and relentlessly objective in his vision. The Homeric Zeus presides over the battle from his mountain fastness, holding the scales of destiny but not intervening. Or, rather, intervening solely to restore equilibrium, to safeguard the mutability of man's life against miraculous aid or the excessive achievements of heroism. As in the detachment of the god, so there is in the clear-sightedness of Homer and Tolstoy both cruelty and compassion.

They saw with those blank, ardent, unswerving eyes which look upon us through the helmet-slits of archaic Greek statues. Their vision was terribly sober. Schiller marvelled at Homer's impassiveness, at his ability to communicate the utmost of grief and terror in perfect evenness of tone. He believed that this quality—this "naïveté"—belonged to an earlier age and would be unrecapturable in the sophisticated and analytic temper of modern literature.

From it Homer derived his most poignant effects. Take, for example, Achilles' slaying of Lykaon in Book XXI of the *Iliad*:

"So, friend, you die also. Why all this clamour about it?
Patroklos also is dead, who was better by far than you are.
Do you not see what a man I am, how huge, how splendid
and born of a great father, and the mother who bore me immortal?
Yet even I have also my death and my strong destiny,
and there shall be a dawn or an afternoon or a noontime
when some man in the fighting will take the life from me also
either with a spearcast or an arrow flown from the bowstring."
So he spoke, and in the other the knees and the inward
heart went slack. He let go of the spear and sat back, spreading
wide both hands; but Achilleus drawing his sharp sword struck him
beside the neck at the collar-bone, and the double-edged sword
plunged full length inside. He dropped to the ground, face downward,
and lay at length, and the black blood flowed, and the ground was soaked with it.

The calm of the narrative is nearly inhuman; but in consequence the horror speaks naked and moves us unutterably. Moreover, Homer never sacrifices the steadiness of his vision to the needs of pathos. Priam and Achilles have met and given vent to their great griefs. But then they bethink themselves of meat and wine. For, as Achilles says of Niobe:

"She remembered to eat when she was worn out with weeping."

Again, it is the dry fidelity to the facts, the poet's refusal to be outwardly moved, which communicate the bitterness of his soul.

In this respect, no one in the western tradition is more akin to Homer than is Tolstoy. As Romain Rolland noted in his journal for 1887, "in the art of Tolstoy a given scene is not perceived from two points of view, but from only one: things are as they are, not otherwise." In *Childhood*, Tolstoy tells of the death of his mother: "I was in great distress at that moment but involuntarily noticed every detail," including the fact that the nurse was "very fair, young, and remarkably handsome." When his mother dies, the boy experiences "a kind of enjoyment," at knowing himself to be unhappy. That night he sleeps "soundly and calmly," as is always the case after great distress. The following day he becomes aware of the smell of decomposition:

It was only then that I understood what the strong, oppressive smell was that mingling with the incense filled the whole room; and the thought that the face that but a few days before had been so full of beauty and tenderness, the face of her I loved more than anything on earth, could evoke horror, seemed to reveal the bitter truth to me for the first time, and filled my soul with despair.

"Keep your eyes steadfastly to the light," says Tolstoy, "this is how things are."

But in the unflinching clarity of the Homeric and Tolstoyan attitude there is far more than resignation. There is joy, the joy that burns in the "ancient glittering eyes" of the sages in Yeats's *Lapis Lazuli*. For they loved and revered the "humanness" of man; they delighted in the life of the body coolly perceived but ardently narrated. Moreover, it was their instinct to close the gap between spirit and gesture, to relate the hand to the sword, the keel to the brine, and the wheel-rim to the singing cobblestones. Both the Homer of the *Iliad* and Tolstoy saw action whole; the air vibrates around their personages and the force of their being electrifies insensate nature. Achilles' horses weep at his impending doom and the oak flowers to persuade Bolkonsky that his heart will live again. This consonance between man and the surrounding world extends even to the cups in which Nestor looks for wisdom when the sun is down and to the birch-leaves that glitter like a sudden riot of jewels after the storm has swept over Levin's estate. The barriers between mind and object, the ambiguities which metaphysicians discern in the very notion of reality and perception, impeded neither Homer nor Tolstoy. Life flooded in upon them like the sea.

And they rejoiced at it. When Simone Weil called the *Iliad* "The Poem of Force" and saw in it a commentary on the tragic futility of war, she was only partially right. The *Iliad* is far removed from the despairing nihilism of Euripides' *Trojan Women*. In the Homeric poem, war is valorous and ultimately ennobling. And even in the midst of carnage, life surges high. Around the burial mound of Patroklus the Greek chieftains wrestle, race, and throw the javelin in celebration of their strength and aliveness. Achilles knows that he is foredoomed, but "bright-cheeked Briseis" comes to him each night. War and mortality cry havoc in the Homeric and Tolstoyan worlds, but the centre holds: it is the affirmation that life is, of itself, a thing of beauty, that the works and days of men are worth recording, and that no catastrophe—not even the burning of Troy or of Moscow—is ultimate. For beyond the charred towers and beyond the battle rolls the wine-dark sea, and when Austerlitz is forgotten the harvest shall, in Pope's image, once again "embrown the slope."

This entire cosmology is gathered into Bosola's reminder to the Duchess of Malfi when she curses nature in agonized rebellion: "Look you, the stars shine still." These are terrible words, full of detachment and the harsh reckoning that the physical world contemplates our afflictions with impassiveness. But go beyond their cruel impact and they convey an assurance that life and star-light endure beyond the momentary chaos.

The Homer of the *Iliad* and Tolstoy are akin in yet another respect. Their image of reality is anthropomorphic; man is the measure and pivot of experience. Moreover, the atmosphere in which the personages of the *Iliad* and of Tolstoyan fiction are shown to us is profoundly humanistic and even secular. What matters is the kingdom of *this* world, here and now. In a sense, that is a paradox; on the plains of Troy mortal and divine affairs are incessantly confounded. But the very descent of the gods among men and their brazen involvement in all-too-human passions give the work its ironic overtones. Musset invoked this paradoxical attitude in his account of archaic Greece in the opening lines of *Rolla*:

Où tout était divin, jusq'aux douleurs humaines;
Où le monde adorait ce qu'il tue aujourd'hui;
Où quatre mille dieux n'avaient pas un athée. . . .

Precisely; with four thousand deities warring in men's quarrels, dallying with mortal women, and behaving in a manner apt to scandalize even liberal codes of morality, there was no need for atheism. Atheism arises in contrariety to the conception of a living and credible God; it is not a response to a partially comic mythology. In the *Iliad* divinity is quintessentially human. The gods are mortals magnified, and often magnified in a satiric vein. When wounded they howl louder than men, when they are enamoured their lusts are more consuming, when they flee before human spears their speed exceeds that of earthly chariots. But morally and intellectually the deities of the *Iliad* resemble giant brutes or malevolent children endowed with an excess of power. The actions of gods and goddesses in the Trojan War enhance the stature of man, for when odds are equal mortal heroes more than hold their own and when the scales are against them a Hector and an Achilles demonstrate that mortality has its own splendours. In lowering the gods to human values, the "first" Homer achieved not only an effect of comedy, though such an effect obviously contributes to the freshness and "fairy-tale" quality of the poem. Rather, he emphasized the excellence and dignity of heroic man. And this, above all, was his theme.

The pantheon in the *Odyssey* plays a subtler and more awesome role, and the *Aeneid* is an epic penetrated with a feeling for religious values and religious practice. But the *Iliad*, while accepting the mythology of the supernatural, treats it ironically and humanizes its material. The true centre of belief lies not on Olympus but in the recognition of *Moira,* of unyielding destiny which maintains through its apparently blind decimations an ultimate principle of justice and equilibrium. The religiosity of Agamemnon and Hector consists in an acceptance of fate, in a belief that certain impulses towards hospitality are sacred, in reverence for sanctified hours or hallowed places, and in a vague but potent realization that there are daemonic forces in the motion of the stars or the obstinacies of the wind. But beyond that, reality is immanent in the world of man and of his senses. I know of no better word to express the non-transcendence and ultimate physicality of the *Iliad*. No poem runs more strongly counter to the belief that "we are such stuff as dreams are made on."

And this is where it touches significantly on the art of Tolstoy. His also is an immanent realism, a world rooted in the veracity of our senses. From it God is strangely absent. . . . There lies behind the literary techniques of the *Iliad* and of Tolstoy a comparable belief in the centrality of the human personage and in the enduring beauty of the natural world. In the case of *War and Peace* the analogy is even more decisive; where the *Iliad* evokes the laws of *Moira,* Tolstoy expounds his philosophy of history. In both works the chaotic individuality of battle stands for the larger randomness in men's lives. And if we consider *War and Peace* as being, in a genuine sense, a heroic epic it is because in it, as in the *Iliad,* war is portrayed in its glitter and joyous ferocity as well as in its pathos. No measure of Tolstoyan pacifism can negate the ecstasy which young Rostov experiences as he charges down on the French stragglers. Finally, there is the fact that *War and Peace* tells of two nations, or rather of two worlds, engaged in mortal combat. This alone has led many of its readers, and led Tolstoy himself, to compare it with the *Iliad.*

But neither the martial theme nor the portrayal of national destinies should blind us to the fact that the philosophy of the novel is anti-heroic. There are moments in the book in which Tolstoy is emphatically preaching that war is wanton carnage and the result of vainglory and stupidity in high places. There are also times at which Tolstoy is concerned solely with seeking to discover "the real truth" in opposition to the alleged truths of official historians and mythographers. Neither the latent pacifism nor this concern with the evidence of history can be compared to the Homeric attitude.

War and Peace is most genuinely akin to the *Iliad* where its philosophy is least engaged, where, in Isaiah Berlin's terms, the fox is least busy trying to be a hedgehog. Actually, Tolstoy is closest to Homer in less manifold works, in *The Cossacks,* the *Tales from the Caucasus,* the sketches of the Crimean War and in the dread sobriety of *The Death of Ivan Ilych.*

But it cannot be emphasized too strongly that the affinity between the poet of the *Iliad* and the Russian novelist was one of temper and vision; there is no question here (or only in the minute instance) of a Tolstoyan imitation of Homer. Rather, it is that when Tolstoy turned to the Homeric epics in the original Greek, in his early forties, he must have felt wondrously at home.

Until now we have been concerned with generalities, with attempting to express along broad lines what is meant when the works of Tolstoy are qualified as "epic" and more precisely as Homeric. But if these generalities are to be of value they must be founded on matters of detail. The major effects and qualities which give the writings of Tolstoy their particular tone arise from a mosaic of technical practices. It is to some of these that I want to turn.

The stock epithet, the recurrent simile and repeated metaphor are a well-known characteristic of the Homeric style. Probably their origin was mnemonic; in oral poetry recurrent phrases assist the memory of both the singer and his audience; they act like interior echoes recalling to mind earlier incidents in the saga. But such tags as "rosy-fingered Dawn" or the "wine-dark sea," and the stock similes in which wrath is compared with the irruption of a savage lion into a herd of sheep or cattle, appeal to more than memory. They form a tapestry of normal life before which the heroic action unfolds. They create a backdrop of stable reality which gives the personages in the poem both their roundedness and their dimensions. For in evoking the pastoral mood or the daily routine of husbandry and fishing, Homer is saying that the Trojan War has not encroached upon the lives of all men. Elsewhere the dolphin leap and the shepherds drowse in the peace of the mountains. In the midst of carnage and the swift revolutions in human fortunes, these unchanging phrases proclaim that dawn will follow on the night, that the tides will surge inland when the location of Troy is a disputed memory, and that mountain lions will assail flocks when the last descendants of Nestor are in their dotage.

Homer juxtaposes the elements in his similes and metaphors to achieve a particular effect. The eye is borne away from an image of vivid and clamorous action and as the angle of vision widens, a scene of tranquil normality comes into focus. The picture of helmeted warriors scattering before Hector grows dim and now we see the grass bending before a storm. By their juxtaposition, both terms in the comparison are made subtler and more immediately a part of our consciousness. There are Flemish painters who handle this effect magnificently; think of Brueghel's Icarus plummeting into the calm sea as the ploughman walks his furrow in the foreground, or of the Passions and massacres painted against the background of an opulent and impassive landscape of walled cities, unruffled meadows, and fantastic alps. This "double awareness" is perhaps the essential device of pathos and serenity in Homer. It is the tragedy of the doomed heroes to recollect that other world of autumnal hunts, harvests, and domestic revels which they have left irremediably behind. But at the same time the clarity of their remembrance and the constant intrusion of a more stable plane of experience into the sound and fury of battle give the poem its strong repose.

There are moments in art (and they strike one as among the summits of imagination) in which this "double awareness" is itself made the theme of formal rendition. Consider the performance of an air from *Figaro* in the last act of Mozart's *Don Giovanni* or the allusion to *La Belle Dame sans Merci* in Keats's *Eve of St. Agnes*. There is such a moment, also, in Homer. It comes in Book VIII of the *Odyssey* when Demodocus sings a portion of the Trojan saga and Odysseus weeps. In this poignant episode the two planes of reality, the two terms in the metaphor, have been reversed. Troy is now the distant memory and Odysseus is once again in the normal world.

Like Homer, Tolstoy uses stock epithets and recurrent phrases both to assist our memory over the vast stretches of his narrative and to create a dual vision of experience. The massiveness and complexity of such works as *War and Peace* and *Anna Karenina*, together with the fact that they were published in successive fragments and over considerable lapses of time, created problems comparable to those of oral poetry. Throughout the opening sections of *War and Peace*, Tolstoy seeks to aid the reader to keep the multitude of characters distinctly in mind. Princess Mary is shown ever and again walking "with her heavy tread." Pierre is firmly associated with his spectacles. Even before Natasha has loomed large in our mind's eye, her lightness of step and vivacity of motion have been emphasized. As a modern poet has written of an altogether different young lady,

> There was such speed in her little body
> And such lightness in her footfall. . . .

The defect in Denisov's speech is introduced not only for purposes of verbal comedy but to distinguish him at once from a host of other military figures. Tolstoy, moreover, continues this practice in later stages of the novel. Napoleon's hands are the subject of constant allusion, and, as Merezhkovsky remarks, Vereshchagin's "thin neck" is noted five times during his brief but harrowing appearance.

It is an important element of Tolstoy's genius that he gradually complicates his portrayals without effacing the broad strokes. Although we come to know Natasha more closely than we do many a woman whom we meet in our own lives, the initial image, the vision of celerity and gracious impulse, remains with us. In fact, one finds it difficult to believe Tolstoy's statement in the First Epilogue that Natasha had "abandoned all her witchery" and grown "stouter and broader." Would we believe Homer if he told us that Odysseus had grown dull-witted?

More significantly, Tolstoy's use of imagery and metaphor seeks to relate and contrast the two planes of experience with which he is most concerned— the rural and the urban. We touch here on what may well be the centre of his art; for the distinction between life on the land and in the city is illustrative, to Tolstoy, of the primordial distinction between good and evil, between the unnatural and inhuman codes of urbanity on the one hand, and the golden age of pastoral life on the other. This fundamental dualism is one of the motives for the double- and triple-plot structure in the Tolstoyan novel and was ultimately systematized in Tolstoy's ethics. For if Tolstoy's thought is indebted to Socrates, Confucius, and Buddha, it is penetrated also with the pastoralism of Rousseau.

As in Homer, so we find in Tolstoy the juxtaposition of the immediate scene with a recollection of rural impressions. The unchanging and finally meaningful level of experience is set, in criticism and illumination, behind the momentary episode. There is a beautiful example of this technique in *Childhood, Boyhood and Youth*. The little boy has failed dismally in his attempts to dance the mazurka and retreats covered with humiliation:

> ". . . Oh, it is terrible! Now if mamma had been here, she would not have blushed for her Nicholas . . ." And my imagination carried me far away after that dear vision. I recalled the meadow in front of the house, the tall lime-trees in the garden, the clear pond over which the swallows circled, the azure sky with motionless transparent clouds, the fragrant heaps of new-mown hay, and many other peaceful and bright memories floated through my distracted imagination.

Thus the narrator is restored to a sense of harmony with what Henry James called, in *The Portrait of a Lady*, "the deeper rhythms of life."

Another instance, in which the technique and the metaphysics are no longer separable, occurs in that formidable sketch, *After the Ball*. (In Tolstoy's vocabulary, a ball has ambiguous overtones; it is both an occasion of grace and elegance and a symbol of consummate artificiality.) In this brief tale, the narrator is enraptured with love and cannot go to sleep after having danced all night. Seeking to release his joyous tension, he walks through the village at dawn: "It was regular carnival weather—foggy, and the road full of water-soaked snow just melting, and water dripping from the eaves." He comes, by chance, upon a horrible spectacle—a soldier being flogged through the ranks for his attempt to desert. The father of the young woman with whom the narrator is in love is presiding over the affair with pedantic savagery. At the ball, only an hour before, he was a model of decorum and affection. Which, now, is the natural man? And the fact that the flogging takes place under the open sky and amid the tranquil routine of an awakening village makes it all the more bestial.

There are two brilliant examples of Tolstoy's divided consciousness in Book IV of *War and Peace*. Chapter III describes the gala dinner held in honour of Bagration at the English Club in Moscow on March 3, 1806. Count Ilya Rostov is in charge of the lavish arrangements and has put aside the financial perplexities which are beginning to gather about his household. Tolstoy portrays, in glittering strokes, the scurrying servants, the members of the club, the young heroes back from their first war. He is enthralled by the artistic "chances" of the scene; he knows how fine a chronicler he is of high society. But the undercurrent of disapproval is manifest. The luxury, the waste, and the inequality of servant and master stick in Tolstoy's throat.

A footman scurries in with a frightened mien to announce that the guest of honour is arriving:

> Bells rang, the stewards rushed forward, and—like rye shaken together in a shovel—the guests who had been scattered about in different rooms came together and crowded in the large drawing-room by the door of the ball-room.

The simile acts in three ways: it gives a precise equivalent for the movement of the guests; it shocks the imagination into alertness because it derives from an area of experience so different from the one before our eyes; and it conveys a subtle but lucid commentary on the values of the entire episode. By identifying the elegant members of the English Club with grains of rye unceremoniously shaken together, Tolstoy reduces them to something automatic and faintly comical. The simile pierces at one stroke to the heart of their frivolity. Moreover, in its deliberate reversion to pastoral life, it contrasts the world of the English Club—the "false" social world—with that of the land and of the harvest cycle.

In chapter VI of the same Book we find Pierre on the verge of a new existence. He has fought his duel with Dolokhov and has no more illusions regarding his wife, the Countess Helen. He contemplates the degradation which has come about through his marriage and seeks the experience of grace that will transform his soul. Helen enters with "imperturbable calm" to mock at Pierre's jealousy. He looks at her "timidly over his spectacles" and tries to continue reading—

> like a hare surrounded by hounds who lays back her ears and continues to crouch motionless before her enemies. . . .

Again, we have here a comparison which moves us in various and conflicting ways. There is an immediate impression of pity, mingled, however, with amusement. Pictorially, Pierre with his spectacles on his nose and his ears laid back is both pathetic and comical. But in reference to the actual situation, the simile strikes one as ironic: it is Helen, despite her brazen advance, who is the much weaker personage. In a moment Pierre will explode to his full stature and nearly kill her with the marble top of a table. The hare will turn and rout the hunters. Once again, moreover, we have an image taken from rural life. It acts like a burst of wind and sunlight in a scene of stifling urban intrigue. But, at the same time, the picture of the crouching hare shatters the surface of social propriety and says clearly that what we are witnessing is a consequence of elementary lusts. High society hunts in packs.

The examples I have cited embody in miniature the major design in Tolstoy's creation. Two ways of life, two primordially disparate forms of experience are presented in contrast. This duality is not always a simple emblem for good and evil; in *War and Peace* urban life is shown in some of its most attractive colours and *The Power of Darkness* depicts the bestiality which can prevail on the land. But, in the main, Tolstoy saw experience morally and aesthetically divided. There is the life of the city with its social injustices, its artificial sexual conventions, its cruel display of wealth, and its power to alienate man from the essential patterns of physical vitality. On the other hand, there is life in the fields and forests with its alliance of mind and body, its acceptance of sexuality as hallowed and creative, and its instinct for the chain of being which relates the phases of the moon to the phases of conception and which associates the coming of the seed-time with the resurrection of the soul. As [George] Lukács observes, nature was to Tolstoy "the effective guarantee that beyond the world of conventionalities there exists a 'real' Life."[2]

This double vision characterized Tolstoy's thought and aesthetics from the start. His later doctrines, the evolution of his instinctive preferences into a coherent philosophic and social discipline, were not a result of sudden changes but rather a maturing of ideas first set forth in adolescence. The young landowner who attempted to improve the lot of his serfs in 1847 and who founded a school for their children in 1849 was the same Tolstoy who conceived "the immense idea" of a rational and fundamentalist Christianity in 1855 and who finally abandoned the imperfections of worldly life and fled from his home in October of 1910. There was no brusque conversion, no sudden renunciation of art in favour of the higher good. As a very young man, Tolstoy knelt and wept before a prostitute and noted in his diaries that the way of the world was the way of damnation. This conviction burned in him always, and the relentless energy of his literary works reflects the fact that each was a victory of his poetic genius over the gnawing belief that it profits a man nothing to gain the high places of artistic renown if he lose his own soul. Even in his most imaginative achievements, Tolstoy reveals the inner struggle and gives it form in an ever recurrent theme—the passage from the city to the land, from moral myopia to self-discovery and salvation.

The most articulate version of this theme is the departure of the hero or principal personage from St. Petersburg and Moscow towards his estates or some remote province of Russia. Both Tolstoy and Dostoevsky experienced in their personal lives this symbolic departure, Tolstoy when he left St. Petersburg for the Caucasus in April 1851, Dostoevsky when he was escorted out of the city in irons on Christmas night 1849 to begin the terrible journey to Omsk and penal servitude. One would have supposed that there could be few moments more charged with anguish. But on the contrary:

> My heart beat with a peculiar flutter, and that numbed its pain. Still, the fresh air was reviving in its effect, and, since it is usual before all new experiences to be aware of a curious vivacity and eagerness, so I was at bottom quite tranquil. I looked attentively at all the festively-lit houses of Petersburg, and said good-bye to each. They drove us past your abode, and at Krayevsky's the windows were brilliantly lit. You had told me that he was giving a Christmas party and tree, and that your children were going to it, with Emilie Fyodorovna; I did feel dreadfully sad as we passed that house. . . . After the eight months' captivity, sixty versts in a sledge gave us appetites of which, even today, I think with pleasure. I was in a good temper.[3]

It is an extraordinary reminiscence. In atrocious personal circumstances, at the parting of the ways between ordinary life, family affections, and physical comfort on the one hand and probable death after long degradation on the other, Dostoevsky—like Raskolnikov under similar circumstances—experiences a sense of physical liberation. The sounds of revelry by night fade behind him and he seems to possess already some insight into the resurrection which lies beyond the term in purgatory. Even where the journey leads toward the house of the dead or, as in the case of Bezukhov in *War and Peace,* to probable execution before a French firing squad, the mere fact of transition from the city to the open land brings with it an element of joy.

Tolstoy may have been exploring this theme as early as 1852 when he worked on a translation of Sterne's *Sentimental Journey.* But it is in *The Cossacks,* sketched later the same year, that Tolstoy fully realized and mastered a situation which was to become a recurrent parable of his philosophy. After a night of drunken farewells, Olenin sets out for military service against the warring tribes in the distant Caucasus. What he leaves behind is unpaid gambling debts and the stale memories of time wasted in the idle pleasures of high society. Though the night is cold and full of snow,

> The departing man felt warm, even hot, in his fur coat. He sat down in the bed of the sleigh and stretched himself; and the shaggy stage-horses flew from one dark street into another, past houses he had never seen. It appeared to Olenin that only those who departed travelled through these streets. Around him it was dark, speechless, gloomy, and his soul was full of recollections, love, regrets, and of pleasurable tears that choked him.

But soon he is out of the city, gazing at the snow-covered fields and rejoicing. All the mundane concerns which have beset his mind fade away into insignificance. "The farther Olenin travelled from the centre of Russia, the more distant his memories seemed to him; and the nearer he approached the Caucasus, the happier he felt." At last he comes to the mountains, "with their delicate contours and the fantastic and sharply defined outline of their summits, against the distant sky." His new life has begun.

In *War and Peace,* Pierre makes premature departures—such as when he abandons the false existence of the wealthy young aristocrat for the equally false haven of Freemasonry. His purgatorial journey really begins when he is led from the charred ruins of Moscow with other prisoners and sets out on the cruel march across the frozen plains. Like Dostoevsky, Pierre has survived the shock of near-execution and sudden reprieve. But "the mainspring of his life" has been wrenched out and "his faith in the right ordering of the universe, in humanity, in his own soul and in God, had been destroyed." A few moments later, however, he meets with Platon Karataev, the "natural man." Karataev offers him a baked potato. It is a trivial gesture, easily intended; but through it is initiated Pierre's pilgrimage and his sufferance of grace. As Tolstoy emphasizes, the strength of Karataev, his acquiescence in life even where it seems most destructive, derives from the fact that, having let his beard grow (a symbol laden with Scriptural associations), "he seemed to have thrown off all that had been forced upon him—everything military and alien to himself—and had returned to his former peasant habits." So he becomes to Pierre an "eternal personification of the spirit of simplicity and truth," a new Virgil conducting him out of the inferno of the burnt city.

Tolstoy suggests that the great fire has broken down the barriers between Moscow and the open country. Pierre sees "the hoar frost on the dusty grass, the Sparrow Hills, and the wooded banks above the winding river vanishing in the purple distance"; he hears the noise of the crows and he feels "a new joy and strength in life such as he had never before known." Moreover, this feeling grows in intensity as the physical hardships of his position increase. As Natasha observes subsequently, he emerges from captivity as from "a moral bath." Pierre is cleansed of his former vices and has discovered the essential Tolstoyan dogma: "While there is life there is happiness."

The First Epilogue of *War and Peace* confirms this equation of life in the country with "the good life." It is a light-hearted stroke of irony that, in one of our last glimpses of Bald Hills, we should see the Countess Mary's children pretending that they are "going to Moscow" in a carriage made of chairs.

In *Anna Karenina* the contrast between the city and the land is, quite obviously, the axis around which the moral and technical structure of the novel revolves. The whole of Levin's salvation is prefigured in his arrival in the country after the unsuccessful proposal to Kitty:

> But when he got out at his own station when he saw his one-eyed coachman, Ignat, with the collar of his coat turned up; when, in the dim light reflected by the station fires, he saw his own sledge, his own horses with their tails tied up; in their harness trimmed with rings and tassels; when the coachman Ignat, as he put in his luggage, told him the village news, that the contractor had arrived, and that Pava had calved,—he felt that little by little the confusion was clearing up, and the shame and self-dissatisfaction were passing away.

On the land even the relations between Anna and Vronsky, which are already haunted with dissolution, take on an idyllic and sanctified quality. No novel (unless it be Lawrence's *White Peacock*) brings language closer to the sensuous actualities of farm life, to the sweet smell of a cow shed on frosty nights or the rustle of the fox through the high grass.

When Tolstoy came to write *Resurrection,* the teacher and prophet in him did violence to the artist. The sense of equilibrium and design which had previously controlled his invention was sacrificed to the urgencies of rhetoric.

In this novel the juxtaposition of two ways of life and the theme of the pilgrimage from falsehood to salvation are set forth with the nakedness of a tract. And yet, *Resurrection* marks the ultimate realization of motifs which Tolstoy had announced in his very first stories. Nekhlioudov is the Prince Nekhlioudov of the early unfinished *Morning of a Landed Proprietor*. Between the two works lie thirty-seven years of thought and creation; but the fragment already contains, in recognizable outline, many of the elements of the last novel. Nekhlioudov is also the protagonist of a strange short story, *Lucerne*, which Tolstoy wrote in 1857. Indeed, this character appears to have served the novelist as a kind of self-portrait whose traits he could alter as his own experience deepened.

In *Resurrection,* moreover, the return to the land, as the physical correlative to the rebirth of the soul, is beautifully rendered. Before following Maslova to Siberia, Nekhlioudov resolves to visit his domains and sell the estate to the peasants. His wearied senses spring to life; he sees himself once more as he was before his "fall." The sun glimmers on the river, the colt nuzzles, and the pastoral scene enforces on Nekhlioudov the full realization that the morality of urban life is founded on injustice. For in the Tolstoyan dialectic, rural life heals the spirit of man not only through its tranquil beauties but also in that it opens his eyes to the frivolity and exploitations inherent in a class society. This emerges clearly from the drafts for *Resurrection*:

> In town we do not fully understand why the tailor, the coachman, the baker work for us, but in the country we see very plainly why the share-croppers work in their green house and gardens, why they bring in the wheat and thresh it and abandon to the landowner half the produce of their labour.

The land is the awakener of the Tolstoyan hero as well as his reward.

I have dwelt on this topic at some length, but it would be difficult to exaggerate its importance towards an understanding of Tolstoy and of our general theme. The contrast between urban and rural pervades both the major groupings and designs in Tolstoy's novels and the particular resources of his style. Moreover, it is the element which binds into essential unity the literary, the moralistic, and the religious aspects of Tolstoy's genius. The dilemmas which first beset Nekhlioudov in 1852 perplex Prince Andrew, Pierre, Levin, Ivan Ilych, and the narrator of the *Kreutzer Sonata.* The question, which Tolstoy used as the title for one of his tracts, is always the same: *What Then Must We Do?* What one can say is that in the end the portrait overcame the painter and seized upon his soul; Nekhlioudov abandoned his worldly possessions and set out on a final pilgrimage in the guise of Tolstoy.

The polarity of city and land is one of the main aspects of any comparison between Tolstoy and Dostoevsky. The motif of departure toward salvation was common to the lives and imaginings of both men, and *Resurrection* is, in many respects, an epilogue to *Crime and Punishment.* But in Dostoevsky we do not actually see the promised land (except for a momentary, shadowy glimpse of Raskolnikov's Siberia). The Dostoevskyan inferno is the *Grosstadt,* the modern metropolis, and more specifically the Petersburg of the "white nights." There are purgatorial departures, but the reconciliation and grace which Tolstoy's protagonists find on the land, the "great sinners" of Dostoevsky will find only in the Kingdom of God. And to Dostoevsky—in utter contrariety to Tolstoy—that Kingdom is not, and cannot be, of this world. It is in this context that one must weigh the often noticed fact that Dostoevsky, who excels in describing city life, nearly never attempts to describe a rural landscape or the open country.

Finally, the twofold plane of experience in the Tolstoyan novel is one of the traits which make a comparison between Homer and Tolstoy possible and illuminating. The point of view in the *Iliad* and the *Odyssey* (the latter can now be pertinently referred to) arises from an association of *bas-relief* with deep perspective. As Erich Auerbach noted in *Mimesis*, the contemporaneity of events in the Homeric narrative gives an impression of "flatness." But behind the surface, and shimmering through it, is the great vista of the marine and pastoral world. It is from this background that the Homeric poems derive their power of suggesting depth and pathos. Only thus, I think, can one understand why certain scenes in Homer and Tolstoy are so uncannily alike in composition and effect. Thomas Mann considered the chapters which tell of Levin mowing with his peasants as archetypal of Tolstoy's philosophy and technique. So they are. Many strands are interwoven: Levin's triumphant return to his own kind of life, his unspoken concord with the land and those who till it, the test of his bodily strength against that of the peasants, the physical exhaustion which revitalizes the mind and which orders past experience in the cleansed and forgiving memory. All this is, in Mann's phrase, *echt tolstoïsch*. But we find a close parallel in Book XVIII of the *Odyssey*. Odysseus, in beggar's rags, sits unrecognized at his own hearth, scorned by Penelope's serving women and mocked by Eurymachus. He replies (in T. E. Lawrence's translation):

> Ah, Eurymachus, if only there might be a working match just between us two during the late springtide when the days are long: in a hay meadow, perhaps; me with a well-curved scythe and you with one like mine; our match to last all day, foodless, and far into the gloaming, with grass yet to spare! Or draught oxen of the finest, great flaming beasts lusty with feed, well matched in age and pulling-power, and fresh: also a four-team field of loam that turns cleanly from the coulter. Then should you see what a long straight furrow I would drive.

The words are uttered in a context of grief and sordid spoliation and Odysseus is evoking memories of the time before he set out for Troy, twenty years earlier. But their poignancy springs also from our knowledge that the suitors shall never again mow in the gloaming.

Set the two passages side by side; compare their tonality and the world image they convey. You may not find a third to match them. From such comparison derives the force of the idea that *War and Peace* and *Anna Karenina* can, in some crucial manner, be qualified as Homeric.

It is tempting to speculate whether the motif of a journey towards material or spiritual resurrection and the sense of two worlds which is so strongly marked in Tolstoy are not typical elements of epic poetry as such. This question raises fascinating and difficult issues. There are voyages, in the actual and allegoric sense, in the *Odyssey,* the *Aeneid,* and the *Divine Comedy.* In many of the major epics, most evidently in *Paradise Lost* and *Paradise Regained,* we find the same theme of the blessed realm, of the pastoral vision or the golden Atlantis. Amid such variety of instance one can hardly generalize. But something of this idea of the voyage and the divided world lies behind the fact that it should be *Don Quixote, Pilgrim's Progress,* and *Moby Dick* to which the mind turns most readily when we think of the notion of "epic novels."

NOTES

1. Quoted in D. S. Merezhkovsky, *Tolstoi as Man and Artist, with an Essay on Dostoievski* (London, 1902).
2. George Lukács, *Die Theorie des Romans* (Berlin, 1920).
3. Dostoevsky to his brother, Michael, February 22, 1854 (*Letters of Fyodor Michailovitch Dostoevsky;* tr. by E. C. Mayne [London, 1914]).

Roy Harvey Pearce

TOWARD AN AMERICAN EPIC

I

One of the most arresting yet practically unnoticed phenomena in the history of our poetry is the regularity with which there occurs an attempt to write nothing less than an American epic. The regularity is of an intensity such as to indicate a virtual compulsion to make such a poem—which is to say, to create such a form. Indeed, one can now say that this phenomenon is of a much more vital significance for the history of our national imagination than is that comparable phenomenon, the urge to create the great American novel. This is so because in order to do it right, to invent an autochthonous American epic, or—to say the same thing—a genuinely American analogue of the traditional epic, the poet would have to break radically with the very tradition which he would be trying to carry on and reinvigorate. He would indeed have, in Pound's phrase, to make it new. Confronted with a society which supplied him with no authentically American epic material, he would yet have to find that material, to transubstantiate what his society gave him so that he could transform it. And this, one concludes, is exactly what has happened—or, perhaps to put it more accurately—what has been intended to happen.

There is no point, at this stage, in trying to recite the history of the American epic; nor of trying to indicate precisely the limits of its achievement. In the present state of our knowledge, it would seem unlikely that such a history could be written, or if such evaluations could be made. Nonetheless, it is possible to establish the dialectic of that history and to begin to assess its significance for the more general history of our aspiration toward not only an American epic but an American poetry. I mean to make such an attempt here—to offer what amounts to a theory of the American epic and a summation of the sort of poetics it has striven so hard, so desperately, to put into action. I shall take as my exemplars three poems—*The Columbiad, Song of Myself,* and the *Cantos.*

"Toward an American Epic" by Roy Harvey Pearce. From *The Hudson Review* 13: 362–77 (1959). Reprinted by permission of *The Hudson Review*. A greatly revised and expanded version appears in Roy Harvey Pearce, *The Continuity of American Poetry* (Princeton, 1961), p.59–136.

These are heroic poems, but of a curious sort. For, instead of celebrating, affirming, and memorializing a hero, as the poet of traditional epic had done, the poet of the American epic (or, quite strictly speaking, proto-epic) tried and continues to try to create a hero. And his means to that creation was, and remains, the very act of the poem itself.

Barlow's *Columbiad* (1807), so dreary in what it is and so exciting in what it is not, is our first instance—and almost a negative one. *Almost.* For if Barlow could not write an adequate American epic, he could at least desiderate one—indeed, desiderate (and how shocked he would have been to learn this!) poems like *Song of Myself* and the *Cantos*.

As we all know, *The Columbiad* is an enlarged and improved version of Barlow's earlier *Vision of Columbus* (1787). The enlargements were by way of clarifying and articulating the idea of democratic order and progress which totally suffuses the poem. As it stands, the poem, so Barlow tells us in his Preface, is meant to celebrate the establishment of democratic order, inculcate its working in those who participate in it, and project its glorious possibilities into the future. Its aim, Barlow says, is "altogether of a moral and political nature." Specifically, he insists that his moral object far supersedes his poetical object. Only thus can he write the true modern epic, uncluttered with the base and false values of the traditional epic, those of *The Iliad* for example. His problem, hence, is to find a heroic center for democratic, progressivist values; and inevitably he fails utterly to do so. The poem begins epically ("I sing the Mariner who first unfurl'd/ An eastern banner o'er the western world/ And taught mankind where future empires lay . . ."). But in fact it is not Columbus's actions which are sung, but rather the inexorable progress of free institutions in the Americas as Columbus is given to envision them. To Columbus, despairing in prison, comes Hesper, the guardian Genius of the western continent, who takes him to a mount of vision. And the poem unfolds in a series of visions in which Columbus cannot be made to take part. Rather, he is tutored by his vision, as a person assuaged by an assurance that all will go off on schedule. He looks on at the origin of the new world, its native populations, Inca heroics, English colonization, the American Revolution—he looks on at all these and, now understanding something of the history and meaning of a national culture, is somehow changed. The vision is meant to do its work on him, as later in *Song of Myself* and the *Cantos,* the vision, the lived-through quality of the poetic experience, is meant to do its work on us. Columbus thus figures the reader, with whom Barlow makes him share his vision, as later Whitman and Pound themselves figure the reader, on whom they make their visions do their work. But, of course—and the contrast with Whitman and Pound makes it all the more obvious—Barlow is not poet enough to give his poetic rendering of Columbus's vision the power to work in this way. The quality of that vision is not substantial enough to make us accept Barlow's Columbus as a hero, as we can accept as heroes—even if we hate to—Whitman and Pound, or the *personae* who speak to us in *Song of Myself* and the *Cantos*. What is unfolded in the twelve books of *The Columbiad* are tiresome, insistent, intemperate, homogenized descriptions of places, people, and events—all of value only as they aspire (in *The Columbiad,* even the places are made to aspire) toward the reason, freedom, and joy of a new society in a new world. The poem, if we look at it closely enough, would have us see how history, as informing milieu and ambiance, literally creates its protagonists—or what is the same thing, creates the values which, as they are embodied by the protagonists of history, give them their worth.

To say this is indeed to look very closely at the poem. I do so here, and so briefly, because I want to remark those implications of Barlow's theory and practice which point the epic away from its traditional mode and function. If it is undoubtedly true that Barlow could write neither a traditional epic nor an adequate American equivalent of that epic, nonetheless he seems, in the act of writing a poem which fails to do what he wanted it to do, to have had a sense of one of the preconditions of the sort of poem which his hero-less culture needed. This precondition was a new poetics, deriving from a new use of imaginative language, this deriving in turn from a new language itself. Barlow's conception is two or three times removed from that of a poetics which would make the new epic immediately possible; but it is nonetheless there, however vaguely, however subliminally—a product, one assumes, of the very logic of his conception of the relation between the American poet and his new world. It occurs as part of Columbus's utopian vision in Book X:

> *At this blest period, when the total race*
> *Shall speak one language and all truths embrace*
> *Instruction clear a speedier course shall find,*
> *And open earlier on the infant mind,*
> *No foreign terms shall crowd with barbarous rules*
> *The dull unmeaning pageantry of schools;*
> *Nor dark authorities nor names unknown*
> *Fill the learnt head with ignorance not its own;*
> *But wisdom's eye with beams unclouded shine,*
> *And simplest rules her native charms define;*
> *One living language, one unborrow'd dress*
> *Her boldest flights with fullest force express;*
> *Triumphant virtue, in the garb of truth*
> *Win[s] a pure passage to the heart of youth....*

This is, on the one hand, an utterly simplistic view of one world as utopia. But it is, in the light of what came after it in the history of American poetry, something more: a description of the sufficient and necessary qualities of a poetic language which, at once carrying a vision like Columbus's and working on its reader as the vision is intended to have worked on him, will have given him a sense of certitude and authenticity, of being fully and creatively at one with his culture, of being defined as a person. This is indeed precisely how Columbus is said to feel at the very end of *The Columbiad*, and presumably how the reader is supposed to feel. It is beyond Barlow's abilities to bring about such a condition, of course. To have done so he would have to have created a radically new kind of epic—an epic which, in its very directness and overwhelming clarity, would have not subordinated poetic to moral purpose but would have made them one; one in which language, transubstantiating and transforming history and milieu, would, in its pure passage to men's hearts, have redefined Columbus's sense of himself and his world, and through him that of Barlow's readers; one which, lacking a traditional hero on which to center, would create him and make the reader participate in that creation. Barlow failed utterly, as we have always known. But we have not known how, in his very failure, he hit upon and tried to understand the necessary and sufficient conditions of an authentic and valid American epic.

II

It is as exemplars of that epic, with all its aspirations, commitments, compulsions, and excesses, that we must finally consider *Song of Myself* and the *Cantos*.

Consider the vexing problem of the form of *Song of Myself*. We have regularly made it out to have been more than it is, or have damned it for not having been so. But if only we consider it in the light of its status as a further stage in the development of that epic which Barlow so painfully desiderated, we can accept the poem for what it is and see how it breaks with all traditional canons of form, just so that it can do the job that an American epic would perforce have to do. It is as if Barlow's Columbus were allowed to have a vision which would demonstrably be his and his alone, not one which had been given to him; as though the structure of that vision were demonstrably the structure of his own native perceptions and his wilful resolution of them into meaning and significance. What the Whitman of *Song of Myself* (he is his own Columbus) does is to survey his whole world, his milieu and his ambiance—but not according to any necessary order and chronology. He looks when he wills and interprets as he wills. There is a dialectic here, but not a form. It is essential to the meaning of the poem that the dialectic be unique; for the dialectic derives from the very motion of the protagonist's sensibility. What is relatively stable and fixed, because it has no end and no beginning, is the world of which that sensibility becomes conscious, the world in and through which that sensibility would discover and define itself. The end of *Song of Myself*, the moral object which synchronizes with its poetic object, is to know that the world is there, and in the knowing, to know itself as there; in effect, through such a transaction to create itself and the possibility for readers to create themselves.

This is, quite briefly, how *Song of Myself* looks when, in gross outline, we trace that dialectic set by the rhythm of the sensibility:

1–5: The initial insight into the creative nature of the self and the initiating of creative power which follows spontaneously upon that insight.

6–16: Recognition of the relation of the self to its world, and a seeking after the creative metamorphosis which follow spontaneously upon that recognition.

17–25: The roles of the self in and through its world; a return to the matter of 1–5, but with this difference—that self-knowledge now exists formally, a product not of sheer inwardness as in 1–5 but of a spontaneously formalized relation between the self and its world. Now the poet is not just a force, but a force defined in terms of its world; now he is fully a person and can even name himself: "Walt Whitman, a kosmos, of Manhattan the son."

26–52: The poet (as person) fully at home in his newly defined world, fully sure of himself and his "procreant urge." He no longer needs to seek his world (as in 6–16); he can openly and lovingly address it as he creates and controls it and as he is created and controlled by it. He is thus a religion, God-like in himself. "I am an acme of things accomplish'd, and I am encloser of things to be."

And this is, quite briefly, how the rhythm of sensibility moves in what we have marked out as the first stage of the poem's total dialectic, in sections 1–5: *Song of Myself* begins epically, but immediately (so sharply in contrast to the traditional epic that one is shocked into awareness of the fact that Whitman has found the tradition inadequate and so has rejected it) turns inward, demanding that its readers do likewise:

> *I celebrate myself, and sing myself,*
> *And what I assume you shall assume,*
> *For every atom belonging to me as good belongs to you.* (1)

The whole first section establishes the dominance of the self when for the first time it is overpoweringly discovered; the language of the section is composed in such a way as to register the overpower. For example, all verbs in the section apply only to the self and its attributes. At the end Whitman writes:

> *Creeds and schools in abeyance,*
> *Retiring back awhile sufficed at what they are, but never forgotten,*
> *I harbor for good or bad, I permit to speak at every hazard,*
> *Nature without check with original energy.*

In this stanza the absence of verbs for the items named in the first and last lines absolutely subordinates them to the newly (or re-) discovered self. What follows in the next sections is a retailing of a complete absorption into the self ("I am mad to be in contact with me" [2]) and a sense that the self possesses "the origin of all poems"; an elucidation of the timeless "Urge and urge and urge,/ Always the procreant urge of the world" (3); a recognition of its difference from other souls ("But they are not the Me myself" [4]); and the final account of how the soul, turning inward upon itself, discovers its true nature:

> *I mind how once we lay such a transparent summer morning,*
> *How you settled your head athwart my hips and gently turn'd over upon me,*
> *And parted the shirt from my bosom-bone, and plunged your tongue to my*
> *   bare-stript heart,*
> *And reach'd till you felt my beard, and reach'd till you held my feet.* (5)

The passage of parallelisms which follows takes its energy from this apocalyptic moment. The items that are named are chaotically scattered in their natural habitat; but the force of the parallelisms is to unify and interrelate them by means of the newly initiated powers of the creative self:

> *Swiftly arose and spread around me the peace and knowledge that pass all the*
> *   argument of the earth,*
> *And I know that the hand of God is the promise of my own,*
> *And I know that the spirit of God is the brother of my own,*
> *And that all the men ever born are also my brothers, and the women my sisters*
> *   and lovers,*

And that a kelson of the creation is love,
And that limitless are leaves stiff or drooping in the fields,
And brown ants in the little wells beneath them,
And mossy scabs of the worm fence, heap'd stones, elder, mullein and poke weed.

Thus, at the very end of this first phase of the discovery, creation, and transubstantiation of the sensibility, the self begins to turn outward toward its world and to unite with it in a heroic transformation. There begins a unique metamorphosis—unique because through its transformation, the self best discovers what it is as self. The rest of *Song of Myself* projects the sensibility in the process of making that discovery.

I venture this quite foreshortened view of the dialectic of *Song of Myself* and of the rhythm of its first phase, because I want to point out just how the poem seems to be intended to do its job. What is particularly important in this connection is that the poet's heroic quality has come about precisely by virtue of the fact that he has made the sort of poem that he has made—one in which he at once creates and controls his world (including his readers) and is created and controlled by it (including his readers). All that is demanded of the readers is that they yield to the poem, as has the world. This done, the "procreant urge," as Whitman calls the drive towards creativity, will be spontaneously released and the readers will be on their way to their own personal, individuated transformations, to their own achievement of heroic status. Thus, we may say, Whitman worked toward what Pound has called a new Paideuma—"a tangle or complex of unrooted ideas": one entirely of process, of guiding, strengthening, energizing, and redefining the sensible self by putting it into direct contact with the world, only in which it would be free, creative, and whole—a self proper to the American democrat. Such a poetry would, to say it again, not memorialize a hero but rather create one.

Song of Myself does make for a new kind of heroic poetry. In it, the hero comes into being, as, releasing the full creative force of the self, he energizes the *realia* of his world and takes from them his name, his office, and his phenomenal qualities. Unlike Barlow's Columbus, he is not given a vision; he makes one—and making it, he becomes it. Part of his heroic act entails his freeing himself from what he has learned is the false hierarchical heroism of traditional societies. The dialectic of *Song of Myself* articulates this act. And as the act is dynamically invertebrate, so is the dialectic. This new heroic poem, this new epic, is one of ordering, not of order; of creation, not confirmation; of energizing, not memorializing. When in 1872 Whitman wrote *Democratic Vistas* and let the trajectory of *Song of Myself* and what followed it carry him forward toward his utopia, he concluded:

> It must still be reiterated . . . that all else in the contributions of nation or age, through its policies, materials, heroic personalities, military eclat &c., remains crude, and defers, in any close and thorough-going estimate, until vitalized by a national, original archetype in literature. They only put the nation in form, finally tell anything—prove, complete anything—perpetrate anything.

Song of Myself, then, as it is the sort of poem which Barlow's Columbus might have envisioned, is such a national, original archetype.

III

The third of my exemplars of the American epic is the *Cantos* of Ezra Pound. Pound, of course, is the ideal type of an anti-Whitmanian poet. Yet this very opposition is quite meaningful, as oppositions in a dialectical series tend inevitably to be. For the question of Whitman has always troubled Pound. Recently we have been told a good deal about Pound's varying appraisals of Whitman: how he seems finally to have come to understand Whitman as a nineteenth-century culture hero who, in Pound's words, went "bail for the nation." But the understanding goes even deeper than that; for in *Canto 82* (one of the Pisan series) Pound finally goes so far as to identify himself with Whitman—both poets, in his view, seeking to understand the deep mystery of birth, death, regeneration as it totally informs man's lonely fate on this earth. It is, however, an identification which we should be careful to limit and define. Pound feels that he too is making the sort of cosmically penetrating poem toward which Whitman aspired; moreover he too feels that he is a culture hero for modern man and that his poem, when read properly, will exhibit to his readers a sense of the possibility for heroic action in our time and thus will redefine, reintegrate and recreate them as total human beings. But his poetics are almost diametrically opposed to Whitman's.

The crux of the opposition lies in two conceptions of style; which is to say, two conceptions of how poetry acts, hence two poetics. This can be illustrated briefly. Whitman wrote in the 1855 preface to *Leaves of Grass:*

> The greatest poet has less a marked style and is more the channel of thoughts and things without increase or diminution, and is the free channel of himself. He swears to his art, I will not be meddlesome, I will not have in my writing any elegance or effect or originality to stand in the way between me and the rest like curtains . . . [my elision]. You shall stand by my side and look in the mirror with me.

And Pound wrote in his *Guide to Kulchur* (1938):

> STYLE, the attainment of a style consists of so knowing words that one will communicate the various parts of what one says with the various degrees and weights of importance which one wishes.

It is, in essence, for Pound, a matter of self-expression and decorum at all costs. Pound's belief in decorum ("knowing words") of this sort, indeed, is at bottom the belief which makes possible his conception of the American epic: one in which degrees and weights are so finely managed that communication is exact and exacting knowledge. The end—its fusion of the artistic and the moral object—of the Poundian epic is such knowledge and insight—the new Paideuma which will make the new man. One thing—and I cannot help but think that, in spite of Pound's marvellous internationalism, it is an American thing—Pound has in common with Whitman: He would create, not confirm, the hero of his epic.

And how is he to do so? Which is to ask: What are the *Cantos?* What would they do? How would they do it? Toward the middle of *Canto 85,* these words suddenly leap off the page:

> *No classics,*
>   *No American history,*
>   *no centre, no general root,*
> *No* prezzo giusto *as core.*

The *Cantos* are an attempt to remedy this radical defect. They supply, however, not a single center but a series—a constellation of exemplars of *prezzo giusto* and its opposites by means of which the center, and the reader who will seek it, may be defined. The *Cantos* consist of a complex of centers, the perception of which is to be ordered by the absolutely decorous management of "degrees and weights of importance." They may be perceived thus because they are intended to exist as ideograms, as Pound now puts it; units of meaning so clearly articulated that they virtually dispense with abstract, discursive effects. Whereas in Whitman, it was the rhythm of the sensibility which was procreantly to urge the reader toward the wonders of the visible world, in Pound it is the commanding power of the ideograms (or images, or vortexes) which is to define the reader's world and so define the reader himself.

There are, to take a quite brief example, these lines from that section of *Canto 82* to which I have already alluded: Pound has had occasion to speak of the "ignorance of locality," modern man's inability to know himself in relation to the culture in which he lives. He speaks of ancient Greece, where things were better. Then:

> *Till forty years since, Reithmuller indignant:*
> *"Fvy! in Tdaenmarck efen dh' beasantz gnow him,"*
>   *meaning Whitman, exotic, still suspect*
> *four miles from Camden*
>   *"O troubled reflection*
>   *"O Throat, O throbbing heart"*
> *How drawn, O GEA TERRA,*
>   *what draws as thou drawest*
>   *till one sink into thee by an arm's width*
>   *embracing thee. Drawest,*
>   *truly thou drawest.*
> *Wisdom lies next thee,*
>   *simple, past metaphor.*
> *Where I lie let the thyme rise*
>   *and basilicum*
>   *let the herbs rise in April abundant*
> *By Ferrara was buried naked, fu Nicolo*
>   *e di qua di la del Po,*
>
> *wind: ἐμὸν τὸν ἄνδρα*
> *lie into earth to the breast bone, to the left shoulder*
>   *Kipling suspected it*
>   *to the height of ten inches or over*
> *man, earth: two halves of the tally. . . .*

The work of the Pound exegetes lets us begin to see what this passage comes to. Riethmuller (Pound misspells the name) was a teacher of Pound's at the University of Pennsylvania and the author of a study of "Whitman and the

Germans." Recalling his teacher's oral statement, Pound then recalls and echoes "Out of the Cradle." He moves to an address to Gea Terra, and so to a definition of his own situation through that of Whitman and the protagonists of his poem. This is the wisdom "past metaphor." And our sense of that wisdom is further sharpened by the image of the herbs rising out of the grave, of the account of the burial place of Nicolo (one of Pound's culture-bearing Renaissance heroes); of the Greek "my man"—a fragmentary quotation from the second idyll of Theocritus in which a woman asks the goddess of the moon to keep her lover faithful; of the (as yet not totally understood) reference to Kipling on burial; and of the use of the Whitmanian "tally" to indicate the ritualistic significance of "man, earth." The passage goes on in this vein, drawing from widely scattered sources, to force us into a realization of the ultimate loneliness—separated like a lover from his lost or dead beloved—of the role of the hero as artist in our culture. It is not so much that Pound speaks, but that he would make his images, quotations, and citations speak—speak so sharply, infra-linguistically, as to define the sensibility of him who makes and/or reads the *Cantos*.

What emerges (or is intended to emerge) from the *Cantos* is a sense of absolute propaedeutic control; the assemblage of centers that is the poem is for Pound the only proper Paideuma. It is intended to constitute a rediscovery, a making new, of the noblest, truest, and surest elements in culture; a rediscovery so powerful in its stylistic precision that it will irresistibly reconstitute the sensibility (and thus the political and economic morality) of him who would give himself over to reading it—someone, in the end, akin to the "cosmic man" whom Pound's friend Wyndham Lewis envisaged for America at the end of the forties. Pound once said of the *Cantos:* "They are openly volitionist, establishing, I think clearly, the effect of the factive personality. . . ." In Pound's hands, the American epic becomes thus openly volitionist and entirely factive—willing and making, through its collocation of ideogrammic centers, a new Paideuma for a new world.

We cannot yet say precisely what the structural principle of the *Cantos* is. Pound has not made up his mind. We can observe, quite briefly (with D. S. Carne-Ross, whose observances I echo here), that there are a series of thematic continuities in the poem: sea-voyages of Odysseus to hell, of Niccolo of Este to the Holy Land, of the Carthaginian Hanno along the west coast of Africa. We can observe, moreover, a reiterated concern with the problem of the artist in society. And we can trace out episodes in early national American history, in that of Renaissance Italy, and of Confucian China. And there are Pound's factive, volitionist heroes, Odysseus, Confucius, Sigismundo, Jefferson, John Adams, and the poet himself—each of whom is marked by a quality of awareness which is transubstantiated by his acts into the monuments of world culture. In all there is the concern to see how the great acts of world history have been acts of creation, not destruction; how such acts have resulted from a resistance to the abstractive, usurous demands which Pound believes the world has put on his heroes. Yet it is not possible to put down even briefly the poem's dialectic; for it has none. That is, it has no linear, composed, structured form; no rhythmic periodicities; rather it consists of decorously managed, ideogrammically set down instants of insight which are to force themselves beyond abstractness into the reader's consciousness and so to make him new. The *Cantos,* Pound has said, "are the tale of the tribe." The point is that Pound has to re-create the tribe in order to tell its tale. The *Cantos* are that act of creation. If it is but done powerfully enough, there will be no longer a need to tell the tale. For it would be ours—ours in such a way that we would not have to have it told to us. As in Barlow's vision, and as in Whitman's practice, the end of poetry is that reconstitution of man which will entail the withering away of poetry.

IV

Pound once declared that the Cantos had a large defect, "the defect inherent in the record of struggle." He did not say, or have to say, that the virtues of the *Cantos* are specifically related to its defects. For they are indeed the virtues of struggle: the struggle to make the poem such a powerful social weapon that it will come to dispense with itself by being itself. And it is thus also with *Song of Myself.* The struggle is one for self-identification and self-preservation, and it is truly the epic subject of modern times, in America and out. The fact that the poet should be obliged to conceive the poetic act as the sole means of self-identification and self-preservation: this is perhaps one of the tragic subjects of modern times. The highest significance that *Song of Myself* and the *Cantos* can have for us is as the most profound of records of that impossible struggle. No poem, I should judge, can do all they are intended to.

And yet I should likewise judge that in the modern world, such poems have to exist just so that they may fail. A sign of their success indeed is their failure. And what is left? A need to question what we have, how far we have come, and how far we may go, I can only think that it is ultimately as an instigator of such questions that the American epic, as given to us by Whitman and Pound (and many others, I should say), has its highest imaginative value for us. Asking such questions, we concern ourselves with the life of our culture; perhaps we will be moved to strive to make it more vital. Doing so, perhaps we will even have one day that kind of community in which we can conceive of an authentic hero, whom the poets among us will finally be able to memorialize and reaffirm in a true epic. We can only hope that he will not be as obtuse as Barlow's Columbus, as manic as Whitman's Whitman, or as distorted from his historical actuality as Pound's Malatesta. Which is to say: We can only hope that he will be a projection of something other than the agonizing desire of his creator to make over the world, and the men in it, in his own heroic image. We would wish him to be a person first and a hero afterwards—a hero in consequence of his being a person.

Indeed, if we ever get to the point of knowing how to define ourselves as persons, maybe we will be able to define our community. And maybe it will turn out to be a community with not one image of the hero but many—a community whose heroes' heroism consists in the fact that they can teach us how to resist a community's inevitable urge to coalesce all its heroes into one. What we long for, in many heroes or one, is a strong, assured image of our full possibilities as persons in our community. And it might well be that for us a definition of the person is *per se* a definition of the hero—instead of the other way around; as it seems to have been in the epic and the epic communities of tradition. And it might well be that Barlow's, Whitman's, and Pound's ultimate failure to create a hero adequate to our needs lies in the fact that such a definition was for them intolerable in its restrictiveness. They lusted (Pound still lusts) after a sheer creative power which would not only let them define the modern heroic self but reformulate it, not only make it new but make it. Thus, we can quite safely say, they went too far. But surely they did what they had to do; and surely we can learn from it. They saw (does Pound still see?) quite clearly what Freud was to see in 1930, in *Civilization and Its Discontents*. Speaking of that "misère psychologique" which is so marked in modern life, he wrote:

> This danger is most menacing where the social forces of cohesion consist predominantly of identifications of the individuals in the group with one another, whilst leading personalities fail to acquire the significance that should fall to them in the process of group-formation. The state of civilization in America at the present day offers a good opportunity for studying this injurious effect of civilization which we have reason to dread.

The Columbiad, Song of Myself, and the *Cantos*—each can be made out to be therapeutic in so far as each is to initiate in us something of a clear understanding of the powers and limitations of our own processes of group-formation. The best, as always, must be yet to come.

But this is utopianism. It is a curious fact, and a painful one, that those of us who might want such a society and who cannot struggle for it imaginatively, as do Whitman and Pound, so often, like Barlow, conclude with such bleak, abstractive, fleshless utopianisms. We cannot really believe in heroes, yet we want them, and so want them created for us. Looking for a hero in an epic, we discover, of course, that the author must first of all be his own hero, as his epic is the struggle of his own creative forces to bring into being something which constitutes his central subject. Thus, we see, in some way or other he must tell all; thus he wills himself to be incapable of dissembling, lest something of the creative self be left out. There is ever the ungainliness of his compulsions, which we cannot escape: some of them, like Whitman's homosexuality and his political sentimentality, no longer much disturb or concern us; others, like Pound's paranoia and his antisemitism, are of a dangerousness which we can only hate and fear, even to the point of cutting off part of the *Cantos* from ourselves. We know all this, know it well. Still, as we used to gather around Whitman and form Fellowships, so we now wait upon Pound at St. Elizabeth's and contribute to *Pound Newsletters*. We seem bound to strive to live in our hero's image in cults with no rituals except those of *explication de texte*. We even publish statements like this:

> "Leaves of Grass" has a tone peculiarly its own and strange in all the annals of literary creation. Whitman speaks in it as would heaven, making unalterable pronouncements, oracular of the mysteries and powers that pervade and guide all life, all death, all purpose.
>
> (Horace Trauble, in *In Re Walt Whitman,* 1883)

And this:

> It would seem that [Pound] has his fingers on the pulse of creation, and like the poet-philosopher Goethe, bequeaths more than he states: a myriad of facets of existence to be explored in coming years, an attempt to understand what this fire is that he . . . kindles in one.
>
> (Louise Myers, in *Pound Newsletter*, 1955)

At second glance, we blush, or should. But then this is our situation; and we all (perhaps secretly, or unknowingly) hope for someone, somewhere, who will make the struggle for us—or at least show us its conditions. Occasionally we find him, as many found Whitman and have found Pound. Whitman and Pound, each knows who the real hero is: himself. This is the root of their virtues and their defects, of the strength of their epics and of their weakness. Their poems are thus doubly propaedeutic—in their strength and in their weakness, in their virtues and in their defects. If we fail to take the two together, we miss their great meaning for us. It is perhaps useful to recall that the *editio princeps* of *Song of Myself* (in the 1855 *Leaves of Grass*) and of the *Cantos* (and, curiously enough, of *The Columbiad* too) has as frontispiece a portrait of its real hero, its author: he who is perforce our hero because he is, in so far as we can bring ourselves to know and admit it, a projection of ourselves into an ultimate American personality. Looking at our ultimate, marginal selves thus, we are bound either to hate or to adore.

And what, in the long run, is the relation between the American epic and the epic of tradition? It is as though Odysseus, or Aeneas, or Beowulf, or Mio Cid, or even Dante, under the *persona* of Adam (in whose fall/ we sinnèd all) had been compelled, out of some deep, dark necessity, to write his own history, and in writing it, to make it. I am reminded of some words of Robert Penn Warren in the prefatory note to *Brother to Dragons*: ". . . if poetry is the little myth we make, history is the big myth we live, and in our living, constantly remake." The struggle to make the big myth into the little one—this is as good a definition as any of the American epic.

SELECTED BIBLIOGRAPHY
FOR FURTHER READING

SELECTED BIBLIOGRAPHY
FOR FURTHER READING

Abercrombie, Lascelles. *The Epic.* London, 1922.

Armato, Rosario P., and John M. Spalek, eds. *Medieval Epic to the "Epic Theater" of Brecht.* (Univ. of Southern California Studies in Comparative Literature, v. 1). Los Angeles, 1968.

Autran, Charles. *L'épopée indoue, étude de l'arrière-fonds ethnographique et religieux.* Paris, 1946.

—— *Homère et les origines sacredotales de l'épopée grecque.* Paris, 1938.

Ball, Lewis F. *Studies in the Structure of the Minor English Renaissance Epics.* Baltimore, 1934.

Bayer, Hans J. *Untersuchungen zum Sprachstil weltlichen Epen des deutschen früh und Hochmittelalters.* Berlin, 1962.

Bedier, Joseph. *Les légendes épiques: recherches sur la formation des chansons de geste.* Paris, 1908.

Bell, Clair H. *Peasant Life in Old German Epics.* New York, 1931.

Bérard, Victor. *Le drame épique.* Paris, 1930.

Beye, Charles Rowan. *The Iliad, the Odyssey and the Epic Tradition.* New York, 1966.

Bowra, C. M. *Heroic Poetry.* London, 1952.

Briggs, H. M. "Tasso's Theory of Epic Poetry." *Modern Language Review* 25:457–73 (1930).

Brkić, Jovan. *Moral Concepts in Traditional Serbian Epic Poetry.* The Hague, 1961.

Brown, Wallace C. *Triumph of Form.* Chapel Hill, 1948.

Bynum, D. E. "Themes of the Young Hero in Serbocroatian Oral Epic Tradition." *PMLA* 83:1296–1303 (1968).

Carson, Ruth. *A Study of Motivation of Action in Greek and Latin Epic.* Columbus, Ohio, 1930.

Chadwick, H. M., and Nora K. Chadwick. *The Growth of Literature.* 3 vs. Cambridge, Eng., 1932–40. Repr. 1968.

Chadwick, Nora K., and Victor Zhirmunsky. *Oral Epics of Central Asia.* Cambridge, Eng., 1969.

Chernaik, W. L. "Heroic Occasional Poem: Panegyric and Satire in the Restoration." *Modern Language Quarterly* 26:523–35 (1965).

Clark, John. *A History of Epic Poetry.* Edinburgh, 1900.

Conway, R. S. *The Architecture of the Epic.* Manchester, 1925.

Cook, Albert. *The Classic Line: A Study in Epic Poetry.* Bloomington and London, 1966.

Cooke, J. P. *Studies in Epic Time-Designations.* Chicago, 1938.

Craigie, P. C. "Song of Deborah and the Epic of Tukulti-Ninurta." *Journal of Biblical Literature* 88:253–65 (1969).

Crosland, Jessie. *The Old French Epic.* Oxford, 1951.

Curran, Stuart, ed. *Le Bossu and Voltaire on the Epic.* Gainesville, Fla., 1970.

Dessau, Albert. "Zum Problem der epischen Kunst." *Beiträge zur Romanischen Philologie* 1:52–69 (1963).

Dixon, W. Macneile. *English Epic and Heroic Poetry.* Glasgow, 1912. Repr. 1964.

Dorfman, Eugene. *The Narreme in the Medieval Romance Epic: An Introduction to Narrative Structures.* Toronto, 1969.

Duckworth, George E. *Foreshadowing and Suspense in the Epics of Homer, Apollonius, and Vergil.* Princeton, 1933. Repr. 1966.

Dumézil, Georges. *Mythe et épopée.* Paris, 1968.

——— *The Destiny of the Warrior.* Tr. by Alf Hiltebeitel. Chicago, 1970.

Durling, Robert M. *The Figure of the Poet in Renaissance Epic.* Cambridge, 1965.

Entwhistle, W. J. "New Light in the Epic-Ballad Problem." *Journal of American Folklore* 62:375–81 (1949).

Evans, Maurice. *Spenser's Anatomy of Heroism: A Commentary on* The Faerie Queene. Cambridge, Eng., 1970.

Fleming, Willi. *Epik und Dramatik: Versuch ihrer Wesendeutung.* Bern, 1955.

Foerster, D. M. "Critical Attack Upon the Epic in the English Romantic Movement." *PMLA* 69:432–47 (1954).

——— "Critical Approval of Epic Poetry in the Age of Wordsworth." *PMLA* 70:682–705 (1955).

——— "Homer, Milton, and the American Revolt Against Epic Poetry: 1812–1860." *Studies in Philology* 53:75–100 (1956).

——— *Fortunes of Epic Poetry: A Study in English and American Criticism, 1750–1950.* Washington, 1962.

Fränkel, Hermann. *Dichtung und Philosophie des frühen Griechentums: eine Geschichte der griechischen Epik, Lyrik und Prosa bis zur Mitte des fünften Jahrhunderts.* München, 1969.

Friedmann, Käte. *Die Rolle der Erzählers in der Epik.* Leipzig, 1910. Repr. 1967.

Giamatti, A. B. *Earthly Paradise and the Renaissance Epic.* Princeton, 1966.

Gilbert, A. H. "Qualities of the Renaissance Epic," *South Atlantic Quarterly* 53:372–78 (1954).

Goldsmith, Margaret E. *The Mode and Meaning of "Beowulf."* London, 1970.

Greene, Thomas. *The Descent from Heaven: A Study in Epic Continuity.* New Haven, 1963.

Grillone, Antonio. *Il Sogno nell'epica latina.* Palermo, 1967.

Hägin, Peter. *The Epic Hero and the Decline of Heroic Poetry.* Bern, 1964.

Higgins, A. I. T. *Secular Heroic Epic Poetry of the Caroline Period.* Bern, 1953.

Hopkins, E. W. *The Great Epic of India.* New York, 1902.

——— *Epic Mythology.* Strasbourg, 1915.

Horrent, Jules. *Le Chanson de Roland dans les littératures française et espagnole au moyen âge.* Paris, 1951.

Hunt, Herbert J. *The Epic in Nineteenth Century France: A Study in Heroic and Humanitarian Poetry from* Les Martyrs *to* Les Siècles Morts. Oxford, 1941.

Huxley, G. L. *Greek Epic Poetry from Eumelos to Panyassis.* Cambridge, 1969.

Ingalls, Jeremy. "The Epic Tradition: A Commentary." *East-West Review* 1:42–69 (1964); 2:173–211, 271–305 (1965).

Isler, A. D. "Heroic Poetry and Sidney's Two Arcadias." *PMLA* 83:368–79 (1968).

Jacobson, Roman, and E. J. Simmons, eds. *Russian Epic Studies.* (Memoirs of the American Folklore Society, v. 42). Philadelphia, 1949.

Kahler, Erich. *The Inward Turn of Narrative.* Tr. by Richard and Clara Winston. (Bollingen Series, 83). Princeton, 1973.

Kailasapathy, K. *Tamil Heroic Poetry.* New York and Oxford, 1968.

Kayser, Wolfgang. *Das sprachliche Kunstwerk: Eine Einführung in die Literaturwissenschaft.* Bern, 1948.

Ker, W. P. *Epic and Romance: Essays on Medieval Literature.* New York, 1908. Repr. 1957.

Lawrence, W. W. *Beowulf and Epic Tradition.* New York, 1961.

Levy, G. R. *Gate of Horn: A Study of the Religious Conceptions of the Stone Age and their Influence on European Thought.* London, 1948.

——— *The Sword from the Rock: An Investigation into the Origins of Epic Literature and the Development of the Hero.* London, 1953.

Lewalski, Barbara K. *Milton's Brief Epic: The Genre, Meaning, and Art of "Paradise Regained."* Providence and London, 1966.

Lot, Ferdinand. *Études sur les légendes épiques françaises.* Paris, 1958.

McNamee, Maurice B. *Honor and the Epic Hero: A Study of the Shifting Concept of Magnanimity in Philosophy and Epic Poetry.* New York, 1960.

Marni, Archimede. *Allegory in the French Heroic Poem of the Seventeenth Century.* Princeton, 1936.

Menéndez-Pidal, Ramón. *La epopeya castellana a travérs de la literatura española.* Buenos Aires, 1945.

——— *Los godos y la epopeya española.* Madrid, 1956.

——— *Historia y epopeya.* Madrid, 1934.

Miniconi, P. J. *Étude des thèmes "guerriers" de la poésie épique grècoromaine.* Paris, 1951.

Morris, Henry F. *The Heroic Recitations of the Bahima of Ankole.* New York and Oxford, 1964.

Nitze, W. A. "Bédier's Epic Theory and the Arthuriana of Nennius." *Modern Philology* 39:1–14 (1941).

Patrides, C. A., ed. *Milton's Epic Poetry.* Harmondsworth, Eng., 1967.

Perkinson, R. H. "Epic in Five Acts and a Discussion of Sidney's *Old Arcadia,* Davenant's *Gondibert,* and Chamberlayne's *Pharonnida.*" *Studies in Philology* 40:465–81 (1946).

Petsch, Robert. *Wesen und Formen der Erzählkunst.* Halle, 1942.

Pierce, Frank. "Some Aspects of the Spanish Religious Epic of the Golden Age." *Hispanic Review* 12:1–10 (1944).

——— "Some Themes and Sources in the Heroic Poem of the Golden Age." *Hispanic Review* 14:95–103 (1946).

Pollman, Leo. *Das Epos in den romanischen Literaturen.* Stuttgart, 1966.

Prescott, Henry W. *The Development of Virgil's Art.* Chicago, 1927.

Pusalker, A. D. *Studies in Epics and Purānas.* Bombay, 1963.

Riquer, Martin de. *La legenda del graal y temas épicos medievales.* Madrid, 1968.

Routh, H. V. *God, 'Man, and Epic Poetry: A Study in Comparative Literature.* Cambridge, 1927. Repr. 1968.

Rychner, Jean. *La chanson de geste, essai sur l'art épique des jongleurs.* Geneva and Lille, 1955.

Sarma, N. M. "Epic Substratum in the Prose of Job." *Journal of Biblical Literature* 76:13–25 (1957).

Sayce, R. A. *French Biblical Epic in the Seventeenth Century.* Oxford, 1955.

Schmidt, Friedrich. *Die Erneuerung des Epos, eine geschichtsphilosophische Betrachtung der Spittelers "Olympischen Frühling."* Leipzig, 1928.

Scholes, Robert, and Robert Kellogg. *The Nature of Narrative.* New York and Oxford, 1966.

Schueler, Heinz J. *The German Verse Epic in the Nineteenth and Twentieth Centuries.* The Hague, 1967.

Sidhanta, N. K. *The Heroic Age of India: A Comparative Study.* London, 1930.

Staiger, Emil. *Grundbegriffe der Poetik.* Zürich, 1946.

Stanford, W. B. *The Ulysses Theme.* Oxford, 1963.

Steadman, John M. *Milton and the Renaissance Hero.* New York and Oxford, 1967.

—— *Milton's Epic Characters: Image and Idol.* Chapel Hill, 1968.

Stein, R. A. *Recherches sur l'épopée et le barde au Tibet.* Paris, 1959.

Swedenberg, H. T. *The Theory of the Epic in England, 1650–1800.* Berkeley and Los Angeles, 1944.

Taube, René Simon. "Paradise Lost Forever; a Study of the German Philosophical Epics of the Nineteenth Century." *Germanic Review* 35:185–201 (1960).

Thornbury, Ethel M. *Henry Fielding's Theory of the Comic Prose Epic.* Madison, Wis., 1931.

Throop, G. R. "Epic and Dramatic." *Washington University Studies* 12:67–104 (1924).

Tillyard, E. M. W. *The English Epic and Its Background.* London, 1954.

—— *The Epic Strain in the English Novel.* London, 1958.

Vries, Jan de. *Heroic Song and Heroic Legend.* Tr. by B. J. Timmer. Oxford, 1963.

Warren, F. M. "Early History of the French National Epic." *Modern Philology* 14: 129–44 (1916).

Watt, Ian. "Defoe and Richardson on Homer: A Study of the Relation of Novel and Epic to the Early Eighteenth Century." *Review of English Studies* 43:325–40 (1952).

Whitman, Cedric H. *Homer and the Heroic Tradition.* Cambridge, 1958.

Williams, R. C. "Epic Unity as Discussed by Sixteenth Century Critics in Italy." *Modern Philology* 17:383–400 (1920).

—— "Metrical Form of the Epic as Discussed by Sixteenth Century Critics." *Modern Language Notes* 36:449–57 (1921).

—— "Two Studies in Epic Theory." *Modern Philology* 22:133–58 (1924).

—— *The Merveilleux in the Epic.* Paris, 1925.

Yu, Anthony C. "Heroic Verse and Heroic Mission: Dimensions of the Epic in the *Hsi-yu Chi.*" *Journal of Asian Studies* 31: 879–97 (1972).

Ziegler, Konrat. *Das hellenistische Epos; ein vergessenes Kapital griechischer Dichtung.* Leipzig, 1966.